*From the rising of the sun to its setting,
the name of the Lord is to be praised.*

PSALM 113:3

WORD on FIRE.

THE
LITURGY
OF THE
HOURS

July 2023

Published by Word on Fire
Elk Grove Village, IL 60007
© 2023 by Word on Fire Catholic Ministries
Printed in the United States of America
All rights reserved

General Editor: Brandon Vogt
Associate Editor: Danny O'Brien
Creative Director: Rozann Lee
Lead Designer: Michael Stevens
Designer: Katherine Spitler
Typesetting by: 2K/DENMARK A/S
Liturgical Consultant: Fr. Randy Stice
Hymn Consultant: Kathleen Pluth
Editing Manager: Daniel Seseske
Proofreaders: Andrew Dushek, Christine Collins,
Sara Lavenduski, Kelly Lombardo Matthews

The English translation of Antiphons, Intercessions,
Responsories, the Canticle of the Lamb, Concluding Prayers from *The Liturgy of the Hours* © 1973, 1974, 1975, International Commission on English in the Liturgy Corporation (ICEL); excerpts from the English translation of *The Roman Missal* © 2010, ICEL.
All rights reserved

English translations of the Magnificat,
Nunc Dimittis, Benedictus, and Doxology by the
International Consultation on English Texts.

The Psalms: A New Translation except Psalm 95 © The Grail (England) 1963, GIA Publications, Inc., exclusive North American agent.
All rights reserved

The texts of all Biblical Readings and Canticles (except the Gospel Canticles and the Canticle of the Lamb) are reproduced with permission from *The New American Bible*, copyright © 1970 by the Confraternity of Christian Doctrine,
Washington, D.C.
All rights reserved

Body text set in Trinité No. 2
Cover titling and inscriptions set in Greenstone

The design of the ornamental patterns in this book was inspired by the graphical experiments of Bram de Does, as presented in his treatise *The Kaba Ornament in Vignettes, Borders and Patterns.*

ISSN: 2771-1285

wordonfire.org

July 2023

SATURDAY, JULY 1   22
Saturday of the Twelfth Week in Ordinary Time

SUNDAY, JULY 2   42
Thirteenth Sunday in Ordinary Time

MONDAY, JULY 3   63
St. Thomas

TUESDAY, JULY 4   83
Tuesday of the Thirteenth Week in Ordinary Time

WEDNESDAY, JULY 5   105
Wednesday of the Thirteenth Week in Ordinary Time

THURSDAY, JULY 6   125
Thursday of the Thirteenth Week in Ordinary Time

FRIDAY, JULY 7   147
Friday of the Thirteenth Week in Ordinary Time

SATURDAY, JULY 8   169
Saturday of the Thirteenth Week in Ordinary Time

SUNDAY, JULY 9   188
Fourteenth Sunday in Ordinary Time

MONDAY, JULY 10   211
Monday of the Fourteenth Week in Ordinary Time

TUESDAY, JULY 11   231
St. Benedict

WEDNESDAY, JULY 12   252
Wednesday of the Fourteenth Week in Ordinary Time

THURSDAY, JULY 13   276
Thursday of the Fourteenth Week in Ordinary Time

FRIDAY, JULY 14   296
St. Kateri Tekakwitha

SATURDAY, JULY 15   318
St. Bonaventure

SUNDAY, JULY 16 *Fifteenth Sunday in Ordinary Time*	340
MONDAY, JULY 17 *Monday of the Fifteenth Week in Ordinary Time*	362
TUESDAY, JULY 18 *Tuesday of the Fifteenth Week in Ordinary Time*	382
WEDNESDAY, JULY 19 *Wednesday of the Fifteenth Week in Ordinary Time*	402
THURSDAY, JULY 20 *Thursday of the Fifteenth Week in Ordinary Time*	422
FRIDAY, JULY 21 *Friday of the Fifteenth Week in Ordinary Time*	442
SATURDAY, JULY 22 *St. Mary Magdalene*	462
SUNDAY, JULY 23 *Sixteenth Sunday in Ordinary Time*	484
MONDAY, JULY 24 *Monday of the Sixteenth Week in Ordinary Time*	506
TUESDAY, JULY 25 *St. James*	527
WEDNESDAY, JULY 26 *Sts. Joachim and Anne*	548
THURSDAY, JULY 27 *Thursday of the Sixteenth Week in Ordinary Time*	569
FRIDAY, JULY 28 *Friday of the Sixteenth Week in Ordinary Time*	589
SATURDAY, JULY 29 *Sts. Martha, Mary, and Lazarus*	610
SUNDAY, JULY 30 *Seventeenth Sunday in Ordinary Time*	631
MONDAY, JULY 31 *St. Ignatius of Loyola*	651
HYMNS	673

Introduction

WORD ON FIRE LITURGY OF THE HOURS BOOKLET

Brandon Vogt

THIS LITURGY OF THE HOURS, which you hold in your hands, is an ancient, structured way of praying Scripture throughout the day, focusing especially on the Psalms. It hearkens back to the Jewish custom of praying at fixed hours, a practice early Christians continued. By the medieval period, monks chanted the entire Psalter, all 150 Psalms, throughout each week, and sometimes in a single day!

Eventually, this form of prayer became known as the Liturgy of the Hours, also called the Divine Office. It is a liturgy because, like the Mass and other sacraments, it is a public prayer of the Church, Christ's Mystical Body, as distinct from private devotions such as the Rosary, novenas, or personal prayer.

Its purpose is to sanctify the day and the whole range of human activity. It does this by bathing the morning, afternoon, and evening in prayer, so that "the whole course of the day and night is made holy by the praises of God."[1]

---

[1] *Sacrosanctum Concilium* 84.

Saints up and down the centuries have prayed the Psalms each day, including John Paul II, Pier Giorgio Frassati, Thérèse of Lisieux, Thomas Aquinas, Augustine, Benedict, and the first Apostles. And, of course, this is how Mary, Joseph, and Jesus prayed too. They knew, loved, and prayed the Psalms. So, you're entering into this same tradition of prayer shared by the greatest men and women in Christian history.

The Liturgy of the Hours is composed of five major "hours" or times of prayer:

Morning Prayer—also known as Lauds, prayed first thing in the morning

Daytime Prayer—prayed sometime between mid-morning and mid-afternoon

Evening Prayer—also known as Vespers, prayed in the early evening

Night Prayer—also known as Compline, offered just before bedtime

Office of Readings—the longest hour, featuring lengthy readings from the Bible, Church Fathers, or other saints, prayed at any point during the day

This booklet contains the core hours of Morning, Evening, and Night Prayer.

The word "hours" can be misleading. It doesn't refer to the time it takes to complete each prayer, but to the hours of the day. None of the liturgical hours takes anywhere close to sixty minutes. In fact, the two main hours, Morning and Evening Prayer, take around fifteen minutes each, while Night Prayer takes only five to ten minutes.

The Liturgy of the Hours is well-known among clergy and religious, who are required to pray the five major hours every day. Permanent deacons are obliged to pray Morning and Evening Prayer. Among the laity, the Liturgy of the Hours has been less popular, but that is starting to change. The Second Vatican Council taught that "the laity, too, are encouraged to recite the divine office, either with the priests, or among themselves, or even individually."[2] Recent popes have repeated this invitation. Pope St. Paul VI especially emphasized the call for families to pray the Liturgy of the Hours, saying, "No avenue should be left unexplored to ensure that this clear and practical recommendation finds within Christian families growing and joyful acceptance."[3]

---

[2] *Sacrosanctum Concilium* 100.
[3] Paul VI, *Marialis Cultus* 53.

Why Pray the Liturgy of the Hours?

There are many reasons why you should pray the Liturgy of the Hours, whether individually or with others, but here are seven.

First, it unites us to Jesus Christ. The Liturgy of the Hours joins us with Christ in singing an eternal hymn of praise to the Father. As Vatican II taught, "It is the very prayer which Christ Himself, together with His body, addresses to the Father."[4] If you want to grow deeper in your relationship with Christ, and you already frequent the sacraments, your next step should be to begin praying the Liturgy of the Hours. Few practices will draw you closer to Jesus.

Second, the Liturgy of the Hours allows you to pray with the Church. Personal prayer is good and necessary, but when the Church offers praise to God through the Liturgy of the Hours, "it unites itself with that hymn of praise sung throughout all ages in the halls of heaven."[5] We join not only people from every tribe and tongue, every people and nation, but the entire communion of saints in heaven.

Third, the Liturgy of the Hours is the highest form of prayer after the Mass. Why? Because the Liturgy of the Hours is not just the private prayer of some Christians, but the unified, sacred prayer

---

[4] *Sacrosanctum Concilium* 84.
[5] *General Instruction on the Liturgy of the Hours* 16. See *Sacrosanctum Concilium* 83.

of the whole Church, uniting all the faithful, from all vocations, in all countries, into one single prayer to the Father, echoing the very Word of God back to its source. (It's also the supreme way to pray as a family. Pope St. Paul VI affirmed this in *Marialis Cultus*, calling it "the high point which family prayer can reach."[6])

Fourth, the Liturgy of the Hours is thoroughly biblical. "Its readings are drawn from sacred Scripture, God's words in the Psalms are sung in his presence, and the intercessions, prayers, and hymns are inspired by Scripture and steeped in its spirit."[7] The more you pray the Hours, the more the Bible saturates your mind and heart. You'll begin noticing yourself memorizing large chunks of Scripture—the Canticles especially, which are repeated each morning and evening—and you'll find that biblical passages spring to mind during your own quiet, personal prayer. All of this will make your prayer more biblical.

Fifth, the Liturgy of the Hours will mature and deepen the rest of your spiritual life. After praying the Hours for some time, you will begin to see the world differently. You will develop a renewed spiritual vision, seeing the world as God sees it, more attuned to the dynamics of justice, love, sin, compassion, and forgiveness. You are changed as a consequence. You will also notice your

---

[6] Paul VI, *Marialis Cultus* 54.
[7] *General Instruction on the Liturgy of the Hours* 14. See *Sacrosanctum Concilium* 24.

times of personal prayer outside the Liturgy of the Hours becoming more elevated and intense. The Liturgy of the Hours incorporates each major dimension of Christian prayer—worship, thanksgiving, petition, and intercession—and by praying the Hours, you become more proficient in each one.

Sixth, the Liturgy of the Hours allows you to "pray without ceasing." Jesus taught about the need to "pray always and not to lose heart" (Luke 18:1), and St. Paul directed us to "pray without ceasing" (1 Thess. 5:17). But for many Christians, these directives seem unrealistic, if not impossible. How can we pray continually, especially when our days are jam-packed with duties and commitments? The Liturgy of the Hours offers a solution, allowing you to lock in times of prayer throughout the day and, more than that, combine your voice with millions of others throughout the world who are also praying the Hours. At every moment, someone somewhere is offering these prayers to God. So, while we might not be able to "pray without ceasing" as individuals, we can do so together as a Church.

Seventh, and finally, the Liturgy of the Hours makes God the center of your day. When you begin each day with Morning Prayer, close it with Evening Prayer, and offer Night Prayer before bed, you establish three fixed pillars during the day around which the rest of your activities turn. For other people, the main pillars of the day might be breakfast, lunch, and dinner, or perhaps work meetings or other activities. Everything else, including spiritual commitments, fits around those moments. But that changes when you pray the Liturgy of the Hours. Prayer becomes the new hinge of your day, reorienting your mind so that you give highest priority to the things of God.

Practical Tips for Praying

So the Liturgy of the Hours is definitely worth praying! Yet the next obvious question is: How do you do it? How do you begin? The answer used to be complicated. It required special books, personal instruction, lots of page flipping and bookmarks, and a solid familiarity with the liturgical calendar. It was confusing, expensive, and difficult.

That is no longer the case. This Word on Fire Liturgy of the Hours booklet, which you hold in your hands, has made it easier than ever to enter into this chorus of praise. It's simple: you just read and pray. No special expertise, no page flipping, no ribbons, no guessing which prayers to say. You can get started right away.

That said, here are some recommendations that will enhance your experience.

First, *start slow*. If you're new to this form of prayer, you might not want to immediately start praying all three hours included in this booklet—Morning, Evening, and Night

Prayer—every day. Instead, perhaps consider starting with just Night Prayer, the shortest and easiest hour. It repeats on a seven-day cycle. So, for example, you pray the exact same Night Prayer each Monday night throughout the year, meaning you'll quickly become familiar and comfortable with it. Start with Night Prayer, and do it consistently for a week or two. From there, add one more hour, either Morning or Evening, before finally working up to all three in this booklet.

Second, be at peace if you aren't able to pray every hour, every day. Unless you are a priest or consecrated religious, you are not required to pray all the hours each day, which means there is no pressure on you. It is, of course, ideal if you can commit to praying Morning, Evening, and Night Prayer every day, and few things will deepen your prayer life more than consistently doing that, but don't feel deflated if you miss an hour here or there or have to take a short break. Like all prayer, the Liturgy of the Hours should be a gift, not a burden. So be at peace with what you can handle.

Third, push through the initial difficulties. Sometimes, those new to the Liturgy of the Hours find it to be stilted and monotonous, especially if they're used to more spontaneous, personal prayer. After all, it follows the same pattern, day after day, repeating the same Psalms and prayers on a cyclical basis. If you feel bored by this initially, that's okay; it's common. But push through it.

The spiritual fruit of the Liturgy of the Hours typically begins to bloom only after a few months of dedicated, consistent praying. It's similar in that way to the Mass and the Rosary. Both of those prayers include formal, repetitive recitation, which can seem monotonous at first. But at some point, after regular dedication, they open up with surprising freshness and power. You learn to appreciate the repetition the same way a child delights in saying "Do it again! Do it again!" to their parents. That will eventually happen, too, with the Liturgy of the Hours, so persevere.

Fourth, get outside of yourself. The Liturgy of the Hours has been described as "the prayer of the Church with Christ and to Christ."[8] This is because you not only pray alongside Christ but, in a mystical way, you pray with him and through him. So, as you pray the Psalms, learn to pray them as if it were Christ within you offering these words to the Father. For example, when praying Psalm 86, imagine yourself as Christ on the cross, and let it be that inner Christ saying, "O give your strength to your servant, and save your handmaid's son. Show me a sign of your favor, that my foes may see to their shame, that you console me and give me your help." You can also offer these prayers on behalf of other Christians throughout the world. You might not feel that enemies "surround me all the day like a flood"

---

[8] *General Instruction on the Liturgy of the Hours* 2.

or that "my one companion is darkness," as we find in Night Prayer each Friday. But certainly there are other Christians in the world in that position, and you can give voice to their laments. Let their cries become your prayer, on their behalf. Remember, this is the prayer of the whole Church: it transcends you and your personal concerns, important as those are. Through it, you become one with Christ and his entire Body.

Fifth, and finally, learn more about the Liturgy of the Hours. A basic principle of the spiritual life is that the more you study a facet of the faith, the more impactful it becomes. For instance, if you want to heighten your experience of the Mass, read some books about it. Understand it better, and it will soon shimmer in a new light. The same applies to the Liturgy of the Hours. The better you understand its history, purpose, and logic, the more profound your experience will be. Here are some excellent books that will help toward that end:

> The Everyday Catholic's Guide to the Liturgy of the Hours by Daria Sockey
>
> A Layman's Guide to the Liturgy of the Hours by Fr. Timothy Gallagher
>
> Praying the Liturgy of the Hours: A Personal Journey by Fr. Timothy Gallagher
>
> General Instruction on the Liturgy of the Hours

You will find other helpful resources at **wordonfire.org/pray**. But don't wait until you become a master at the Liturgy of the Hours to start praying it. Begin now. Start with this booklet: flip to the correct day, and commence with Morning, Evening, or Night Prayer. Then find other people—in your family, your parish, your community—and invite them to pray the Liturgy of the Hours with you.

Join your voice to this great chorus of praise as you begin now to sanctify each day.

Brandon Vogt

General Editor of Word on Fire Liturgy of the Hours
Senior Publishing Director at Word on Fire

Using Alternate Melodies to Sing the Hymns

If you are unfamiliar with the hymn assigned to a particular hour and you do not read music, you can still sing most of the hymns in this book.

The great majority of Latin hymns sung in the Liturgy of the Hours over the past two millennia are written in a metrical pattern called "Long Meter." Each stanza or verse in Long Meter contains four lines, with eight syllables per line (8.8.8.8), stressing the even-numbered syllables (with some stress variation allowed on the first two and last two syllables in each line). An example of an English hymn in Long Meter is the well-known Advent hymn "Creator of the Stars of Night":

> Cre - **a** - tor **of** the **stars** of **night**,
> Your **peo** - ple's **ev** - er - **last** - ing **Light**,
> **Je** - **sus**, Re - **deem** - er **of** us **all**,
> We **pray** you **hear** us **when** we **call**.

For well over a thousand years, both in its original Latin and in translation, this particular hymn has ordinarily been set to a single Gregorian chant melody known as CONDITOR ALME SIDERUM (the melody we used in our December 2022 issue). Yet throughout the history of

Christian hymnody, most tunes have been shared quite freely among multiple texts, and many texts can be sung to more than one tune. Any text and tune that share the same metrical pattern can be paired (although some melodies tend better than others to suit a given text's mood, arc, or patterns of emphasis).

In addition to "Creator of the Stars of Night," familiar Long Meter hymns include "All People That on Earth Do Dwell," "Jesus Shall Reign," "Lift Up Your Heads," "O Radiant Light," "Take Up Your Cross," "The God Whom Earth and Sea and Sky," and "When I Survey the Wondrous Cross." Many Christians know one or several of these hymns, and any Long Meter text can be set to any Long Meter melody.

Likewise, most hymn texts in other meters can also fit more than one melody. For instance, almost any text with the syllable pattern 8.7.8.7 D can be sung to Beethoven's HYMN TO JOY ("Joyful, Joyful, We Adore Thee") or to the Welsh tune HYFRYDOL ("Alleluia! Sing to Jesus!" and "Love Divine, All Loves Excelling"). To use another well-known example, almost any text with the syllables 8.6.8.6 can be sung to "Amazing Grace."

At the end of this booklet you will find an index of hymns included in this month's issue of *Word on Fire Liturgy of the Hours* with metrical information and alternate melody options for most texts. If you or your group do not know the tune we have assigned to a given hymn text, you can use these suggestions to sing the same lyrics to a more familiar melody.

July 2023

Saturday, July 1, 2023
Saturday of the Twelfth Week in Ordinary Time

MORNING PRAYER

God, + come to my assistance.
— Lord, make haste to help me.

Glory to the Father, and to the Son,
   and to the Holy Spirit:
— as it was in the beginning, is now,
and will be for ever. Amen. Alleluia.

Hymn — *The Heavens Declare Your Glory, p. 704*

Psalmody

Ant. 1 **We do well to sing to your name, Most High, and proclaim your mercy at daybreak.**

Psalm 92

It is good to give thanks to the Lord,
to make music to your name, O Most High,
to proclaim your love in the morning
and your truth in the watches of the night,
on the ten-stringed lyre and the lute,
with the murmuring sound of the harp.

Your deeds, O Lord, have made me glad;
for the work of your hands I shout with joy.
O Lord, how great are your works!
How deep are your designs!
The foolish man cannot know this
and the fool cannot understand.

Though the wicked spring up like grass
and all who do evil thrive:
they are doomed to be eternally destroyed.
But you, Lord, are eternally on high.
See how your enemies perish;
all doers of evil are scattered.

To me you give the wild-ox's strength;
you anoint me with the purest oil.
My eyes looked in triumph on my foes;
my ears heard gladly of their fall.
The just will flourish like the palm-tree
and grow like a Lebanon cedar.

Planted in the house of the Lord,
they will flourish in the courts of our God,
still bearing fruit when they are old,
still full of sap, still green,
to proclaim that the Lord is just.
In him, my rock, there is no wrong.

Glory to the Father, and to the Son,
    and to the Holy Spirit:
—as it was in the beginning, is now,
and will be for ever. Amen.

Ant. **We do well to sing to your name, Most High, and proclaim your mercy at daybreak.**

Ant. 2 **I will create a new heart in you, and breathe into you a new spirit.**

Canticle:
Ezekiel 36:24–28

I will take you away from among the nations,
gather you from all the foreign lands,
and bring you back to your own land.

I will sprinkle clean water upon you
to cleanse you from all your impurities,
and from all your idols I will cleanse you.

I will give you a new heart
and place a new spirit within you,
taking from your bodies your stony hearts
and giving you natural hearts.

I will put my spirit within you
and make you live by my statutes,
careful to observe my decrees.

You shall live in the land I gave your fathers;
you shall be my people,
and I will be your God.

Glory to the Father, and to the Son,
   and to the Holy Spirit:
—as it was in the beginning, is now,
and will be for ever. Amen.

Ant. **I will create a new heart in you, and breathe into you a new spirit.**

Ant. 3 **On the lips of children and infants you have found perfect praise.**

Psalm 8

How great is your name, O Lord our God,
through all the earth!

Your majesty is praised above the heavens;
on the lips of children and of babes
you have found praise to foil your enemy,
to silence the foe and the rebel.

When I see the heavens, the work of
    your hands,
the moon and the stars which you arranged,
what is man that you should keep
    him in mind,
mortal man that you care for him?

Yet you have made him little less than a god;
with glory and honor you crowned him,
gave him power over the works of your hand,
put all things under his feet.

All of them, sheep and cattle,
yes, even the savage beasts,
birds of the air, and fish
that make their way through the waters.

How great is your name, O Lord our God,
through all the earth!

Glory to the Father, and to the Son,
    and to the Holy Spirit:
—as it was in the beginning, is now,
and will be for ever. Amen.

JULY 1 SAT MORNING PRAYER

Ant. **On the lips of children and infants you have found perfect praise.**

Reading
2 Peter 3:13–15a

What we await are new heavens and a new earth where, according to his promise, the justice of God will reside. So, beloved, while waiting for this, make every effort to be found without stain or defilement, and at peace in his sight. Consider that our Lord's patience is directed toward salvation.

Responsory

It is my joy, O God, to praise you with song.
—It is my joy, O God, to praise you with song.

To sing as I ponder your goodness,
—to praise you with song.

Glory to the Father, and to the Son,
    and to the Holy Spirit.
—It is my joy, O God, to praise you with song.

Gospel Canticle

Ant. **Lord, guide our feet into the way of peace.**

Canticle of Zechariah
Luke 1:68–79

Blessed + be the Lord, the God of Israel;
he has come to his people and set them free.

He has raised up for us a mighty savior,
born of the house of his servant David.

Through his holy prophets he
    promised of old
that he would save us from our enemies,
from the hands of all who hate us.

He promised to show mercy to our fathers
and to remember his holy covenant.

This was the oath he swore to our
    father Abraham:
to set us free from the hands of our enemies,
free to worship him without fear,
holy and righteous in his sight
    all the days of our life.

You, my child, shall be called the prophet of
    the Most High;
for you will go before the Lord to
    prepare his way,
to give his people knowledge of salvation
by the forgiveness of their sins.

In the tender compassion of our God
the dawn from on high shall break upon us,
to shine on those who dwell in darkness and
    the shadow of death,
and to guide our feet into the way of peace.

Glory to the Father, and to the Son,
    and to the Holy Spirit:
as it was in the beginning, is now,
and will be for ever. Amen.

Ant. **Lord, guide our feet into the way of peace.**

Intercessions Let us adore God, who has given hope and life to the world through his Son, and let us humbly ask him:
Lord, hear us.

Lord, Father of all, you have brought us to the dawn of this day,
— make us live with Christ and praise your glory.

You have poured out faith, hope and love upon us,
— keep them firmly rooted in our hearts.

Lord, let our eyes be always raised up to you,
— so that we may swiftly answer your call.

Protect us from the snares and enticements of evil,
— keep our feet from stumbling.

The Lord's Prayer
Our Father, who art in heaven,
hallowed be thy name;
thy kingdom come,
thy will be done
on earth as it is in heaven.
Give us this day our daily bread,
and forgive us our trespasses,
as we forgive those who trespass against us;
and lead us not into temptation,
but deliver us from evil.

Pater noster, qui es in cælis:
sanctificetur nomen tuum;
adveniat regnum tuum;
fiat voluntas tua,
sicut in cælo, et in terra.
Panem nostrum cotidianum da nobis hodie;
et dimitte nobis debita nostra,
sicut et nos dimittimus debitoribus nostris;
et ne nos inducas in tentationem;
sed libera nos a malo.

Concluding Prayer

All-powerful and ever-living God,
splendor of true light, and never ending day:
let the radiance of your coming
banish from our minds
the darkness of sin.
We ask this through our Lord Jesus Christ,
    your Son,
who lives and reigns with you and
    the Holy Spirit,
God, for ever and ever.
—Amen.

Dismissal

If praying individually, or in a group without a priest or deacon:

May the Lord + bless us,
protect us from all evil
and bring us to everlasting life.
—Amen.

If praying with a priest or deacon, he dismisses the people:

The Lord be with you.
—And with your spirit.

May almighty God bless you,
the Father, and the Son, ✢ and the Holy Spirit.
—Amen.

Go in peace.
—Thanks be to God.

EVENING PRAYER

BEGINS THE THIRTEENTH SUNDAY IN ORDINARY TIME

God, ✢ come to my assistance.
—Lord, make haste to help me.

Glory to the Father, and to the Son,
    and to the Holy Spirit:
—as it was in the beginning, is now,
and will be for ever. Amen. Alleluia.

Hymn *Praise to the Lord, the Almighty, p. 696*

Psalmody Ant. 1 **Like burning incense, Lord, let my prayer rise up to you.**

Psalm 141:1–9

I have called to you, Lord; hasten to help me!
Hear my voice when I cry to you.
Let my prayer arise before you like incense,
the raising of my hands like an
    evening oblation.

Set, O Lord, a guard over my mouth;
keep watch at the door of my lips!
Do not turn my heart to things that
    are wrong,
to evil deeds with men who are sinners.

Never allow me to share in their feasting.
If a good man strikes or reproves me it
    is kindness;
but let the oil of the wicked not
    anoint my head.
Let my prayer be ever against their malice.

Their princes were thrown down by the side
    of the rock:
then they understood that my words
    were kind.
As a millstone is shattered to pieces on
    the ground,
so their bones were strewn at the mouth of
    the grave.

To you, Lord God, my eyes are turned:
in you I take refuge; spare my soul!
From the trap they have laid for me
    keep me safe:
keep me from the snares of those who do evil.

Glory to the Father, and to the Son,
    and to the Holy Spirit:
—as it was in the beginning, is now,
and will be for ever. Amen.

Ant. **Like burning incense, Lord, let my prayer rise up to you.**

Ant. 2 **You are my refuge, Lord; you are all that I desire in life.**

Psalm 142

With all my voice I cry to the Lord,
with all my voice I entreat the Lord.
I pour out my trouble before him;
I tell him all my distress
while my spirit faints within me.
But you, O Lord, know my path.

On the way where I shall walk
they have hidden a snare to entrap me.
Look on my right and see:
there is not one who takes my part.
I have no means of escape,
not one who cares for my soul.

I cry to you, O Lord.
I have said: "You are my refuge,
all I have left in the land of the living."
Listen then to my cry
for I am in the depths of distress.

Rescue me from those who pursue me
for they are stronger than I.
Bring my soul out of this prison
and then I shall praise your name.
Around me the just will assemble
because of your goodness to me.

Glory to the Father, and to the Son,
    and to the Holy Spirit:
—as it was in the beginning, is now,
and will be for ever. Amen.

Ant.

You are my refuge, Lord; you are all that I desire in life.

Ant. 3 **The Lord Jesus humbled himself, and God exalted him for ever.**

Canticle: Philippians 2:6–11

Though he was in the form of God,
Jesus did not deem equality with God
something to be grasped at.

Rather, he emptied himself
and took the form of a slave,
being born in the likeness of men.

He was known to be of human estate,
and it was thus that he humbled himself,
obediently accepting even death,
death on a cross!

Because of this,
God highly exalted him
and bestowed on him the name
above every other name,

So that at Jesus' name
every knee must bend
in the heavens, on the earth,
and under the earth,
and every tongue proclaim
to the glory of God the Father:
JESUS CHRIST IS LORD!

Glory to the Father, and to the Son,
    and to the Holy Spirit:
—as it was in the beginning, is now,
and will be for ever. Amen.

JULY 1　　SAT　　EVENING PRAYER

Ant. **The Lord Jesus humbled himself, and God exalted him for ever.**

Reading
Romans 11:33–36

How deep are the riches and the wisdom and the knowledge of God! How inscrutable his judgments, how unsearchable his ways! For "who has known the mind of the Lord? Or who has been his counselor? Who has given him anything so as to deserve return?" For from him and through him and for him all things are. To him be glory forever. Amen.

Responsory

Our hearts are filled with wonder as we
　　contemplate your works, O Lord.
—Our hearts are filled with wonder as we
　　contemplate your works, O Lord.

We praise the wisdom which
　　wrought them all,
—as we contemplate your works, O Lord.

Glory to the Father, and to the Son,
　　and to the Holy Spirit.
—Our hearts are filled with wonder as we
　　contemplate your works, O Lord.

Gospel Canticle

Ant. **Those who welcome you are welcoming me, and those who welcome me are welcoming him who sent me.**

Canticle of Mary
Luke 1:46–55

My + soul proclaims the greatness of the Lord,
my spirit rejoices in God my Savior
for he has looked with favor on his
　　lowly servant.

From this day all generations will
　　call me blessed:
the Almighty has done great things for me,
and holy is his Name.

He has mercy on those who fear him
in every generation.

He has shown the strength of his arm,
he has scattered the proud in their conceit.

He has cast down the mighty from
　　their thrones,
and has lifted up the lowly.

He has filled the hungry with good things,
and the rich he has sent away empty.

He has come to the help of his servant Israel
for he has remembered his promise of mercy,
the promise he made to our fathers,
to Abraham and his children for ever.

Glory to the Father, and to the Son,
　　and to the Holy Spirit:
—as it was in the beginning, is now,
and will be for ever. Amen.

Ant. **Those who welcome you are welcoming me, and those who welcome me are welcoming him who sent me.**

Intercessions We give glory to the one God—Father,
Son and Holy Spirit—and in our
weakness we pray:
Lord, be with your people.

Holy Lord, Father all-powerful, let justice
spring up on the earth,
—then your people will dwell in the
beauty of peace.

Let every nation come into your kingdom,
—so that all peoples will be saved.

Let married couples live in your peace,
—and grow in mutual love.

Reward all who have done good to us, Lord,
—and grant them eternal life.

Look with compassion on victims of
hatred and war,
—grant them heavenly peace.

The Lord's Prayer Our Father, who art in heaven,
hallowed be thy name;
thy kingdom come,
thy will be done
on earth as it is in heaven.
Give us this day our daily bread,
and forgive us our trespasses,
as we forgive those who trespass against us;
and lead us not into temptation,
but deliver us from evil.

Pater noster, qui es in cælis:
sanctificetur nomen tuum;
adveniat regnum tuum;
fiat voluntas tua,
sicut in cælo, et in terra.
Panem nostrum cotidianum da nobis hodie;
et dimitte nobis debita nostra,
sicut et nos dimittimus debitoribus nostris;
et ne nos inducas in tentationem;
sed libera nos a malo.

Concluding Prayer

Father,
you call your children
to walk in the light of Christ.
Free us from darkness
and keep us in the radiance of your truth.
We ask this through our Lord Jesus Christ,
    your Son,
who lives and reigns with you and
    the Holy Spirit,
God, for ever and ever.
—Amen.

Dismissal

If praying individually, or in a group without a priest or deacon:

May the Lord + bless us,
protect us from all evil
and bring us to everlasting life.
—Amen.

If praying with a priest or deacon, he dismisses the people:

The Lord be with you.
—And with your spirit.

May almighty God bless you,
the Father, and the Son, ✠ and the Holy Spirit.
—Amen.

Go in peace.
—Thanks be to God.

NIGHT PRAYER

God, + come to my assistance.
—Lord, make haste to help me.

Glory to the Father, and to the Son,
and to the Holy Spirit:
—as it was in the beginning, is now,
and will be for ever. Amen. Alleluia.

Examen *An optional brief examination of conscience may be made. Call to mind your sins and failings this day.*

Hymn *Abide with Me, p. 675*

Psalmody Ant. 1 **Have mercy, Lord, and hear my prayer.**

Psalm 4

When I call, answer me, O God of justice;
from anguish you released me; have mercy
    and hear me!

O men, how long will your hearts be closed,
will you love what is futile and seek
    what is false?

It is the Lord who grants favors to those
    whom he loves;
the Lord hears me whenever I call him.

Fear him; do not sin: ponder on your bed
    and be still.
Make justice your sacrifice and trust
    in the Lord.

"What can bring us happiness?" many say.
Let the light of your face shine on us, O Lord.

You have put into my heart a greater joy
than they have from abundance of corn
    and new wine.

I will lie down in peace and sleep
    comes at once
for you alone, Lord, make me dwell in safety.

Glory to the Father, and to the Son,
    and to the Holy Spirit:
—as it was in the beginning, is now,
and will be for ever. Amen.

Ant. **Have mercy, Lord, and hear my prayer.**

Ant. 2 **In the silent hours of night, bless the Lord.**

Psalm 134

O come, bless the Lord,
all you who serve the Lord,
who stand in the house of the Lord,
in the courts of the house of our God.

Lift up your hands to the holy place
and bless the Lord through the night.

May the Lord bless you from Zion,
he who made both heaven and earth.

Glory to the Father, and to the Son,
   and to the Holy Spirit:
—as it was in the beginning, is now,
and will be for ever. Amen.

Ant. **In the silent hours of night, bless the Lord.**

Reading
Deuteronomy 6:4-7

Hear, O Israel! The Lord is our God, the Lord alone! Therefore, you shall love the Lord, your God, with all your heart, and with all your soul, and with all your strength. Take to heart these words which I enjoin on you today. Drill them into your children. Speak of them at home and abroad, whether you are busy or at rest.

Responsory

Into your hands, Lord, I commend my spirit.
—Into your hands, Lord, I commend my spirit.

You have redeemed us, Lord God of truth.
—I commend my spirit.

Glory to the Father, and to the Son,
   and to the Holy Spirit.
—Into your hands, Lord, I commend my spirit.

Gospel Canticle

Ant. **Protect us, Lord, as we stay awake; watch over us as we sleep, that awake, we may keep watch with Christ, and asleep, rest in his peace.**

NIGHT PRAYER	SAT JULY 1

Canticle of Simeon
Luke 2:29–32

Lord, + now you let your servant go in peace;
your word has been fulfilled:
my own eyes have seen the salvation
which you have prepared in the sight of
    every people:
a light to reveal you to the nations
and the glory of your people Israel.

Glory to the Father, and to the Son,
    and to the Holy Spirit:
—as it was in the beginning, is now,
and will be for ever. Amen.

Ant.

Protect us, Lord, as we stay awake; watch over us as we sleep, that awake, we may keep watch with Christ, and asleep, rest in his peace.

Concluding Prayer

Let us pray.
Lord,
be with us throughout this night.
When day comes may we rise from sleep
to rejoice in the resurrection of your Christ,
who lives and reigns for ever and ever.
—Amen.

Blessing

May the all-powerful Lord
grant us a restful night
and a peaceful death.
—Amen.

Marian Antiphon

Sing the "Salve Regina," found on p. 698, or pray a Hail Mary.

Sunday, July 2, 2023
Thirteenth Sunday in Ordinary Time

MORNING PRAYER

God, + come to my assistance.
—Lord, make haste to help me.

Glory to the Father, and to the Son,
   and to the Holy Spirit:
—as it was in the beginning, is now,
and will be for ever. Amen. Alleluia.

Hymn   *This Day the First of Days Was Made, p. 695*

Psalmody   Ant. 1 **As morning breaks I look to you, O God, to be my strength this day, alleluia.**

Psalm 63:2–9

O God, you are my God, for you I long;
for you my soul is thirsting.
My body pines for you
like a dry, weary land without water.
So I gaze on you in the sanctuary
to see your strength and your glory.

For your love is better than life,
my lips will speak your praise.
So I will bless you all my life,
in your name I will lift up my hands.
My soul shall be filled as with a banquet,
my mouth shall praise you with joy.

On my bed I remember you.
On you I muse through the night
for you have been my help;
in the shadow of your wings I rejoice.
My soul clings to you;
your right hand holds me fast.

Glory to the Father, and to the Son,
    and to the Holy Spirit:
—as it was in the beginning, is now,
and will be for ever. Amen.

Ant.

As morning breaks I look to you, O God, to be my strength this day, alleluia.

Ant. 2

From the midst of the flames the three young men cried out with one voice: Blessed be God, alleluia.

Canticle:
Daniel
3:57–88, 56

Bless the Lord, all you works of the Lord.
Praise and exalt him above all forever.
Angels of the Lord, bless the Lord.
You heavens, bless the Lord.
All you waters above the heavens,
    bless the Lord.
All you hosts of the Lord, bless the Lord.
Sun and moon, bless the Lord.
Stars of heaven, bless the Lord.

Glory to the Father, and to the Son,
>   and to the Holy Spirit:
— as it was in the beginning, is now,
and will be for ever. Amen.

Ant. **Let the people of Zion rejoice in their King, alleluia.**

Reading
Revelation
7:10, 12

Salvation is from our God, who is seated on the throne, and from the Lamb! Praise and glory, wisdom and thanksgiving and honor, power and might, to our God forever and ever. Amen!

Responsory

Christ, Son of the living God,
>   have mercy on us.
— Christ, Son of the living God,
>   have mercy on us.

You are seated at the right hand of the Father,
— have mercy on us.

Glory to the Father, and to the Son,
>   and to the Holy Spirit.
— Christ, Son of the living God,
>   have mercy on us.

Gospel
Canticle

Ant. **Jesus, turning, saw the woman and said: Take courage, daughter; your faith has saved you, alleluia.**

Canticle of Zechariah
Luke 1:68–79

Blessed + be the Lord, the God of Israel;
he has come to his people and set them free.

He has raised up for us a mighty savior,
born of the house of his servant David.

Through his holy prophets he
 promised of old
that he would save us from our enemies,
from the hands of all who hate us.

He promised to show mercy to our fathers
and to remember his holy covenant.

This was the oath he swore to our
 father Abraham:
to set us free from the hands of our enemies,
free to worship him without fear,
holy and righteous in his sight
 all the days of our life.

You, my child, shall be called the prophet of
 the Most High;
for you will go before the Lord to
 prepare his way,
to give his people knowledge of salvation
by the forgiveness of their sins.

In the tender compassion of our God
the dawn from on high shall break upon us,
to shine on those who dwell in darkness and
 the shadow of death,
and to guide our feet into the way of peace.

Glory to the Father, and to the Son,
> and to the Holy Spirit:
— as it was in the beginning, is now,
and will be for ever. Amen.

Ant. **Jesus, turning, saw the woman and said: Take courage, daughter; your faith has saved you, alleluia.**

Intercessions Christ is the sun that never sets, the true light that shines on every man. Let us call out to him in praise:
Lord, you are our life and our salvation.

Creator of the stars, we thank you for your gift, the first rays of the dawn,
— and we commemorate your resurrection.

May your Holy Spirit teach us to do your will today,
— and may your Wisdom guide us always.

Each Sunday give us the joy of gathering as your people,
— around the table of your Word and your Body.

From our hearts we thank you,
— for your countless blessings.

The Lord's Prayer

Our Father, who art in heaven,
hallowed be thy name;
thy kingdom come,
thy will be done
on earth as it is in heaven.
Give us this day our daily bread,
and forgive us our trespasses,
as we forgive those who trespass against us;
and lead us not into temptation,
but deliver us from evil.

Pater noster, qui es in cælis:
sanctificetur nomen tuum;
adveniat regnum tuum;
fiat voluntas tua,
sicut in cælo, et in terra.
Panem nostrum cotidianum da nobis hodie;
et dimitte nobis debita nostra,
sicut et nos dimittimus debitoribus nostris;
et ne nos inducas in tentationem;
sed libera nos a malo.

Concluding Prayer

Father,
you call your children
to walk in the light of Christ.
Free us from darkness
and keep us in the radiance of your truth.
We ask this through our Lord Jesus Christ,
    your Son,
who lives and reigns with you and
    the Holy Spirit,
God, for ever and ever.
—Amen.

Dismissal *If praying individually, or in a group without a priest or deacon:*

May the Lord + bless us,
protect us from all evil
and bring us to everlasting life.
—Amen.

If praying with a priest or deacon, he dismisses the people:

The Lord be with you.
—And with your spirit.

May almighty God bless you,
the Father, and the Son, ✠ and the Holy Spirit.
—Amen.

Go in peace.
—Thanks be to God.

EVENING PRAYER

God, + come to my assistance.
—Lord, make haste to help me.

Glory to the Father, and to the Son,
    and to the Holy Spirit:
—as it was in the beginning, is now,
and will be for ever. Amen. Alleluia.

Hymn *Holy God, We Praise Thy Name, p. 686*

Psalmody Ant. 1 **The Lord will stretch forth his mighty scepter from Zion, and he will reign for ever, alleluia.**

Psalm 110:1-5, 7 The Lord's revelation to my Master:
"Sit on my right:
your foes I will put beneath your feet."

The Lord will wield from Zion
your scepter of power:
rule in the midst of all your foes.

A prince from the day of your birth
on the holy mountains;
from the womb before the dawn I begot you.

The Lord has sworn an oath he will
    not change.
"You are a priest for ever,
a priest like Melchizedek of old."

The Master standing at your right hand
will shatter kings in the day of his
    great wrath.

He shall drink from the stream by
    the wayside
and therefore he shall lift up his head.

Glory to the Father, and to the Son,
    and to the Holy Spirit:
—as it was in the beginning, is now,
and will be for ever. Amen.

Ant. **The Lord will stretch forth his mighty scepter from Zion, and he will reign for ever, alleluia.**

JULY 2　　SUN　　　　　　　　　　EVENING PRAYER

Reading
2 Corinthians 1:3–4

Praised be God, the Father of our Lord Jesus Christ, the Father of mercies and the God of all consolation! He comforts us in all our afflictions and thus enables us to comfort those who are in trouble, with the same consolation we have received from him.

Responsory

The whole creation proclaims the greatness
　of your glory.
—The whole creation proclaims the greatness
　of your glory.

Eternal ages praise
—the greatness of your glory.

Glory to the Father, and to the Son,
　and to the Holy Spirit.
—The whole creation proclaims the greatness
　of your glory.

Gospel Canticle

Ant. **The Son of Man did not come to condemn men but to save them.**

Canticle of Mary
Luke 1:46–55

My + soul proclaims the greatness of the Lord,
my spirit rejoices in God my Savior
for he has looked with favor on his
　lowly servant.

From this day all generations will
　call me blessed:
the Almighty has done great things for me,
and holy is his Name.

He has mercy on those who fear him
in every generation.

He has shown the strength of his arm,
he has scattered the proud in their conceit.

He has cast down the mighty from
   their thrones,
and has lifted up the lowly.

He has filled the hungry with good things,
and the rich he has sent away empty.

He has come to the help of his servant Israel
for he has remembered his promise of mercy,
the promise he made to our fathers,
to Abraham and his children for ever.

Glory to the Father, and to the Son,
   and to the Holy Spirit:
—as it was in the beginning, is now,
and will be for ever. Amen.

Ant. **The Son of Man did not come to condemn men but to save them.**

Intercessions Christ the Lord is our head; we are his members. In joy let us call out to him:
Lord, may your kingdom come.

Christ our Savior, make your Church a more vivid symbol of the unity of all mankind,
—make it more effectively the sacrament of salvation for all peoples.

Through your presence, guide the college of bishops in union with the Pope,
—give them the gifts of unity, love and peace.

Bind all Christians more closely to yourself,
> their divine Head,
—lead them to proclaim your kingdom by the
> witness of their lives.

Grant peace to the world,
—let every land flourish in justice and security.

Grant to the dead the glory of resurrection,
—and give us a share in their happiness.

The Lord's Prayer

Our Father, who art in heaven,
hallowed be thy name;
thy kingdom come,
thy will be done
on earth as it is in heaven.
Give us this day our daily bread,
and forgive us our trespasses,
as we forgive those who trespass against us;
and lead us not into temptation,
but deliver us from evil.

Pater noster, qui es in cælis:
sanctificetur nomen tuum;
adveniat regnum tuum;
fiat voluntas tua,
sicut in cælo, et in terra.
Panem nostrum cotidianum da nobis hodie;
et dimitte nobis debita nostra,
sicut et nos dimittimus debitoribus nostris;
et ne nos inducas in tentationem;
sed libera nos a malo.

Concluding Prayer

Father,
you call your children
to walk in the light of Christ.
Free us from darkness
and keep us in the radiance of your truth.
We ask this through our Lord Jesus Christ,
 your Son,
who lives and reigns with you and
 the Holy Spirit,
God, for ever and ever.
—Amen.

Dismissal

If praying individually, or in a group without a priest or deacon:

May the Lord + bless us,
protect us from all evil
and bring us to everlasting life.
—Amen.

If praying with a priest or deacon, he dismisses the people:

The Lord be with you.
—And with your spirit.

May almighty God bless you,
the Father, and the Son, ✠ and the Holy Spirit.
—Amen.

Go in peace.
—Thanks be to God.

MY REFUGE, MY STRONGHOLD, MY GOD IN WHOM I TRUST!

NIGHT PRAYER

God, + come to my assistance.
—Lord, make haste to help me.

Glory to the Father, and to the Son,
 and to the Holy Spirit:
—as it was in the beginning, is now,
and will be for ever. Amen. Alleluia.

Examen *An optional brief examination of conscience may be made. Call to mind your sins and failings this day.*

Hymn *Before the Final Light of Day, p. 676*

Psalmody Ant. **Night holds no terrors for me sleeping under God's wings.**

Psalm 91
He who dwells in the shelter of the Most High
and abides in the shade of the Almighty
says to the Lord: "My refuge,
my stronghold, my God in whom I trust!"

It is he who will free you from the snare
of the fowler who seeks to destroy you;
he will conceal you with his pinions
and under his wings you will find refuge.

You will not fear the terror of the night
nor the arrow that flies by day,
nor the plague that prowls in the darkness
nor the scourge that lays waste at noon.

A thousand may fall at your side,
ten thousand fall at your right,
you, it will never approach;
his faithfulness is buckler and shield.

Your eyes have only to look
to see how the wicked are repaid,
you who have said: "Lord, my refuge!"
and have made the Most High your dwelling.

Upon you no evil shall fall,
no plague approach where you dwell.
For you has he commanded his angels,
to keep you in all your ways.

They shall bear you upon their hands
lest you strike your foot against a stone.
On the lion and the viper you will tread
and trample the young lion and the dragon.

Since he clings to me in love, I will free him;
protect him for he knows my name.
When he calls I shall answer: "I am with you."
I will save him in distress and give him glory.

With length of life I will content him;
I shall let him see my saving power.

Glory to the Father, and to the Son,
    and to the Holy Spirit:
as it was in the beginning, is now,
and will be for ever. Amen.

Ant. **Night holds no terrors for me sleeping under God's wings.**

Reading
Revelation 22:4–5

They shall see the Lord face to face and bear his name on their foreheads. The night shall be no more. They will need no light from lamps or the sun, for the Lord God shall give them light, and they shall reign forever.

Responsory

Into your hands, Lord, I commend my spirit.
—Into your hands, Lord, I commend my spirit.

You have redeemed us, Lord God of truth.
—I commend my spirit.

Glory to the Father, and to the Son,
   and to the Holy Spirit.
—Into your hands, Lord, I commend my spirit.

Gospel Canticle

Ant. **Protect us, Lord, as we stay awake; watch over us as we sleep, that awake, we may keep watch with Christ, and asleep, rest in his peace.**

Canticle of Simeon
Luke 2:29–32

Lord, + now you let your servant go in peace;
   your word has been fulfilled:
my own eyes have seen the salvation
which you have prepared in the sight of
      every people:
a light to reveal you to the nations
and the glory of your people Israel.

Glory to the Father, and to the Son,
   and to the Holy Spirit:
—as it was in the beginning, is now,
   and will be for ever. Amen.

Ant. **Protect us, Lord, as we stay awake; watch over us as we sleep, that awake, we may keep watch with Christ, and asleep, rest in his peace.**

Concluding Prayer
Let us pray.
Lord,
we have celebrated today
the mystery of the rising of Christ to new life.
May we now rest in your peace,
safe from all that could harm us,
and rise again refreshed and joyful,
to praise you throughout another day.
We ask this through Christ our Lord.
—Amen.

Blessing
May the all-powerful Lord
grant us a restful night
and a peaceful death.
—Amen.

Marian Antiphon
Sing the "Salve Regina," found on p. 698, or pray a Hail Mary.

Monday, July 3, 2023
St. Thomas

MORNING PRAYER

God, + come to my assistance.
—Lord, make haste to help me.

Glory to the Father, and to the Son,
    and to the Holy Spirit:
—as it was in the beginning, is now,
and will be for ever. Amen. Alleluia.

Hymn — *Let All on Earth Their Voices Raise, p. 690*

Psalmody   Ant. 1 **Lord, we do not know where you are going; how can we know the way? Jesus replied: I am the way, the truth and the life.**

Psalm 63:2–9

O God, you are my God, for you I long;
for you my soul is thirsting.
My body pines for you
like a dry, weary land without water.
So I gaze on you in the sanctuary
to see your strength and your glory.

For your love is better than life,
my lips will speak your praise.
So I will bless you all my life,
in your name I will lift up my hands.
My soul shall be filled as with a banquet,
my mouth shall praise you with joy.

On my bed I remember you.
On you I muse through the night
for you have been my help;
in the shadow of your wings I rejoice.
My soul clings to you;
your right hand holds me fast.

Glory to the Father, and to the Son,
    and to the Holy Spirit:
—as it was in the beginning, is now,
and will be for ever. Amen.

Ant. **Lord, we do not know where you are going; how can we know the way? Jesus replied: I am the way, the truth and the life.**

Ant. 2 **Thomas, who was called the Twin, was not present when Jesus appeared to the apostles; so they told him: We have seen the Lord, alleluia.**

Canticle:
Daniel
3:57–88, 56

Bless the Lord, all you works of the Lord.
Praise and exalt him above all forever.
Angels of the Lord, bless the Lord.
You heavens, bless the Lord.
All you waters above the heavens,
    bless the Lord.
All you hosts of the Lord, bless the Lord.
Sun and moon, bless the Lord.
Stars of heaven, bless the Lord.

Every shower and dew, bless the Lord.
All you winds, bless the Lord.
Fire and heat, bless the Lord.
Cold and chill, bless the Lord.
Dew and rain, bless the Lord.
Frost and chill, bless the Lord.
Ice and snow, bless the Lord.
Nights and days, bless the Lord.
Light and darkness, bless the Lord.
Lightnings and clouds, bless the Lord.

Let the earth bless the Lord.
Praise and exalt him above all forever.
Mountains and hills, bless the Lord.
Everything growing from the earth,
    bless the Lord.
You springs, bless the Lord.
Seas and rivers, bless the Lord.
You dolphins and all water creatures,
    bless the Lord.
All you birds of the air, bless the Lord.
All you beasts, wild and tame, bless the Lord.
You sons of men, bless the Lord.

O Israel, bless the Lord.
Praise and exalt him above all forever.
Priests of the Lord, bless the Lord.
Servants of the Lord, bless the Lord.
Spirits and souls of the just, bless the Lord.
Holy men of humble heart, bless the Lord.
Hananiah, Azariah, Mishael, bless the Lord.
Praise and exalt him above all forever.

Let us bless the Father, and the Son,
   and the Holy Spirit.
Let us praise and exalt him above all forever.
Blessed are you, Lord, in the firmament
   of heaven.
Praiseworthy and glorious and exalted above
   all forever.

Ant. **Thomas, who was called the Twin, was not present when Jesus appeared to the apostles; so they told him: We have seen the Lord, alleluia.**

Ant. 3 **With your hand, touch the mark of the nails; doubt no longer, but believe, alleluia.**

Psalm 149
Sing a new song to the Lord,
his praise in the assembly of the faithful.
Let Israel rejoice in its maker,
let Zion's sons exult in their king.
Let them praise his name with dancing
and make music with timbrel and harp.

For the Lord takes delight in his people.
He crowns the poor with salvation.
Let the faithful rejoice in their glory,
shout for joy and take their rest.
Let the praise of God be on their lips
and a two-edged sword in their hand,

to deal out vengeance to the nations
and punishment on all the peoples;
to bind their kings in chains
and their nobles in fetters of iron;
to carry out the sentence pre-ordained;
this honor is for all his faithful.

Glory to the Father, and to the Son,
    and to the Holy Spirit:
—as it was in the beginning, is now,
and will be for ever. Amen.

Ant. **With your hand, touch the mark of the nails; doubt no longer, but believe, alleluia.**

Reading
Ephesians 2:19–22

You are strangers and aliens no longer. No, you are fellow citizens of the saints and members of the household of God. You form a building which rises on the foundation of the apostles and prophets, with Christ Jesus himself as the capstone. Through him the whole structure is fitted together and takes shape as a holy temple in the Lord; in him you are being built into this temple, to become a dwelling place for God in the Spirit.

Responsory

You have made them rulers over all the earth.
—You have made them rulers over all the earth.

They will always remember your name, O Lord,
—over all the earth.

Glory to the Father, and to the Son,
    and to the Holy Spirit.
—You have made them rulers over all the earth.

Gospel Canticle

Ant. **Because you have seen me, Thomas, you have believed; blessed are they who have not seen me and yet believe.**

Canticle of Zechariah
Luke 1:68–79

Blessed + be the Lord, the God of Israel;
he has come to his people and set them free.

He has raised up for us a mighty savior,
born of the house of his servant David.

Through his holy prophets he
    promised of old
that he would save us from our enemies,
from the hands of all who hate us.

He promised to show mercy to our fathers
and to remember his holy covenant.

This was the oath he swore to our
    father Abraham:
to set us free from the hands of our enemies,
free to worship him without fear,
holy and righteous in his sight
    all the days of our life.

You, my child, shall be called the prophet of
    the Most High;
for you will go before the Lord to
    prepare his way,
to give his people knowledge of salvation
by the forgiveness of their sins.

In the tender compassion of our God
the dawn from on high shall break upon us,
to shine on those who dwell in darkness and
    the shadow of death,
and to guide our feet into the way of peace.

Glory to the Father, and to the Son,
    and to the Holy Spirit:
—as it was in the beginning, is now,
    and will be for ever. Amen.

Ant. **Because you have seen me, Thomas, you have believed; blessed are they who have not seen me and yet believe.**

Intercessions

Beloved friends, we have inherited heaven along with the apostles. Let us give thanks to the Father for all his gifts:
The company of apostles praises you, O Lord.

Praise be to you, Lord, for the banquet of Christ's body and blood given us through the apostles,
—which refreshes us and gives us life.

Praise be to you, Lord, for the feast of your word prepared for us by the apostles,
—giving us light and joy.

Praise be to you, Lord, for your holy Church, founded on the apostles,
—where we are gathered together into your community.

Praise be to you, Lord, for the cleansing power of baptism and penance that you have entrusted to your apostles,
—through which we are cleansed of our sins.

The Lord's Prayer

Our Father, who art in heaven,
hallowed be thy name;
thy kingdom come,
thy will be done
on earth as it is in heaven.
Give us this day our daily bread,
and forgive us our trespasses,
as we forgive those who trespass against us;
and lead us not into temptation,
but deliver us from evil.

Pater noster, qui es in cælis:
sanctificetur nomen tuum;
adveniat regnum tuum;
fiat voluntas tua,
sicut in cælo, et in terra.
Panem nostrum cotidianum da nobis hodie;
et dimitte nobis debita nostra,
sicut et nos dimittimus debitoribus nostris;
et ne nos inducas in tentationem;
sed libera nos a malo.

Concluding Prayer

Almighty Father,
as we honor Thomas the apostle,
let us always experience the help of his prayers.
May we have eternal life by believing in Jesus,
whom Thomas acknowledged as Lord,
for he lives and reigns with you and
 the Holy Spirit,
God, for ever and ever.
—Amen.

Dismissal *If praying individually, or in a group without a priest or deacon:*

May the Lord + bless us,
protect us from all evil
and bring us to everlasting life.
—Amen.

If praying with a priest or deacon, he dismisses the people:

The Lord be with you.
—And with your spirit.

May almighty God bless you,
the Father, and the Son, ✠ and the Holy Spirit.
—Amen.

Go in peace.
—Thanks be to God.

EVENING PRAYER

God, + come to my assistance.
—Lord, make haste to help me.

Glory to the Father, and to the Son,
    and to the Holy Spirit:
—as it was in the beginning, is now,
and will be for ever. Amen. Alleluia.

Hymn *Captains of the Saintly Band, p. 677*

Psalmody Ant. 1 **Lord, we do not know where you are going; how can we know the way? Jesus replied: I am the way, the truth and the life.**

Psalm 116:10–19 I trusted, even when I said:
"I am sorely afflicted,"
 and when I said in my alarm:
"No man can be trusted."

How can I repay the Lord
for his goodness to me?
The cup of salvation I will raise;
I will call on the Lord's name.

My vows to the Lord I will fulfill
before all his people.
O precious in the eyes of the Lord
is the death of his faithful.

Your servant, Lord, your servant am I;
you have loosened my bonds.
A thanksgiving sacrifice I make:
I will call on the Lord's name.

My vows to the Lord I will fulfill
before all his people,
in the courts of the house of the Lord,
in your midst, O Jerusalem.

Glory to the Father, and to the Son,
 and to the Holy Spirit:
—as it was in the beginning, is now,
and will be for ever. Amen.

Ant. **Lord, we do not know where you are going; how can we know the way? Jesus replied: I am the way, the truth and the life.**

EVENING PRAYER   MON   JULY 3

Ant. 2   **Thomas, who was called the Twin, was
not present when Jesus appeared to the
apostles; so they told him: We have seen
the Lord, alleluia.**

Psalm 126   When the Lord delivered Zion from bondage,
it seemed like a dream.
Then was our mouth filled with laughter,
on our lips there were songs.

The heathens themselves said: "What marvels
the Lord worked for them!"
What marvels the Lord worked for us!
Indeed we were glad.

Deliver us, O Lord, from our bondage
as streams in dry land.
Those who are sowing in tears
will sing when they reap.

They go out, they go out, full of tears,
carrying seed for the sowing:
they come back, they come back, full of song,
carrying their sheaves.

Glory to the Father, and to the Son,
   and to the Holy Spirit:
—as it was in the beginning, is now,
and will be for ever. Amen.

Ant.   **Thomas, who was called the Twin, was
not present when Jesus appeared to the
apostles; so they told him: We have seen
the Lord, alleluia.**

Ant. 3 **With your hand, touch the mark of the nails; doubt no longer, but believe, alleluia.**

Canticle:
Ephesians 1:3–10

Praised be the God and Father
of our Lord Jesus Christ,
who has bestowed on us in Christ
every spiritual blessing in the heavens.

God chose us in him
before the world began
to be holy
and blameless in his sight.

He predestined us
to be his adopted sons through Jesus Christ,
such was his will and pleasure,
that all might praise the glorious favor
he has bestowed on us in his beloved.

In him and through his blood, we have
    been redeemed,
and our sins forgiven,
so immeasurably generous
is God's favor to us.

God has given us the wisdom
to understand fully the mystery,
the plan he was pleased
to decree in Christ.

A plan to be carried out
in Christ, in the fullness of time,
to bring all things into one in him,
in the heavens and on the earth.

Glory to the Father, and to the Son,
  and to the Holy Spirit:
—as it was in the beginning, is now,
  and will be for ever. Amen.

Ant. **With your hand, touch the mark of the nails; doubt no longer, but believe, alleluia.**

Reading
Ephesians
4:11–13

Christ gave apostles, prophets, evangelists, pastors and teachers in roles of service for the faithful to build up the body of Christ, till we become one in faith and in the knowledge of God's Son, and form that perfect man who is Christ come to full stature.

Responsory Tell all the nations how glorious God is.
—Tell all the nations how glorious God is.

Make known his wonders to every people.
—How glorious God is.

Glory to the Father, and to the Son,
  and to the Holy Spirit.
—Tell all the nations how glorious God is.

Gospel Canticle Ant. **I touched the mark of the nails with my fingers; I put my hand into his side and said: My Lord and my God, alleluia.**

Canticle of
Mary
Luke 1:46–55

My + soul proclaims the greatness of the Lord,
my spirit rejoices in God my Savior
for he has looked with favor on his
  lowly servant.

From this day all generations will
    call me blessed:
the Almighty has done great things for me,
and holy is his Name.

He has mercy on those who fear him
in every generation.

He has shown the strength of his arm,
he has scattered the proud in their conceit.

He has cast down the mighty from
    their thrones,
and has lifted up the lowly.

He has filled the hungry with good things,
and the rich he has sent away empty.

He has come to the help of his servant Israel
for he has remembered his promise of mercy,
the promise he made to our fathers,
to Abraham and his children for ever.

Glory to the Father, and to the Son,
    and to the Holy Spirit:
as it was in the beginning, is now,
and will be for ever. Amen.

Ant. **I touched the mark of the nails with my fingers; I put my hand into his side and said: My Lord and my God, alleluia.**

Intercessions My brothers, we build on the foundation of the apostles. Let us pray to our almighty Father for his holy people and say:
Be mindful of your Church, O Lord.

Father, you wanted your Son to be seen first by the apostles after the resurrection from the dead,
—we ask you to make us his witnesses to the farthest corners of the world.

You sent your Son to preach the good news to the poor,
—help us to preach this Gospel to every creature.

You sent your Son to sow the seed of unending life,
—grant that we who work at sowing the seed may share the joy of the harvest.

You sent your Son to reconcile all men to you through his blood,
—help us all to work toward achieving this reconciliation.

Your Son sits at your right hand in heaven,
—let the dead enter your kingdom of joy.

The Lord's Prayer

Our Father, who art in heaven,
hallowed be thy name;
thy kingdom come,
thy will be done
on earth as it is in heaven.
Give us this day our daily bread,
and forgive us our trespasses,
as we forgive those who trespass against us;
and lead us not into temptation,
but deliver us from evil.

Pater noster, qui es in cælis:
sanctificetur nomen tuum;
adveniat regnum tuum;
fiat voluntas tua,
sicut in cælo, et in terra.
Panem nostrum cotidianum da nobis hodie;
et dimitte nobis debita nostra,
sicut et nos dimittimus debitoribus nostris;
et ne nos inducas in tentationem;
sed libera nos a malo.

Concluding Prayer

Almighty Father,
as we honor Thomas the apostle,
let us always experience the help of his prayers.
May we have eternal life by believing in Jesus,
whom Thomas acknowledged as Lord,
for he lives and reigns with you and
    the Holy Spirit,
God, for ever and ever.
—Amen.

Dismissal *If praying individually, or in a group without a priest or deacon:*

May the Lord + bless us,
protect us from all evil
and bring us to everlasting life.
—Amen.

If praying with a priest or deacon, he dismisses the people:

The Lord be with you.
—And with your spirit.

May almighty God bless you,
the Father, and the Son, ✠ and the Holy Spirit.
—Amen.

Go in peace.
—Thanks be to God.

NIGHT PRAYER

God, + come to my assistance.
—Lord, make haste to help me.

Glory to the Father, and to the Son,
 and to the Holy Spirit:
—as it was in the beginning, is now,
and will be for ever. Amen. Alleluia.

Examen *An optional brief examination of conscience may be made. Call to mind your sins and failings this day.*

Hymn *O Joyful Light of God Most High, p. 693*

Psalmody Ant. **O Lord, our God, unwearied is your love for us.**

JULY 3   MON   NIGHT PRAYER

Psalm 86

Turn your ear, O Lord, and give answer
for I am poor and needy.
Preserve my life, for I am faithful:
save the servant who trusts in you.

You are my God; have mercy on me, Lord,
for I cry to you all the day long.
Give joy to your servant, O Lord,
for to you I lift up my soul.

O Lord, you are good and forgiving,
full of love to all who call.
Give heed, O Lord, to my prayer
and attend to the sound of my voice.

In the day of distress I will call
and surely you will reply.
Among the gods there is none like you, O Lord;
nor work to compare with yours.

All the nations shall come to adore you
and glorify your name, O Lord:
for you are great and do marvelous deeds,
you who alone are God.

Show me, Lord, your way
so that I may walk in your truth.
Guide my heart to fear your name.

I will praise you, Lord my God, with
    all my heart
and glorify your name for ever;
for your love to me has been great:
you have saved me from the depths of
    the grave.

The proud have risen against me;
ruthless men seek my life:
to you they pay no heed.

But you, God of mercy and compassion,
slow to anger, O Lord,
abounding in love and truth,
turn and take pity on me.

O give your strength to your servant
and save your handmaid's son.
Show me a sign of your favor
that my foes may see to their shame
that you console me and give me your help.

Glory to the Father, and to the Son,
  and to the Holy Spirit:
—as it was in the beginning, is now,
and will be for ever. Amen.

Ant. **O Lord, our God, unwearied is your love for us.**

Reading
1 Thessalonians 5:9–10

God has destined us for acquiring salvation through our Lord Jesus Christ. He died for us, that all of us, whether awake or asleep, together might live with him.

Responsory

Into your hands, Lord, I commend my spirit.
—Into your hands, Lord, I commend my spirit.

You have redeemed us, Lord God of truth.
—I commend my spirit.

Glory to the Father, and to the Son,
    and to the Holy Spirit.
—Into your hands, Lord, I commend my spirit.

Gospel Canticle

Ant. **Protect us, Lord, as we stay awake; watch over us as we sleep, that awake, we may keep watch with Christ, and asleep, rest in his peace.**

Canticle of Simeon
Luke 2:29–32

Lord, + now you let your servant go in peace;
your word has been fulfilled:
my own eyes have seen the salvation
which you have prepared in the sight of
    every people:
a light to reveal you to the nations
and the glory of your people Israel.

Glory to the Father, and to the Son,
    and to the Holy Spirit:
—as it was in the beginning, is now,
and will be for ever. Amen.

Ant. **Protect us, Lord, as we stay awake; watch over us as we sleep, that awake, we may keep watch with Christ, and asleep, rest in his peace.**

Concluding Prayer

Let us pray.
Lord,
give our bodies restful sleep
and let the work we have done today
bear fruit in eternal life.
We ask this through Christ our Lord.
—Amen.

Blessing May the all-powerful Lord
grant us a restful night
and a peaceful death.
—Amen.

Marian Antiphon *Sing the "Salve Regina," found on p. 698, or pray a Hail Mary.*

Tuesday, July 4, 2023
Tuesday of the Thirteenth Week in Ordinary Time

MORNING PRAYER

God, + come to my assistance.
—Lord, make haste to help me.

Glory to the Father, and to the Son,
   and to the Holy Spirit:
—as it was in the beginning, is now,
and will be for ever. Amen. Alleluia.

Hymn *O Splendor of God's Glory Bright, p. 694*

Psalmody Ant. 1 **The man whose deeds are blameless and whose heart is pure will climb the mountain of the Lord.**

Psalm 24 The Lord's is the earth and its fullness,
the world and all its peoples.
It is he who set it on the seas;
on the waters he made it firm.

Who shall climb the mountain of the Lord?
Who shall stand in his holy place?
The man with clean hands and pure heart,
who desires not worthless things,
who has not sworn so as to deceive
　　his neighbor.

He shall receive blessings from the Lord
and reward from the God who saves him.
Such are the men who seek him,
seek the face of the God of Jacob.

O gates, lift high your heads;
grow higher, ancient doors.
Let him enter, the king of glory!

Who is the king of glory?
The Lord, the mighty, the valiant,
the Lord, the valiant in war.

O gates, lift high your heads;
grow higher, ancient doors.
Let him enter, the king of glory!

Who is he, the king of glory?
He, the Lord of armies,
he is the king of glory.

Glory to the Father, and to the Son,
　　and to the Holy Spirit:
—as it was in the beginning, is now,
　and will be for ever. Amen.

Ant. **The man whose deeds are blameless and whose heart is pure will climb the mountain of the Lord.**

Ant. 2 **Praise the eternal King in all your deeds.**

Canticle:
Tobit 13:1–8

Blessed be God who lives forever,
because his kingdom lasts for all ages.

For he scourges and then has mercy;
he casts down to the depths of the
    nether world,
and he brings up from the great abyss.
No one can escape his hand.

Praise him, you Israelites, before the Gentiles,
for though he has scattered you among them,
he has shown you his greatness even there.

Exalt him before every living being,
because he is the Lord our God,
our Father and God forever.

He scourged you for your iniquities,
but will again have mercy on you all.
He will gather you from all the Gentiles
among whom you have been scattered.

When you turn back to him with all
    your heart,
to do what is right before him,
then he will turn back to you,
and no longer hide his face from you.

So now consider what he has done for you,
and praise him with full voice.
Bless the Lord of righteousness,
and exalt the King of the ages.

In the land of my exile I praise him,
and show his power and majesty to a
    sinful nation.
"Turn back, you sinners! do the right
    before him:
perhaps he may look with favor upon you
and show you mercy.

"As for me, I exalt my God,
and my spirit rejoices in the King of heaven.
Let all people speak of his majesty,
and sing his praises in Jerusalem."

Glory to the Father, and to the Son,
    and to the Holy Spirit:
as it was in the beginning, is now,
and will be for ever. Amen.

Ant. **Praise the eternal King in all your deeds.**

Ant. 3 **The loyal heart must praise the Lord.**

Psalm 33 Ring out your joy to the Lord, O you just;
for praise is fitting for loyal hearts.

Give thanks to the Lord upon the harp,
with a ten-stringed lute sing him songs.
O sing him a song that is new,
play loudly, with all your skill.

For the word of the Lord is faithful
and all his works to be trusted.
The Lord loves justice and right
and fills the earth with his love.

By his word the heavens were made,
by the breath of his mouth all the stars.
He collects the waves of the ocean;
he stores up the depths of the sea.

Let all the earth fear the Lord,
all who live in the world revere him.
He spoke; and it came to be.
He commanded; it sprang into being.

He frustrates the designs of the nations,
he defeats the plans of the peoples.
His own designs shall stand for ever,
the plans of his heart from age to age.

They are happy, whose God is the Lord,
the people he has chosen as his own.
From the heavens the Lord looks forth,
he sees all the children of men.

From the place where he dwells he gazes
on all the dwellers on the earth,
he who shapes the hearts of them all
and considers all their deeds.

A king is not saved by his army,
nor a warrior preserved by his strength.
A vain hope for safety is the horse;
despite its power it cannot save.

The Lord looks on those who revere him,
on those who hope in his love,
to rescue their souls from death,
to keep them alive in famine.

Our soul is waiting for the Lord.
The Lord is our help and our shield.
In him do our hearts find joy.
We trust in his holy name.

May your love be upon us, O Lord,
as we place all our hope in you.

Glory to the Father, and to the Son,
    and to the Holy Spirit:
—as it was in the beginning, is now,
and will be for ever. Amen.

Ant. **The loyal heart must praise the Lord.**

Reading
Romans 13:11b, 12–13a

It is now the hour for you to wake from sleep. The night is far spent; the day draws near. Let us cast off deeds of darkness and put on the armor of light. Let us live honorably as in daylight.

Responsory

My God stands by me, all my trust is in him.
—My God stands by me, all my trust is in him.

I find refuge in him, and I am truly free;
—all my trust is in him.

Glory to the Father, and to the Son,
    and to the Holy Spirit.
—My God stands by me, all my trust is in him.

Gospel Canticle

Ant. **God has raised up for us a mighty Savior, as he promised through the words of his holy prophets.**

Canticle of Zechariah
Luke 1:68–79

Blessed + be the Lord, the God of Israel;
he has come to his people and set them free.

He has raised up for us a mighty savior,
born of the house of his servant David.

Through his holy prophets he
    promised of old
that he would save us from our enemies,
from the hands of all who hate us.

He promised to show mercy to our fathers
and to remember his holy covenant.

This was the oath he swore to our
    father Abraham:
to set us free from the hands of our enemies,
free to worship him without fear,
holy and righteous in his sight
    all the days of our life.

You, my child, shall be called the prophet of
    the Most High;
for you will go before the Lord to
    prepare his way,
to give his people knowledge of salvation
by the forgiveness of their sins.

In the tender compassion of our God
the dawn from on high shall break upon us,
to shine on those who dwell in darkness and
   the shadow of death,
and to guide our feet into the way of peace.

Glory to the Father, and to the Son,
   and to the Holy Spirit:
—as it was in the beginning, is now,
and will be for ever. Amen.

Ant. **God has raised up for us a mighty Savior, as he promised through the words of his holy prophets.**

Intercessions Beloved brothers and sisters, we share a heavenly calling under Christ, our high priest. Let us praise him with shouts of joy:
Lord, our God and our Savior.

Almighty King, through baptism you
   conferred on us a royal priesthood,
—inspire us to offer you a continual sacrifice
   of praise.

Help us to keep your commandments,
—that through the power of the Holy Spirit we
   may live in you and you in us.

Give us your eternal wisdom,
—to be with us today and to guide us.

May our companions today be free of sorrow,
—and filled with joy.

The Lord's Prayer

Our Father, who art in heaven,
hallowed be thy name;
thy kingdom come,
thy will be done
on earth as it is in heaven.
Give us this day our daily bread,
and forgive us our trespasses,
as we forgive those who trespass against us;
and lead us not into temptation,
but deliver us from evil.

Pater noster, qui es in cælis:
sanctificetur nomen tuum;
adveniat regnum tuum;
fiat voluntas tua,
sicut in cælo, et in terra.
Panem nostrum cotidianum da nobis hodie;
et dimitte nobis debita nostra,
sicut et nos dimittimus debitoribus nostris;
et ne nos inducas in tentationem;
sed libera nos a malo.

Concluding Prayer

God our Father,
hear our morning prayer
and let the radiance of your love
scatter the gloom of our hearts.
The light of heaven's love has restored
    us to life:
free us from the desires that belong to darkness.
We ask this through our Lord Jesus Christ,
    your Son,
who lives and reigns with you and
    the Holy Spirit,
God, for ever and ever.
—Amen.

JULY 4 TUE EVENING PRAYER

Dismissal *If praying individually, or in a group without a priest or deacon:*

May the Lord + bless us,
protect us from all evil
and bring us to everlasting life.
—Amen.

If praying with a priest or deacon, he dismisses the people:

The Lord be with you.
—And with your spirit.

May almighty God bless you,
the Father, and the Son, ✠ and the Holy Spirit.
—Amen.

Go in peace.
—Thanks be to God.

EVENING PRAYER

God, + come to my assistance.
—Lord, make haste to help me.

Glory to the Father, and to the Son,
   and to the Holy Spirit:
—as it was in the beginning, is now,
and will be for ever. Amen. Alleluia.

Hymn *Immortal, Invisible, God Only Wise, p. 688*

Psalmody Ant. 1 **God has crowned his Christ with victory.**

Psalm 20

May the Lord answer in time of trial;
may the name of Jacob's God protect you.

May he send you help from his shrine
and give you support from Zion.
May he remember all your offerings
and receive your sacrifice with favor.

May he give you your heart's desire
and fulfill every one of your plans.
May we ring out our joy at your victory
and rejoice in the name of our God.
May the Lord grant all your prayers.

I am sure now that the Lord
will give victory to his anointed,
will reply from his holy heaven
with the mighty victory of his hand.

Some trust in chariots or horses,
but we in the name of the Lord.
They will collapse and fall,
but we shall hold and stand firm.

Give victory to the king, O Lord,
give answer on the day we call.

Glory to the Father, and to the Son,
    and to the Holy Spirit:
—as it was in the beginning, is now,
and will be for ever. Amen.

Ant. **God has crowned his Christ with victory.**

Ant. 2 **We celebrate your mighty works with songs of praise, O Lord.**

Psalm 21:2–8, 14

O Lord, your strength gives joy to the king;
how your saving help makes him glad!
You have granted him his heart's desire;
you have not refused the prayer of his lips.

You came to meet him with the blessings
    of success,
you have set on his head a crown of pure gold.
He asked you for life and this you have given,
days that will last from age to age.

Your saving help has given him glory.
You have laid upon him majesty
    and splendor,
you have granted your blessings to
    him for ever.
You have made him rejoice with the joy of
    your presence.

The king has put his trust in the Lord:
through the mercy of the Most High he shall
    stand firm.
O Lord, arise in your strength;
we shall sing and praise your power.

Glory to the Father, and to the Son,
    and to the Holy Spirit:
—as it was in the beginning, is now,
and will be for ever. Amen.

Ant. **We celebrate your mighty works with songs of praise, O Lord.**

Ant. 3 **Lord, you have made us a kingdom and priests for God our Father.**

Canticle:
Revelation 4:11;
5:9, 10, 12

O Lord our God, you are worthy
to receive glory and honor and power.

For you have created all things;
by your will they came to be and were made.

Worthy are you, O Lord,
to receive the scroll and break open its seals.

For you were slain;
with your blood you purchased for God
men of every race and tongue,
of every people and nation.

You made of them a kingdom,
and priests to serve our God,
and they shall reign on the earth.

Worthy is the Lamb that was slain
to receive power and riches,
wisdom and strength,
honor and glory and praise.

Glory to the Father, and to the Son,
    and to the Holy Spirit:
—as it was in the beginning, is now,
and will be for ever. Amen.

Ant. **Lord, you have made us a kingdom and priests for God our Father.**

Reading
1 John 3:1a, 2

See what love the Father has bestowed on us
in letting us be called the children of God!
Yet that is what we are.
Dearly beloved,
we are God's children now;
what we shall later be has not yet
   come to light.
We know that when it comes to light
we shall be like him,
for we shall see him as he is.

Responsory

Through all eternity, O Lord, your promise
   stands unshaken.
—Through all eternity, O Lord, your promise
   stands unshaken.

Your faithfulness will never fail;
—your promise stands unshaken.

Glory to the Father, and to the Son,
   and to the Holy Spirit.
—Through all eternity, O Lord, your promise
   stands unshaken.

Gospel Canticle

Ant. **My spirit rejoices in God my Savior.**

Canticle of Mary
Luke 1:46–55

My + soul proclaims the greatness of the Lord,
my spirit rejoices in God my Savior
for he has looked with favor on his
   lowly servant.

From this day all generations will
   call me blessed:
the Almighty has done great things for me,
and holy is his Name.

He has mercy on those who fear him
in every generation.

He has shown the strength of his arm,
he has scattered the proud in their conceit.

He has cast down the mighty from
    their thrones,
and has lifted up the lowly.

He has filled the hungry with good things,
and the rich he has sent away empty.

He has come to the help of his servant Israel
for he has remembered his promise of mercy,
the promise he made to our fathers,
to Abraham and his children for ever.

Glory to the Father, and to the Son,
    and to the Holy Spirit:
—as it was in the beginning, is now,
and will be for ever. Amen.

Ant. **My spirit rejoices in God my Savior.**

Intercessions Let us praise Christ the Lord, who lives among us, the people he redeemed, and let us say:
Lord, hear our prayer.

Lord, king and ruler of nations, be with all your people and their governments,
—inspire them to pursue the good of all according to your law.

You made captive our captivity,
—to our brothers who are enduring bodily or
    spiritual chains, grant the freedom of the
    sons of God.

May our young people be concerned with
    remaining blameless in your sight,
—and may they generously follow your call.

May our children imitate your example,
—and grow in wisdom and grace.

Accept our dead brothers and sisters into
    your eternal kingdom,
—where we hope to reign with you.

The Lord's Prayer

Our Father, who art in heaven,
hallowed be thy name;
thy kingdom come,
thy will be done
on earth as it is in heaven.
Give us this day our daily bread,
and forgive us our trespasses,
as we forgive those who trespass against us;
and lead us not into temptation,
but deliver us from evil.

Pater noster, qui es in cælis:
sanctificetur nomen tuum;
adveniat regnum tuum;
fiat voluntas tua,
sicut in cælo, et in terra.
Panem nostrum cotidianum da nobis hodie;
et dimitte nobis debita nostra,
sicut et nos dimittimus debitoribus nostris;
et ne nos inducas in tentationem;
sed libera nos a malo.

Concluding Prayer

Almighty God,
we give you thanks
for bringing us safely
to this evening hour.
May this lifting up of our hands in prayer
be a sacrifice pleasing in your sight.
We ask this through our Lord Jesus Christ,
    your Son,
who lives and reigns with you and
    the Holy Spirit,
God, for ever and ever.
—Amen.

Dismissal

If praying individually, or in a group without a priest or deacon:

May the Lord + bless us,
protect us from all evil
and bring us to everlasting life.
—Amen.

If praying with a priest or deacon, he dismisses the people:

The Lord be with you.
—And with your spirit.

May almighty God bless you,
the Father, and the Son, ✠ and the Holy Spirit.
—Amen.

Go in peace.
—Thanks be to God.

NIGHT PRAYER

God, ✠ come to my assistance.
—Lord, make haste to help me.

Glory to the Father, and to the Son,
and to the Holy Spirit:
—as it was in the beginning, is now,
and will be for ever. Amen. Alleluia.

Examen — *An optional brief examination of conscience may be made. Call to mind your sins and failings this day.*

Hymn — *Abide with Me, p. 675*

Psalmody — Ant. **Do not hide your face from me; in you I put my trust.**

Psalm 143:1–11

Lord, listen to my prayer:
turn your ear to my appeal.
You are faithful, you are just; give answer.
Do not call your servant to judgment
for no one is just in your sight.

The enemy pursues my soul;
he has crushed my life to the ground;
he has made me dwell in darkness
like the dead, long forgotten.
Therefore my spirit fails;
my heart is numb within me.

I remember the days that are past:
I ponder all your works.
I muse on what your hand has wrought
and to you I stretch out my hands.
Like a parched land my soul thirsts for you.

Lord, make haste and answer;
for my spirit fails within me.
Do not hide your face
lest I become like those in the grave.

In the morning let me know your love
for I put my trust in you.
Make me know the way I should walk:
to you I lift up my soul.

Rescue me, Lord, from my enemies;
I have fled to you for refuge.
Teach me to do your will
for you, O Lord, are my God.
Let your good spirit guide me
in ways that are level and smooth.

For your name's sake, Lord, save my life;
in your justice save my soul from distress.

Glory to the Father, and to the Son,
    and to the Holy Spirit:
as it was in the beginning, is now,
and will be for ever. Amen.

Ant. **Do not hide your face from me; in you I put my trust.**

JULY 4   TUE   NIGHT PRAYER

Reading
1 Peter 5:8–9a

Stay sober and alert. Your opponent the devil is prowling like a roaring lion looking for someone to devour. Resist him, solid in your faith.

Responsory

Into your hands, Lord, I commend my spirit.
—Into your hands, Lord, I commend my spirit.

You have redeemed us, Lord God of truth.
—I commend my spirit.

Glory to the Father, and to the Son,
   and to the Holy Spirit.
—Into your hands, Lord, I commend my spirit.

Gospel Canticle

Ant. **Protect us, Lord, as we stay awake; watch over us as we sleep, that awake, we may keep watch with Christ, and asleep, rest in his peace.**

Canticle of Simeon
Luke 2:29–32

Lord, + now you let your servant go in peace;
your word has been fulfilled:
my own eyes have seen the salvation
which you have prepared in the sight of
   every people:
a light to reveal you to the nations
and the glory of your people Israel.

Glory to the Father, and to the Son,
   and to the Holy Spirit:
—as it was in the beginning, is now,
and will be for ever. Amen.

Ant. **Protect us, Lord, as we stay awake; watch over us as we sleep, that awake, we may keep watch with Christ, and asleep, rest in his peace.**

Concluding Prayer
Let us pray.
Lord,
fill this night with your radiance.
May we sleep in peace and rise with joy
to welcome the light of a new day in
 your name.
We ask this through Christ our Lord.
—Amen.

Blessing
May the all-powerful Lord
grant us a restful night
and a peaceful death.
—Amen.

Marian Antiphon
Sing the "Salve Regina," found on p. 698, or pray a Hail Mary.

YOUR LOVE,
LORD, REACHES
TO HEAVEN;
YOUR TRUTH
TO THE SKIES.

YOUR JUSTICE
IS LIKE GOD'S
MOUNTAIN,
YOUR JUDGMENTS
LIKE THE DEEP.

Wednesday, July 5, 2023
Wednesday of the Thirteenth Week in Ordinary Time

MORNING PRAYER

God, + come to my assistance.
—Lord, make haste to help me.

Glory to the Father, and to the Son,
   and to the Holy Spirit:
—as it was in the beginning, is now,
   and will be for ever. Amen. Alleluia.

Hymn — *From All That Dwell Below the Skies, p. 679*

Psalmody — Ant. 1 **O Lord, in your light we see light itself.**

Psalm 36

Sin speaks to the sinner
in the depths of his heart.
There is no fear of God
before his eyes.

He so flatters himself in his mind
that he knows not his guilt.
In his mouth are mischief and deceit.
All wisdom is gone.

He plots the defeat of goodness
as he lies on his bed.
He has set his foot on evil ways,
he clings to what is evil.

Your love, Lord, reaches to heaven;
your truth to the skies.
Your justice is like God's mountain,
your judgments like the deep.

To both man and beast you give protection.
O Lord, how precious is your love.
My God, the sons of men
find refuge in the shelter of your wings.

They feast on the riches of your house;
they drink from the stream of your delight.
In you is the source of life
and in your light we see light.

Keep on loving those who know you,
doing justice for upright hearts.
Let the foot of the proud not crush me
nor the hand of the wicked cast me out.

See how the evil-doers fall!
Flung down, they shall never arise.

Glory to the Father, and to the Son,
    and to the Holy Spirit:
—as it was in the beginning, is now,
and will be for ever. Amen.

Ant. **O Lord, in your light we see light itself.**

Ant. 2 **O God, you are great and glorious; we marvel at your power.**

Canticle:
Judith 16:2–3a,
13–15

Strike up the instruments,
a song to my God with timbrels,
chant to the Lord with cymbals.
Sing to him a new song,
exalt and acclaim his name.

A new hymn I will sing to my God.
O Lord, great are you and glorious,
wonderful in power and unsurpassable.

Let your every creature serve you;
for you spoke, and they were made,
you sent forth your spirit, and they
    were created;
no one can resist your word.

The mountains to their bases, and the seas,
    are shaken;
the rocks, like wax, melt before your glance.
But to those who fear you,
you are very merciful.

Glory to the Father, and to the Son,
    and to the Holy Spirit:
—as it was in the beginning, is now,
and will be for ever. Amen.

Ant. **O God, you are great and glorious; we marvel at your power.**

Ant. 3 **Exult in God's presence with hymns of praise.**

Psalm 47

All peoples, clap your hands,
cry to God with shouts of joy!
For the Lord, the Most High, we must fear,
great king over all the earth.

He subdues peoples under us
and nations under our feet.
Our inheritance, our glory, is from him,
given to Jacob out of love.

God goes up with shouts of joy;
the Lord goes up with trumpet blast.
Sing praise for God, sing praise,
sing praise to our king, sing praise.

God is king of all the earth.
Sing praise with all your skill.
God is king over the nations;
God reigns on his holy throne.

The princes of the peoples are assembled
with the people of Abraham's God.
The rulers of the earth belong to God,
to God who reigns over all.

Glory to the Father, and to the Son,
    and to the Holy Spirit:
as it was in the beginning, is now,
and will be for ever. Amen.

Ant. **Exult in God's presence with hymns of praise.**

Reading
Tobit 4:15a, 16a, 18a, 19

Do to no one what you yourself dislike. Give to the hungry some of your bread, and to the naked some of your clothing. Seek counsel from every wise man. At all times bless the Lord God, and ask him to make all your paths straight and to grant success to all your endeavors and plans.

Responsory

Incline my heart according to your
　　will, O God.
—Incline my heart according to your
　　will, O God.

Speed my steps along your path,
—according to your will, O God.

Glory to the Father, and to the Son,
　　and to the Holy Spirit.
—Incline my heart according to your
　　will, O God.

Gospel Canticle

Ant. **Show us your mercy, Lord; remember your holy covenant.**

Canticle of Zechariah
Luke 1:68–79

Blessed + be the Lord, the God of Israel;
he has come to his people and set them free.

He has raised up for us a mighty savior,
born of the house of his servant David.

Through his holy prophets he
　　promised of old
that he would save us from our enemies,
from the hands of all who hate us.

He promised to show mercy to our fathers
and to remember his holy covenant.

This was the oath he swore to our
    father Abraham:
to set us free from the hands of our enemies,
free to worship him without fear,
holy and righteous in his sight
    all the days of our life.

You, my child, shall be called the prophet of
    the Most High;
for you will go before the Lord to
    prepare his way,
to give his people knowledge of salvation
by the forgiveness of their sins.

In the tender compassion of our God
the dawn from on high shall break upon us,
to shine on those who dwell in darkness and
    the shadow of death,
and to guide our feet into the way of peace.

Glory to the Father, and to the Son,
    and to the Holy Spirit:
as it was in the beginning, is now,
and will be for ever. Amen.

Ant. **Show us your mercy, Lord; remember your holy covenant.**

Intercessions Let us give thanks to Christ and offer him
continual praise, for he sanctifies us and
calls us his brothers:
Lord, help your brothers to grow in holiness.

With single-minded devotion we dedicate
the beginnings of this day to the honor of
your resurrection,
—may we make the whole day pleasing to you
by our works of holiness.

As a sign of your love, you renew each day for
the sake of our well-being and happiness,
—renew us daily for the sake of your glory.

Teach us today to recognize your presence
in all men,
—especially in the poor and in those
who mourn.

Grant that we may live today in peace
with all men,
—never rendering evil for evil.

The Lord's Prayer Our Father, who art in heaven,
hallowed be thy name;
thy kingdom come,
thy will be done
on earth as it is in heaven.
Give us this day our daily bread,
and forgive us our trespasses,
as we forgive those who trespass against us;
and lead us not into temptation,
but deliver us from evil.

Pater noster, qui es in cælis:
sanctificetur nomen tuum;
adveniat regnum tuum;
fiat voluntas tua,
sicut in cælo, et in terra.
Panem nostrum cotidianum da nobis hodie;
et dimitte nobis debita nostra,
sicut et nos dimittimus debitoribus nostris;
et ne nos inducas in tentationem;
sed libera nos a malo.

Concluding Prayer

God our Savior,
hear our morning prayer:
help us to follow the light
and live the truth.
In you we have been born again
as sons and daughters of light:
may we be your witnesses before all
　the world.
We ask this through our Lord Jesus Christ,
　your Son,
who lives and reigns with you and
　the Holy Spirit,
God, for ever and ever.
—Amen.

Dismissal

If praying individually, or in a group without a priest or deacon:

May the Lord + bless us,
protect us from all evil
and bring us to everlasting life.
—Amen.

If praying with a priest or deacon, he dismisses the people:

The Lord be with you.
—And with your spirit.

May almighty God bless you,
the Father, and the Son, ✢ and the Holy Spirit.
—Amen.

Go in peace.
—Thanks be to God.

EVENING PRAYER

God, + come to my assistance.
—Lord, make haste to help me.

Glory to the Father, and to the Son,
  and to the Holy Spirit:
—as it was in the beginning, is now,
  and will be for ever. Amen. Alleluia.

Hymn *Sing Praise to God Who Reigns Above, p. 700*

Psalmody Ant. 1 **The Lord is my light and my help; whom shall I fear?**

Psalm 27 The Lord is my light and my help;
whom shall I fear?
The Lord is the stronghold of my life;
before whom shall I shrink?

When evil-doers draw near
to devour my flesh,
it is they, my enemies and foes,
who stumble and fall.

Though an army encamp against me
my heart would not fear.
Though war break out against me
even then would I trust.

There is one thing I ask of the Lord,
for this I long,
to live in the house of the Lord,
all the days of my life,
to savor the sweetness of the Lord,
to behold his temple.

For there he keeps me safe in his tent
in the day of evil.
He hides me in the shelter of his tent,
on a rock he sets me safe.

And now my head shall be raised
above my foes who surround me
and I shall offer within his tent
a sacrifice of joy.

I will sing and make music for the Lord.

Glory to the Father, and to the Son,
   and to the Holy Spirit:
—as it was in the beginning, is now,
and will be for ever. Amen.

Ant. **The Lord is my light and my help; whom shall I fear?**

Ant. 2 **I long to look on you, O Lord; do not turn your face from me.**

Psalm 27
(continued)

O Lord, hear my voice when I call;
have mercy and answer.
Of you my heart has spoken:
"Seek his face."

It is your face, O Lord, that I seek;
hide not your face.
Dismiss not your servant in anger;
you have been my help.

Do not abandon or forsake me,
O God my help!
Though father and mother forsake me,
the Lord will receive me.

Instruct me, Lord, in your way;
on an even path lead me.
When they lie in ambush, protect me
from my enemy's greed.
False witnesses rise against me,
breathing out fury.

I am sure I shall see the Lord's goodness
in the land of the living.
Hope in him, hold firm and take heart.
Hope in the Lord!

Glory to the Father, and to the Son,
    and to the Holy Spirit:
—as it was in the beginning, is now,
and will be for ever. Amen.

Ant. **I long to look on you, O Lord; do not turn your face from me.**

Ant. 3 **He is the first-born of all creation; in every way the primacy is his.**

Canticle:
Colossians
1:12–20

Let us give thanks to the Father
for having made you worthy
to share the lot of the saints
in light.

He rescued us
from the power of darkness
and brought us
into the kingdom of his beloved Son.
Through him we have redemption,
the forgiveness of our sins.

He is the image of the invisible God,
the first-born of all creatures.
In him everything in heaven and on earth
    was created,
things visible and invisible.

All were created through him;
all were created for him.
He is before all else that is.
In him everything continues in being.

It is he who is head of the body, the church!
he who is the beginning,
the first-born of the dead,
so that primacy may be his in everything.

It pleased God to make absolute fullness
    reside in him
and, by means of him, to reconcile
    everything in his person,
both on earth and in the heavens,
making peace through the blood of his cross.

Glory to the Father, and to the Son,
    and to the Holy Spirit:
as it was in the beginning, is now,
and will be for ever. Amen.

Ant. **He is the first-born of all creation; in every way the primacy is his.**

Reading
James 1:22, 25

Act on this word. If all you do is listen to it, you are deceiving yourselves. There is, on the other hand, the man who peers into freedom's ideal law and abides by it. He is no forgetful listener, but one who carries out the law in practice. Blest will this man be in whatever he does.

Responsory

Claim me once more as your own, Lord,
    and have mercy on me.
—Claim me once more as your own, Lord,
    and have mercy on me.

Do not abandon me with the wicked;
—have mercy on me.

Glory to the Father, and to the Son,
    and to the Holy Spirit.
—Claim me once more as your own, Lord,
    and have mercy on me.

Gospel Canticle   **Ant. The Almighty has done great things for me, and holy is his Name.**

Canticle of Mary
Luke 1:46–55

My + soul proclaims the greatness of the Lord,
my spirit rejoices in God my Savior
for he has looked with favor on his
    lowly servant.

From this day all generations will
    call me blessed:
the Almighty has done great things for me,
and holy is his Name.

He has mercy on those who fear him
in every generation.

He has shown the strength of his arm,
he has scattered the proud in their conceit.

He has cast down the mighty from
    their thrones,
and has lifted up the lowly.

He has filled the hungry with good things,
and the rich he has sent away empty.

He has come to the help of his servant Israel
for he has remembered his promise of mercy,
the promise he made to our fathers,
to Abraham and his children for ever.

Glory to the Father, and to the Son,
    and to the Holy Spirit:
—as it was in the beginning, is now,
    and will be for ever. Amen.

Ant. **The Almighty has done great things for me, and holy is his Name.**

Intercessions In all that we do, let the name of the Lord be praised, for he surrounds his chosen people with boundless love. Let our prayer rise up to him:
Lord, show us your love.

Remember your Church, Lord,
—keep her from every evil and let her grow to the fullness of your love.

Let the nations recognize you as the one true God,
—and Jesus your Son, as the Messiah whom you sent.

Grant prosperity to our neighbors,
—give them life and happiness for ever.

Console those who are burdened with oppressive work and daily hardships,
—preserve the dignity of workers.

Open wide the doors of your compassion to those who have died today,
—and in your mercy receive them into your kingdom.

JULY 5   WED   EVENING PRAYER

The Lord's Prayer

Our Father, who art in heaven,
hallowed be thy name;
thy kingdom come,
thy will be done
on earth as it is in heaven.
Give us this day our daily bread,
and forgive us our trespasses,
as we forgive those who trespass against us;
and lead us not into temptation,
but deliver us from evil.

Pater noster, qui es in cælis:
sanctificetur nomen tuum;
adveniat regnum tuum;
fiat voluntas tua,
sicut in cælo, et in terra.
Panem nostrum cotidianum da nobis hodie;
et dimitte nobis debita nostra,
sicut et nos dimittimus debitoribus nostris;
et ne nos inducas in tentationem;
sed libera nos a malo.

Concluding Prayer

Lord,
watch over us by day and by night.
In the midst of life's countless changes
strengthen us with your never-changing love.
We ask this through our Lord Jesus Christ,
    your Son,
who lives and reigns with you and
    the Holy Spirit,
God, for ever and ever.
—Amen.

Dismissal *If praying individually, or in a group without a priest or deacon:*

May the Lord + bless us,
protect us from all evil
and bring us to everlasting life.
—Amen.

If praying with a priest or deacon, he dismisses the people:

The Lord be with you.
—And with your spirit.

May almighty God bless you,
the Father, and the Son, ✠ and the Holy Spirit.
—Amen.

Go in peace.
—Thanks be to God.

NIGHT PRAYER

God, + come to my assistance.
—Lord, make haste to help me.

Glory to the Father, and to the Son,
    and to the Holy Spirit:
—as it was in the beginning, is now,
and will be for ever. Amen. Alleluia.

Examen *An optional brief examination of conscience may be made. Call to mind your sins and failings this day.*

Hymn *Before the Final Light of Day, p. 676*

Psalmody Ant. 1 **Lord God, be my refuge and my strength.**

JULY 5   WED   NIGHT PRAYER

Psalm 31:1–6

In you, O Lord, I take refuge.
Let me never be put to shame.
In your justice, set me free,
hear me and speedily rescue me.

Be a rock of refuge for me,
a mighty stronghold to save me,
for you are my rock, my stronghold.
For your name's sake, lead me and guide me.

Release me from the snares they have hidden
for you are my refuge, Lord.
Into your hands I commend my spirit.
It is you who will redeem me, Lord.

Glory to the Father, and to the Son,
    and to the Holy Spirit:
—as it was in the beginning, is now,
and will be for ever. Amen.

Ant. **Lord God, be my refuge and my strength.**

Ant. 2 **Out of the depths I cry to you, Lord.**

Psalm 130

Out of the depths I cry to you, O Lord,
Lord, hear my voice!
O let your ears be attentive
to the voice of my pleading.

If you, O Lord, should mark our guilt,
Lord, who would survive?
But with you is found forgiveness:
for this we revere you.

My soul is waiting for the Lord,
I count on his word.
My soul is longing for the Lord
more than watchman for daybreak.
Let the watchman count on daybreak
and Israel on the Lord.

Because with the Lord there is mercy
and fullness of redemption,
Israel indeed he will redeem
from all its iniquity.

Glory to the Father, and to the Son,
    and to the Holy Spirit:
—as it was in the beginning, is now,
and will be for ever. Amen.

Ant. **Out of the depths I cry to you, Lord.**

Reading
Ephesians 4:26–27

If you are angry, let it be without sin. The sun must not go down on your wrath; do not give the devil a chance to work on you.

Responsory

Into your hands, Lord, I commend my spirit.
—Into your hands, Lord, I commend my spirit.

You have redeemed us, Lord God of truth.
—I commend my spirit.

Glory to the Father, and to the Son,
    and to the Holy Spirit.
—Into your hands, Lord, I commend my spirit.

Gospel Canticle

Ant. **Protect us, Lord, as we stay awake; watch over us as we sleep, that awake, we may keep watch with Christ, and asleep, rest in his peace.**

Canticle of Simeon
Luke 2:29–32

Lord, ✠ now you let your servant go in peace;
your word has been fulfilled:
my own eyes have seen the salvation
which you have prepared in the sight of
    every people:
a light to reveal you to the nations
and the glory of your people Israel.

Glory to the Father, and to the Son,
    and to the Holy Spirit:
—as it was in the beginning, is now,
and will be for ever. Amen.

Ant. **Protect us, Lord, as we stay awake; watch over us as we sleep, that awake, we may keep watch with Christ, and asleep, rest in his peace.**

Concluding Prayer

Let us pray.
Lord Jesus Christ,
you have given your followers
an example of gentleness and humility,
a task that is easy, a burden that is light.
Accept the prayers and work of this day,
and give us the rest that will strengthen us
to render more faithful service to you
who live and reign for ever and ever.
—Amen.

Blessing May the all-powerful Lord
grant us a restful night
and a peaceful death.
—Amen.

Marian Antiphon *Sing the "Salve Regina," found on p. 698, or pray a Hail Mary.*

Thursday, July 6, 2023
Thursday of the Thirteenth Week in Ordinary Time

MORNING PRAYER

God, + come to my assistance.
—Lord, make haste to help me.

Glory to the Father, and to the Son,
    and to the Holy Spirit:
—as it was in the beginning, is now,
and will be for ever. Amen. Alleluia.

Hymn *Now That the Sun Is Gleaming Bright, p. 692*

Psalmody Ant. 1 **Awake, lyre and harp, with praise let us awake the dawn.**

Psalm 57 Have mercy on me, God, have mercy
for in you my soul has taken refuge.
In the shadow of your wings I take refuge
till the storms of destruction pass by.

JULY 6 THU MORNING PRAYER

I call to God the Most High,
to God who has always been my help.
May he send from heaven and save me
and shame those who assail me.

May God send his truth and his love.

My soul lies down among lions,
who would devour the sons of men.
Their teeth are spears and arrows,
their tongue a sharpened sword.

O God, arise above the heavens;
may your glory shine on earth!

They laid a snare for my steps,
my soul was bowed down.
They dug a pit in my path
but fell in it themselves.

My heart is ready, O God,
my heart is ready.
I will sing, I will sing your praise.
Awake, my soul,
awake, lyre and harp,
I will awake the dawn.

I will thank you, Lord, among the peoples,
among the nations I will praise you
for your love reaches to the heavens
and your truth to the skies.

O God, arise above the heavens;
may your glory shine on earth!

Glory to the Father, and to the Son,
    and to the Holy Spirit:
—as it was in the beginning, is now,
and will be for ever. Amen.

Ant. **Awake, lyre and harp, with praise let us awake the dawn.**

Ant. 2 **My people, says the Lord, will be filled with my blessings.**

Canticle:
Jeremiah
31:10–14

Hear the word of the Lord, O nations,
proclaim it on distant coasts, and say:
He who scattered Israel, now gathers
    them together,
he guards them as a shepherd his flock.

The Lord shall ransom Jacob,
he shall redeem him from the hand of his
    conqueror.

Shouting, they shall mount the
    heights of Zion,
they shall come streaming to the Lord's
    blessings:
the grain, the wine, and the oil,
the sheep and the oxen;
they themselves shall be like
    watered gardens,
never again shall they languish.

Then the virgins shall make merry and dance,
and young men and old as well.
I will turn their mourning into joy,
I will console and gladden them after
  their sorrows.
I will lavish choice portions upon the priests,
and my people shall be filled with my
  blessings,
says the Lord.

Glory to the Father, and to the Son,
  and to the Holy Spirit:
—as it was in the beginning, is now,
and will be for ever. Amen.

Ant. **My people, says the Lord, will be filled with my blessings.**

Ant. 3 **The Lord is great and worthy to be praised in the city of our God.**

Psalm 48

The Lord is great and worthy to be praised
in the city of our God.
His holy mountain rises in beauty,
the joy of all the earth.

Mount Zion, true pole of the earth,
the Great King's city!
God, in the midst of its citadels,
has shown himself its stronghold.

For the kings assembled together,
together they advanced.
They saw; at once they were astounded;
dismayed, they fled in fear.

A trembling seized them there,
like the pangs of birth.
By the east wind you have destroyed
the ships of Tarshish.

As we have heard, so we have seen
in the city of our God,
in the city of the Lord of hosts
which God upholds for ever.

O God, we ponder your love
within your temple.
Your praise, O God, like your name
reaches the ends of the earth.

With justice your right hand is filled.
Mount Zion rejoices;
the people of Judah rejoice
at the sight of your judgments.

Walk through Zion, walk all round it;
count the number of its towers.
Review all its ramparts,
examine its castles,

that you may tell the next generation
that such is our God,
our God for ever and always.
It is he who leads us.

Glory to the Father, and to the Son,
    and to the Holy Spirit:
—as it was in the beginning, is now,
    and will be for ever. Amen.

JULY 6 THU MORNING PRAYER

Ant. **The Lord is great and worthy to be praised in the city of our God.**

Reading
Isaiah 66:1–2

Thus says the Lord:
The heavens are my throne,
   and the earth is my footstool.
What kind of house can you build for me;
   what is to be my resting place?
My hand made all these things
   when all of them came to be, says the Lord.
This is the one whom I approve:
   the lowly and afflicted man who trembles
      at my word.

Responsory

From the depths of my heart I cry to you;
   hear me, O Lord.
—From the depths of my heart I cry to you;
   hear me, O Lord.

I will do what you desire;
—hear me, O Lord.

Glory to the Father, and to the Son,
   and to the Holy Spirit.
—From the depths of my heart I cry to you;
   hear me, O Lord.

Gospel Canticle

Ant. Let us serve the Lord in holiness, and he will save us from our enemies.

Canticle of Zechariah
Luke 1:68–79

Blessed + be the Lord, the God of Israel;
he has come to his people and set them free.

He has raised up for us a mighty savior,
born of the house of his servant David.

Through his holy prophets he
    promised of old
that he would save us from our enemies,
from the hands of all who hate us.

He promised to show mercy to our fathers
and to remember his holy covenant.

This was the oath he swore to our
    father Abraham:
to set us free from the hands of our enemies,
free to worship him without fear,
holy and righteous in his sight
    all the days of our life.

You, my child, shall be called the prophet of
    the Most High;
for you will go before the Lord to
    prepare his way,
to give his people knowledge of salvation
by the forgiveness of their sins.

In the tender compassion of our God
the dawn from on high shall break upon us,
to shine on those who dwell in darkness and
    the shadow of death,
and to guide our feet into the way of peace.

Glory to the Father, and to the Son,
    and to the Holy Spirit:
—as it was in the beginning, is now,
    and will be for ever. Amen.

JULY 6   THU   MORNING PRAYER

Ant.   **Let us serve the Lord in holiness, and he will save us from our enemies.**

Intercessions   The Lord Jesus Christ has given us the light of another day. In return we thank him as we cry out:
Lord, bless us and bring us close to you.

You offered yourself in sacrifice for our sins,
—accept our intentions and our work today.

You bring us joy by the light of another day,
—let the morning star rise in our hearts.

Give us strength to be patient with those we meet today,
—and so imitate you.

Make us aware of your mercy this morning, Lord,
—and let your strength be our delight.

The Lord's Prayer   Our Father, who art in heaven,
hallowed be thy name;
thy kingdom come,
thy will be done
on earth as it is in heaven.
Give us this day our daily bread,
and forgive us our trespasses,
as we forgive those who trespass against us;
and lead us not into temptation,
but deliver us from evil.

Pater noster, qui es in cælis:
sanctificetur nomen tuum;
adveniat regnum tuum;
fiat voluntas tua,
sicut in cælo, et in terra.
Panem nostrum cotidianum da nobis hodie;
et dimitte nobis debita nostra,
sicut et nos dimittimus debitoribus nostris;
et ne nos inducas in tentationem;
sed libera nos a malo.

Concluding Prayer

All-powerful and ever-living God,
at morning, noon, and evening we pray:
cast out from our hearts the darkness of sin
and bring us to the light of your truth,
Jesus Christ, who lives and reigns with you
    and the Holy Spirit,
God, for ever and ever.
—Amen.

Dismissal

If praying individually, or in a group without a priest or deacon:

May the Lord + bless us,
protect us from all evil
and bring us to everlasting life.
—Amen.

If praying with a priest or deacon, he dismisses the people:

The Lord be with you.
—And with your spirit.

May almighty God bless you,
the Father, and the Son, ✣ and the Holy Spirit.
—Amen.

JULY 6   THU   EVENING PRAYER

Go in peace.
—Thanks be to God.

EVENING PRAYER ————————————

God, + come to my assistance.
—Lord, make haste to help me.

Glory to the Father, and to the Son,
 and to the Holy Spirit:
—as it was in the beginning, is now,
 and will be for ever. Amen. Alleluia.

Hymn *Go, Labor On, p. 684*

Psalmody Ant. 1 **I cried to you, Lord, and you healed me; I will praise you for ever.**

Psalm 30 I will praise you, Lord, you have rescued me
and have not let my enemies rejoice over me.

O Lord, I cried to you for help
and you, my God, have healed me.
O Lord, you have raised my soul
 from the dead,
restored me to life from those who sink into
 the grave.

Sing psalms to the Lord, you who love him,
give thanks to his holy name.
His anger lasts a moment; his favor
 through life.
At night there are tears, but joy comes
 with dawn.

I said to myself in my good fortune:
"Nothing will ever disturb me."
Your favor had set me on a mountain fastness,
then you hid your face and I was put to
confusion.

To you, Lord, I cried,
to my God I made appeal:
"What profit would my death be, my going to
the grave?
Can dust give you praise or proclaim
your truth?"

The Lord listened and had pity.
The Lord came to my help.
For me you have changed my mourning
into dancing,
you removed my sackcloth and clothed
me with joy.
So my soul sings psalms to you unceasingly.
O Lord my God, I will thank you for ever.

Glory to the Father, and to the Son,
and to the Holy Spirit:
—as it was in the beginning, is now,
and will be for ever. Amen.

Ant. **I cried to you, Lord, and you healed me; I will praise you for ever.**

Ant. 2 **The one who is sinless in the eyes of God is blessed indeed.**

Psalm 32

Happy the man whose offense is forgiven,
whose sin is remitted.
O happy the man to whom the Lord
imputes no guilt,
in whose spirit is no guile.

I kept it secret and my frame was wasted.
I groaned all the day long
for night and day your hand
was heavy upon me.
Indeed, my strength was dried up
as by the summer's heat.

But now I have acknowledged my sins;
my guilt I did not hide.
I said: "I will confess
my offense to the Lord."
And you, Lord, have forgiven
the guilt of my sin.

So let every good man pray to you
in the time of need.
The floods of water may reach high
but him they shall not reach.
You are my hiding place, O Lord;
you save me from distress.
You surround me with cries of deliverance.

I will instruct you and teach you
the way you should go;
I will give you counsel
with my eye upon you.

Be not like horse and mule, unintelligent,
needing bridle and bit,
else they will not approach you.
Many sorrows has the wicked
but he who trusts in the Lord,
loving mercy surrounds him.

Rejoice, rejoice in the Lord,
exult, you just!
O come, ring out your joy,
all you upright of heart.

Glory to the Father, and to the Son,
    and to the Holy Spirit:
—as it was in the beginning, is now,
and will be for ever. Amen.

Ant. **The one who is sinless in the eyes of God is blessed indeed.**

Ant. 3 **The Father has given Christ all power, honor and kingship; all people will obey him.**

Canticle:
Revelation
11:17–18;
12:10b–12a

We praise you, the Lord God Almighty,
who is and who was.
You have assumed your great power,
you have begun your reign.

The nations have raged in anger,
but then came your day of wrath
and the moment to judge the dead:
the time to reward your servants the prophets
and the holy ones who revere you,
the great and the small alike.

Now have salvation and power come,
the reign of our God and the authority
of his Anointed One.
For the accuser of our brothers is cast out,
who night and day accused them before God.

They defeated him by the blood of the Lamb
and by the word of their testimony;
love for life did not deter them from death.
So rejoice, you heavens,
and you that dwell therein!

Glory to the Father, and to the Son,
   and to the Holy Spirit:
as it was in the beginning, is now,
and will be for ever. Amen.

Ant. **The Father has given Christ all power, honor and kingship; all people will obey him.**

Reading
1 Peter 1:6–9

There is cause for rejoicing here. You may for a time have to suffer the distress of many trials; but this is so that your faith, which is more precious than the passing splendor of fire-tried gold, may by its genuineness lead to praise, glory, and honor when Jesus Christ appears. Although you have never seen him, you love him, and without seeing you now believe in him, and rejoice with inexpressible joy touched with glory because you are achieving faith's goal, your salvation.

Responsory

The Lord has given us food, bread of the
    finest wheat.
—The Lord has given us food, bread of the
    finest wheat.

Honey from the rock to our heart's content,
—bread of the finest wheat.

Glory to the Father, and to the Son,
    and to the Holy Spirit.
—The Lord has given us food, bread of the
    finest wheat.

Gospel Canticle

Ant. **God has cast down the mighty from their thrones, and has lifted up the lowly.**

Canticle of Mary
Luke 1:46–55

My + soul proclaims the greatness of the Lord,
my spirit rejoices in God my Savior
for he has looked with favor on his
    lowly servant.

From this day all generations will
    call me blessed:
the Almighty has done great things for me,
and holy is his Name.

He has mercy on those who fear him
in every generation.

He has shown the strength of his arm,
he has scattered the proud in their conceit.

He has cast down the mighty from
    their thrones,
and has lifted up the lowly.

He has filled the hungry with good things,
and the rich he has sent away empty.

He has come to the help of his servant Israel
for he has remembered his promise of mercy,
the promise he made to our fathers,
to Abraham and his children for ever.

Glory to the Father, and to the Son,
   and to the Holy Spirit:
—as it was in the beginning, is now,
and will be for ever. Amen.

Ant. **God has cast down the mighty from their thrones, and has lifted up the lowly.**

Intercessions Our hope is in God, who gives us help.
   Let us call upon him, and say:
Look kindly on your children, Lord.

Lord, our God, you made an eternal covenant
   with your people,
—keep us ever mindful of your mighty deeds.

Let your ordained ministers grow toward
   perfect love,
—and preserve your faithful people in unity by
   the bond of peace.

Be with us in our work of building the
   earthly city,
—that in building we may not labor in vain.

Send workers into your vineyard,
—and glorify your name among the nations.

Welcome into the company of your saints our relatives and benefactors who have died,
—may we share their happiness one day.

The Lord's Prayer

Our Father, who art in heaven,
hallowed be thy name;
thy kingdom come,
thy will be done
on earth as it is in heaven.
Give us this day our daily bread,
and forgive us our trespasses,
as we forgive those who trespass against us;
and lead us not into temptation,
but deliver us from evil.

Pater noster, qui es in cælis:
sanctificetur nomen tuum;
adveniat regnum tuum;
fiat voluntas tua,
sicut in cælo, et in terra.
Panem nostrum cotidianum da nobis hodie;
et dimitte nobis debita nostra,
sicut et nos dimittimus debitoribus nostris;
et ne nos inducas in tentationem;
sed libera nos a malo.

Concluding Prayer

Father,
you illumine the night
and bring the dawn to scatter darkness.
Let us pass this night in safety,
free from Satan's power,
and rise when morning comes
to give you thanks and praise.
We ask this through our Lord Jesus Christ,
  your Son,
who lives and reigns with you and
  the Holy Spirit,
God, for ever and ever.
—Amen.

Dismissal

If praying individually, or in a group without a priest or deacon:

May the Lord + bless us,
protect us from all evil
and bring us to everlasting life.
—Amen.

If praying with a priest or deacon, he dismisses the people:

The Lord be with you.
—And with your spirit.

May almighty God bless you,
the Father, and the Son, ✠ and the Holy Spirit.
—Amen.

Go in peace.
—Thanks be to God.

HE HAS MERCY
ON THOSE
WHO FEAR HIM
IN EVERY
GENERATION.

NIGHT PRAYER

God, + come to my assistance.
—Lord, make haste to help me.

Glory to the Father, and to the Son,
    and to the Holy Spirit:
—as it was in the beginning, is now,
    and will be for ever. Amen. Alleluia.

Examen — *An optional brief examination of conscience may be made. Call to mind your sins and failings this day.*

Hymn — *O Joyful Light of God Most High, p. 693*

Psalmody   Ant. **In you, my God, my body will rest in hope.**

Psalm 16

Preserve me, God, I take refuge in you.
I say to the Lord: "You are my God.
My happiness lies in you alone."

He has put into my heart a marvelous love
for the faithful ones who dwell in his land.
Those who choose other gods increase
    their sorrows.
Never will I offer their offerings of blood.
Never will I take their name upon my lips.

O Lord, it is you who are my portion and cup;
it is you yourself who are my prize.
The lot marked out for me is my delight:
welcome indeed the heritage that falls to me!

I will bless the Lord who gives me counsel,
who even at night directs my heart.
I keep the Lord ever in my sight:
since he is at my right hand, I shall stand firm.

And so my heart rejoices, my soul is glad;
even my body shall rest in safety.
For you will not leave my soul
    among the dead,
nor let your beloved know decay.

You will show me the path of life,
the fullness of joy in your presence,
at your right hand happiness for ever.

Glory to the Father, and to the Son,
    and to the Holy Spirit:
—as it was in the beginning, is now,
and will be for ever. Amen.

Ant. **In you, my God, my body will rest in hope.**

Reading
1 Thessalonians 5:23

May the God of peace make you perfect in holiness. May he preserve you whole and entire, spirit, soul, and body, irreproachable at the coming of our Lord Jesus Christ.

Responsory
Into your hands, Lord, I commend my spirit.
—Into your hands, Lord, I commend my spirit.

You have redeemed us, Lord God of truth.
—I commend my spirit.

Glory to the Father, and to the Son,
    and to the Holy Spirit.
—Into your hands, Lord, I commend my spirit.

Gospel Canticle

Ant. **Protect us, Lord, as we stay awake; watch over us as we sleep, that awake, we may keep watch with Christ, and asleep, rest in his peace.**

Canticle of Simeon
Luke 2:29–32

Lord, + now you let your servant go in peace;
your word has been fulfilled:
my own eyes have seen the salvation
which you have prepared in the sight of
    every people:
a light to reveal you to the nations
and the glory of your people Israel.

Glory to the Father, and to the Son,
    and to the Holy Spirit:
—as it was in the beginning, is now,
and will be for ever. Amen.

Ant. **Protect us, Lord, as we stay awake; watch over us as we sleep, that awake, we may keep watch with Christ, and asleep, rest in his peace.**

Concluding Prayer

Let us pray.
Lord God,
send peaceful sleep
to refresh our tired bodies.
May your help always renew us
and keep us strong in your service.
We ask this through Christ our Lord.
—Amen.

Blessing May the all-powerful Lord
grant us a restful night
and a peaceful death.
—Amen.

Marian Antiphon *Sing the "Salve Regina," found on p. 698, or pray a Hail Mary.*

Friday, July 7, 2023
Friday of the Thirteenth Week in Ordinary Time

MORNING PRAYER

God, + come to my assistance.
—Lord, make haste to help me.

Glory to the Father, and to the Son,
and to the Holy Spirit:
—as it was in the beginning, is now,
and will be for ever. Amen. Alleluia.

Hymn *God Who Made Both Earth and Heaven, p. 682*

Psalmody Ant. 1 **Lord, you will accept the true sacrifice offered on your altar.**

Psalm 51 Have mercy on me, God, in your kindness.
In your compassion blot out my offense.
O wash me more and more from my guilt
and cleanse me from my sin.

My offenses truly I know them;
my sin is always before me.
Against you, you alone, have I sinned;
what is evil in your sight I have done.

That you may be justified when you
    give sentence
and be without reproach when you judge.
O see, in guilt I was born,
a sinner was I conceived.

Indeed you love truth in the heart;
then in the secret of my heart teach
    me wisdom.
O purify me, then I shall be clean;
O wash me, I shall be whiter than snow.

Make me hear rejoicing and gladness,
that the bones you have crushed may revive.
From my sins turn away your face
and blot out all my guilt.

A pure heart create for me, O God,
put a steadfast spirit within me.
Do not cast me away from your presence,
nor deprive me of your holy spirit.

Give me again the joy of your help;
with a spirit of fervor sustain me,
that I may teach transgressors your ways
and sinners may return to you.

O rescue me, God, my helper,
and my tongue shall ring out your goodness.
O Lord, open my lips
and my mouth shall declare your praise.

For in sacrifice you take no delight,
burnt offering from me you would refuse,
my sacrifice, a contrite spirit.
A humbled, contrite heart you will not spurn.

In your goodness, show favor to Zion:
rebuild the walls of Jerusalem.
Then you will be pleased with lawful sacrifice,
holocausts offered on your altar.

Glory to the Father, and to the Son,
    and to the Holy Spirit:
—as it was in the beginning, is now,
and will be for ever. Amen.

Ant. **Lord, you will accept the true sacrifice offered on your altar.**

Ant. 2 **All the descendants of Israel will glory in the Lord's gift of victory.**

Canticle:
Isaiah 45:15-25

Truly with you God is hidden,
the God of Israel, the savior!
Those are put to shame and disgrace
who vent their anger against him.
Those go in disgrace
who carve images.

Israel, you are saved by the Lord,
  saved forever!
You shall never be put to shame or disgrace
in future ages.

For thus says the Lord,
the creator of the heavens,
who is God,
the designer and maker of the earth
who established it,
not creating it to be a waste,
but designing it to be lived in:

I am the Lord, and there is no other.
I have not spoken from hiding
nor from some dark place of the earth.
And I have not said to the
  descendants of Jacob,
"Look for me in an empty waste."
I, the Lord, promise justice,
I foretell what is right.

Come and assemble, gather together,
you fugitives from among the Gentiles!
They are without knowledge who bear
  wooden idols
and pray to gods that cannot save.

Come here and declare
in counsel together:
Who announced this from the beginning
and foretold it from of old?
Was it not I, the Lord,
besides whom there is no other God?
There is no just and saving God but me.

Turn to me and be safe,
all you ends of the earth,
for I am God; there is no other!

By myself I swear,
uttering my just decree
and my unalterable word:

To me every knee shall bend;
by me every tongue shall swear,
saying, "Only in the Lord
are just deeds and power.

Before him in shame shall come
all who vent their anger against him.
In the Lord shall be the vindication
    and the glory
of all the descendants of Israel."

Glory to the Father, and to the Son,
    and to the Holy Spirit:
—as it was in the beginning, is now,
and will be for ever. Amen.

Ant. **All the descendants of Israel will glory in the Lord's gift of victory.**

Ant. 3 **Let us go into God's presence singing for joy.**

Psalm 100
Cry out with joy to the Lord, all the earth.
Serve the Lord with gladness.
Come before him, singing for joy.

Know that he, the Lord, is God.
He made us, we belong to him,
we are his people, the sheep of his flock.

Go within his gates, giving thanks.
Enter his courts with songs of praise.
Give thanks to him and bless his name.

Indeed, how good is the Lord,
eternal his merciful love.
He is faithful from age to age.

Glory to the Father, and to the Son,
 and to the Holy Spirit:
—as it was in the beginning, is now,
and will be for ever. Amen.

Ant. **Let us go into God's presence singing for joy.**

Reading
Ephesians 4:29–32

Never let evil talk pass your lips; say only the good things men need to hear, things that will really help them. Do nothing that will sadden the Holy Spirit with whom you were sealed against the day of redemption. Get rid of all bitterness, all passion and anger, harsh words, slander, and malice of every kind. In place of these, be kind to one another, compassionate, and mutually forgiving, just as God has forgiven you in Christ.

Responsory At daybreak, be merciful to me.
—At daybreak, be merciful to me.

Make known to me the path that I must walk.
—Be merciful to me.

Glory to the Father, and to the Son,
  and to the Holy Spirit.
—At daybreak, be merciful to me.

Gospel Canticle

Ant. **The Lord has come to his people and set them free.**

Canticle of Zechariah
Luke 1:68–79

Blessed + be the Lord, the God of Israel;
he has come to his people and set them free.

He has raised up for us a mighty savior,
born of the house of his servant David.

Through his holy prophets he
  promised of old
that he would save us from our enemies,
from the hands of all who hate us.

He promised to show mercy to our fathers
and to remember his holy covenant.

This was the oath he swore to our
  father Abraham:
to set us free from the hands of our enemies,
free to worship him without fear,
holy and righteous in his sight
  all the days of our life.

You, my child, shall be called the prophet of
  the Most High;
for you will go before the Lord to
  prepare his way,
to give his people knowledge of salvation
by the forgiveness of their sins.

In the tender compassion of our God
the dawn from on high shall break upon us,
to shine on those who dwell in darkness and
    the shadow of death,
and to guide our feet into the way of peace.

Glory to the Father, and to the Son,
    and to the Holy Spirit:
—as it was in the beginning, is now,
and will be for ever. Amen.

Ant. **The Lord has come to his people and set them free.**

Intercessions Through his cross the Lord Jesus brought salvation to the human race. We adore him and in faith we call out to him:
Lord, pour out your mercy upon us.

Christ, Rising Sun, warm us with your rays,
—and restrain us from every evil impulse.

Keep guard over our thoughts, words
    and actions,
—and make us pleasing in your sight this day.

Turn your gaze from our sinfulness,
—and cleanse us from our iniquities.

Through your cross and resurrection,
—fill us with the consolation of the Spirit.

The Lord's Prayer

Our Father, who art in heaven,
hallowed be thy name;
thy kingdom come,
thy will be done
on earth as it is in heaven.
Give us this day our daily bread,
and forgive us our trespasses,
as we forgive those who trespass against us;
and lead us not into temptation,
but deliver us from evil.

Pater noster, qui es in cælis:
sanctificetur nomen tuum;
adveniat regnum tuum;
fiat voluntas tua,
sicut in cælo, et in terra.
Panem nostrum cotidianum da nobis hodie;
et dimitte nobis debita nostra,
sicut et nos dimittimus debitoribus nostris;
et ne nos inducas in tentationem;
sed libera nos a malo.

Concluding Prayer

God our Father,
you conquer the darkness of ignorance
by the light of your Word.
Strengthen within our hearts
the faith you have given us;
let not temptation ever quench the fire
that your love has kindled within us.
We ask this through our Lord Jesus Christ,
    your Son,
who lives and reigns with you and
    the Holy Spirit,
God, for ever and ever.
—Amen.

Dismissal *If praying individually, or in a group without a priest or deacon:*

May the Lord + bless us,
protect us from all evil
and bring us to everlasting life.
—Amen.

If praying with a priest or deacon, he dismisses the people:

The Lord be with you.
—And with your spirit.

May almighty God bless you,
the Father, and the Son, ✠ and the Holy Spirit.
—Amen.

Go in peace.
—Thanks be to God.

EVENING PRAYER

God, + come to my assistance.
—Lord, make haste to help me.

Glory to the Father, and to the Son,
 and to the Holy Spirit:
—as it was in the beginning, is now,
and will be for ever. Amen. Alleluia.

Hymn *Come, My Way, My Truth, My Life, p. 678*

Psalmody Ant. 1 **Lord, lay your healing hand upon me, for I have sinned.**

Psalm 41

Happy the man who considers the poor
    and the weak.
The Lord will save him in the day of evil,
will guard him, give him life, make him
    happy in the land
and will not give him up to the will
    of his foes.
The Lord will help him on his bed of pain,
he will bring him back from sickness
    to health.

As for me, I said: "Lord, have mercy on me,
heal my soul for I have sinned against you."
My foes are speaking evil against me.
"How long before he dies and his name be
    forgotten?"
They come to visit me and speak
    empty words,
their hearts full of malice, they spread
    it abroad.

My enemies whisper together against me.
They all weigh up the evil which is on me:
"Some deadly thing has fastened upon him,
he will not rise again from where he lies."
Thus even my friend, in whom I trusted,
who ate my bread, has turned against me.

But you, O Lord, have mercy on me.
Let me rise once more and I will repay them.
By this I shall know that you are my friend,
if my foes do not shout in triumph over me.
If you uphold me I shall be unharmed
and set in your presence for evermore.

Blessed be the Lord, the God of Israel
from age to age. Amen. Amen.

Glory to the Father, and to the Son,
    and to the Holy Spirit:
—as it was in the beginning, is now,
and will be for ever. Amen.

Ant. **Lord, lay your healing hand upon me, for I have sinned.**

Ant. 2 **The mighty Lord is with us; the God of Jacob is our stronghold.**

Psalm 46

God is for us a refuge and strength,
a helper close at hand, in time of distress:
so we shall not fear though the earth
    should rock,
though the mountains fall into the depths
    of the sea,
even though its waters rage and foam,
even though the mountains be shaken by
    its waves.

The Lord of hosts is with us:
the God of Jacob is our stronghold.

The waters of a river give joy to God's city,
the holy place where the Most High dwells.
God is within, it cannot be shaken;
God will help it at the dawning of the day.
Nations are in tumult, kingdoms are shaken:
he lifts his voice, the earth shrinks away.

The Lord of hosts is with us:
the God of Jacob is our stronghold.

Come, consider the works of the Lord,
the redoubtable deeds he has done on
    the earth.
He puts an end to wars over all the earth;
the bow he breaks, the spear he snaps.
He burns the shields with fire.
"Be still and know that I am God,
    supreme among the nations, supreme on
    the earth!"

The Lord of hosts is with us:
the God of Jacob is our stronghold.

Glory to the Father, and to the Son,
    and to the Holy Spirit:
—as it was in the beginning, is now,
and will be for ever. Amen.

Ant. **The mighty Lord is with us; the God of Jacob is our stronghold.**

Ant. 3 **All nations will come and worship before you, O Lord.**

Canticle:
Revelation
15:3–4

Mighty and wonderful are your works,
Lord God Almighty!
Righteous and true are your ways,
O King of the nations!

Who would dare refuse you honor,
or the glory due your name, O Lord?

Since you alone are holy,
all nations shall come
and worship in your presence.
Your mighty deeds are clearly seen.

Glory to the Father, and to the Son,
    and to the Holy Spirit:
—as it was in the beginning, is now,
and will be for ever. Amen.

Ant. **All nations will come and worship before you, O Lord.**

Reading
Romans 15:1–3

We who are strong in faith should be patient with the scruples of those whose faith is weak; we must not be selfish. Each should please his neighbor so as to do him good by building up his spirit. Thus, in accord with Scripture, Christ did not please himself: "The reproaches they uttered against you fell on me."

Responsory

Christ loved us and washed away our sins,
    in his own blood.
—Christ loved us and washed away our sins,
    in his own blood.

He made us a nation of kings and priests,
—in his own blood.

Glory to the Father, and to the Son,
    and to the Holy Spirit.
—Christ loved us and washed away our sins,
    in his own blood.

Gospel Canticle

Ant. **The Lord has come to the help of his servants, for he has remembered his promise of mercy.**

Canticle of Mary
Luke 1:46–55

My + soul proclaims the greatness of the Lord,
my spirit rejoices in God my Savior
for he has looked with favor on his
    lowly servant.

From this day all generations will
    call me blessed:
the Almighty has done great things for me,
and holy is his Name.

He has mercy on those who fear him
in every generation.

He has shown the strength of his arm,
he has scattered the proud in their conceit.

He has cast down the mighty from
    their thrones,
and has lifted up the lowly.

He has filled the hungry with good things,
and the rich he has sent away empty.

He has come to the help of his servant Israel
for he has remembered his promise of mercy,
the promise he made to our fathers,
to Abraham and his children for ever.

Glory to the Father, and to the Son,
    and to the Holy Spirit:
—as it was in the beginning, is now,
and will be for ever. Amen.

Ant. **The Lord has come to the help of his servants, for he has remembered his promise of mercy.**

Intercessions Blessed be God, who hears the prayers of the needy, and fills the hungry with good things. Let us pray to him in confidence:
Lord, show us your mercy.

Merciful Father, upon the cross Jesus offered you the perfect evening sacrifice,
—we pray now for all the suffering members of his Church.

Release those in bondage, give sight to the blind,
—shelter the widow and the orphan.

Clothe your faithful people in the armor of salvation,
—and shield them from the deceptions of the devil.

Let your merciful presence be with us, Lord, at the hour of our death,
—may we be found faithful and leave this world in your peace.

Lead the departed into the light of your
   dwelling place,
—that they may gaze upon you for all eternity.

The Lord's Prayer

Our Father, who art in heaven,
hallowed be thy name;
thy kingdom come,
thy will be done
on earth as it is in heaven.
Give us this day our daily bread,
and forgive us our trespasses,
as we forgive those who trespass against us;
and lead us not into temptation,
but deliver us from evil.

Pater noster, qui es in cælis:
sanctificetur nomen tuum;
adveniat regnum tuum;
fiat voluntas tua,
sicut in cælo, et in terra.
Panem nostrum cotidianum da nobis hodie;
et dimitte nobis debita nostra,
sicut et nos dimittimus debitoribus nostris;
et ne nos inducas in tentationem;
sed libera nos a malo.

Concluding Prayer

God our Father,
help us to follow the example
of your Son's patience in suffering.
By sharing the burden he carries,
may we come to share his glory
in the kingdom where he lives with you and
   the Holy Spirit,
God, for ever and ever.
—Amen.

Dismissal	*If praying individually, or in a group without a priest or deacon:*

May the Lord + bless us,
protect us from all evil
and bring us to everlasting life.
—Amen.

If praying with a priest or deacon, he dismisses the people:

The Lord be with you.
—And with your spirit.

May almighty God bless you,
the Father, and the Son, ✠ and the Holy Spirit.
—Amen.

Go in peace.
—Thanks be to God.

NIGHT PRAYER

God, + come to my assistance.
—Lord, make haste to help me.

Glory to the Father, and to the Son,
    and to the Holy Spirit:
—as it was in the beginning, is now,
    and will be for ever. Amen. Alleluia.

Examen	*An optional brief examination of conscience may be made. Call to mind your sins and failings this day.*
Hymn	*Abide with Me, p. 675*
Psalmody	Ant. **Day and night I cry to you, my God.**

Psalm 88

Lord my God, I call for help by day;
I cry at night before you.
Let my prayer come into your presence.
O turn your ear to my cry.

For my soul is filled with evils;
my life is on the brink of the grave.
I am reckoned as one in the tomb:
I have reached the end of my strength,

like one alone among the dead;
like the slain lying in their graves;
like those you remember no more,
cut off, as they are, from your hand.

You have laid me in the depths of the tomb,
in places that are dark, in the depths.
Your anger weighs down upon me:
I am drowned beneath your waves.

You have taken away my friends
and made me hateful in their sight.
Imprisoned, I cannot escape;
my eyes are sunken with grief.

I call to you, Lord, all the day long;
to you I stretch out my hands.
Will you work your wonders for the dead?
Will the shades stand and praise you?

Will your love be told in the grave
or your faithfulness among the dead?
Will your wonders be known in the dark
or your justice in the land of oblivion?

As for me, Lord, I call to you for help:
in the morning my prayer comes before you.
Lord, why do you reject me?
Why do you hide your face?

Wretched, close to death from my youth,
I have borne your trials; I am numb.
Your fury has swept down upon me;
your terrors have utterly destroyed me.

They surround me all the day like a flood,
they assail me all together.
Friend and neighbor you have taken away:
my one companion is darkness.

Glory to the Father, and to the Son,
    and to the Holy Spirit:
—as it was in the beginning, is now,
and will be for ever. Amen.

Ant. **Day and night I cry to you, my God.**

Reading
Jeremiah 14:9a

You are in our midst, O Lord,
    your name we bear:
        do not forsake us, O Lord, our God!

Responsory Into your hands, Lord, I commend my spirit.
—Into your hands, Lord, I commend my spirit.

You have redeemed us, Lord God of truth.
—I commend my spirit.

Glory to the Father, and to the Son,
    and to the Holy Spirit.
—Into your hands, Lord, I commend my spirit.

NIGHT PRAYER   FRI   JULY 7

Gospel Canticle   Ant. **Protect us, Lord, as we stay awake; watch over us as we sleep, that awake, we may keep watch with Christ, and asleep, rest in his peace.**

Canticle of Simeon
Luke 2:29–32

Lord, + now you let your servant go in peace;
your word has been fulfilled:
my own eyes have seen the salvation
which you have prepared in the sight of
    every people:
a light to reveal you to the nations
and the glory of your people Israel.

Glory to the Father, and to the Son,
    and to the Holy Spirit:
—as it was in the beginning, is now,
and will be for ever. Amen.

Ant. **Protect us, Lord, as we stay awake; watch over us as we sleep, that awake, we may keep watch with Christ, and asleep, rest in his peace.**

Concluding Prayer

Let us pray.
All-powerful God,
keep us united with your Son
in his death and burial
so that we may rise to new life with him,
who lives and reigns for ever and ever.
—Amen.

Blessing

May the all-powerful Lord
grant us a restful night
and a peaceful death.
—Amen.

Marian Antiphon

Sing the "Salve Regina," found on p. 698, or pray a Hail Mary.

IN YOUR LOVE
HEAR MY VOICE,
O LORD;
GIVE ME LIFE BY
YOUR DECREES.

Saturday, July 8, 2023
Saturday of the Thirteenth Week in Ordinary Time

MORNING PRAYER

God, + come to my assistance.
—Lord, make haste to help me.

Glory to the Father, and to the Son,
    and to the Holy Spirit:
—as it was in the beginning, is now,
and will be for ever. Amen. Alleluia.

Hymn   *The Heavens Declare Your Glory, p. 704*

Psalmody   Ant. 1 **Dawn finds me ready to welcome you, my God.**

Psalm 119:145–152 I call with all my heart; Lord, hear me,
I will keep your commands.
I call upon you, save me
and I will do your will.

I rise before dawn and cry for help,
I hope in your word.
My eyes watch through the night
to ponder your promise.

In your love hear my voice, O Lord;
give me life by your decrees.
Those who harm me unjustly draw near:
they are far from your law.

But you, O Lord, are close:
your commands are truth.
Long have I known that your will
is established for ever.

Glory to the Father, and to the Son,
   and to the Holy Spirit:
—as it was in the beginning, is now,
and will be for ever. Amen.

Ant. **Dawn finds me ready to welcome you, my God.**

Ant. 2 **The Lord is my strength, and I shall sing his praise, for he has become my Savior.**

Canticle:
Exodus 15:1–4a,
8–13, 17–18

I will sing to the Lord, for he is gloriously
   triumphant;
horse and chariot he has cast into the sea.

My strength and my courage is the Lord,
and he has been my savior.
He is my God, I praise him;
the God of my father, I extol him.

The Lord is a warrior,
Lord is his name!
Pharaoh's chariots and army he hurled
   into the sea.
At a breath of your anger the waters piled up,
the flowing waters stood like a mound,
the flood waters congealed in the midst
   of the sea.

The enemy boasted, "I will pursue and
  overtake them;
I will divide the spoils and have my
  fill of them;
I will draw my sword; my hand shall
  despoil them!"
When your wind blew, the sea covered them;
like lead they sank in the mighty waters.

Who is like to you among the gods, O Lord?
Who is like to you, magnificent in holiness?
O terrible in renown, worker of wonders,
when you stretched out your right hand, the
  earth swallowed them!

In your mercy you led the people
  you redeemed;
in your strength you guided them to your
  holy dwelling.

And you brought them in and planted them
  on the mountain of your inheritance—
the place where you made your seat, O Lord,
the sanctuary, O Lord, which your hands
  established.
The Lord shall reign forever and ever.

Glory to the Father, and to the Son,
  and to the Holy Spirit:
—as it was in the beginning, is now,
and will be for ever. Amen.

Ant. **The Lord is my strength, and I shall sing his praise, for he has become my Savior.**

Ant. 3 **O praise the Lord, all you nations.**

Psalm 117
O praise the Lord, all you nations,
acclaim him, all you peoples!

Strong is his love for us;
he is faithful for ever.

Glory to the Father, and to the Son,
 and to the Holy Spirit:
—as it was in the beginning, is now,
and will be for ever. Amen.

Ant. **O praise the Lord, all you nations.**

Reading
2 Peter 1:10–11
Be solicitous to make your call and election permanent, brothers; surely those who do so will never be lost. On the contrary, your entry into the everlasting kingdom of our Lord and Savior Jesus Christ will be richly provided for.

Responsory
I cry to you, O Lord, for you are my refuge.
—I cry to you, O Lord, for you are my refuge.

You are all I desire in the land of the living;
—for you are my refuge.

Glory to the Father, and to the Son,
 and to the Holy Spirit.
—I cry to you, O Lord, for you are my refuge.

Gospel Canticle
Ant. **Lord, shine on those who dwell in darkness and the shadow of death.**

Canticle of Zechariah
Luke 1:68–79

Blessed + be the Lord, the God of Israel;
he has come to his people and set them free.

He has raised up for us a mighty savior,
born of the house of his servant David.

Through his holy prophets he
    promised of old
that he would save us from our enemies,
from the hands of all who hate us.

He promised to show mercy to our fathers
and to remember his holy covenant.

This was the oath he swore to our
    father Abraham:
to set us free from the hands of our enemies,
free to worship him without fear,
holy and righteous in his sight
    all the days of our life.

You, my child, shall be called the prophet of
    the Most High;
for you will go before the Lord to
    prepare his way,
to give his people knowledge of salvation
by the forgiveness of their sins.

In the tender compassion of our God
the dawn from on high shall break upon us,
to shine on those who dwell in darkness and
    the shadow of death,
and to guide our feet into the way of peace.

Glory to the Father, and to the Son,
and to the Holy Spirit:
— as it was in the beginning, is now,
and will be for ever. Amen.

Ant. **Lord, shine on those who dwell in darkness and the shadow of death.**

Intercessions Let us all praise Christ. In order to become our faithful and merciful high priest before the Father's throne, he chose to become one of us, a brother in all things. In prayer we ask of him:
Lord, share with us the treasure of your love.

Sun of Justice, you filled us with light at our baptism,
— we dedicate this day to you.

At every hour of the day, we give you glory,
— in all our deeds, we offer you praise.

Mary, your mother, was obedient to your word,
— direct our lives in accordance with that word.

Our lives are surrounded with passing things; set our hearts on things of heaven,
— so that through faith, hope and charity we may come to enjoy the vision of your glory.

The Lord's Prayer

Our Father, who art in heaven,
hallowed be thy name;
thy kingdom come,
thy will be done
on earth as it is in heaven.
Give us this day our daily bread,
and forgive us our trespasses,
as we forgive those who trespass against us;
and lead us not into temptation,
but deliver us from evil.

Pater noster, qui es in cælis:
sanctificetur nomen tuum;
adveniat regnum tuum;
fiat voluntas tua,
sicut in cælo, et in terra.
Panem nostrum cotidianum da nobis hodie;
et dimitte nobis debita nostra,
sicut et nos dimittimus debitoribus nostris;
et ne nos inducas in tentationem;
sed libera nos a malo.

Concluding Prayer

Lord,
free us from the dark night of death.
Let the light of resurrection
dawn within our hearts
to bring us to the radiance of eternal life.
We ask this through our Lord Jesus Christ,
    your Son,
who lives and reigns with you and
    the Holy Spirit,
God, for ever and ever.
—Amen.

Dismissal *If praying individually, or in a group without a priest or deacon:*

May the Lord + bless us,
protect us from all evil
and bring us to everlasting life.
—Amen.

If praying with a priest or deacon, he dismisses the people:

The Lord be with you.
—And with your spirit.

May almighty God bless you,
the Father, and the Son, ✠ and the Holy Spirit.
—Amen.

Go in peace.
—Thanks be to God.

EVENING PRAYER

BEGINS THE FOURTEENTH SUNDAY IN ORDINARY TIME

God, + come to my assistance.
—Lord, make haste to help me.

Glory to the Father, and to the Son,
 and to the Holy Spirit:
—as it was in the beginning, is now,
and will be for ever. Amen. Alleluia.

Hymn *Praise to the Lord, the Almighty, p. 696*

Psalmody Ant. 1 **Your word, O Lord, is the lantern to light our way, alleluia.**

Psalm 119:105-112 Your word is a lamp for my steps
and a light for my path.
I have sworn and have made up my mind
to obey your decrees.

Lord, I am deeply afflicted:
by your word give me life.
Accept, Lord, the homage of my lips
and teach me your decrees.

Though I carry my life in my hands,
I remember your law.
Though the wicked try to ensnare me
I do not stray from your precepts.

Your will is my heritage for ever,
the joy of my heart.
I set myself to carry out your will
in fullness, for ever.

Glory to the Father, and to the Son,
    and to the Holy Spirit:
—as it was in the beginning, is now,
and will be for ever. Amen.

Ant. **Your word, O Lord, is the lantern to light our way, alleluia.**

Ant. 2 **When I see your face, O Lord, I shall know the fullness of joy, alleluia.**

Psalm 16 Preserve me, God, I take refuge in you.
I say to the Lord: "You are my God.
My happiness lies in you alone."

He has put into my heart a marvelous love
for the faithful ones who dwell in his land.
Those who choose other gods increase
 their sorrows.
Never will I offer their offerings of blood.
Never will I take their name upon my lips.

O Lord, it is you who are my portion and cup;
it is you yourself who are my prize.
The lot marked out for me is my delight:
welcome indeed the heritage that falls to me!

I will bless the Lord who gives me counsel,
who even at night directs my heart.
I keep the Lord ever in my sight:
since he is at my right hand, I shall stand firm.

And so my heart rejoices, my soul is glad;
even my body shall rest in safety.
For you will not leave my soul
 among the dead,
nor let your beloved know decay.

You will show me the path of life,
the fullness of joy in your presence,
at your right hand happiness for ever.

Glory to the Father, and to the Son,
 and to the Holy Spirit:
as it was in the beginning, is now,
and will be for ever. Amen.

Ant. **When I see your face, O Lord, I shall know the fullness of joy, alleluia.**

Ant. 3 **Let everything in heaven and on earth bend the knee at the name of Jesus, alleluia.**

Canticle:
Philippians
2:6–11

Though he was in the form of God,
Jesus did not deem equality with God
something to be grasped at.

Rather, he emptied himself
and took the form of a slave,
being born in the likeness of men.

He was known to be of human estate,
and it was thus that he humbled himself,
obediently accepting even death,
death on a cross!

Because of this,
God highly exalted him
and bestowed on him the name
above every other name,

So that at Jesus' name
every knee must bend
in the heavens, on the earth,
and under the earth,
and every tongue proclaim
to the glory of God the Father:
JESUS CHRIST IS LORD!

Glory to the Father, and to the Son,
    and to the Holy Spirit:
—as it was in the beginning, is now,
and will be for ever. Amen.

Ant. **Let everything in heaven and on earth bend the knee at the name of Jesus, alleluia.**

Reading
Colossians 1:2b–6a

May God our Father give you grace and peace. We always give thanks to God, the Father of our Lord Jesus Christ, in our prayers for you because we have heard of your faith in Christ Jesus and the love you bear toward all the saints—moved as you are by the hope held in store for you in heaven. You heard of this hope through the message of truth, the gospel, which has come to you, has borne fruit, and has continued to grow in your midst, as it has everywhere in the world.

Responsory

From the rising of the sun to its setting,
may the name of the Lord be praised.
—From the rising of the sun to its setting,
may the name of the Lord be praised.

His splendor reaches far beyond the heavens;
—may the name of the Lord be praised.

Glory to the Father, and to the Son,
and to the Holy Spirit.
—From the rising of the sun to its setting,
may the name of the Lord be praised.

Gospel Canticle

Ant. **My yoke is easy and my burden is light, says the Lord.**

Canticle of Mary
Luke 1:46–55

My + soul proclaims the greatness of the Lord,
my spirit rejoices in God my Savior
for he has looked with favor on his
    lowly servant.

From this day all generations will
    call me blessed:
the Almighty has done great things for me,
and holy is his Name.

He has mercy on those who fear him
in every generation.

He has shown the strength of his arm,
he has scattered the proud in their conceit.

He has cast down the mighty from
    their thrones,
and has lifted up the lowly.

He has filled the hungry with good things,
and the rich he has sent away empty.

He has come to the help of his servant Israel
for he has remembered his promise of mercy,
the promise he made to our fathers,
to Abraham and his children for ever.

Glory to the Father, and to the Son,
    and to the Holy Spirit:
—as it was in the beginning, is now,
    and will be for ever. Amen.

Ant. **My yoke is easy and my burden is light, says the Lord.**

Intercessions God aids and protects the people he has chosen for his inheritance. Let us give thanks to him and proclaim his goodness:
Lord, we trust in you.

We pray for N., our Pope, and N., our bishop,
—protect them and in your goodness make them holy.

May the sick feel their companionship with the suffering Christ,
—and know that they will enjoy his eternal consolation.

In your goodness have compassion on the homeless,
—help them to find proper housing.

In your goodness give and preserve the fruits of the earth,
—so that each day there may be bread enough for all.

Lord, you attend the dying with great mercy,
—grant them an eternal dwelling.

The Lord's Prayer

Our Father, who art in heaven,
hallowed be thy name;
thy kingdom come,
thy will be done
on earth as it is in heaven.
Give us this day our daily bread,
and forgive us our trespasses,
as we forgive those who trespass against us;
and lead us not into temptation,
but deliver us from evil.

Pater noster, qui es in cælis:
sanctificetur nomen tuum;
adveniat regnum tuum;
fiat voluntas tua,
sicut in cælo, et in terra.
Panem nostrum cotidianum da nobis hodie;
et dimitte nobis debita nostra,
sicut et nos dimittimus debitoribus nostris;
et ne nos inducas in tentationem;
sed libera nos a malo.

Concluding Prayer

Father,
through the obedience of Jesus,
your servant and your Son,
you raised a fallen world.
Free us from sin
and bring us the joy that lasts for ever.
We ask this through our Lord Jesus Christ,
    your Son,
who lives and reigns with you and
    the Holy Spirit,
God, for ever and ever.
—Amen.

Dismissal *If praying individually, or in a group without a priest or deacon:*

May the Lord + bless us,
protect us from all evil
and bring us to everlasting life.
—Amen.

If praying with a priest or deacon, he dismisses the people:

The Lord be with you.
—And with your spirit.

May almighty God bless you,
the Father, and the Son, ✠ and the Holy Spirit.
—Amen.

Go in peace.
—Thanks be to God.

NIGHT PRAYER

God, + come to my assistance.
—Lord, make haste to help me.

Glory to the Father, and to the Son,
 and to the Holy Spirit:
—as it was in the beginning, is now,
and will be for ever. Amen. Alleluia.

Examen *An optional brief examination of conscience may be made. Call to mind your sins and failings this day.*

Hymn *Before the Final Light of Day, p. 676*

Psalmody Ant. 1 **Have mercy, Lord, and hear my prayer.**

Psalm 4

When I call, answer me, O God of justice;
from anguish you released me; have mercy
    and hear me!

O men, how long will your hearts be closed,
will you love what is futile and seek
    what is false?

It is the Lord who grants favors to those
    whom he loves;
the Lord hears me whenever I call him.

Fear him; do not sin: ponder on your bed
    and be still.
Make justice your sacrifice and trust
    in the Lord.

"What can bring us happiness?" many say.
Let the light of your face shine on us, O Lord.

You have put into my heart a greater joy
than they have from abundance of corn
    and new wine.

I will lie down in peace and sleep
    comes at once
for you alone, Lord, make me dwell in safety.

Glory to the Father, and to the Son,
    and to the Holy Spirit:
—as it was in the beginning, is now,
and will be for ever. Amen.

Ant. **Have mercy, Lord, and hear my prayer.**

Ant. 2 — **In the silent hours of night, bless the Lord.**

Psalm 134

O come, bless the Lord,
all you who serve the Lord,
who stand in the house of the Lord,
in the courts of the house of our God.

Lift up your hands to the holy place
and bless the Lord through the night.

May the Lord bless you from Zion,
he who made both heaven and earth.

Glory to the Father, and to the Son,
   and to the Holy Spirit:
—as it was in the beginning, is now,
and will be for ever. Amen.

Ant. — **In the silent hours of night, bless the Lord.**

Reading
Deuteronomy 6:4-7

Hear, O Israel! The Lord is our God, the Lord alone! Therefore, you shall love the Lord, your God, with all your heart, and with all your soul, and with all your strength. Take to heart these words which I enjoin on you today. Drill them into your children. Speak of them at home and abroad, whether you are busy or at rest.

Responsory

Into your hands, Lord, I commend my spirit.
—Into your hands, Lord, I commend my spirit.

You have redeemed us, Lord God of truth.
—I commend my spirit.

Glory to the Father, and to the Son,
 and to the Holy Spirit.
—Into your hands, Lord, I commend my spirit.

Gospel Canticle

Ant. **Protect us, Lord, as we stay awake; watch over us as we sleep, that awake, we may keep watch with Christ, and asleep, rest in his peace.**

Canticle of Simeon
Luke 2:29–32

Lord, + now you let your servant go in peace;
 your word has been fulfilled:
my own eyes have seen the salvation
which you have prepared in the sight of
 every people:
a light to reveal you to the nations
and the glory of your people Israel.

Glory to the Father, and to the Son,
 and to the Holy Spirit:
—as it was in the beginning, is now,
and will be for ever. Amen.

Ant. **Protect us, Lord, as we stay awake; watch over us as we sleep, that awake, we may keep watch with Christ, and asleep, rest in his peace.**

Concluding Prayer

Let us pray.
Lord,
be with us throughout this night.
When day comes may we rise from sleep
to rejoice in the resurrection of your Christ,
who lives and reigns for ever and ever.
—Amen.

Blessing

May the all-powerful Lord
grant us a restful night
and a peaceful death.
—Amen.

Marian Antiphon

Sing the "Salve Regina," found on p. 698, or pray a Hail Mary.

Sunday, July 9, 2023
Fourteenth Sunday in Ordinary Time

MORNING PRAYER

God, + come to my assistance.
—Lord, make haste to help me.

Glory to the Father, and to the Son,
    and to the Holy Spirit:
—as it was in the beginning, is now,
and will be for ever. Amen. Alleluia.

Hymn

This Day the First of Days Was Made, p. 695

Psalmody

Ant. 1 **Blessed is he who comes in the name of the Lord, alleluia.**

Psalm 118

Give thanks to the Lord for he is good,
for his love endures forever.

Let the sons of Israel say:
"His love endures for ever."
Let the sons of Aaron say:
"His love endures for ever."
Let those who fear the Lord say:
"His love endures for ever."

I called to the Lord in my distress;
he answered and freed me.
The Lord is at my side; I do not fear.
What can man do against me?
The Lord is at my side as my helper:
I shall look down on my foes.

It is better to take refuge in the Lord
than to trust in men:
it is better to take refuge in the Lord
than to trust in princes.

The nations all encompassed me;
in the Lord's name I crushed them.
They compassed me, compassed me about;
in the Lord's name I crushed them.
They compassed me about like bees;
they blazed like a fire among thorns.
In the Lord's name I crushed them.

I was hard-pressed and was falling
but the Lord came to help me.
The Lord is my strength and my song;
he is my savior.
There are shouts of joy and victory
in the tents of the just.

The Lord's right hand has triumphed;
his right hand raised me.
The Lord's right hand has triumphed;
I shall not die, I shall live
and recount his deeds.
I was punished, I was punished by the Lord,
but not doomed to die.

Open to me the gates of holiness:
I will enter and give thanks.
This is the Lord's own gate
where the just may enter.
I will thank you for you have answered
and you are my savior.

The stone which the builders rejected
has become the corner stone.
This is the work of the Lord,
a marvel in our eyes.
This day was made by the Lord;
we rejoice and are glad.

O Lord, grant us salvation;
O Lord, grant success.
Blessed in the name of the Lord
is he who comes.
We bless you from the house of the Lord;
the Lord God is our light.

Go forward in procession with branches
even to the altar.
You are my God, I thank you.
My God, I praise you.
Give thanks to the Lord for he is good;
for his love endures for ever.

Glory to the Father, and to the Son,
    and to the Holy Spirit:
—as it was in the beginning, is now,
and will be for ever. Amen.

Ant. **Blessed is he who comes in the name of the Lord, alleluia.**

Ant. 2 **Let us sing a hymn of praise to our God, alleluia.**

Canticle:
Daniel 3:52–57

Blessed are you, O Lord, the God of
 our fathers,
praiseworthy and exalted above all forever.

And blessed is your holy and glorious name,
praiseworthy and exalted above all
 for all ages.

Blessed are you in the temple of your
 holy glory,
praiseworthy and glorious above all forever.

Blessed are you on the throne of
 your kingdom,
praiseworthy and exalted above all forever.

Blessed are you who look into the depths
from your throne upon the cherubim,
praiseworthy and exalted above all forever.

Blessed are you in the firmament of heaven,
praiseworthy and glorious forever.

Bless the Lord, all you works of the Lord,
praise and exalt him above all forever.

Glory to the Father, and to the Son,
 and to the Holy Spirit:
—as it was in the beginning, is now,
and will be for ever. Amen.

JULY 9 SUN MORNING PRAYER

Ant. **Let us sing a hymn of praise to our God, alleluia.**

Ant. 3 **Praise the Lord for his infinite greatness, alleluia.**

Psalm 150
Praise God in his holy place,
praise him in his mighty heavens.
Praise him for his powerful deeds,
praise his surpassing greatness.

O praise him with sound of trumpet,
praise him with lute and harp.
Praise him with timbrel and dance,
praise him with strings and pipes.

O praise him with resounding cymbals,
praise him with clashing of cymbals.
Let everything that lives and that breathes
give praise to the Lord.

Glory to the Father, and to the Son,
   and to the Holy Spirit:
—as it was in the beginning, is now,
and will be for ever. Amen.

Ant. **Praise the Lord for his infinite greatness, alleluia.**

Reading
Ezekiel 36:25–27

I will sprinkle clean water upon you to cleanse you from all your impurities, and from all your idols I will cleanse you. I will give you a new heart and place a new spirit within you, taking from your bodies your stony hearts and giving you natural hearts. I will put my spirit within you and make you live by my statutes, careful to observe my decrees.

Responsory

We give thanks to you, O God,
 as we call upon your name.
—We give thanks to you, O God,
 as we call upon your name.

We cry aloud how marvelous you are,
—as we call upon your name.

Glory to the Father, and to the Son,
 and to the Holy Spirit.
—We give thanks to you, O God,
 as we call upon your name.

Gospel Canticle

Ant. **Many who heard the teaching of Jesus were astonished and said: Where did he get all this? Is he not the carpenter, the son of Mary?**

Canticle of Zechariah
Luke 1:68–79

Blessed + be the Lord, the God of Israel;
he has come to his people and set them free.

He has raised up for us a mighty savior,
born of the house of his servant David.

Through his holy prophets he
 promised of old
that he would save us from our enemies,
from the hands of all who hate us.

He promised to show mercy to our fathers
and to remember his holy covenant.

This was the oath he swore to our
 father Abraham:
to set us free from the hands of our enemies,
free to worship him without fear,
holy and righteous in his sight
 all the days of our life.

You, my child, shall be called the prophet of
 the Most High;
for you will go before the Lord to
 prepare his way,
to give his people knowledge of salvation
by the forgiveness of their sins.

In the tender compassion of our God
the dawn from on high shall break upon us,
to shine on those who dwell in darkness and
 the shadow of death,
and to guide our feet into the way of peace.

Glory to the Father, and to the Son,
 and to the Holy Spirit:
—as it was in the beginning, is now,
 and will be for ever. Amen.

Ant. **Many who heard the teaching of Jesus were astonished and said: Where did he get all this? Is he not the carpenter, the son of Mary?**

Intercessions Let us give thanks to our Savior who came into this world as God's presence among us. Let us call upon him:
Christ, King of Glory, be our light and our joy.

Lord Jesus, you are the rising Sun, the firstfruits of the future resurrection,
—grant that we may not sit in the shadow of death but walk in the light of life.

Show us your goodness, present in every creature,
—that we may contemplate your glory everywhere.

Do not allow us to be overcome by evil today,
—but grant that we may overcome evil through the power of good.

You were baptized in the Jordan and anointed by the Holy Spirit,
—grant that we may this day give thanks to your Holy Spirit.

The Lord's Prayer

Our Father, who art in heaven,
hallowed be thy name;
thy kingdom come,
thy will be done
on earth as it is in heaven.
Give us this day our daily bread,
and forgive us our trespasses,
as we forgive those who trespass against us;
and lead us not into temptation,
but deliver us from evil.

Pater noster, qui es in cælis:
sanctificetur nomen tuum;
adveniat regnum tuum;
fiat voluntas tua,
sicut in cælo, et in terra.
Panem nostrum cotidianum da nobis hodie;
et dimitte nobis debita nostra,
sicut et nos dimittimus debitoribus nostris;
et ne nos inducas in tentationem;
sed libera nos a malo.

Concluding Prayer

Father,
through the obedience of Jesus,
your servant and your Son,
you raised a fallen world.
Free us from sin
and bring us the joy that lasts for ever.
We ask this through our Lord Jesus Christ,
   your Son,
who lives and reigns with you and
   the Holy Spirit,
God, for ever and ever.
—Amen.

Dismissal   *If praying individually, or in a group without a priest or deacon:*

> May the Lord + bless us,
> protect us from all evil
> and bring us to everlasting life.
> —Amen.

If praying with a priest or deacon, he dismisses the people:

> The Lord be with you.
> —And with your spirit.

> May almighty God bless you,
> the Father, and the Son, ✠ and the Holy Spirit.
> —Amen.

> Go in peace.
> —Thanks be to God.

EVENING PRAYER

> God, + come to my assistance.
> —Lord, make haste to help me.

> Glory to the Father, and to the Son,
>   and to the Holy Spirit:
> —as it was in the beginning, is now,
> and will be for ever. Amen. Alleluia.

Hymn   *Holy God, We Praise Thy Name, p. 686*

Psalmody   Ant. 1 **Christ our Lord is a priest for ever, like Melchizedek of old, alleluia.**

Psalm 110:1–5, 7   The Lord's revelation to my Master:
  "Sit on my right:
  your foes I will put beneath your feet."

The Lord will wield from Zion
your scepter of power:
rule in the midst of all your foes.

A prince from the day of your birth
on the holy mountains;
from the womb before the dawn I begot you.

The Lord has sworn an oath he will
    not change.
"You are a priest for ever,
a priest like Melchizedek of old."

The Master standing at your right hand
will shatter kings in the day of his
    great wrath.

He shall drink from the stream by the wayside
and therefore he shall lift up his head.

Glory to the Father, and to the Son,
    and to the Holy Spirit:
as it was in the beginning, is now,
and will be for ever. Amen.

Ant. **Christ our Lord is a priest for ever, like Melchizedek of old, alleluia.**

Ant. 2 **God dwells in highest heaven; he has power to do all he wills, alleluia.**

Psalm 115
Not to us, Lord, not to us,
but to your name give the glory
for the sake of your love and your truth,
lest the heathen say: "Where is their God?"

But our God is in the heavens;
he does whatever he wills.
Their idols are silver and gold,
the work of human hands.

They have mouths but they cannot speak;
they have eyes but they cannot see;
they have ears but they cannot hear;
they have nostrils but they cannot smell.

With their hands they cannot feel;
with their feet they cannot walk.
No sound comes from their throats.
Their makers will come to be like them
and so will all who trust in them.

Sons of Israel, trust in the Lord;
he is their help and their shield.
Sons of Aaron, trust in the Lord;
he is their help and their shield.

You who fear him, trust in the Lord;
he is their help and their shield.
He remembers us, and he will bless us;
he will bless the sons of Israel.
He will bless the sons of Aaron.

The Lord will bless those who fear him,
the little no less than the great:
to you may the Lord grant increase,
to you and all your children.

May you be blessed by the Lord,
the maker of heaven and earth.
The heavens belong to the Lord
but the earth he has given to men.

The dead shall not praise the Lord,
nor those who go down into the silence.
But we who live bless the Lord
now and for ever. Amen.

Glory to the Father, and to the Son,
   and to the Holy Spirit:
—as it was in the beginning, is now,
and will be for ever. Amen.

Ant. **God dwells in highest heaven; he has power to do all he wills, alleluia.**

Ant. 3 **Praise God, all you who serve him, both great and small, alleluia.**

Canticle: See Revelation 19:1–7

Alleluia.
Salvation, glory, and power to our God:
his judgments are honest and true.
Alleluia.

Alleluia.
Sing praise to our God, all you his servants,
all who worship him reverently,
   great and small.
Alleluia.

Alleluia.
The Lord our all-powerful God is King;
let us rejoice, sing praise, and give him glory.
Alleluia.

Alleluia.
The wedding feast of the Lamb has begun,
and his bride is prepared to welcome him.
Alleluia.

Alleluia.
Glory to the Father, and to the Son,
    and to the Holy Spirit:
Alleluia.

Alleluia.
as it was in the beginning, is now,
and will be for ever. Amen.
Alleluia.

Ant. **Praise God, all you who serve him, both great and small, alleluia.**

Reading
2 Thessalonians
2:13–14

We are bound to thank God for you always, beloved brothers in the Lord, because you are the first fruits of those whom God has chosen for salvation, in holiness of spirit and fidelity to truth. He called you through our preaching of the good news so that you might achieve the glory of our Lord Jesus Christ.

JULY 9   SUN   EVENING PRAYER

Responsory   Our Lord is great, mighty is his power.
—Our Lord is great, mighty is his power.

His wisdom is beyond compare,
—mighty is his power.

Glory to the Father, and to the Son,
    and to the Holy Spirit.
—Our Lord is great, mighty is his power.

Gospel Canticle   Ant. **So great a harvest, and so few to gather it in; pray to the Lord of the harvest; beg him to send out laborers for his harvest.**

Canticle of Mary
Luke 1:46–55

My + soul proclaims the greatness of the Lord,
my spirit rejoices in God my Savior
for he has looked with favor on his
    lowly servant.

From this day all generations will
    call me blessed:
the Almighty has done great things for me,
and holy is his Name.

He has mercy on those who fear him
in every generation.

He has shown the strength of his arm,
he has scattered the proud in their conceit.

He has cast down the mighty from
    their thrones,
and has lifted up the lowly.

He has filled the hungry with good things,
and the rich he has sent away empty.

He has come to the help of his servant Israel
for he has remembered his promise of mercy,
the promise he made to our fathers,
to Abraham and his children for ever.

Glory to the Father, and to the Son,
   and to the Holy Spirit:
—as it was in the beginning, is now,
and will be for ever. Amen.

Ant. **So great a harvest, and so few to gather it in; pray to the Lord of the harvest; beg him to send out laborers for his harvest.**

Intercessions All praise and honor to Christ! He lives for ever to intercede for us, and he is able to save those who approach the Father in his name. Sustained by our faith, let us call upon him:
Remember your people, Lord.

As the day draws to a close, Sun of Justice,
   we invoke your name upon the whole human race,
—so that all men may enjoy your never failing light.

Preserve the covenant which you have ratified in your blood,
—cleanse and sanctify your Church.

Remember your assembly, Lord,
—your dwelling place.

Guide travelers along the path of peace and prosperity,
—so that they may reach their destinations in safety and joy.

Receive the souls of the dead, Lord,
—grant them your favor and the gift of eternal glory.

The Lord's Prayer

Our Father, who art in heaven,
hallowed be thy name;
thy kingdom come,
thy will be done
on earth as it is in heaven.
Give us this day our daily bread,
and forgive us our trespasses,
as we forgive those who trespass against us;
and lead us not into temptation,
but deliver us from evil.

Pater noster, qui es in cælis:
sanctificetur nomen tuum;
adveniat regnum tuum;
fiat voluntas tua,
sicut in cælo, et in terra.
Panem nostrum cotidianum da nobis hodie;
et dimitte nobis debita nostra,
sicut et nos dimittimus debitoribus nostris;
et ne nos inducas in tentationem;
sed libera nos a malo.

Concluding Prayer

Father,
through the obedience of Jesus,
your servant and your Son,
you raised a fallen world.
Free us from sin
and bring us the joy that lasts for ever.
We ask this through our Lord Jesus Christ,
    your Son,
who lives and reigns with you and
    the Holy Spirit,
God, for ever and ever.
—Amen.

Dismissal

If praying individually, or in a group without a priest or deacon:

May the Lord + bless us,
protect us from all evil
and bring us to everlasting life.
—Amen.

If praying with a priest or deacon, he dismisses the people:

The Lord be with you.
—And with your spirit.

May almighty God bless you,
the Father, and the Son, ✠ and the Holy Spirit.
—Amen.

Go in peace.
—Thanks be to God.

FOR YOU HAS
HE COMMANDED
HIS ANGELS,
TO KEEP YOU IN
ALL YOUR WAYS.

NIGHT PRAYER

God, + come to my assistance.
—Lord, make haste to help me.

Glory to the Father, and to the Son,
    and to the Holy Spirit:
—as it was in the beginning, is now,
and will be for ever. Amen. Alleluia.

Examen — *An optional brief examination of conscience may be made. Call to mind your sins and failings this day.*

Hymn — *O Joyful Light of God Most High, p. 693*

Psalmody   Ant. **Night holds no terrors for me sleeping under God's wings.**

Psalm 91

He who dwells in the shelter of the Most High
and abides in the shade of the Almighty
says to the Lord: "My refuge,
my stronghold, my God in whom I trust!"

It is he who will free you from the snare
of the fowler who seeks to destroy you;
he will conceal you with his pinions
and under his wings you will find refuge.

You will not fear the terror of the night
nor the arrow that flies by day,
nor the plague that prowls in the darkness
nor the scourge that lays waste at noon.

A thousand may fall at your side,
ten thousand fall at your right,
you, it will never approach;
his faithfulness is buckler and shield.

Your eyes have only to look
to see how the wicked are repaid,
you who have said: "Lord, my refuge!"
and have made the Most High your dwelling.

Upon you no evil shall fall,
no plague approach where you dwell.
For you has he commanded his angels,
to keep you in all your ways.

They shall bear you upon their hands
lest you strike your foot against a stone.
On the lion and the viper you will tread
and trample the young lion and the dragon.

Since he clings to me in love, I will free him;
protect him for he knows my name.
When he calls I shall answer: "I am with you."
I will save him in distress and give him glory.

With length of life I will content him;
I shall let him see my saving power.

Glory to the Father, and to the Son,
    and to the Holy Spirit:
—as it was in the beginning, is now,
and will be for ever. Amen.

Ant. **Night holds no terrors for me sleeping under God's wings.**

Reading
Revelation 22:4-5

They shall see the Lord face to face and bear his name on their foreheads. The night shall be no more. They will need no light from lamps or the sun, for the Lord God shall give them light, and they shall reign forever.

Responsory

Into your hands, Lord, I commend my spirit.
—Into your hands, Lord, I commend my spirit.

You have redeemed us, Lord God of truth.
—I commend my spirit.

Glory to the Father, and to the Son,
  and to the Holy Spirit.
—Into your hands, Lord, I commend my spirit.

Gospel Canticle

Ant. **Protect us, Lord, as we stay awake; watch over us as we sleep, that awake, we may keep watch with Christ, and asleep, rest in his peace.**

Canticle of Simeon
Luke 2:29-32

Lord, + now you let your servant go in peace;
your word has been fulfilled:
my own eyes have seen the salvation
which you have prepared in the sight of
  every people:
a light to reveal you to the nations
and the glory of your people Israel.

Glory to the Father, and to the Son,
  and to the Holy Spirit:
—as it was in the beginning, is now,
  and will be for ever. Amen.

JULY 9   SUN   NIGHT PRAYER

Ant. **Protect us, Lord, as we stay awake; watch over us as we sleep, that awake, we may keep watch with Christ, and asleep, rest in his peace.**

Concluding Prayer
Let us pray.
Lord,
we have celebrated today
the mystery of the rising of Christ to new life.
May we now rest in your peace,
safe from all that could harm us,
and rise again refreshed and joyful,
to praise you throughout another day.
We ask this through Christ our Lord.
—Amen.

Blessing
May the all-powerful Lord
grant us a restful night
and a peaceful death.
—Amen.

Marian Antiphon *Sing the "Salve Regina," found on p. 698, or pray a Hail Mary.*

Monday, July 10, 2023
Monday of the Fourteenth Week in Ordinary Time

MORNING PRAYER

God, + come to my assistance.
—Lord, make haste to help me.

Glory to the Father, and to the Son,
   and to the Holy Spirit:
—as it was in the beginning, is now,
   and will be for ever. Amen. Alleluia.

Hymn   *O Splendor of God's Glory Bright, p. 694*

Psalmody   Ant. 1 **When will I come to the end of my pilgrimage and enter the presence of God?**

Psalm 42

Like the deer that yearns
for running streams,
so my soul is yearning
for you, my God.

My soul is thirsting for God,
the God of my life;
when can I enter and see
the face of God?

My tears have become my bread,
by night, by day,
as I hear it said all the day long:
"Where is your God?"

These things will I remember
as I pour out my soul:
how I would lead the rejoicing crowd
into the house of God,
amid cries of gladness and thanksgiving,
the throng wild with joy.

Why are you cast down, my soul,
why groan within me?
Hope in God; I will praise him still,
my savior and my God.

My soul is cast down within me
as I think of you,
from the country of Jordan and
    Mount Hermon,
from the Hill of Mizar.

Deep is calling on deep,
in the roar of waters:
your torrents and all your waves
swept over me.

By day the Lord will send
his loving kindness;
by night I will sing to him,
praise the God of my life.

I will say to God, my rock:
"Why have you forgotten me?
Why do I go mourning,
oppressed by the foe?"

With cries that pierce me to the heart,
my enemies revile me,
saying to me all the day long:
"Where is your God?"

Why are you cast down, my soul,
why groan within me?
Hope in God; I will praise him still,
my savior and my God.

Glory to the Father, and to the Son,
    and to the Holy Spirit:
as it was in the beginning, is now,
and will be for ever. Amen.

Ant. **When will I come to the end of my pilgrimage and enter the presence of God?**

Ant. 2 **Lord, show us the radiance of your mercy.**

Canticle:
Sirach 36:1–5,
10–13

Come to our aid, O God of the universe,
and put all the nations in dread of you!
Raise your hand against the heathen,
that they may realize your power.

As you have used us to show them
    your holiness,
so now use them to show us your glory.
Thus they will know, as we know,
that there is no God but you.

Give new signs and work new wonders;
show forth the splendor of your right
    hand and arm.

Gather all the tribes of Jacob,
that they may inherit the land as of old.
Show mercy to the people called by
    your name;
Israel, whom you named your first-born.

Take pity on your holy city,
Jerusalem, your dwelling place.
Fill Zion with your majesty,
your temple with your glory.

Glory to the Father, and to the Son,
    and to the Holy Spirit:
as it was in the beginning, is now,
and will be for ever. Amen.

Ant. **Lord, show us the radiance of your mercy.**

Ant. 3 **The vaults of heaven ring with your praise, O Lord.**

Psalm 19A

The heavens proclaim the glory of God
and the firmament shows forth the work of
    his hands.
Day unto day takes up the story
and night unto night makes known
    the message.

No speech, no word, no voice is heard
yet their span extends through all the earth,
their words to the utmost bounds of
    the world.

There he has placed a tent for the sun;
it comes forth like a bridegroom coming
  from his tent,
rejoices like a champion to run its course.

At the end of the sky is the rising of the sun;
to the furthest end of the sky is its course.
There is nothing concealed from its
  burning heat.

Glory to the Father, and to the Son,
  and to the Holy Spirit:
—as it was in the beginning, is now,
and will be for ever. Amen.

Ant. **The vaults of heaven ring with your praise, O Lord.**

Reading
Jeremiah 15:16

When I found your words, I devoured them;
  they became my joy and the happiness
  of my heart,
Because I bore your name,
  O Lord, God of hosts.

Responsory

Sing for joy, God's chosen ones, give him the
  praise that is due.
—Sing for joy, God's chosen ones, give him the
  praise that is due.

Sing a new song to the Lord;
—give him the praise that is due.

Glory to the Father, and to the Son,
> and to the Holy Spirit.
—Sing for joy, God's chosen ones, give him the
> praise that is due.

Gospel Canticle

Ant. **Blessed be the Lord, for he has come to his people and set them free.**

Canticle of Zechariah Luke 1:68–79

Blessed + be the Lord, the God of Israel;
he has come to his people and set them free.

He has raised up for us a mighty savior,
born of the house of his servant David.

Through his holy prophets he
> promised of old
that he would save us from our enemies,
from the hands of all who hate us.

He promised to show mercy to our fathers
and to remember his holy covenant.

This was the oath he swore to our
> father Abraham:
to set us free from the hands of our enemies,
free to worship him without fear,
holy and righteous in his sight
> all the days of our life.

You, my child, shall be called the prophet of
> the Most High;
for you will go before the Lord to
> prepare his way,
to give his people knowledge of salvation
by the forgiveness of their sins.

In the tender compassion of our God
the dawn from on high shall break upon us,
to shine on those who dwell in darkness and
    the shadow of death,
and to guide our feet into the way of peace.

Glory to the Father, and to the Son,
    and to the Holy Spirit:
—as it was in the beginning, is now,
and will be for ever. Amen.

Ant. **Blessed be the Lord, for he has come to his people and set them free.**

Intercessions Our Savior has made us a nation of priests to offer acceptable sacrifice to the Father. Let us call upon him in gratitude:
Preserve us in your ministry, Lord.

Christ, eternal priest, you conferred the holy priesthood on your people,
—grant that we may offer spiritual sacrifices acceptable to the Father.

In your goodness pour out on us the fruits of your Spirit,
—patience, kindness and gentleness.

May we love you and possess you, for you are love,
—and may every action of our lives praise you.

May we seek those things which are beneficial to our brothers, without counting the cost,
—to help them on the way to salvation.

JULY 10   MON   MORNING PRAYER

The Lord's Prayer

Our Father, who art in heaven,
hallowed be thy name;
thy kingdom come,
thy will be done
on earth as it is in heaven.
Give us this day our daily bread,
and forgive us our trespasses,
as we forgive those who trespass against us;
and lead us not into temptation,
but deliver us from evil.

Pater noster, qui es in cælis:
sanctificetur nomen tuum;
adveniat regnum tuum;
fiat voluntas tua,
sicut in cælo, et in terra.
Panem nostrum cotidianum da nobis hodie;
et dimitte nobis debita nostra,
sicut et nos dimittimus debitoribus nostris;
et ne nos inducas in tentationem;
sed libera nos a malo.

Concluding Prayer

Almighty Father,
you have brought us to the light of
    a new day:
keep us safe the whole day through
from every sinful inclination.
May all our thoughts, words and actions
aim at doing what is pleasing in your sight.
We ask this through our Lord Jesus Christ,
    your Son,
who lives and reigns with you and
    the Holy Spirit,
God, for ever and ever.
—Amen.

Dismissal   *If praying individually, or in a group without a priest or deacon:*

> May the Lord + bless us,
> protect us from all evil
> and bring us to everlasting life.
> —Amen.

If praying with a priest or deacon, he dismisses the people:

> The Lord be with you.
> —And with your spirit.

> May almighty God bless you,
> the Father, and the Son, ☩ and the Holy Spirit.
> —Amen.

> Go in peace.
> —Thanks be to God.

EVENING PRAYER

> God, + come to my assistance.
> —Lord, make haste to help me.

> Glory to the Father, and to the Son,
>   and to the Holy Spirit:
> —as it was in the beginning, is now,
> and will be for ever. Amen. Alleluia.

Hymn   *Immortal, Invisible, God Only Wise, p. 688*

Psalmody   Ant. 1 **Yours is more than mortal beauty;
every word you speak is full of grace.**

Psalm 45   My heart overflows with noble words.
To the king I must speak the song I have made;
my tongue as nimble as the pen of a scribe.

You are the fairest of the children of men
and graciousness is poured upon your lips:
because God has blessed you for evermore.

O mighty one, gird your sword upon
    your thigh;
in splendor and state, ride on in triumph
for the cause of truth and goodness and right.

Take aim with your bow in your dread
    right hand.
Your arrows are sharp: peoples fall
    beneath you.
The foes of the king fall down and lose heart.

Your throne, O God, shall endure for ever.
A scepter of justice is the scepter of
    your kingdom.
Your love is for justice; your hatred for evil.

Therefore God, your God, has anointed you
with the oil of gladness above other kings:
your robes are fragrant with aloes and myrrh.

From the ivory palace you are greeted
    with music.
The daughters of kings are among your
    loved ones.
On your right stands the queen in
    gold of Ophir.

Glory to the Father, and to the Son,
    and to the Holy Spirit:
—as it was in the beginning, is now,
    and will be for ever. Amen.

Ant. **Yours is more than mortal beauty; every word you speak is full of grace.**

Ant. 2 **The Bridegroom is here; go out and welcome him.**

Psalm 45 (continued)

Listen, O daughter, give ear to my words:
forget your own people and your
   father's house.
So will the king desire your beauty:
he is your lord, pay homage to him.

And the people of Tyre shall come with gifts,
the richest of the people shall seek your favor.
The daughter of the king is clothed
   with splendor,
her robes embroidered with pearls
   set in gold.

She is led to the king with her maiden
   companions.
They are escorted amid gladness and joy;
they pass within the palace of the king.

Sons shall be yours in place of your fathers:
you will make them princes over all the earth.
May this song make your name for ever
   remembered.
May the peoples praise you from age to age.

Glory to the Father, and to the Son,
   and to the Holy Spirit:
—as it was in the beginning, is now,
   and will be for ever. Amen.

Ant.	**The Bridegroom is here; go out and welcome him.**
Ant. 3	**God planned in the fullness of time to restore all things in Christ.**
Canticle: Ephesians 1:3–10	Praised be the God and Father of our Lord Jesus Christ, who has bestowed on us in Christ every spiritual blessing in the heavens.

God chose us in him
before the world began
to be holy
and blameless in his sight.

He predestined us
to be his adopted sons through Jesus Christ,
such was his will and pleasure,
that all might praise the glorious favor
he has bestowed on us in his beloved.

In him and through his blood, we have
    been redeemed,
and our sins forgiven,
so immeasurably generous
is God's favor to us.

God has given us the wisdom
to understand fully the mystery,
the plan he was pleased
to decree in Christ.

A plan to be carried out
in Christ, in the fullness of time,
to bring all things into one in him,
in the heavens and on earth.

Glory to the Father, and to the Son,
    and to the Holy Spirit:
—as it was in the beginning, is now,
and will be for ever. Amen.

Ant. **God planned in the fullness of time to restore all things in Christ.**

Reading
1 Thessalonians 2:13

We thank God constantly that in receiving his message from us you took it, not as the word of men, but as it truly is, the word of God at work within you who believe.

Responsory

Accept my prayer, O Lord, which rises
    up to you.
—Accept my prayer, O Lord, which rises
    up to you.

Like burning incense in your sight,
—which rises up to you.

Glory to the Father, and to the Son,
    and to the Holy Spirit.
—Accept my prayer, O Lord, which rises
    up to you.

Gospel Canticle

Ant. **For ever will my soul proclaim the greatness of the Lord.**

Canticle of Mary
Luke 1:46-55

My + soul proclaims the greatness of the Lord,
my spirit rejoices in God my Savior
for he has looked with favor on his
    lowly servant.

From this day all generations will
    call me blessed:
the Almighty has done great things for me,
and holy is his Name.

He has mercy on those who fear him
in every generation.

He has shown the strength of his arm,
he has scattered the proud in their conceit.

He has cast down the mighty from
    their thrones,
and has lifted up the lowly.

He has filled the hungry with good things,
and the rich he has sent away empty.

He has come to the help of his servant Israel
for he has remembered his promise of mercy,
the promise he made to our fathers,
to Abraham and his children for ever.

Glory to the Father, and to the Son,
    and to the Holy Spirit:
—as it was in the beginning, is now,
and will be for ever. Amen.

Ant. **For ever will my soul proclaim the greatness of the Lord.**

Intercessions Let us praise Christ, who loves, nourishes and supports his Church. With faith let us cry out to him:
Answer the prayers of your people, Lord.

Lord Jesus, grant that all men be saved,
—and come to the knowledge of truth.

Preserve our holy father, Pope N., and N., our bishop,
—come with your power to help them.

Remember those who long for honest work,
—so that they may lead a life of peaceful security.

Lord, be the refuge of the poor,
—their help in distress.

We commend to your care all bishops, priests and deacons who have died,
—may they sing your praises for ever around your heavenly throne.

The Lord's Prayer Our Father, who art in heaven,
hallowed be thy name;
thy kingdom come,
thy will be done
on earth as it is in heaven.
Give us this day our daily bread,
and forgive us our trespasses,
as we forgive those who trespass against us;
and lead us not into temptation,
but deliver us from evil.

Pater noster, qui es in cælis:
sanctificetur nomen tuum;
adveniat regnum tuum;
fiat voluntas tua,
sicut in cælo, et in terra.
Panem nostrum cotidianum da nobis hodie;
et dimitte nobis debita nostra,
sicut et nos dimittimus debitoribus nostris;
et ne nos inducas in tentationem;
sed libera nos a malo.

Concluding Prayer

Almighty Father,
you have given us the strength
to work throughout this day.
Receive our evening sacrifice of praise
in thanksgiving for your countless gifts.
We ask this through our Lord Jesus Christ,
    your Son,
who lives and reigns with you and
    the Holy Spirit,
God, for ever and ever.
—Amen.

Dismissal

If praying individually, or in a group without a priest or deacon:

May the Lord + bless us,
protect us from all evil
and bring us to everlasting life.
—Amen.

If praying with a priest or deacon, he dismisses the people:

The Lord be with you.
—And with your spirit.

May almighty God bless you,
the Father, and the Son, ✠ and the Holy Spirit.
—Amen.

Go in peace.
—Thanks be to God.

NIGHT PRAYER

God, + come to my assistance.
—Lord, make haste to help me.

Glory to the Father, and to the Son,
    and to the Holy Spirit:
—as it was in the beginning, is now,
and will be for ever. Amen. Alleluia.

Examen *An optional brief examination of conscience may be made. Call to mind your sins and failings this day.*

Hymn *Abide with Me, p. 675*

Psalmody Ant. **O Lord, our God, unwearied is your love for us.**

Psalm 86 Turn your ear, O Lord, and give answer
for I am poor and needy.
Preserve my life, for I am faithful:
save the servant who trusts in you.

You are my God; have mercy on me, Lord,
for I cry to you all the day long.
Give joy to your servant, O Lord,
for to you I lift up my soul.

O Lord, you are good and forgiving,
full of love to all who call.
Give heed, O Lord, to my prayer
and attend to the sound of my voice.

In the day of distress I will call
and surely you will reply.
Among the gods there is none like you, O Lord;
nor work to compare with yours.

All the nations shall come to adore you
and glorify your name, O Lord:
for you are great and do marvelous deeds,
you who alone are God.

Show me, Lord, your way
so that I may walk in your truth.
Guide my heart to fear your name.

I will praise you, Lord my God, with
    all my heart
and glorify your name for ever;
for your love to me has been great:
you have saved me from the depths of
    the grave.

The proud have risen against me;
ruthless men seek my life:
to you they pay no heed.

But you, God of mercy and compassion,
slow to anger, O Lord,
abounding in love and truth,
turn and take pity on me.

O give your strength to your servant
and save your handmaid's son.
Show me a sign of your favor
that my foes may see to their shame
that you console me and give me your help.

Glory to the Father, and to the Son,
    and to the Holy Spirit:
—as it was in the beginning, is now,
and will be for ever. Amen.

Ant. **O Lord, our God, unwearied is your love for us.**

Reading
1 Thessalonians 5:9–10

God has destined us for acquiring salvation through our Lord Jesus Christ. He died for us, that all of us, whether awake or asleep, together might live with him.

Responsory

Into your hands, Lord, I commend my spirit.
—Into your hands, Lord, I commend my spirit.

You have redeemed us, Lord God of truth.
—I commend my spirit.

Glory to the Father, and to the Son,
    and to the Holy Spirit.
—Into your hands, Lord, I commend my spirit.

Gospel Canticle

Ant. **Protect us, Lord, as we stay awake; watch over us as we sleep, that awake, we may keep watch with Christ, and asleep, rest in his peace.**

Canticle of Simeon
Luke 2:29–32

Lord, + now you let your servant go in peace;
your word has been fulfilled:
my own eyes have seen the salvation
which you have prepared in the sight of
   every people:
a light to reveal you to the nations
and the glory of your people Israel.

Glory to the Father, and to the Son,
   and to the Holy Spirit:
—as it was in the beginning, is now,
and will be for ever. Amen.

Ant. **Protect us, Lord, as we stay awake; watch over us as we sleep, that awake, we may keep watch with Christ, and asleep, rest in his peace.**

Concluding Prayer
Let us pray.
Lord,
give our bodies restful sleep
and let the work we have done today
bear fruit in eternal life.
We ask this through Christ our Lord.
—Amen.

Blessing
May the all-powerful Lord
grant us a restful night
and a peaceful death.
—Amen.

Marian Antiphon
Sing the "Salve Regina," found on p. 698, or pray a Hail Mary.

Tuesday, July 11, 2023
St. Benedict

MORNING PRAYER

God, + come to my assistance.
—Lord, make haste to help me.

Glory to the Father, and to the Son,
    and to the Holy Spirit:
—as it was in the beginning, is now,
and will be for ever. Amen. Alleluia.

Hymn   *Jesus, Eternal Truth Sublime, p. 689*

Psalmody   Ant. 1 **Lord, send forth your light and your truth.**

Psalm 43

Defend me, O God, and plead my cause
against a godless nation.
From deceitful and cunning men
rescue me, O God.

Since you, O God, are my stronghold,
why have you rejected me?
Why do I go mourning
oppressed by the foe?

O send forth your light and your truth;
let these be my guide.
Let them bring me to your holy mountain
to the place where you dwell.

And I will come to the altar of God,
the God of my joy.
My redeemer, I will thank you on the harp,
O God, my God.

Why are you cast down, my soul,
why groan within me?
Hope in God; I will praise him still,
my savior and my God.

Glory to the Father, and to the Son,
    and to the Holy Spirit:
as it was in the beginning, is now,
and will be for ever. Amen.

Ant. **Lord, send forth your light and your truth.**

Ant. 2 **Lord, keep us safe all the days of our life.**

Canticle:
Isaiah 38:10–14,
17–20

Once I said,
"In the noontime of life I must depart!
To the gates of the nether world I shall
    be consigned
for the rest of my years."

I said, "I shall see the Lord no more
in the land of the living.
No longer shall I behold my fellow men
among those who dwell in the world."

My dwelling, like a shepherd's tent,
is struck down and borne away from me;
you have folded up my life, like a weaver
who severs the last thread.

Day and night you give me over to torment;
I cry out until the dawn.
Like a lion he breaks all my bones;
day and night you give me over to torment.

Like a swallow I utter shrill cries;
I moan like a dove.
My eyes grow weak, gazing heaven-ward:
O Lord, I am in straits; be my surety!

You have preserved my life
from the pit of destruction,
when you cast behind your back
all my sins.

For it is not the nether world that gives
   you thanks,
nor death that praises you;
neither do those who go down into the pit
await your kindness.

The living, the living give you thanks,
as I do today.
Fathers declare to their sons,
O God, your faithfulness.

The Lord is our savior;
we shall sing to stringed instruments
in the house of the Lord
all the days of our life.

Glory to the Father, and to the Son,
   and to the Holy Spirit:
—as it was in the beginning, is now,
   and will be for ever. Amen.

Ant. **Lord, keep us safe all the days of our life.**

Ant. 3 **To you, O God, our praise is due in Zion.**

Psalm 65

To you our praise is due
in Zion, O God.
To you we pay our vows,
you who hear our prayer.

To you all flesh will come
with its burden of sin.
Too heavy for us, our offenses,
but you wipe them away.

Blessed is he whom you choose and call
to dwell in your courts.
We are filled with the blessings of your house,
of your holy temple.

You keep your pledge with wonders,
O God our savior,
the hope of all the earth
and of far distant isles.

You uphold the mountains with
    your strength,
you are girded with power.
You still the roaring of the seas,
the roaring of their waves
and the tumult of the peoples.

The ends of the earth stand in awe
at the sight of your wonders.
The lands of sunrise and sunset
you fill with your joy.

You care for the earth, give it water,
you fill it with riches.
Your river in heaven brims over
to provide its grain.

And thus you provide for the earth;
you drench its furrows,
you level it, soften it with showers,
you bless its growth.

You crown the year with your goodness.
Abundance flows in your steps,
in the pastures of the wilderness it flows.

The hills are girded with joy,
the meadows covered with flocks,
the valleys are decked with wheat.
They shout for joy, yes, they sing.

Glory to the Father, and to the Son,
   and to the Holy Spirit:
as it was in the beginning, is now,
and will be for ever. Amen.

Ant. **To you, O God, our praise is due in Zion.**

Reading
Romans 12:1–2

Brothers, I beg you through the mercy of God to offer your bodies as a living sacrifice holy and acceptable to God, your spiritual worship. Do not conform yourselves to this age but be transformed by the renewal of your mind, so that you may judge what is God's will, what is good, pleasing and perfect.

Responsory

In the depths of his heart,
    the law of God is his guide.
—In the depths of his heart,
    the law of God is his guide.

He will never lose his way;
—the law of God is his guide.

Glory to the Father, and to the Son,
    and to the Holy Spirit.
—In the depths of his heart,
    the law of God is his guide.

Gospel Canticle

Ant. **He lived a holy life; Benedict, blessed in name and in grace.**

Canticle of Zechariah
Luke 1:68–79

Blessed + be the Lord, the God of Israel;
he has come to his people and set them free.

He has raised up for us a mighty savior,
born of the house of his servant David.

Through his holy prophets he
    promised of old
that he would save us from our enemies,
from the hands of all who hate us.

He promised to show mercy to our fathers
and to remember his holy covenant.

This was the oath he swore to our
> father Abraham:
to set us free from the hands of our enemies,
free to worship him without fear,
holy and righteous in his sight
> all the days of our life.

You, my child, shall be called the prophet of
> the Most High;
for you will go before the Lord to
> prepare his way,
to give his people knowledge of salvation
by the forgiveness of their sins.

In the tender compassion of our God
the dawn from on high shall break upon us,
to shine on those who dwell in darkness and
> the shadow of death,
and to guide our feet into the way of peace.

Glory to the Father, and to the Son,
> and to the Holy Spirit:
—as it was in the beginning, is now,
and will be for ever. Amen.

Ant. **He lived a holy life; Benedict, blessed in name and in grace.**

Intercessions My brothers, let us praise Christ, asking to serve him and to be holy and righteous in his sight all the days of our life. Let us acclaim him:
Lord, you alone are the holy one.

You desired to experience everything we
    experience but sin,
—have mercy on us, Lord Jesus.

You called us to love perfectly,
—make us holy, Lord Jesus.

You commissioned us to be the salt of the
    earth and the light of the world,
—let your light shine on us, Lord Jesus.

You desired to serve, not to be served,
—help us, Lord Jesus, to give humble service to
    you and to our neighbors.

You are in the form of God sharing in the
    splendor of the Father,
—Lord Jesus, let us see the glory of your face.

The Lord's Prayer

Our Father, who art in heaven,
hallowed be thy name;
thy kingdom come,
thy will be done
on earth as it is in heaven.
Give us this day our daily bread,
and forgive us our trespasses,
as we forgive those who trespass against us;
and lead us not into temptation,
but deliver us from evil.

Pater noster, qui es in cælis:
sanctificetur nomen tuum;
adveniat regnum tuum;
fiat voluntas tua,
sicut in cælo, et in terra.
Panem nostrum cotidianum da nobis hodie;
et dimitte nobis debita nostra,
sicut et nos dimittimus debitoribus nostris;
et ne nos inducas in tentationem;
sed libera nos a malo.

Concluding Prayer

God our Father,
you made Saint Benedict an outstanding guide
to teach men how to live in your service.
Grant that by preferring your love to
    everything else,
we may walk in the way of your
    commandments.
We ask this through our Lord Jesus Christ,
    your Son,
who lives and reigns with you and
    the Holy Spirit,
God, forever and ever.
—Amen.

Dismissal

If praying individually, or in a group without a priest or deacon:

May the Lord + bless us,
protect us from all evil
and bring us to everlasting life.
—Amen.

If praying with a priest or deacon, he dismisses the people:

The Lord be with you.
—And with your spirit.

May almighty God bless you,
the Father, and the Son, ✠ and the Holy Spirit.
—Amen.

Go in peace.
—Thanks be to God.

EVENING PRAYER

God, + come to my assistance.
—Lord, make haste to help me.

Glory to the Father, and to the Son,
 and to the Holy Spirit:
—as it was in the beginning, is now,
and will be for ever. Amen. Alleluia.

Hymn *Sing with All the Saints in Glory, p. 702*

Psalmody Ant. 1 **You cannot serve both God and mammon.**

Psalm 49

Hear this, all you peoples,
give heed, all who dwell in the world,
men both high and low,
rich and poor alike!

My lips will speak words of wisdom.
My heart is full of insight.
I will turn my mind to a parable,
with the harp I will solve my problem.

Why should I fear in evil days
the malice of the foes who surround me,
men who trust in their wealth,
and boast of the vastness of their riches?

For no man can buy his own ransom,
or pay a price to God for his life.
The ransom of his soul is beyond him.
He cannot buy life without end,
nor avoid coming to the grave.

He knows that wise men and fools must
    both perish
and leave their wealth to others.
Their graves are their homes for ever,
their dwelling place from age to age,
though their names spread wide
    through the land.

In his riches, man lacks wisdom:
he is like the beasts that are destroyed.

Glory to the Father, and to the Son,
    and to the Holy Spirit:
—as it was in the beginning, is now,
and will be for ever. Amen.

Ant. **You cannot serve both God and mammon.**

Ant. 2 **Store up for yourselves treasure in heaven, says the Lord.**

Psalm 49 (continued)

This is the lot of those who trust in themselves,
who have others at their beck and call.
Like sheep they are driven to the grave,
where death shall be their shepherd
and the just shall become their rulers.

With the morning their outward
    show vanishes
and the grave becomes their home.
But God will ransom me from death
and take my soul to himself.

Then do not fear when a man grows rich,
when the glory of his house increases.
He takes nothing with him when he dies,
his glory does not follow him below.

Though he flattered himself while he lived:
"Men will praise me for all my success,"
yet he will go to join his fathers,
and will never see the light any more.

In his riches, man lacks wisdom:
he is like the beasts that are destroyed.

Glory to the Father, and to the Son,
    and to the Holy Spirit:
—as it was in the beginning, is now,
and will be for ever. Amen.

Ant. **Store up for yourselves treasure in heaven, says the Lord.**

Ant. 3 **Adoration and glory belong by right to the Lamb who was slain.**

Canticle:
Revelation 4:11;
5:9, 10, 12

O Lord our God, you are worthy
to receive glory and honor and power.

For you have created all things;
by your will they came to be and were made.

Worthy are you, O Lord,
to receive the scroll and break open its seals.

For you were slain;
with your blood you purchased for God
men of every race and tongue,
of every people and nation.

You made of them a kingdom,
and priests to serve our God,
and they shall reign on the earth.

Worthy is the Lamb that was slain
to receive power and riches,
wisdom and strength,
honor and glory and praise.

Glory to the Father, and to the Son,
    and to the Holy Spirit:
—as it was in the beginning, is now,
and will be for ever. Amen.

Ant. **Adoration and glory belong by right to the Lamb who was slain.**

Reading
Romans 8:28-30

We know that God makes all things work together for the good of those who have been called according to his decree. Those whom he foreknew he predestined to share the image of his Son, that the Son might be the first-born of many brothers. Those he predestined he likewise called; those he called he also justified; and those he justified he in turn glorified.

Responsory

Just is the Lord, in justice he delights.
—Just is the Lord, in justice he delights.

He looks with favor on the upright man;
—in justice he delights.

Glory to the Father, and to the Son,
 and to the Holy Spirit.
—Just is the Lord, in justice he delights.

Gospel Canticle

Ant. **He received the Lord's blessing and the merciful saving power of God; such is the fortune of those who seek the Lord.**

Canticle of Mary
Luke 1:46-55

My + soul proclaims the greatness of the Lord,
my spirit rejoices in God my Savior
for he has looked with favor on his
 lowly servant.

From this day all generations will
 call me blessed:
the Almighty has done great things for me,
and holy is his Name.

He has mercy on those who fear him
in every generation.

He has shown the strength of his arm,
he has scattered the proud in their conceit.

He has cast down the mighty from
 their thrones,
and has lifted up the lowly.

He has filled the hungry with good things,
and the rich he has sent away empty.

He has come to the help of his servant Israel
for he has remembered his promise of mercy,
the promise he made to our fathers,
to Abraham and his children for ever.

Glory to the Father, and to the Son,
   and to the Holy Spirit:
as it was in the beginning, is now,
and will be for ever. Amen.

Ant. **He received the Lord's blessing and the merciful saving power of God; such is the fortune of those who seek the Lord.**

Intercessions Let us pray to the Father, the source of all holiness, and ask him to lead us to holiness of life through the example and intercession of his saints:
May we be holy as you are holy.

Holy Father, you want us to be called your sons and truly to be such,
—grant that your holy Church may proclaim you throughout the world.

Holy Father, you want us to walk worthily and please you in all we do,
—let us abound in doing good works.

Holy Father, you have reconciled us to yourself through Christ,
—preserve us in your name so that all may be one.

Holy Father, you have called us to a
 heavenly banquet,
—through the bread that came down from
 heaven make us worthy to grow in
 perfect love.

Holy Father, forgive the offenses of
 every sinner,
—let the dead perceive the light of your
 countenance.

The Lord's Prayer

Our Father, who art in heaven,
hallowed be thy name;
thy kingdom come,
thy will be done
on earth as it is in heaven.
Give us this day our daily bread,
and forgive us our trespasses,
as we forgive those who trespass against us;
and lead us not into temptation,
but deliver us from evil.

Pater noster, qui es in cælis:
sanctificetur nomen tuum;
adveniat regnum tuum;
fiat voluntas tua,
sicut in cælo, et in terra.
Panem nostrum cotidianum da nobis hodie;
et dimitte nobis debita nostra,
sicut et nos dimittimus debitoribus nostris;
et ne nos inducas in tentationem;
sed libera nos a malo.

Concluding Prayer

God our Father,
you made Saint Benedict an outstanding guide
to teach men how to live in your service.
Grant that by preferring your love to
everything else,
we may walk in the way of your
commandments.
We ask this through our Lord Jesus Christ,
your Son,
who lives and reigns with you and
the Holy Spirit,
God, forever and ever.
—Amen.

Dismissal

If praying individually, or in a group without a priest or deacon:

May the Lord ✛ bless us,
protect us from all evil
and bring us to everlasting life.
—Amen.

If praying with a priest or deacon, he dismisses the people:

The Lord be with you.
—And with your spirit.

May almighty God bless you,
the Father, and the Son, ✛ and the Holy Spirit.
—Amen.

Go in peace.
—Thanks be to God.

I MUSE ON WHAT YOUR HAND HAS WROUGHT AND TO YOU I STRETCH OUT MY HANDS.

NIGHT PRAYER

God, + come to my assistance.
—Lord, make haste to help me.

Glory to the Father, and to the Son,
    and to the Holy Spirit:
—as it was in the beginning, is now,
and will be for ever. Amen. Alleluia.

Examen — *An optional brief examination of conscience may be made. Call to mind your sins and failings this day.*

Hymn — *Before the Final Light of Day, p. 676*

Psalmody   Ant. **Do not hide your face from me; in you I put my trust.**

Psalm 143:1–11

Lord, listen to my prayer:
turn your ear to my appeal.
You are faithful, you are just; give answer.
Do not call your servant to judgment
for no one is just in your sight.

The enemy pursues my soul;
he has crushed my life to the ground;
he has made me dwell in darkness
like the dead, long forgotten.
Therefore my spirit fails;
my heart is numb within me.

I remember the days that are past:
I ponder all your works.
I muse on what your hand has wrought
and to you I stretch out my hands.
Like a parched land my soul thirsts for you.

Lord, make haste and answer;
for my spirit fails within me.
Do not hide your face
lest I become like those in the grave.

In the morning let me know your love
for I put my trust in you.
Make me know the way I should walk:
to you I lift up my soul.

Rescue me, Lord, from my enemies;
I have fled to you for refuge.
Teach me to do your will
for you, O Lord, are my God.
Let your good spirit guide me
in ways that are level and smooth.

For your name's sake, Lord, save my life;
in your justice save my soul from distress.

Glory to the Father, and to the Son,
    and to the Holy Spirit:
—as it was in the beginning, is now,
and will be for ever. Amen.

Ant. **Do not hide your face from me; in you I put my trust.**

Reading
1 Peter 5:8–9a

Stay sober and alert. Your opponent the devil is prowling like a roaring lion looking for someone to devour. Resist him, solid in your faith.

Responsory Into your hands, Lord, I commend my spirit.
—Into your hands, Lord, I commend my spirit.

You have redeemed us, Lord God of truth.
—I commend my spirit.

Glory to the Father, and to the Son,
 and to the Holy Spirit.
—Into your hands, Lord, I commend my spirit.

Gospel Canticle

Ant. **Protect us, Lord, as we stay awake; watch over us as we sleep, that awake, we may keep watch with Christ, and asleep, rest in his peace.**

Canticle of Simeon
Luke 2:29–32

Lord, ✛ now you let your servant go in peace;
your word has been fulfilled:
my own eyes have seen the salvation
which you have prepared in the sight of
 every people:
a light to reveal you to the nations
and the glory of your people Israel.

Glory to the Father, and to the Son,
 and to the Holy Spirit:
—as it was in the beginning, is now,
and will be for ever. Amen.

Ant. **Protect us, Lord, as we stay awake; watch over us as we sleep, that awake, we may keep watch with Christ, and asleep, rest in his peace.**

Concluding Prayer

Let us pray.
Lord,
fill this night with your radiance.
May we sleep in peace and rise with joy
to welcome the light of a new day in
 your name.
We ask this through Christ our Lord.
—Amen.

Blessing

May the all-powerful Lord
grant us a restful night
and a peaceful death.
—Amen.

Marian Antiphon

Sing the "Salve Regina," found on p. 698, or pray a Hail Mary.

Wednesday, July 12, 2023
Wednesday of the Fourteenth Week in Ordinary Time

MORNING PRAYER ———————————————

God, + come to my assistance.
—Lord, make haste to help me.

Glory to the Father, and to the Son,
 and to the Holy Spirit:
—as it was in the beginning, is now,
 and will be for ever. Amen. Alleluia.

Hymn

From All That Dwell Below the Skies, p. 679

Psalmody Ant. 1 **O God, all your ways are holy; what god can compare with our God?**

Psalm 77

I cry aloud to God,
cry aloud to God that he may hear me.

In the day of my distress I sought the Lord.
My hands were raised at night
    without ceasing;
my soul refused to be consoled.
I remembered my God and I groaned.
I pondered and my spirit fainted.

You withheld sleep from my eyes.
I was troubled, I could not speak.
I thought of the days of long ago
and remembered the years long past.
At night I mused within my heart.
I pondered and my spirit questioned.

"Will the Lord reject us for ever?
Will he show us his favor no more?
Has his love vanished for ever?
Has his promise come to an end?
Does God forget his mercy
or in anger withhold his compassion?"

I said: "This is what causes my grief;
that the way of the Most High has changed."
I remember the deeds of the Lord,
I remember your wonders of old,
I muse on all your works
and ponder your mighty deeds.

Your ways, O God, are holy.
What god is great as our God?
You are the God who works wonders.
You showed your power among the peoples.
Your strong arm redeemed your people,
the sons of Jacob and Joseph.

The waters saw you, O God,
the waters saw you and trembled;
the depths were moved with terror.
The clouds poured down rain,
the skies sent forth their voice;
your arrows flashed to and fro.

Your thunder rolled round the sky,
your flashes lighted up the world.
The earth was moved and trembled
when your way led through the sea,
your path through the mighty waters,
and no one saw your footprints.

You guided your people like a flock
by the hand of Moses and Aaron.

Glory to the Father, and to the Son,
    and to the Holy Spirit:
—as it was in the beginning, is now,
and will be for ever. Amen.

Ant. **O God, all your ways are holy; what god can compare with our God?**

Ant. 2 **My heart leaps up with joy to the Lord, for he humbles only to exalt us.**

Canticle:
1 Samuel 2:1–10

My heart exults in the Lord,
my horn is exalted in my God.

I have swallowed up my enemies;
I rejoice in my victory.
There is no Holy One like the Lord;
there is no Rock like our God.

Speak boastfully no longer,
nor let arrogance issue from your mouths.
For an all-knowing God is the Lord,
a God who judges deeds.

The bows of the mighty are broken,
while the tottering gird on strength.
The well-fed hire themselves out for bread,
while the hungry batten on spoil.
The barren wife bears seven sons,
while the mother of many languishes.

The Lord puts to death and gives life;
he casts down to the nether world;
he raises up again.
The Lord makes poor and makes rich,
he humbles, he also exalts.

He raises the needy from the dust;
from the ash heap he lifts up the poor,
to seat them with nobles
and make a glorious throne their heritage.

For the pillars of the earth are the Lord's,
and he has set the world upon them.
He will guard the footsteps of his
 faithful ones,
but the wicked shall perish in the darkness.
For not by strength does man prevail;
the Lord's foes shall be shattered.

The Most High in heaven thunders;
the Lord judges the ends of the earth.
Now may he give strength to his king
and exalt the horn of his anointed!

Glory to the Father, and to the Son,
 and to the Holy Spirit:
—as it was in the beginning, is now,
and will be for ever. Amen.

Ant. **My heart leaps up with joy to the Lord, for he humbles only to exalt us.**

Ant. 3 **The Lord is king, let the earth rejoice.**

Psalm 97

The Lord is king, let earth rejoice,
let all the coastlands be glad.
Cloud and darkness are his raiment;
his throne, justice and right.

A fire prepares his path;
it burns up his foes on every side.
His lightnings light up the world,
the earth trembles at the sight.

The mountains melt like wax
before the Lord of all the earth.
The skies proclaim his justice;
all peoples see his glory.

Let those who serve idols be ashamed,
those who boast of their worthless gods.
All you spirits, worship him.

Zion hears and is glad;
the people of Judah rejoice
because of your judgments, O Lord.

For you indeed are the Lord,
most high above all the earth,
exalted far above all spirits.

The Lord loves those who hate evil:
he guards the souls of his saints;
he sets them free from the wicked.

Light shines forth for the just
and joy for the upright of heart.
Rejoice, you just, in the Lord;
give glory to his holy name.

Glory to the Father, and to the Son,
    and to the Holy Spirit:
—as it was in the beginning, is now,
and will be for ever. Amen.

Ant. **The Lord is king, let the earth rejoice.**

Reading
Romans 8:35, 37

Who will separate us from the love of Christ? Trial, or distress, or persecution, or hunger, or nakedness, or danger, or the sword? Yet in all this we are more than conquerors because of him who has loved us.

Responsory

I will bless the Lord all my life long.
—I will bless the Lord all my life long.

With a song of praise ever on my lips,
—all my life long.

Glory to the Father, and to the Son,
 and to the Holy Spirit.
—I will bless the Lord all my life long.

Gospel Canticle

Ant. **Let us serve the Lord in holiness all the days of our life.**

Canticle of Zechariah
Luke 1:68–79

Blessed + be the Lord, the God of Israel;
he has come to his people and set them free.

He has raised up for us a mighty savior,
born of the house of his servant David.

Through his holy prophets he
 promised of old
that he would save us from our enemies,
from the hands of all who hate us.

He promised to show mercy to our fathers
and to remember his holy covenant.

This was the oath he swore to our
    father Abraham:
to set us free from the hands of our enemies,
free to worship him without fear,
holy and righteous in his sight
    all the days of our life.

You, my child, shall be called the prophet of
    the Most High;
for you will go before the Lord to
    prepare his way,
to give his people knowledge of salvation
by the forgiveness of their sins.

In the tender compassion of our God
the dawn from on high shall break upon us,
to shine on those who dwell in darkness and
    the shadow of death,
and to guide our feet into the way of peace.

Glory to the Father, and to the Son,
    and to the Holy Spirit:
—as it was in the beginning, is now,
and will be for ever. Amen.

Ant. **Let us serve the Lord in holiness all the days of our life.**

Intercessions Blessed be God our Savior, who promised to remain with his Church all days, until the end of the world. Let us give him thanks and call out:
Remain with us, Lord.

Remain with us the whole day, Lord,
—let your grace be a sun that never sets.

We dedicate this day to you as an offering,
—do not let us offer anything that is evil.

May your gift of light pervade this whole day,
—that we may be the salt of the earth and the light of the world.

May the love of your Holy Spirit direct our hearts and our lips,
—and may we always act in accordance with your will.

The Lord's Prayer
Our Father, who art in heaven,
hallowed be thy name;
thy kingdom come,
thy will be done
on earth as it is in heaven.
Give us this day our daily bread,
and forgive us our trespasses,
as we forgive those who trespass against us;
and lead us not into temptation,
but deliver us from evil.

Pater noster, qui es in cælis:
sanctificetur nomen tuum;
adveniat regnum tuum;
fiat voluntas tua,
sicut in cælo, et in terra.
Panem nostrum cotidianum da nobis hodie;
et dimitte nobis debita nostra,
sicut et nos dimittimus debitoribus nostris;
et ne nos inducas in tentationem;
sed libera nos a malo.

Concluding Prayer

Lord,
as a new day dawns
send the radiance of your light
to shine in our hearts.
Make us true to your teaching;
keep us free from error and sin.
We ask this through our Lord Jesus Christ,
 your Son,
who lives and reigns with you and
 the Holy Spirit,
God, for ever and ever.
—Amen.

Dismissal

If praying individually, or in a group without a priest or deacon:

May the Lord + bless us,
protect us from all evil
and bring us to everlasting life.
—Amen.

If praying with a priest or deacon, he dismisses the people:

The Lord be with you.
—And with your spirit.

May almighty God bless you,
the Father, and the Son, ✠ and the Holy Spirit.
—Amen.

Go in peace.
—Thanks be to God.

EVENING PRAYER

God, + come to my assistance.
—Lord, make haste to help me.

Glory to the Father, and to the Son,
 and to the Holy Spirit:
—as it was in the beginning, is now,
and will be for ever. Amen. Alleluia.

Hymn *Sing Praise to God Who Reigns Above, p. 700*

Psalmody Ant. 1 **Eagerly we await the fulfillment of our hope, the glorious coming of our Savior.**

Psalm 62

In God alone is my soul at rest;
my help comes from him.
He alone is my rock, my stronghold,
my fortress: I stand firm.

How long will you all attack one man
to break him down,
as though he were a tottering wall,
or a tumbling fence?

Their plan is only to destroy:
they take pleasure in lies.
With their mouth they utter blessing
but in their heart they curse.

In God alone be at rest, my soul;
for my hope comes from him.
He alone is my rock, my stronghold,
my fortress: I stand firm.

In God is my safety and glory,
the rock of my strength.
Take refuge in God, all you people.
Trust him at all times.
Pour out your hearts before him
for God is our refuge.

Common folk are only a breath,
great men an illusion.
Placed in the scales, they rise;
they weigh less than a breath.

Do not put your trust in oppression
nor vain hopes on plunder.
Do not set your heart on riches
even when they increase.

For God has said only one thing:
only two do I know:
that to God alone belongs power
and to you, Lord, love;
and that you repay each man
according to his deeds.

Glory to the Father, and to the Son,
   and to the Holy Spirit:
as it was in the beginning, is now,
and will be for ever. Amen.

Ant. **Eagerly we await the fulfillment of our hope, the glorious coming of our Savior.**

Ant. 2 **May God turn his radiant face toward us, and fill us with his blessings.**

Psalm 67

O God, be gracious and bless us
and let your face shed its light upon us.
So will your ways be known upon earth
and all nations learn your saving help.

Let the peoples praise you, O God;
let all the peoples praise you.

Let the nations be glad and exult
for you rule the world with justice.
With fairness you rule the peoples,
you guide the nations on earth.

Let the peoples praise you, O God;
let all the peoples praise you.

The earth has yielded its fruit
for God, our God, has blessed us.
May God still give us his blessing
till the ends of the earth revere him.

EVENING PRAYER   WED   JULY 12

Glory to the Father, and to the Son,
>   and to the Holy Spirit:
— as it was in the beginning, is now,
and will be for ever. Amen.

Ant. **May God turn his radiant face toward us, and fill us with his blessings.**

Ant. 3 **Through him all things were made; he holds all creation together in himself.**

Canticle:
Colossians
1:12–20

Let us give thanks to the Father
for having made you worthy
to share the lot of the saints
in light.

He rescued us
from the power of darkness
and brought us
into the kingdom of his beloved Son.
Through him we have redemption,
the forgiveness of our sins.

He is the image of the invisible God,
the first-born of all creatures.
In him everything in heaven and on earth
    was created,
things visible and invisible.

All were created through him;
all were created for him.
He is before all else that is.
In him everything continues in being.

It is he who is head of the body, the church!
he who is the beginning,
the first-born of the dead,
so that primacy may be his in everything.

It pleased God to make absolute fullness
　　reside in him
and, by means of him, to reconcile
　　everything in his person,
both on earth and in the heavens,
making peace through the blood of his cross.

Glory to the Father, and to the Son,
　　and to the Holy Spirit:
—as it was in the beginning, is now,
and will be for ever. Amen.

Ant. **Through him all things were made; he holds all creation together in himself.**

Reading
1 Peter 5:5b–7

In your relations with one another, clothe yourselves with humility, because God "is stern with the arrogant but to the humble he shows kindness." Bow humbly under God's mighty hand, so that in due time he may lift you high. Cast all your cares on him because he cares for you.

Responsory Keep us, O Lord, as the apple of your eye.
—Keep us, O Lord, as the apple of your eye.

Gather us under the shadow of your wings,
　　and keep us,
—as the apple of your eye.

Glory to the Father, and to the Son,
    and to the Holy Spirit.
—Keep us, O Lord, as the apple of your eye.

Gospel Canticle

Ant. **Lord, with the strength of your arm scatter the proud and lift up the lowly.**

Canticle of Mary
Luke 1:46–55

My + soul proclaims the greatness of the Lord,
my spirit rejoices in God my Savior
for he has looked with favor on his
    lowly servant.

From this day all generations will
    call me blessed:
the Almighty has done great things for me,
and holy is his Name.

He has mercy on those who fear him
in every generation.

He has shown the strength of his arm,
he has scattered the proud in their conceit.

He has cast down the mighty from
    their thrones,
and has lifted up the lowly.

He has filled the hungry with good things,
and the rich he has sent away empty.

He has come to the help of his servant Israel
for he has remembered his promise of mercy,
the promise he made to our fathers,
to Abraham and his children for ever.

Glory to the Father, and to the Son,
   and to the Holy Spirit:
—as it was in the beginning, is now,
   and will be for ever. Amen.

Ant. **Lord, with the strength of your arm scatter the proud and lift up the lowly.**

Intercessions Beloved brothers and sisters, let us rejoice in our God, for he takes great delight in bestowing benefits on his people. Let us fervently pray:
Increase your grace and your peace, Lord.

Eternal God, for whom a thousand years are
   like the passing day,
—help us to remember that life is like a flower
   which blossoms in the morning, but
   withers in the evening.

Give your people manna to satisfy
   their hunger,
—and living water to quench their thirst for
   all eternity.

Let your faithful ones seek and taste the
   things that are above,
—and let them direct their work and their
   leisure to your glory.

Grant us good weather, Lord,
—that we may reap the copious fruits of
   the earth.

Show the faithful departed the vision of
>   your face,
— let them rejoice in the contemplation of
>   your presence.

The Lord's Prayer

Our Father, who art in heaven,
hallowed be thy name;
thy kingdom come,
thy will be done
on earth as it is in heaven.
Give us this day our daily bread,
and forgive us our trespasses,
as we forgive those who trespass against us;
and lead us not into temptation,
but deliver us from evil.

Pater noster, qui es in cælis:
sanctificetur nomen tuum;
adveniat regnum tuum;
fiat voluntas tua,
sicut in cælo, et in terra.
Panem nostrum cotidianum da nobis hodie;
et dimitte nobis debita nostra,
sicut et nos dimittimus debitoribus nostris;
et ne nos inducas in tentationem;
sed libera nos a malo.

Concluding Prayer

Lord God,
holy is your name,
and renowned your compassion,
cherished by every generation.
Hear our evening prayer
and let us sing your praise,
and proclaim your greatness for ever.
We ask this through our Lord Jesus Christ,
    your Son,
who lives and reigns with you and
    the Holy Spirit,
God, for ever and ever.
—Amen.

Dismissal

If praying individually, or in a group without a priest or deacon:

May the Lord + bless us,
protect us from all evil
and bring us to everlasting life.
—Amen.

If praying with a priest or deacon, he dismisses the people:

The Lord be with you.
—And with your spirit.

May almighty God bless you,
the Father, and the Son, ✚ and the Holy Spirit.
—Amen.

Go in peace.
—Thanks be to God.

NIGHT PRAYER

God, + come to my assistance.
—Lord, make haste to help me.

Glory to the Father, and to the Son,
 and to the Holy Spirit:
—as it was in the beginning, is now,
 and will be for ever. Amen. Alleluia.

Examen *An optional brief examination of conscience may be made. Call to mind your sins and failings this day.*

Hymn *O Joyful Light of God Most High, p. 693*

Psalmody Ant. 1 **Lord God, be my refuge and my strength.**

Psalm 31:1–6
In you, O Lord, I take refuge.
Let me never be put to shame.
In your justice, set me free,
hear me and speedily rescue me.

Be a rock of refuge for me,
a mighty stronghold to save me,
for you are my rock, my stronghold.
For your name's sake, lead me and guide me.

Release me from the snares they have hidden
for you are my refuge, Lord.
Into your hands I commend my spirit.
It is you who will redeem me, Lord.

Glory to the Father, and to the Son,
 and to the Holy Spirit:
—as it was in the beginning, is now,
 and will be for ever. Amen.

Ant. **Lord God, be my refuge and my strength.**

Ant. 2 **Out of the depths I cry to you, Lord.**

Psalm 130

Out of the depths I cry to you, O Lord,
Lord, hear my voice!
O let your ears be attentive
to the voice of my pleading.

If you, O Lord, should mark our guilt,
Lord, who would survive?
But with you is found forgiveness:
for this we revere you.

My soul is waiting for the Lord,
I count on his word.
My soul is longing for the Lord
more than watchman for daybreak.
Let the watchman count on daybreak
and Israel on the Lord.

Because with the Lord there is mercy
and fullness of redemption,
Israel indeed he will redeem
from all its iniquity.

Glory to the Father, and to the Son,
  and to the Holy Spirit:
—as it was in the beginning, is now,
  and will be for ever. Amen.

Ant. **Out of the depths I cry to you, Lord.**

Reading
Ephesians 4:26–27

If you are angry, let it be without sin. The sun must not go down on your wrath; do not give the devil a chance to work on you.

Responsory

Into your hands, Lord, I commend my spirit.
—Into your hands, Lord, I commend my spirit.

You have redeemed us, Lord God of truth.
—I commend my spirit.

Glory to the Father, and to the Son,
 and to the Holy Spirit.
—Into your hands, Lord, I commend my spirit.

Gospel Canticle

Ant. **Protect us, Lord, as we stay awake; watch over us as we sleep, that awake, we may keep watch with Christ, and asleep, rest in his peace.**

Canticle of Simeon
Luke 2:29–32

Lord, + now you let your servant go in peace;
your word has been fulfilled:
my own eyes have seen the salvation
which you have prepared in the sight of
 every people:
a light to reveal you to the nations
and the glory of your people Israel.

Glory to the Father, and to the Son,
 and to the Holy Spirit:
—as it was in the beginning, is now,
 and will be for ever. Amen.

JULY 12　　WED　　　　　　　　　　　　NIGHT PRAYER

Ant. **Protect us, Lord, as we stay awake; watch over us as we sleep, that awake, we may keep watch with Christ, and asleep, rest in his peace.**

Concluding Prayer
Let us pray.
Lord Jesus Christ,
you have given your followers
an example of gentleness and humility,
a task that is easy, a burden that is light.
Accept the prayers and work of this day,
and give us the rest that will strengthen us
to render more faithful service to you
who live and reign for ever and ever.
—Amen.

Blessing
May the all-powerful Lord
grant us a restful night
and a peaceful death.
—Amen.

Marian Antiphon
Sing the "Salve Regina," found on p. 698, or pray a Hail Mary.

MY SOUL IS
WAITING FOR
THE LORD,
I COUNT ON
HIS WORD.

Thursday, July 13, 2023
Thursday of the Fourteenth Week in Ordinary Time

MORNING PRAYER

God, + come to my assistance.
—Lord, make haste to help me.

Glory to the Father, and to the Son,
   and to the Holy Spirit:
—as it was in the beginning, is now,
   and will be for ever. Amen. Alleluia.

Hymn — *Now That the Sun Is Gleaming Bright, p. 692*

Psalmody — Ant. 1 **Stir up your mighty power, Lord; come to our aid.**

Psalm 80

O shepherd of Israel, hear us,
you who lead Joseph's flock,
shine forth from your cherubim throne
upon Ephraim, Benjamin, Manasseh.
O Lord, rouse up your might,
O Lord, come to our help.

God of hosts, bring us back;
let your face shine on us and we
    shall be saved.

Lord God of hosts, how long
will you frown on your people's plea?
You have fed them with tears for their bread,
an abundance of tears for their drink.
You have made us the taunt of our neighbors,
our enemies laugh us to scorn.

God of hosts, bring us back;
let your face shine on us and we
    shall be saved.

You brought a vine out of Egypt;
to plant it you drove out the nations.
Before it you cleared the ground;
it took root and spread through the land.

The mountains were covered with its shadow,
the cedars of God with its boughs.
It stretched out its branches to the sea,
to the Great River it stretched out its shoots.

Then why have you broken down its walls?
It is plucked by all who pass by.
It is ravaged by the boar of the forest,
devoured by the beasts of the field.

God of hosts, turn again, we implore,
look down from heaven and see.
Visit this vine and protect it,
the vine your right hand has planted.
Men have burnt it with fire and destroyed it.
May they perish at the frown of your face.

May your hand be on the man you
    have chosen,
the man you have given your strength.
And we shall never forsake you again:
give us life that we may call upon your name.

God of hosts, bring us back;
let your face shine on us and we
    shall be saved.

Glory to the Father, and to the Son,
    and to the Holy Spirit:
as it was in the beginning, is now,
and will be for ever. Amen.

Ant. **Stir up your mighty power, Lord; come to our aid.**

Ant. 2 **The Lord has worked marvels for us; make it known to the ends of the world.**

Canticle: Isaiah 12:1–6

I give you thanks, O Lord;
though you have been angry with me,
your anger has abated, and you have
    consoled me.

God indeed is my savior;
I am confident and unafraid.
My strength and my courage is the Lord,
and he has been my savior.

With joy you will draw water
at the fountain of salvation, and say
    on that day:
Give thanks to the Lord, acclaim his name;
among the nations make known his deeds,
proclaim how exalted is his name.

Sing praise to the Lord for his glorious
    achievement;
let this be known throughout all the earth.

Shout with exultation, O city of Zion,
for great in your midst
is the Holy One of Israel!

Glory to the Father, and to the Son,
    and to the Holy Spirit:
as it was in the beginning, is now,
and will be for ever. Amen.

Ant. **The Lord has worked marvels for us; make it known to the ends of the world.**

Ant. 3 **Ring out your joy to God our strength.**

Psalm 81

Ring out your joy to God our strength,
shout in triumph to the God of Jacob.

Raise a song and sound the timbrel,
the sweet-sounding harp and the lute,
blow the trumpet at the new moon,
when the moon is full, on our feast.

For this is Israel's law,
a command of the God of Jacob.
He imposed it as a rule on Joseph,
when he went out against the land of Egypt.

A voice I did not know said to me:
"I freed your shoulder from the burden;
your hands were freed from the load.
You called in distress and I saved you.

I answered, concealed in the storm cloud,
at the waters of Meribah I tested you.
Listen, my people, to my warning,
O Israel, if only you would heed!

Let there be no foreign god among you,
no worship of an alien god.
I am the Lord your God,
who brought you from the land of Egypt.
Open wide your mouth and I will fill it.

But my people did not heed my voice
and Israel would not obey,
so I left them in their stubbornness of heart
to follow their own designs.

O that my people would heed me,
that Israel would walk in my ways!
At once I would subdue their foes,
turn my hand against their enemies.

The Lord's enemies would cringe at their feet
and their subjection would last for ever.
But Israel I would feed with finest wheat
and fill them with honey from the rock."

Glory to the Father, and to the Son,
    and to the Holy Spirit:
—as it was in the beginning, is now,
and will be for ever. Amen.

Ant. **Ring out your joy to God our strength.**

Reading
Romans 14:17-19

The kingdom of God is not a matter of eating or drinking, but of justice, peace, and the joy that is given by the Holy Spirit. Whoever serves Christ in this way pleases God and wins the esteem of men. Let us, then, make it our aim to work for peace and to strengthen one another.

Responsory

In the early hours of the morning, I think of you, O Lord.
—In the early hours of the morning, I think of you, O Lord.

Always you are there to help me.
—I think of you, O Lord.

Glory to the Father, and to the Son, and to the Holy Spirit.
—In the early hours of the morning, I think of you, O Lord.

Gospel Canticle

Ant. **Give your people knowledge of salvation, Lord, and forgive us our sins.**

Canticle of Zechariah
Luke 1:68-79

Blessed + be the Lord, the God of Israel;
he has come to his people and set them free.

He has raised up for us a mighty savior,
born of the house of his servant David.

Through his holy prophets he
    promised of old
that he would save us from our enemies,
from the hands of all who hate us.

He promised to show mercy to our fathers
and to remember his holy covenant.

This was the oath he swore to our
   father Abraham:
to set us free from the hands of our enemies,
free to worship him without fear,
holy and righteous in his sight
   all the days of our life.

You, my child, shall be called the prophet of
   the Most High;
for you will go before the Lord to
   prepare his way,
to give his people knowledge of salvation
by the forgiveness of their sins.

In the tender compassion of our God
the dawn from on high shall break upon us,
to shine on those who dwell in darkness and
   the shadow of death,
and to guide our feet into the way of peace.

Glory to the Father, and to the Son,
   and to the Holy Spirit:
— as it was in the beginning, is now,
and will be for ever. Amen.

Ant. **Give your people knowledge of salvation,
Lord, and forgive us our sins.**

Intercessions Blessed be God, our Father, who protects his
children and never spurns their prayers.
Let us humbly implore him:
Enlighten us, Lord.

We thank you, Lord, for enlightening us
through your Son,
—fill us with his light throughout the day.

Let your wisdom lead us today, Lord,
—that we may walk in the newness of life.

May we bear hardships with courage for your
name's sake,
—and be generous in serving you.

Direct our thoughts, feelings and
actions this day,
—help us to follow your providential guidance.

The Lord's Prayer Our Father, who art in heaven,
hallowed be thy name;
thy kingdom come,
thy will be done
on earth as it is in heaven.
Give us this day our daily bread,
and forgive us our trespasses,
as we forgive those who trespass against us;
and lead us not into temptation,
but deliver us from evil.

Pater noster, qui es in cælis:
sanctificetur nomen tuum;
adveniat regnum tuum;
fiat voluntas tua,
sicut in cælo, et in terra.
Panem nostrum cotidianum da nobis hodie;
et dimitte nobis debita nostra,
sicut et nos dimittimus debitoribus nostris;
et ne nos inducas in tentationem;
sed libera nos a malo.

Concluding Prayer

Lord,
true light and source of all light,
listen to our morning prayer.
Turn our thoughts to what is holy
and may we ever live in the light of your love.
We ask this through our Lord Jesus Christ,
    your Son,
who lives and reigns with you and
    the Holy Spirit,
God, for ever and ever.
—Amen.

Dismissal

If praying individually, or in a group without a priest or deacon:

May the Lord + bless us,
protect us from all evil
and bring us to everlasting life.
—Amen.

If praying with a priest or deacon, he dismisses the people:

The Lord be with you.
—And with your spirit.

May almighty God bless you,
the Father, and the Son, ✢ and the Holy Spirit.
—Amen.

Go in peace.
—Thanks be to God.

EVENING PRAYER

God, + come to my assistance.
—Lord, make haste to help me.

Glory to the Father, and to the Son,
    and to the Holy Spirit:
—as it was in the beginning, is now,
and will be for ever. Amen. Alleluia.

Hymn   *Go, Labor On, p. 684*

Psalmody   Ant. 1 **I have made you the light of all nations to carry my salvation to the ends of the earth.**

Psalm 72   O God, give your judgment to the king,
to a king's son your justice,
that he may judge your people in justice
and your poor in right judgment.

May the mountains bring forth peace for
    the people
and the hills, justice.
May he defend the poor of the people
and save the children of the needy
and crush the oppressor.

He shall endure like the sun and the moon
from age to age.
He shall descend like rain on the meadow,
like raindrops on the earth.

In his days justice shall flourish
and peace till the moon fails.
He shall rule from sea to sea,
from the Great River to earth's bounds.

Before him his enemies shall fall,
his foes lick the dust.
The kings of Tarshish and the sea coasts
shall pay him tribute.

The kings of Sheba and Seba
shall bring him gifts.
Before him all kings shall fall prostrate,
all nations shall serve him.

Glory to the Father, and to the Son,
   and to the Holy Spirit:
—as it was in the beginning, is now,
and will be for ever. Amen.

Ant. **I have made you the light of all nations to carry my salvation to the ends of the earth.**

Ant. 2 **The Lord will save the children of the poor and rescue them from slavery.**

Psalm 72 (continued)

For he shall save the poor when they cry
and the needy who are helpless.
He will have pity on the weak
and save the lives of the poor.

From oppression he will rescue their lives,
to him their blood is dear.
Long may he live,
may the gold of Sheba be given him.
They shall pray for him without ceasing
and bless him all the day.

May corn be abundant in the land
to the peaks of the mountains.
May its fruit rustle like Lebanon;
may men flourish in the cities
like grass on the earth.

May his name be blessed for ever
and endure like the sun.
Every tribe shall be blessed in him,
all nations bless his name.

Blessed be the Lord, God of Israel,
who alone works wonders,
ever blessed his glorious name.
Let his glory fill the earth.

Amen! Amen!

Glory to the Father, and to the Son,
    and to the Holy Spirit:
—as it was in the beginning, is now,
and will be for ever. Amen.

Ant. **The Lord will save the children of the poor and rescue them from slavery.**

Ant. 3 **Now the victorious reign of our God has begun.**

Canticle: Revelation 11:17–18; 12:10b–12a

We praise you, the Lord God Almighty,
who is and who was.
You have assumed your great power,
you have begun your reign.

The nations have raged in anger,
but then came your day of wrath
and the moment to judge the dead:
the time to reward your servants the prophets
and the holy ones who revere you,
the great and the small alike.

Now have salvation and power come,
the reign of our God and the authority
of his Anointed One.
For the accuser of our brothers is cast out,
who night and day accused them before God.

They defeated him by the blood of the Lamb
and by the word of their testimony;
love for life did not deter them from death.
So rejoice, you heavens,
and you that dwell therein!

Glory to the Father, and to the Son,
   and to the Holy Spirit:
—as it was in the beginning, is now,
and will be for ever. Amen.

Ant. **Now the victorious reign of our God has begun.**

Reading
1 Peter 1:22–23

By obedience to the truth you have purified yourselves for a genuine love of your brothers; therefore, love one another constantly from the heart. Your rebirth has come, not from a destructible but from an indestructible seed, through the living and enduring word of God.

Responsory

The Lord is my shepherd,
> I shall want for nothing.
—The Lord is my shepherd,
> I shall want for nothing.

He has brought me to green pastures.
—I shall want for nothing.

Glory to the Father, and to the Son,
> and to the Holy Spirit.
—The Lord is my shepherd,
> I shall want for nothing.

Gospel Canticle

Ant. **If you hunger for holiness, God will satisfy your longing, good measure, and flowing over.**

Canticle of Mary
Luke 1:46–55

My + soul proclaims the greatness of the Lord,
my spirit rejoices in God my Savior
for he has looked with favor on his
> lowly servant.

From this day all generations will
> call me blessed:
the Almighty has done great things for me,
and holy is his Name.

He has mercy on those who fear him
in every generation.

He has shown the strength of his arm,
he has scattered the proud in their conceit.

He has cast down the mighty from
 their thrones,
and has lifted up the lowly.

He has filled the hungry with good things,
and the rich he has sent away empty.

He has come to the help of his servant Israel
for he has remembered his promise of mercy,
the promise he made to our fathers,
to Abraham and his children for ever.

Glory to the Father, and to the Son,
 and to the Holy Spirit:
—as it was in the beginning, is now,
and will be for ever. Amen.

Ant. **If you hunger for holiness, God will satisfy your longing, good measure, and flowing over.**

Intercessions Lift up your hearts to our Lord and Savior who gives his people every spiritual blessing. In the spirit of devotion, let us ask him:
Bless your people, Lord.

Merciful God, strengthen N., our Pope, and
 N., our bishop,
—keep them free from harm.

Look favorably on our country, Lord,
—free us from all evil.

Call men to serve at your altar,
—and to follow you more closely in chastity,
 poverty and obedience.

Take care of your handmaidens vowed to
 virginity,
—that they may follow you, the divine Lamb,
 wherever you go.

May the dead rest in eternal peace,
—may their union with us be strengthened
 through the sharing of spiritual goods.

The Lord's Prayer

Our Father, who art in heaven,
hallowed be thy name;
thy kingdom come,
thy will be done
on earth as it is in heaven.
Give us this day our daily bread,
and forgive us our trespasses,
as we forgive those who trespass against us;
and lead us not into temptation,
but deliver us from evil.

Pater noster, qui es in cælis:
sanctificetur nomen tuum;
adveniat regnum tuum;
fiat voluntas tua,
sicut in cælo, et in terra.
Panem nostrum cotidianum da nobis hodie;
et dimitte nobis debita nostra,
sicut et nos dimittimus debitoribus nostris;
et ne nos inducas in tentationem;
sed libera nos a malo.

Concluding Prayer

Father of mercy,
hear our evening prayer of praise,
and let our hearts never waver
from the love of your law.
Lead us on through night's darkness
to the dawning of eternal life.
We ask this through our Lord Jesus Christ,
    your Son,
who lives and reigns with you and
    the Holy Spirit,
God, for ever and ever.
—Amen.

Dismissal

If praying individually, or in a group without a priest or deacon:

May the Lord + bless us,
protect us from all evil
and bring us to everlasting life.
—Amen.

If praying with a priest or deacon, he dismisses the people:

The Lord be with you.
—And with your spirit.

May almighty God bless you,
the Father, and the Son, ✢ and the Holy Spirit.
—Amen.

Go in peace.
—Thanks be to God.

NIGHT PRAYER

God, + come to my assistance.
—Lord, make haste to help me.

Glory to the Father, and to the Son,
    and to the Holy Spirit:
—as it was in the beginning, is now,
and will be for ever. Amen. Alleluia.

Examen   *An optional brief examination of conscience may be made. Call to mind your sins and failings this day.*

Hymn   *Abide with Me, p. 675*

Psalmody   **Ant. In you, my God, my body will rest in hope.**

Psalm 16

Preserve me, God, I take refuge in you.
I say to the Lord: "You are my God.
My happiness lies in you alone."

He has put into my heart a marvelous love
for the faithful ones who dwell in his land.
Those who choose other gods increase
    their sorrows.
Never will I offer their offerings of blood.
Never will I take their name upon my lips.

O Lord, it is you who are my portion and cup;
it is you yourself who are my prize.
The lot marked out for me is my delight:
welcome indeed the heritage that falls to me!

I will bless the Lord who gives me counsel,
who even at night directs my heart.
I keep the Lord ever in my sight:
since he is at my right hand, I shall stand firm.

And so my heart rejoices, my soul is glad;
even my body shall rest in safety.
For you will not leave my soul
    among the dead,
nor let your beloved know decay.

You will show me the path of life,
the fullness of joy in your presence,
at your right hand happiness for ever.

Glory to the Father, and to the Son,
    and to the Holy Spirit:
—as it was in the beginning, is now,
and will be for ever. Amen.

Ant. **In you, my God, my body will rest in hope.**

Reading (1 Thessalonians 5:23)

May the God of peace make you perfect in holiness. May he preserve you whole and entire, spirit, soul, and body, irreproachable at the coming of our Lord Jesus Christ.

Responsory Into your hands, Lord, I commend my spirit.
—Into your hands, Lord, I commend my spirit.

You have redeemed us, Lord God of truth.
—I commend my spirit.

Glory to the Father, and to the Son,
    and to the Holy Spirit.
—Into your hands, Lord, I commend my spirit.

Gospel Canticle   Ant. **Protect us, Lord, as we stay awake; watch over us as we sleep, that awake, we may keep watch with Christ, and asleep, rest in his peace.**

Canticle of Simeon
Luke 2:29–32

Lord, ✝ now you let your servant go in peace;
your word has been fulfilled:
my own eyes have seen the salvation
which you have prepared in the sight of
    every people:
a light to reveal you to the nations
and the glory of your people Israel.

Glory to the Father, and to the Son,
    and to the Holy Spirit:
—as it was in the beginning, is now,
and will be for ever. Amen.

Ant. **Protect us, Lord, as we stay awake; watch over us as we sleep, that awake, we may keep watch with Christ, and asleep, rest in his peace.**

Concluding Prayer

Let us pray.
Lord God,
send peaceful sleep
to refresh our tired bodies.
May your help always renew us
and keep us strong in your service.
We ask this through Christ our Lord.
—Amen.

Blessing

May the all-powerful Lord
grant us a restful night
and a peaceful death.
—Amen.

Marian Antiphon

Sing the "Salve Regina," found on p. 698, or pray a Hail Mary.

Friday, July 14, 2023
St. Kateri Tekakwitha

MORNING PRAYER ——————————————

God, + come to my assistance.
—Lord, make haste to help me.

Glory to the Father, and to the Son,
 and to the Holy Spirit:
—as it was in the beginning, is now,
and will be for ever. Amen. Alleluia.

Hymn

High Let Us All Our Voices Raise, p. 685

Psalmody

Ant. 1 **A humble, contrite heart, O God, you will not spurn.**

Psalm 51

Have mercy on me, God, in your kindness.
In your compassion blot out my offense.
O wash me more and more from my guilt
and cleanse me from my sin.

My offenses truly I know them;
my sin is always before me.
Against you, you alone, have I sinned;
what is evil in your sight I have done.

That you may be justified when you
    give sentence
and be without reproach when you judge.
O see, in guilt I was born,
a sinner was I conceived.

Indeed you love truth in the heart;
then in the secret of my heart teach
    me wisdom.
O purify me, then I shall be clean;
O wash me, I shall be whiter than snow.

Make me hear rejoicing and gladness,
that the bones you have crushed may revive.
From my sins turn away your face
and blot out all my guilt.

A pure heart create for me, O God,
put a steadfast spirit within me.
Do not cast me away from your presence,
nor deprive me of your holy spirit.

Give me again the joy of your help;
with a spirit of fervor sustain me,
that I may teach transgressors your ways
and sinners may return to you.

O rescue me, God, my helper,
and my tongue shall ring out your goodness.
O Lord, open my lips
and my mouth shall declare your praise.

For in sacrifice you take no delight,
burnt offering from me you would refuse,
my sacrifice, a contrite spirit.
A humbled, contrite heart you will not spurn.

In your goodness, show favor to Zion:
rebuild the walls of Jerusalem.
Then you will be pleased with lawful sacrifice,
holocausts offered on your altar.

Glory to the Father, and to the Son,
    and to the Holy Spirit:
as it was in the beginning, is now,
and will be for ever. Amen.

Ant. **A humble, contrite heart, O God, you will not spurn.**

Ant. 2 **Even in your anger, Lord, you will remember compassion.**

Canticle:
Habakkuk 3:2–4,
13a, 15–19

O Lord, I have heard your renown,
and feared, O Lord, your work.
In the course of the years revive it,
in the course of the years make it known;
in your wrath remember compassion!

God comes from Teman,
the Holy One from Mount Paran.
Covered are the heavens with his glory,
and with his praise the earth is filled.

His splendor spreads like the light;
rays shine forth from beside him,
where his power is concealed.
You come forth to save your people,
to save your anointed one.

You tread the sea with your steeds
amid the churning of the deep waters.
I hear, and my body trembles;
at the sound, my lips quiver.

Decay invades my bones,
my legs tremble beneath me.
I await the day of distress
that will come upon the people who
    attack us.

For though the fig tree blossom not
nor fruit be on the vines,
though the yield of the olive fail
and the terraces produce no nourishment,

Though the flocks disappear from the fold
and there be no herd in the stalls,
yet will I rejoice in the Lord
and exult in my saving God.

God, my Lord, is my strength;
he makes my feet swift as those of hinds
and enables me to go upon the heights.

Glory to the Father, and to the Son,
 and to the Holy Spirit:
as it was in the beginning, is now,
and will be for ever. Amen.

Ant. **Even in your anger, Lord, you will remember compassion.**

Ant. 3 **O praise the Lord, Jerusalem!**

Psalm 147:12-20
O praise the Lord, Jerusalem!
Zion, praise your God!

He has strengthened the bars of your gates,
he has blessed the children within you.
He established peace on your borders,
he feeds you with finest wheat.

He sends out his word to the earth
and swiftly runs his command.
He showers down snow white as wool,
he scatters hoar-frost like ashes.

He hurls down hailstones like crumbs.
The waters are frozen at his touch;
he sends forth his word and it melts them:
at the breath of his mouth the waters flow.

He makes his word known to Jacob,
to Israel his laws and decrees.
He has not dealt thus with other nations;
he has not taught them his decrees.

Glory to the Father, and to the Son,
    and to the Holy Spirit:
—as it was in the beginning, is now,
and will be for ever. Amen.

Ant. **O praise the Lord, Jerusalem!**

Reading
Song of Songs 8:7

Deep waters cannot quench love,
    nor floods sweep it away.
Were one to offer all he owns to purchase love,
    he would be roundly mocked.

Responsory

My heart is ever pleading, show me your face.
—My heart is ever pleading, show me your face.

I long to gaze upon you, Lord.
—Show me your face.

Glory to the Father, and to the Son,
    and to the Holy Spirit.
—My heart is ever pleading, show me your face.

Gospel Canticle

Ant. **Now this wise virgin has gone to Christ. Among the choirs of virgins she is radiant as the sun in the heavens.**

JULY 14   FRI   MORNING PRAYER

Canticle of
Zechariah
Luke 1:68–79

Blessed + be the Lord, the God of Israel;
he has come to his people and set them free.

He has raised up for us a mighty savior,
born of the house of his servant David.

Through his holy prophets he
    promised of old
that he would save us from our enemies,
from the hands of all who hate us.

He promised to show mercy to our fathers
and to remember his holy covenant.

This was the oath he swore to our
    father Abraham:
to set us free from the hands of our enemies,
free to worship him without fear,
holy and righteous in his sight
    all the days of our life.

You, my child, shall be called the prophet of
    the Most High;
for you will go before the Lord to
    prepare his way,
to give his people knowledge of salvation
by the forgiveness of their sins.

In the tender compassion of our God
the dawn from on high shall break upon us,
to shine on those who dwell in darkness and
    the shadow of death,
and to guide our feet into the way of peace.

Glory to the Father, and to the Son,
    and to the Holy Spirit:
—as it was in the beginning, is now,
    and will be for ever. Amen.

Ant. **Now this wise virgin has gone to Christ. Among the choirs of virgins she is radiant as the sun in the heavens.**

Intercessions Christ is the spouse and crowning glory of virgins. Let us praise him with joy in our voices and pray to him with sincerity in our hearts:
Jesus, crown of virgins, hear us.

Christ, the holy virgins loved you as their one true spouse,
—grant that nothing may separate us from your love.

You crowned Mary, your mother, queen of virgins,
—through her intercession, let us continually serve you with pure hearts.

Your handmaids were always careful to love you with whole and undivided attention, that they might be holy in body and spirit,
—through their intercession grant that the lure of this passing world may not distract our attention from you.

Lord Jesus, you are the spouse whose coming was anticipated by the wise virgins,
—grant that we may wait for you in hope and expectation.

Through the intercession of Saint Kateri, who was one of the wise and prudent virgins,
—grant us wisdom and innocence of life.

The Lord's Prayer

Our Father, who art in heaven,
hallowed be thy name;
thy kingdom come,
thy will be done
on earth as it is in heaven.
Give us this day our daily bread,
and forgive us our trespasses,
as we forgive those who trespass against us;
and lead us not into temptation,
but deliver us from evil.

Pater noster, qui es in cælis:
sanctificetur nomen tuum;
adveniat regnum tuum;
fiat voluntas tua,
sicut in cælo, et in terra.
Panem nostrum cotidianum da nobis hodie;
et dimitte nobis debita nostra,
sicut et nos dimittimus debitoribus nostris;
et ne nos inducas in tentationem;
sed libera nos a malo.

Concluding Prayer

Lord God,
you called the virgin Saint Kateri Tekakwitha
to shine among the Indian people
as an example of innocence of life.
Through her intercession,
may all peoples of every tribe, tongue,
    and nation,
having been gathered into your Church,
proclaim your greatness
in one song of praise.
We ask this through our Lord Jesus Christ,
    your Son,
who lives and reigns with you and
    the Holy Spirit,
God, for ever and ever
—Amen.

Dismissal

If praying individually, or in a group without a priest or deacon:

May the Lord + bless us,
protect us from all evil
and bring us to everlasting life.
—Amen.

If praying with a priest or deacon, he dismisses the people:

The Lord be with you.
—And with your spirit.

May almighty God bless you,
the Father, and the Son, ✠ and the Holy Spirit.
—Amen.

Go in peace.
—Thanks be to God.

HOW GRACIOUS
IS THE LORD,
AND JUST;
OUR GOD HAS
COMPASSION.

EVENING PRAYER

God, + come to my assistance.
—Lord, make haste to help me.

Glory to the Father, and to the Son,
    and to the Holy Spirit:
—as it was in the beginning, is now,
and will be for ever. Amen. Alleluia.

Hymn *Sing with All the Saints in Glory, p. 702*

Psalmody Ant. 1 **Lord, keep my soul from death, never let me stumble.**

Psalm 116:1–9

I love the Lord for he has heard
the cry of my appeal;
for he turned his ear to me
in the day when I called him.

They surrounded me, the snares of death,
with the anguish of the tomb;
they caught me, sorrow and distress.
I called on the Lord's name.

O Lord my God, deliver me!

How gracious is the Lord, and just;
our God has compassion.
The Lord protects the simple hearts;
I was helpless so he saved me.

Turn back, my soul, to your rest
for the Lord has been good;
he has kept my soul from death,
my eyes from tears
and my feet from stumbling.

I will walk in the presence of the Lord
in the land of the living.

Glory to the Father, and to the Son,
    and to the Holy Spirit:
—as it was in the beginning, is now,
and will be for ever. Amen.

Ant. **Lord, keep my soul from death, never let me stumble.**

Ant. 2 **My help comes from the Lord, who made heaven and earth.**

Psalm 121

I lift up my eyes to the mountains:
from where shall come my help?
My help shall come from the Lord
who made heaven and earth.

May he never allow you to stumble!
Let him sleep not, your guard.
No, he sleeps not nor slumbers,
Israel's guard.

The Lord is your guard and your shade;
at your right side he stands.
By day the sun shall not smite you
nor the moon in the night.

The Lord will guard you from evil,
he will guard your soul.
The Lord will guard your going and coming
both now and for ever.

Glory to the Father, and to the Son,
   and to the Holy Spirit:
—as it was in the beginning, is now,
and will be for ever. Amen.

Ant. **My help comes from the Lord, who made heaven and earth.**

Ant. 3 **King of all the ages, your ways are perfect and true.**

Canticle: Revelation 15:3–4

Mighty and wonderful are your works,
Lord God Almighty!
Righteous and true are your ways,
O King of the nations!

Who would dare refuse you honor,
or the glory due your name, O Lord?

Since you alone are holy,
all nations shall come
and worship in your presence.
Your mighty deeds are clearly seen.

Glory to the Father, and to the Son,
   and to the Holy Spirit:
—as it was in the beginning, is now,
and will be for ever. Amen.

Ant. **King of all the ages, your ways are perfect and true.**

JULY 14   FRI   EVENING PRAYER

Reading
1 Corinthians 7:32b, 34a

The unmarried man is busy with the Lord's affairs, concerned with pleasing the Lord. The virgin—indeed, any unmarried woman—is concerned with things of the Lord, in pursuit of holiness in body and spirit.

Responsory

The virgins are led into the presence of
  the King, amid gladness and joy.
—The virgins are led into the presence of
  the King, amid gladness and joy.

They are brought into the King's
  dwelling place,
—amid gladness and joy.

Glory to the Father, and to the Son,
  and to the Holy Spirit.
—The virgins are led into the presence of
  the King, amid gladness and joy.

Gospel Canticle

Ant. **Come, spouse of Christ, receive the crown the Lord has prepared for you from all eternity.**

Canticle of Mary
Luke 1:46–55

My ✢ soul proclaims the greatness of the Lord,
my spirit rejoices in God my Savior
for he has looked with favor on his
  lowly servant.

From this day all generations will
  call me blessed:
the Almighty has done great things for me,
and holy is his Name.

He has mercy on those who fear him
in every generation.

He has shown the strength of his arm,
he has scattered the proud in their conceit.

He has cast down the mighty from
    their thrones,
and has lifted up the lowly.

He has filled the hungry with good things,
and the rich he has sent away empty.

He has come to the help of his servant Israel
for he has remembered his promise of mercy,
the promise he made to our fathers,
to Abraham and his children for ever.

Glory to the Father, and to the Son,
    and to the Holy Spirit:
—as it was in the beginning, is now,
and will be for ever. Amen.

Ant. **Come, spouse of Christ, receive the crown the Lord has prepared for you from all eternity.**

Intercessions Christ extolled those who practiced virginity for the sake of the kingdom. Let us praise him joyfully and pray to him:
Jesus, example of virgins, hear us.

Christ, you presented the Church to yourself
    as a chaste virgin to her spouse,
—keep her holy and inviolate.

Christ, the holy virgins went out to meet you
   with their lamps alight,
— keep the fidelity of your consecrated
   handmaids burning brightly.

Lord, your virgin Church has always kept its
   faith whole and untarnished,
— grant all Christians a whole and
   untarnished faith.

You have given your people joy in celebrating
   the feast of your holy virgin Saint Kateri,
— give us constant joy through her intercession.

You have admitted the holy virgins to your
   marriage banquet,
— in your mercy lead the dead to your
   heavenly feast.

The Lord's Prayer

Our Father, who art in heaven,
hallowed be thy name;
thy kingdom come,
thy will be done
on earth as it is in heaven.
Give us this day our daily bread,
and forgive us our trespasses,
as we forgive those who trespass against us;
and lead us not into temptation,
but deliver us from evil.

Pater noster, qui es in cælis:
sanctificetur nomen tuum;
adveniat regnum tuum;
fiat voluntas tua,
sicut in cælo, et in terra.
Panem nostrum cotidianum da nobis hodie;
et dimitte nobis debita nostra,
sicut et nos dimittimus debitoribus nostris;
et ne nos inducas in tentationem;
sed libera nos a malo.

Concluding Prayer

Lord God,
you called the virgin Saint Kateri Tekakwitha
to shine among the Indian people
as an example of innocence of life.
Through her intercession,
may all peoples of every tribe, tongue,
    and nation,
having been gathered into your Church,
proclaim your greatness
in one song of praise.
We ask this through our Lord Jesus Christ,
    your Son,
who lives and reigns with you and
    the Holy Spirit,
God, for ever and ever
—Amen.

Dismissal

If praying individually, or in a group without a priest or deacon:

May the Lord + bless us,
protect us from all evil
and bring us to everlasting life.
—Amen.

If praying with a priest or deacon, he dismisses the people:

The Lord be with you.
—And with your spirit.

May almighty God bless you,
the Father, and the Son, ✛ and the Holy Spirit.
—Amen.

Go in peace.
—Thanks be to God.

NIGHT PRAYER

God, ✛ come to my assistance.
—Lord, make haste to help me.

Glory to the Father, and to the Son,
    and to the Holy Spirit:
—as it was in the beginning, is now,
    and will be for ever. Amen. Alleluia.

Examen — *An optional brief examination of conscience may be made. Call to mind your sins and failings this day.*

Hymn — *Before the Final Light of Day, p. 676*

Psalmody — Ant. **Day and night I cry to you, my God.**

Psalm 88

Lord my God, I call for help by day;
I cry at night before you.
Let my prayer come into your presence.
O turn your ear to my cry.

For my soul is filled with evils;
my life is on the brink of the grave.
I am reckoned as one in the tomb:
I have reached the end of my strength,

like one alone among the dead;
like the slain lying in their graves;
like those you remember no more,
cut off, as they are, from your hand.

You have laid me in the depths of the tomb,
in places that are dark, in the depths.
Your anger weighs down upon me:
I am drowned beneath your waves.

You have taken away my friends
and made me hateful in their sight.
Imprisoned, I cannot escape;
my eyes are sunken with grief.

I call to you, Lord, all the day long;
to you I stretch out my hands.
Will you work your wonders for the dead?
Will the shades stand and praise you?

Will your love be told in the grave
or your faithfulness among the dead?
Will your wonders be known in the dark
or your justice in the land of oblivion?

As for me, Lord, I call to you for help:
in the morning my prayer comes before you.
Lord, why do you reject me?
Why do you hide your face?

Wretched, close to death from my youth,
I have borne your trials; I am numb.
Your fury has swept down upon me;
your terrors have utterly destroyed me.

They surround me all the day like a flood,
they assail me all together.
Friend and neighbor you have taken away:
my one companion is darkness.

Glory to the Father, and to the Son,
   and to the Holy Spirit:
—as it was in the beginning, is now,
and will be for ever. Amen.

Ant. **Day and night I cry to you, my God.**

Reading
Jeremiah 14:9a

You are in our midst, O Lord,
   your name we bear:
     do not forsake us, O Lord, our God!

Responsory

Into your hands, Lord, I commend my spirit.
—Into your hands, Lord, I commend my spirit.

You have redeemed us, Lord God of truth.
—I commend my spirit.

Glory to the Father, and to the Son,
   and to the Holy Spirit.
—Into your hands, Lord, I commend my spirit.

Gospel Canticle

Ant. **Protect us, Lord, as we stay awake; watch over us as we sleep, that awake, we may keep watch with Christ, and asleep, rest in his peace.**

Canticle of Simeon
Luke 2:29–32

Lord, + now you let your servant go in peace;
your word has been fulfilled:
my own eyes have seen the salvation
which you have prepared in the sight of
   every people:
a light to reveal you to the nations
and the glory of your people Israel.

Glory to the Father, and to the Son,
   and to the Holy Spirit:
—as it was in the beginning, is now,
and will be for ever. Amen.

Ant. **Protect us, Lord, as we stay awake; watch over us as we sleep, that awake, we may keep watch with Christ, and asleep, rest in his peace.**

Concluding Prayer
Let us pray.
All-powerful God,
keep us united with your Son
in his death and burial
so that we may rise to new life with him,
who lives and reigns for ever and ever.
—Amen.

Blessing
May the all-powerful Lord
grant us a restful night
and a peaceful death.
—Amen.

Marian Antiphon
Sing the "Salve Regina," found on p. 698, or pray a Hail Mary.

Saturday, July 15, 2023
St. Bonaventure

MORNING PRAYER

God, + come to my assistance.
—Lord, make haste to help me.

Glory to the Father, and to the Son,
    and to the Holy Spirit:
—as it was in the beginning, is now,
    and will be for ever. Amen. Alleluia.

Hymn   *Let Heaven Highest Praises Bring, p. 691*

Psalmody   Ant. 1 **As morning breaks we sing of your mercy, Lord, and night will find us proclaiming your fidelity.**

Psalm 92

It is good to give thanks to the Lord,
    to make music to your name, O Most High,
to proclaim your love in the morning
    and your truth in the watches of the night,
on the ten-stringed lyre and the lute,
    with the murmuring sound of the harp.

Your deeds, O Lord, have made me glad;
    for the work of your hands I shout with joy.
O Lord, how great are your works!
How deep are your designs!
The foolish man cannot know this
    and the fool cannot understand.

Though the wicked spring up like grass
and all who do evil thrive:
they are doomed to be eternally destroyed.
But you, Lord, are eternally on high.
See how your enemies perish;
all doers of evil are scattered.

To me you give the wild-ox's strength;
you anoint me with the purest oil.
My eyes looked in triumph on my foes;
my ears heard gladly of their fall.
The just will flourish like the palm-tree
and grow like a Lebanon cedar.

Planted in the house of the Lord
they will flourish in the courts of our God,
still bearing fruit when they are old,
still full of sap, still green,
to proclaim that the Lord is just;
in him, my rock, there is no wrong.

Glory to the Father, and to the Son,
    and to the Holy Spirit:
—as it was in the beginning, is now,
and will be for ever. Amen.

Ant. **As morning breaks we sing of your mercy, Lord, and night will find us proclaiming your fidelity.**

Ant. 2 **Extol the greatness of our God.**

Canticle:
Deuteronomy
32:1–12

Give ear, O heavens, while I speak;
let the earth hearken to the words
    of my mouth!
May my instruction soak in like the rain,
and my discourse permeate like the dew,
like a downpour upon the grass,
like a shower upon the crops:

For I will sing the Lord's renown.
Oh, proclaim the greatness of our God!
The Rock—how faultless are his deeds,
how right all his ways!
A faithful God, without deceit,
how just and upright he is!

Yet basely has he been treated by his
    degenerate children,
a perverse and crooked race!
Is the Lord to be thus repaid by you,
O stupid and foolish people?
Is he not your father who created you?
Has he not made you and established you?

Think back on the days of old,
reflect on the years of age upon age.
Ask your father and he will inform you,
ask your elders and they will tell you:

When the Most High assigned the nations
    their heritage,
when he parceled out the descendants of Adam,
he set up the boundaries of the peoples
after the number of the sons of God;
while the Lord's own portion was Jacob,
his hereditary share was Israel.

He found them in a wilderness,
a wasteland of howling desert.
He shielded them and cared for them,
guarding them as the apple of his eye.

As an eagle incites its nestlings forth
by hovering over its brood,
so he spread his wings to receive them
and bore them up on his pinions.
The Lord alone was their leader,
no strange god was with him.

Glory to the Father, and to the Son,
    and to the Holy Spirit:
—as it was in the beginning, is now,
and will be for ever. Amen.

Ant. **Extol the greatness of our God.**

Ant. 3 **How wonderful is your name, O Lord, in all creation.**

Psalm 8

How great is your name, O Lord our God,
through all the earth!

Your majesty is praised above the heavens;
on the lips of children and of babes
you have found praise to foil your enemy,
to silence the foe and the rebel.

When I see the heavens, the work of
    your hands,
the moon and the stars which you arranged,
what is man that you should keep him in mind,
mortal man that you care for him?

Yet you have made him little less than a god;
with glory and honor you crowned him,
gave him power over the works of your hand,
put all things under his feet.

All of them, sheep and cattle,
yes, even the savage beasts,
birds of the air, and fish
that make their way through the waters.

How great is your name, O Lord our God,
through all the earth!

Glory to the Father, and to the Son,
   and to the Holy Spirit:
—as it was in the beginning, is now,
and will be for ever. Amen.

Ant. **How wonderful is your name, O Lord, in all creation.**

Reading
Wisdom 7:13–14

Simply I learned about Wisdom, and
   ungrudgingly do I share—
her riches I do not hide away;
For to men she is an unfailing treasure;
   those who gain this treasure win the
     friendship of God,
   to whom the gifts they have from
     discipline commend them.

Responsory Let the peoples proclaim the wisdom of
   the saints.
   —Let the peoples proclaim the wisdom of
   the saints.

With joyful praise let the Church tell forth
—the wisdom of the saints.

Glory to the Father, and to the Son,
and to the Holy Spirit.
—Let the peoples proclaim the wisdom of
the saints.

Gospel Canticle

Ant. **Those who are learned will be as radiant as the sky in all its beauty; those who instruct the people in goodness will shine like the stars for all eternity.**

Canticle of Zechariah
Luke 1:68–79

Blessed + be the Lord, the God of Israel;
he has come to his people and set them free.

He has raised up for us a mighty savior,
born of the house of his servant David.

Through his holy prophets he
promised of old
that he would save us from our enemies,
from the hands of all who hate us.

He promised to show mercy to our fathers
and to remember his holy covenant.

This was the oath he swore to our
father Abraham:
to set us free from the hands of our enemies,
free to worship him without fear,
holy and righteous in his sight
all the days of our life.

You, my child, shall be called the prophet of
>> the Most High;
for you will go before the Lord to
>> prepare his way,
to give his people knowledge of salvation
by the forgiveness of their sins.

In the tender compassion of our God
the dawn from on high shall break upon us,
to shine on those who dwell in darkness and
>> the shadow of death,
and to guide our feet into the way of peace.

Glory to the Father, and to the Son,
>> and to the Holy Spirit:
—as it was in the beginning, is now,
and will be for ever. Amen.

Ant. **Those who are learned will be as radiant as the sky in all its beauty; those who instruct the people in goodness will shine like the stars for all eternity.**

Intercessions Christ is the Good Shepherd who laid down his life for his sheep. Let us praise and thank him as we pray:
Nourish your people, Lord.

Christ, you decided to show your merciful
>> love through your holy shepherds,
—let your mercy always reach us through them.

Through your vicars you continue to
>> perform the ministry of shepherd of souls,
—direct us always through our leaders.

Through your holy ones, the leaders of your
    people, you served as physician of our
    bodies and our spirits,
— continue to fulfill your ministry of life and
    holiness in us.

You taught your flock through the prudence
    and love of your saints,
— grant us continual growth in holiness under
    the direction of our pastors.

The Lord's Prayer

Our Father, who art in heaven,
hallowed be thy name;
thy kingdom come,
thy will be done
on earth as it is in heaven.
Give us this day our daily bread,
and forgive us our trespasses,
as we forgive those who trespass against us;
and lead us not into temptation,
but deliver us from evil.

Pater noster, qui es in cælis:
sanctificetur nomen tuum;
adveniat regnum tuum;
fiat voluntas tua,
sicut in cælo, et in terra.
Panem nostrum cotidianum da nobis hodie;
et dimitte nobis debita nostra,
sicut et nos dimittimus debitoribus nostris;
et ne nos inducas in tentationem;
sed libera nos a malo.

Concluding Prayer

All-powerful Father,
may we who celebrate the feast of Saint
    Bonaventure
always benefit from his wisdom
and follow the example of his love.
Grant this through our Lord Jesus Christ,
    your Son,
who lives and reigns with you and
    the Holy Spirit,
God, for ever and ever.
—Amen.

Dismissal

If praying individually, or in a group without a priest or deacon:

May the Lord ✛ bless us,
protect us from all evil
and bring us to everlasting life.
—Amen.

If praying with a priest or deacon, he dismisses the people:

The Lord be with you.
—And with your spirit.

May almighty God bless you,
the Father, and the Son, ✛ and the Holy Spirit.
—Amen.

Go in peace.
—Thanks be to God.

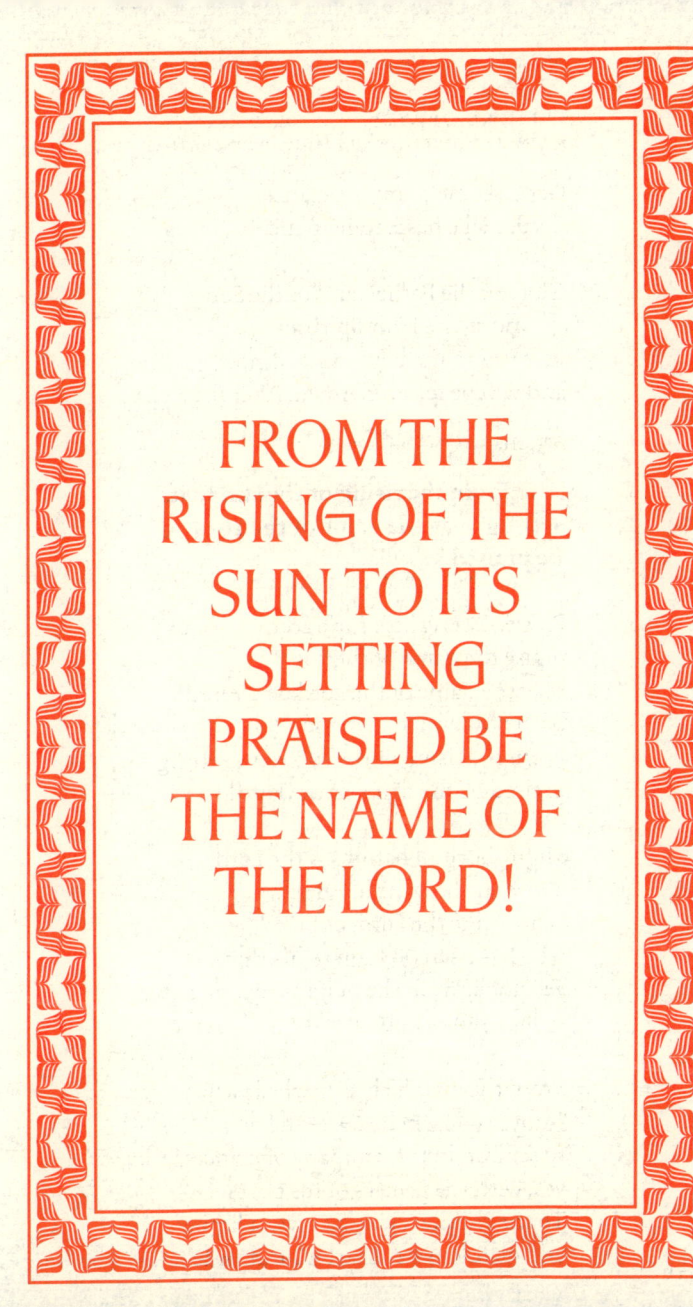

FROM THE RISING OF THE SUN TO ITS SETTING PRAISED BE THE NAME OF THE LORD!

EVENING PRAYER
BEGINS THE FIFTEENTH SUNDAY IN ORDINARY TIME

God, +come to my assistance.
—Lord, make haste to help me.

Glory to the Father, and to the Son,
    and to the Holy Spirit:
—as it was in the beginning, is now,
and will be for ever. Amen. Alleluia.

Hymn   *Praise to the Lord, the Almighty, p. 696*

Psalmody   Ant. 1 **From the rising of the sun to its setting, may the name of the Lord be praised.**

Psalm 113

Praise, O servants of the Lord,
praise the name of the Lord!
May the name of the Lord be blessed
both now and for evermore!
From the rising of the sun to its setting
praised be the name of the Lord!

High above all nations is the Lord,
above the heavens his glory.
Who is like the Lord, our God,
who has risen on high to his throne
yet stoops from the heights to look down,
to look down upon heaven and earth?

From the dust he lifts up the lowly,
from his misery he raises the poor
to set him in the company of princes,
yes, with the princes of his people.
To the childless wife he gives a home
and gladdens her heart with children.

Glory to the Father, and to the Son,
    and to the Holy Spirit:
—as it was in the beginning, is now,
    and will be for ever. Amen.

Ant. **From the rising of the sun to its setting,
may the name of the Lord be praised.**

Ant. 2 **I shall take into my hand the saving chalice
and invoke the name of the Lord.**

Psalm 116:10–19 I trusted, even when I said:
"I am sorely afflicted,"
    and when I said in my alarm:
"No man can be trusted."

How can I repay the Lord
for his goodness to me?
The cup of salvation I will raise;
I will call on the Lord's name.

My vows to the Lord I will fulfill
before all his people.
O precious in the eyes of the Lord
is the death of his faithful.

Your servant, Lord, your servant am I;
you have loosened my bonds.
A thanksgiving sacrifice I make:
I will call on the Lord's name.

My vows to the Lord I will fulfill
before all his people,
in the courts of the house of the Lord,
in your midst, O Jerusalem.

Glory to the Father, and to the Son,
   and to the Holy Spirit:
—as it was in the beginning, is now,
   and will be for ever. Amen.

Ant. **I shall take into my hand the saving chalice and invoke the name of the Lord.**

Ant. 3 **The Lord Jesus humbled himself and God exalted him for ever.**

Canticle: Philippians 2:6–11

Though he was in the form of God,
Jesus did not deem equality with God
something to be grasped at.

Rather, he emptied himself
and took the form of a slave,
being born in the likeness of men.

He was known to be of human estate,
and it was thus that he humbled himself,
obediently accepting even death,
death on a cross!

Because of this,
God highly exalted him
and bestowed on him the name
above every other name,

So that at Jesus' name
every knee must bend
in the heavens, on the earth,
and under the earth,
and every tongue proclaim
to the glory of God the Father:
JESUS CHRIST IS LORD!

Glory to the Father, and to the Son,
    and to the Holy Spirit:
—as it was in the beginning, is now,
and will be for ever. Amen.

Ant. **The Lord Jesus humbled himself and God exalted him for ever.**

Reading
Hebrews 13:20–21

May the God of peace, who brought up from the dead the great Shepherd of the sheep by the blood of the eternal covenant, Jesus our Lord, furnish you with all that is good, that you may do his will. Through Jesus Christ may he carry out in you all that is pleasing to him. To Christ be glory forever! Amen.

Responsory

Our hearts are filled with wonder as we
    contemplate your works, O Lord.
—Our hearts are filled with wonder as we
    contemplate your works, O Lord.

We praise the wisdom which
    wrought them all,
—as we contemplate your works, O Lord.

Glory to the Father, and to the Son,
>   and to the Holy Spirit.
—Our hearts are filled with wonder as we
>   contemplate your works, O Lord.

Gospel Canticle

Ant. **The seed is the word of God; the sower is Christ; all who listen to his words will live for ever.**

Canticle of Mary
Luke 1:46–55

My ✛ soul proclaims the greatness of the Lord,
my spirit rejoices in God my Savior
for he has looked with favor on his
>   lowly servant.

From this day all generations will
>   call me blessed:
the Almighty has done great things for me,
and holy is his Name.

He has mercy on those who fear him
in every generation.

He has shown the strength of his arm,
he has scattered the proud in their conceit.

He has cast down the mighty from
>   their thrones,
and has lifted up the lowly.

He has filled the hungry with good things,
and the rich he has sent away empty.

He has come to the help of his servant Israel
for he has remembered his promise of mercy,
the promise he made to our fathers,
to Abraham and his children for ever.

Glory to the Father, and to the Son,
   and to the Holy Spirit:
—as it was in the beginning, is now,
and will be for ever. Amen.

Ant. **The seed is the word of God; the sower is Christ; all who listen to his words will live for ever.**

Intercessions Christ had compassion on the hungry and performed a miracle of love for them. Mindful of this, let us pray:
Show us your love, Lord.

Lord, we recognize that all the favors we have received today come through your generosity,
—do not let them return to you empty, but let them bear fruit.

Light and salvation of all nations, protect the missionaries you have sent into the world,
—enkindle in them the fire of your Spirit.

Grant that man may shape the world in keeping with human dignity,
—and respond generously to the needs of our time.

Healer of body and spirit, comfort the sick
    and be present to the dying,
— in your mercy visit and refresh us.

May the faithful departed be numbered
    among the saints,
— whose names are in the Book of Life.

The Lord's Prayer

Our Father, who art in heaven,
hallowed be thy name;
thy kingdom come,
thy will be done
on earth as it is in heaven.
Give us this day our daily bread,
and forgive us our trespasses,
as we forgive those who trespass against us;
and lead us not into temptation,
but deliver us from evil.

Pater noster, qui es in cælis:
sanctificetur nomen tuum;
adveniat regnum tuum;
fiat voluntas tua,
sicut in cælo, et in terra.
Panem nostrum cotidianum da nobis hodie;
et dimitte nobis debita nostra,
sicut et nos dimittimus debitoribus nostris;
et ne nos inducas in tentationem;
sed libera nos a malo.

Concluding Prayer

God, our Father,
your light of truth
guides us to the way of Christ.
May all who follow him
reject what is contrary to the Gospel.
We ask this through our Lord Jesus Christ,
    your Son,
who lives and reigns with you and
    the Holy Spirit,
God, for ever and ever.
—Amen.

Dismissal

If praying individually, or in a group without a priest or deacon:

May the Lord + bless us,
protect us from all evil
and bring us to everlasting life.
—Amen.

If praying with a priest or deacon, he dismisses the people:

The Lord be with you.
—And with your spirit.

May almighty God bless you,
the Father, and the Son, ✠ and the Holy Spirit.
—Amen.

Go in peace.
—Thanks be to God.

NIGHT PRAYER

God, + come to my assistance.
—Lord, make haste to help me.

Glory to the Father, and to the Son,
    and to the Holy Spirit:
—as it was in the beginning, is now,
    and will be for ever. Amen. Alleluia.

Examen *An optional brief examination of conscience may be made. Call to mind your sins and failings this day.*

Hymn *O Joyful Light of God Most High, p. 693*

Psalmody   Ant. 1 **Have mercy, Lord, and hear my prayer.**

Psalm 4

When I call, answer me, O God of justice;
from anguish you released me; have mercy
    and hear me!

O men, how long will your hearts be closed,
will you love what is futile and seek
    what is false?

It is the Lord who grants favors to those
    whom he loves;
the Lord hears me whenever I call him.

Fear him; do not sin: ponder on your bed
    and be still.
Make justice your sacrifice and trust
    in the Lord.

"What can bring us happiness?" many say.
Let the light of your face shine on us, O Lord.

You have put into my heart a greater joy
than they have from abundance of corn
    and new wine.

I will lie down in peace and sleep
    comes at once
for you alone, Lord, make me dwell in safety.

Glory to the Father, and to the Son,
    and to the Holy Spirit:
—as it was in the beginning, is now,
and will be for ever. Amen.

Ant. **Have mercy, Lord, and hear my prayer.**

Ant. 2 **In the silent hours of night, bless the Lord.**

Psalm 134

O come, bless the Lord,
all you who serve the Lord,
who stand in the house of the Lord,
in the courts of the house of our God.

Lift up your hands to the holy place
and bless the Lord through the night.

May the Lord bless you from Zion,
he who made both heaven and earth.

Glory to the Father, and to the Son,
    and to the Holy Spirit:
—as it was in the beginning, is now,
and will be for ever. Amen.

Ant. **In the silent hours of night, bless the Lord.**

Reading
Deuteronomy 6:4-7

Hear, O Israel! The Lord is our God, the Lord alone! Therefore, you shall love the Lord, your God, with all your heart, and with all your soul, and with all your strength. Take to heart these words which I enjoin on you today. Drill them into your children. Speak of them at home and abroad, whether you are busy or at rest.

Responsory

Into your hands, Lord, I commend my spirit.
—Into your hands, Lord, I commend my spirit.

You have redeemed us, Lord God of truth.
—I commend my spirit.

Glory to the Father, and to the Son,
 and to the Holy Spirit.
—Into your hands, Lord, I commend my spirit.

Gospel Canticle

Ant. **Protect us, Lord, as we stay awake; watch over us as we sleep, that awake, we may keep watch with Christ, and asleep, rest in his peace.**

Canticle of Simeon
Luke 2:29-32

Lord, + now you let your servant go in peace;
your word has been fulfilled:
my own eyes have seen the salvation
which you have prepared in the sight of
 every people:
a light to reveal you to the nations
and the glory of your people Israel.

Glory to the Father, and to the Son,
    and to the Holy Spirit:
—as it was in the beginning, is now,
and will be for ever. Amen.

Ant. **Protect us, Lord, as we stay awake; watch over us as we sleep, that awake, we may keep watch with Christ, and asleep, rest in his peace.**

Concluding Prayer

Let us pray.
Lord,
be with us throughout this night.
When day comes may we rise from sleep
to rejoice in the resurrection of your Christ,
who lives and reigns for ever and ever.
—Amen.

Blessing

May the all-powerful Lord
grant us a restful night
and a peaceful death.
—Amen.

Marian Antiphon

Sing the "Salve Regina," found on p. 698, or pray a Hail Mary.

Sunday, July 16, 2023
Fifteenth Sunday in Ordinary Time

MORNING PRAYER

God, + come to my assistance.
—Lord, make haste to help me.

Glory to the Father, and to the Son,
    and to the Holy Spirit:
—as it was in the beginning, is now,
and will be for ever. Amen. Alleluia.

Hymn   *This Day the First of Days Was Made, p. 695*

Psalmody   Ant. 1 **Glorious is the Lord on high, alleluia.**

Psalm 93

The Lord is king, with majesty enrobed;
the Lord has robed himself with might,
he has girded himself with power.

The world you made firm, not to be moved;
your throne has stood firm from of old.
From all eternity, O Lord, you are.

The waters have lifted up, O Lord,
the waters have lifted up their voice,
the waters have lifted up their thunder.

Greater than the roar of mighty waters,
more glorious than the surgings of the sea,
the Lord is glorious on high.

Truly your decrees are to be trusted.
Holiness is fitting to your house,
O Lord, until the end of time.

Glory to the Father, and to the Son,
    and to the Holy Spirit:
as it was in the beginning, is now,
and will be for ever. Amen.

Ant. **Glorious is the Lord on high, alleluia.**

Ant. 2 **To you, Lord, be highest glory and praise for ever, alleluia.**

Canticle: Daniel 3:57–88, 56

Bless the Lord, all you works of the Lord.
Praise and exalt him above all forever.
Angels of the Lord, bless the Lord.
You heavens, bless the Lord.
All you waters above the heavens,
    bless the Lord.
All you hosts of the Lord, bless the Lord.
Sun and moon, bless the Lord.
Stars of heaven, bless the Lord.

Every shower and dew, bless the Lord.
All you winds, bless the Lord.
Fire and heat, bless the Lord.
Cold and chill, bless the Lord.
Dew and rain, bless the Lord.
Frost and chill, bless the Lord.
Ice and snow, bless the Lord.
Nights and days, bless the Lord.
Light and darkness, bless the Lord.
Lightnings and clouds, bless the Lord.

Let the earth bless the Lord.
Praise and exalt him above all forever.
Mountains and hills, bless the Lord.
Everything growing from the earth,
 bless the Lord.
You springs, bless the Lord.
Seas and rivers, bless the Lord.
You dolphins and all water creatures,
 bless the Lord.
All you birds of the air, bless the Lord.
All you beasts, wild and tame, bless the Lord.
You sons of men, bless the Lord.

O Israel, bless the Lord.
Praise and exalt him above all forever.
Priests of the Lord, bless the Lord.
Servants of the Lord, bless the Lord.
Spirits and souls of the just, bless the Lord.
Holy men of humble heart, bless the Lord.
Hananiah, Azariah, Mishael, bless the Lord.
Praise and exalt him above all forever.

Let us bless the Father, and the Son,
 and the Holy Spirit.
Let us praise and exalt him above all forever.
Blessed are you, Lord, in the firmament
 of heaven.
Praiseworthy and glorious and exalted above
 all for ever.

Ant. **To you, Lord, be highest glory and praise for ever, alleluia.**

Ant. 3 **Praise the Lord from the heavens, alleluia.**

Psalm 148

Praise the Lord from the heavens,
praise him in the heights.
Praise him, all his angels,
praise him, all his host.

Praise him, sun and moon,
praise him, shining stars.
Praise him, highest heavens
and the waters above the heavens.

Let them praise the name of the Lord.
He commanded: they were made.
He fixed them for ever,
gave a law which shall not pass away.

Praise the Lord from the earth,
sea creatures and all oceans,
fire and hail, snow and mist,
stormy winds that obey his word;

all mountains and hills,
all fruit trees and cedars,
beasts, wild and tame,
reptiles and birds on the wing;

all earth's kings and peoples,
earth's princes and rulers;
young men and maidens,
old men together with children.

Let them praise the name of the Lord
for he alone is exalted.
The splendor of his name
reaches beyond heaven and earth.

He exalts the strength of his people.
He is the praise of all his saints,
of the sons of Israel,
of the people to whom he comes close.

Glory to the Father, and to the Son,
    and to the Holy Spirit:
—as it was in the beginning, is now,
and will be for ever. Amen.

Ant. **Praise the Lord from the heavens, alleluia.**

Reading
Ezekiel 37:12b–14

Thus says the Lord God: O my people, I will open your graves and have you rise from them, and bring you back to the land of Israel. Then you shall know that I am the Lord, when I open your graves and have you rise from them, O my people! I will put my spirit in you that you may live, and I will settle you upon your land; thus you shall know that I am the Lord. I have promised, and I will do it, says the Lord.

Responsory

Christ, Son of the living God,
    have mercy on us.
—Christ, Son of the living God,
    have mercy on us.

You are seated at the right hand of the Father,
—have mercy on us.

Glory to the Father, and to the Son,
    and to the Holy Spirit.
—Christ, Son of the living God,
    have mercy on us.

Gospel Canticle

Ant. **The disciples went out and preached repentance. They anointed many sick people with oil and healed them.**

Canticle of Zechariah Luke 1:68–79

Blessed + be the Lord, the God of Israel;
he has come to his people and set them free.

He has raised up for us a mighty savior,
born of the house of his servant David.

Through his holy prophets he
    promised of old
that he would save us from our enemies,
from the hands of all who hate us.

He promised to show mercy to our fathers
and to remember his holy covenant.

This was the oath he swore to our
    father Abraham:
to set us free from the hands of our enemies,
free to worship him without fear,
holy and righteous in his sight
    all the days of our life.

You, my child, shall be called the prophet of
    the Most High;
for you will go before the Lord to
    prepare his way,
to give his people knowledge of salvation
by the forgiveness of their sins.

In the tender compassion of our God
the dawn from on high shall break upon us,
to shine on those who dwell in darkness and
   the shadow of death,
and to guide our feet into the way of peace.

Glory to the Father, and to the Son,
   and to the Holy Spirit:
—as it was in the beginning, is now,
and will be for ever. Amen.

Ant. **The disciples went out and preached repentance. They anointed many sick people with oil and healed them.**

Intercessions Father, you sent the Holy Spirit to enlighten
   the hearts of men; hear us as we pray:
Enlighten your people, Lord.

Blessed are you, O God, our light,
—you have given us a new day resplendent
   with your glory.

You enlightened the world through the
   resurrection of your Son,
—through your Church shed this light
   on all men.

You gave the disciples of your only-begotten
   Son the Spirit's gift of understanding,
—through the same Spirit keep the Church
   faithful to you.

Light of nations, remember those who
>   remain in darkness,
—open their eyes and let them recognize you,
>   the only true God.

The Lord's Prayer

Our Father, who art in heaven,
hallowed be thy name;
thy kingdom come,
thy will be done
on earth as it is in heaven.
Give us this day our daily bread,
and forgive us our trespasses,
as we forgive those who trespass against us;
and lead us not into temptation,
but deliver us from evil.

Pater noster, qui es in cælis:
sanctificetur nomen tuum;
adveniat regnum tuum;
fiat voluntas tua,
sicut in cælo, et in terra.
Panem nostrum cotidianum da nobis hodie;
et dimitte nobis debita nostra,
sicut et nos dimittimus debitoribus nostris;
et ne nos inducas in tentationem;
sed libera nos a malo.

Concluding Prayer

God, our Father,
your light of truth
guides us to the way of Christ.
May all who follow him
reject what is contrary to the Gospel.
We ask this through our Lord Jesus Christ,
     your Son,
who lives and reigns with you and
     the Holy Spirit,
God, for ever and ever.
—Amen.

Dismissal

If praying individually, or in a group without a priest or deacon:

May the Lord + bless us,
protect us from all evil
and bring us to everlasting life.
—Amen.

If praying with a priest or deacon, he dismisses the people:

The Lord be with you.
—And with your spirit.

May almighty God bless you,
the Father, and the Son, ✚ and the Holy Spirit.
—Amen.

Go in peace.
—Thanks be to God.

EVENING PRAYER

God, + come to my assistance.
—Lord, make haste to help me.

Glory to the Father, and to the Son,
    and to the Holy Spirit:
—as it was in the beginning, is now,
    and will be for ever. Amen. Alleluia.

Hymn   *Holy God, We Praise Thy Name, p. 686*

Psalmody   Ant. 1 **The Lord said to my Master: Sit at my right hand, alleluia.**

Psalm 110:1–5, 7

The Lord's revelation to my Master:
    "Sit on my right:
    your foes I will put beneath your feet."

The Lord will wield from Zion
your scepter of power:
rule in the midst of all your foes.

A prince from the day of your birth
on the holy mountains;
from the womb before the dawn I begot you.

The Lord has sworn an oath he will
    not change.
"You are a priest for ever,
a priest like Melchizedek of old."

The Master standing at your right hand
will shatter kings in the day of his
    great wrath.

He shall drink from the stream by
    the wayside
and therefore he shall lift up his head.

Glory to the Father, and to the Son,
    and to the Holy Spirit:
—as it was in the beginning, is now,
and will be for ever. Amen.

Ant. **The Lord said to my Master: Sit at my right hand, alleluia.**

Ant. 2 **Our compassionate Lord has left us a memorial of his wonderful work, alleluia.**

Psalm 111

I will thank the Lord with all my heart
in the meeting of the just and their assembly.
Great are the works of the Lord;
to be pondered by all who love them.

Majestic and glorious his work,
his justice stands firm for ever.
He makes us remember his wonders.
The Lord is compassion and love.

He gives food to those who fear him;
keeps his covenant ever in mind.
He has shown his might to his people
by giving them the lands of the nations.

His works are justice and truth:
his precepts are all of them sure,
standing firm for ever and ever:
they are made in uprightness and truth.

He has sent deliverance to his people
and established his covenant for ever.
Holy his name, to be feared.

To fear the Lord is the first stage of wisdom;
all who do so prove themselves wise.
His praise shall last for ever!

Glory to the Father, and to the Son,
   and to the Holy Spirit:
as it was in the beginning, is now,
and will be for ever. Amen.

Ant. **Our compassionate Lord has left us a memorial of his wonderful work, alleluia.**

Ant. 3 **All power is yours, Lord God, our mighty King, alleluia.**

Canticle: See Revelation 19:1–7

Alleluia.
Salvation, glory, and power to our God:
his judgments are honest and true.
Alleluia.

Alleluia.
Sing praise to our God, all you his servants,
all who worship him reverently,
   great and small.
Alleluia.

Alleluia.
The Lord our all-powerful God is King;
let us rejoice, sing praise, and give him glory.
Alleluia.

Alleluia.
The wedding feast of the Lamb has begun,
and his bride is prepared to welcome him.
Alleluia.

Alleluia.
Glory to the Father, and to the Son,
and to the Holy Spirit:
Alleluia.

Alleluia.
as it was in the beginning, is now,
and will be for ever. Amen.
Alleluia.

Ant. **All power is yours, Lord God, our mighty King, alleluia.**

Reading
1 Peter 1:3–5

Praised be the God and Father
of our Lord Jesus Christ,
he who in his great mercy
gave us new birth;
a birth unto hope which draws its life
from the resurrection of Jesus Christ
 from the dead;
a birth to an imperishable inheritance,
incapable of fading or defilement,
which is kept in heaven for you
who are guarded with God's power
 through faith;
a birth to a salvation which stands ready
to be revealed in the last days.

Responsory

The whole creation proclaims the greatness
 of your glory.
—The whole creation proclaims the greatness
 of your glory.

Eternal ages praise
—the greatness of your glory.

Glory to the Father, and to the Son,
    and to the Holy Spirit.
—The whole creation proclaims the greatness
    of your glory.

Gospel Canticle

Ant. **Teacher, what is the greatest commandment in the law? Jesus said to him: You shall love the Lord your God with your whole heart.**

Canticle of Mary
Luke 1:46–55

My + soul proclaims the greatness of the Lord,
my spirit rejoices in God my Savior
for he has looked with favor on his
    lowly servant.

From this day all generations will
    call me blessed:
the Almighty has done great things for me,
and holy is his Name.

He has mercy on those who fear him
in every generation.

He has shown the strength of his arm,
he has scattered the proud in their conceit.

He has cast down the mighty from
    their thrones,
and has lifted up the lowly.

He has filled the hungry with good things,
and the rich he has sent away empty.

He has come to the help of his servant Israel
for he has remembered his promise of mercy,
the promise he made to our fathers,
to Abraham and his children for ever.

Glory to the Father, and to the Son,
    and to the Holy Spirit:
—as it was in the beginning, is now,
and will be for ever. Amen.

Ant. **Teacher, what is the greatest commandment in the law? Jesus said to him: You shall love the Lord your God with your whole heart.**

Intercessions The world was created by the Word of God, re-created by his redemption, and it is continually renewed by his love. Rejoicing in him we call out:
Renew the wonders of your love, Lord.

We give thanks to God whose power is revealed in nature,
—and whose providence is revealed in history.

Through your Son, the herald of reconciliation, the victor of the cross,
—free us from empty fear and hopelessness.

May all those who love and pursue justice,
—work together without deceit to build a world of true peace.

Be with the oppressed, free the captives,
>   console the sorrowing, feed the hungry,
>   strengthen the weak,
— in all people reveal the victory of your cross.

After your Son's death and burial you raised
>   him up again in glory,
— grant that the faithful departed may
>   live with him.

The Lord's Prayer

Our Father, who art in heaven,
hallowed be thy name;
thy kingdom come,
thy will be done
on earth as it is in heaven.
Give us this day our daily bread,
and forgive us our trespasses,
as we forgive those who trespass against us;
and lead us not into temptation,
but deliver us from evil.

Pater noster, qui es in cælis:
sanctificetur nomen tuum;
adveniat regnum tuum;
fiat voluntas tua,
sicut in cælo, et in terra.
Panem nostrum cotidianum da nobis hodie;
et dimitte nobis debita nostra,
sicut et nos dimittimus debitoribus nostris;
et ne nos inducas in tentationem;
sed libera nos a malo.

Concluding Prayer

God, our Father,
your light of truth
guides us to the way of Christ.
May all who follow him
reject what is contrary to the Gospel.
We ask this through our Lord Jesus Christ,
   your Son,
who lives and reigns with you and
   the Holy Spirit,
God, for ever and ever.
—Amen.

Dismissal

If praying individually, or in a group without a priest or deacon:

May the Lord ✚ bless us,
protect us from all evil
and bring us to everlasting life.
—Amen.

If praying with a priest or deacon, he dismisses the people:

The Lord be with you.
—And with your spirit.

May almighty God bless you,
the Father, and the Son, ✚ and the Holy Spirit.
—Amen.

Go in peace.
—Thanks be to God.

MY SOUL
PROCLAIMS
THE GREATNESS
OF THE LORD,
MY SPIRIT
REJOICES IN GOD
MY SAVIOR
FOR HE HAS
LOOKED WITH
FAVOR ON HIS
LOWLY SERVANT.

NIGHT PRAYER

God, + come to my assistance.
—Lord, make haste to help me.

Glory to the Father, and to the Son,
    and to the Holy Spirit:
—as it was in the beginning, is now,
and will be for ever. Amen. Alleluia.

Examen *An optional brief examination of conscience may be made. Call to mind your sins and failings this day.*

Hymn *Abide with Me, p. 675*

Psalmody Ant. **Night holds no terrors for me sleeping under God's wings.**

Psalm 91

He who dwells in the shelter of the Most High
and abides in the shade of the Almighty
says to the Lord: "My refuge,
my stronghold, my God in whom I trust!"

It is he who will free you from the snare
of the fowler who seeks to destroy you;
he will conceal you with his pinions
and under his wings you will find refuge.

You will not fear the terror of the night
nor the arrow that flies by day,
nor the plague that prowls in the darkness
nor the scourge that lays waste at noon.

A thousand may fall at your side,
ten thousand fall at your right,
you, it will never approach;
his faithfulness is buckler and shield.

Your eyes have only to look
to see how the wicked are repaid,
you who have said: "Lord, my refuge!"
and have made the Most High your dwelling.

Upon you no evil shall fall,
no plague approach where you dwell.
For you has he commanded his angels,
to keep you in all your ways.

They shall bear you upon their hands
lest you strike your foot against a stone.
On the lion and the viper you will tread
and trample the young lion and the dragon.

Since he clings to me in love, I will free him;
protect him for he knows my name.
When he calls I shall answer: "I am with you."
I will save him in distress and give him glory.

With length of life I will content him;
I shall let him see my saving power.

Glory to the Father, and to the Son,
 and to the Holy Spirit:
—as it was in the beginning, is now,
and will be for ever. Amen.

Ant. **Night holds no terrors for me sleeping under God's wings.**

Reading
Revelation 22:4–5

They shall see the Lord face to face and bear his name on their foreheads. The night shall be no more. They will need no light from lamps or the sun, for the Lord God shall give them light, and they shall reign forever.

Responsory

Into your hands, Lord, I commend my spirit.
—Into your hands, Lord, I commend my spirit.

You have redeemed us, Lord God of truth.
—I commend my spirit.

Glory to the Father, and to the Son,
 and to the Holy Spirit.
—Into your hands, Lord, I commend my spirit.

Gospel Canticle

Ant. **Protect us, Lord, as we stay awake; watch over us as we sleep, that awake, we may keep watch with Christ, and asleep, rest in his peace.**

Canticle of Simeon
Luke 2:29–32

Lord, + now you let your servant go in peace;
your word has been fulfilled:
my own eyes have seen the salvation
which you have prepared in the sight of
 every people:
a light to reveal you to the nations
and the glory of your people Israel.

Glory to the Father, and to the Son,
 and to the Holy Spirit:
—as it was in the beginning, is now,
 and will be for ever. Amen.

Ant. **Protect us, Lord, as we stay awake; watch over us as we sleep, that awake, we may keep watch with Christ, and asleep, rest in his peace.**

Concluding Prayer

Let us pray.
Lord,
we have celebrated today
the mystery of the rising of Christ to new life.
May we now rest in your peace,
safe from all that could harm us,
and rise again refreshed and joyful,
to praise you throughout another day.
We ask this through Christ our Lord.
—Amen.

Blessing

May the all-powerful Lord
grant us a restful night
and a peaceful death.
—Amen.

Marian Antiphon

Sing the "Salve Regina," found on p. 698, or pray a Hail Mary.

Monday, July 17, 2023
Monday of the Fifteenth Week in Ordinary Time

MORNING PRAYER

God, + come to my assistance.
—Lord, make haste to help me.

Glory to the Father, and to the Son,
    and to the Holy Spirit:
—as it was in the beginning, is now,
and will be for ever. Amen. Alleluia.

Hymn *God Who Made Both Earth and Heaven, p. 682*

Psalmody Ant. 1 **Blessed are they who dwell in your house, O Lord.**

Psalm 84
How lovely is your dwelling place,
Lord, God of hosts.

My soul is longing and yearning,
is yearning for the courts of the Lord.
My heart and my soul ring out their joy
to God, the living God.

The sparrow herself finds a home
and the swallow a nest for her brood;
she lays her young by your altars,
Lord of hosts, my king and my God.

They are happy, who dwell in your house,
for ever singing your praise.
They are happy, whose strength is in you,
in whose hearts are the roads to Zion.

As they go through the Bitter Valley
they make it a place of springs,
the autumn rain covers it with blessings.
They walk with ever growing strength,
they will see the God of gods in Zion.

O Lord God of hosts, hear my prayer,
give ear, O God of Jacob.
Turn your eyes, O God, our shield,
look on the face of your anointed.

One day within your courts
is better than a thousand elsewhere.
The threshold of the house of God
I prefer to the dwellings of the wicked.

For the Lord God is a rampart, a shield;
he will give us his favor and glory.
The Lord will not refuse any good
to those who walk without blame.

Lord, God of hosts,
happy the man who trusts in you!

Glory to the Father, and to the Son,
    and to the Holy Spirit:
—as it was in the beginning, is now,
and will be for ever. Amen.

Ant. **Blessed are they who dwell in your house, O Lord.**

Ant. 2 **Come, let us climb the mountain of the Lord.**

JULY 17 MON MORNING PRAYER

Canticle:
Isaiah 2:2–5

In days to come,
the mountain of the Lord's house
shall be established as the highest mountain
and raised above the hills.

All nations shall stream toward it;
many peoples shall come and say:
"Come, let us climb the Lord's mountain,
to the house of the God of Jacob,
that he may instruct us in his ways,
and we may walk in his paths."

For from Zion shall go forth instruction,
and the word of the Lord from Jerusalem.

He shall judge between the nations,
and impose terms on many peoples.
They shall beat their swords into plowshares
and their spears into pruning hooks;
one nation shall not raise the sword
   against another,
nor shall they train for war again.

O house of Jacob, come,
let us walk in the light of the Lord!

Glory to the Father, and to the Son,
   and to the Holy Spirit:
—as it was in the beginning, is now,
and will be for ever. Amen.

Ant. **Come, let us climb the mountain of the Lord.**

Ant. 3 **Sing to the Lord and bless his name.**

Psalm 96

O sing a new song to the Lord,
sing to the Lord, all the earth.
O sing to the Lord, bless his name.

Proclaim his help day by day,
tell among the nations his glory
and his wonders among all the peoples.

The Lord is great and worthy of praise,
to be feared above all gods;
the gods of the heathens are naught.

It was the Lord who made the heavens,
his are majesty and state and power
and splendor in his holy place.

Give the Lord, you families of peoples,
give the Lord glory and power,
give the Lord the glory of his name.

Bring an offering and enter his courts,
worship the Lord in his temple.
O earth, tremble before him.

Proclaim to the nations: "God is king."
The world he made firm in its place;
he will judge the peoples in fairness.

Let the heavens rejoice and earth be glad,
let the sea and all within it thunder praise,
let the land and all it bears rejoice,
all the trees of the wood shout for joy

at the presence of the Lord for he comes,
he comes to rule the earth.
With justice he will rule the world,
he will judge the peoples with his truth.

Glory to the Father, and to the Son,
   and to the Holy Spirit:
—as it was in the beginning, is now,
and will be for ever. Amen.

Ant. **Sing to the Lord and bless his name.**

Reading *James 2:12-13*
Always speak and act as men destined for judgment under the law of freedom. Merciless is the judgment on the man who has not shown mercy; but mercy triumphs over judgment.

Responsory
Blessed be the Lord our God,
   blessed from age to age.
—Blessed be the Lord our God,
   blessed from age to age.

His marvelous works are beyond compare,
—blessed from age to age.

Glory to the Father, and to the Son,
   and to the Holy Spirit.
—Blessed be the Lord our God,
   blessed from age to age.

Gospel Canticle Ant. **Blessed be the Lord our God.**

Canticle of Zechariah
Luke 1:68–79

Blessed + be the Lord, the God of Israel;
he has come to his people and set them free.

He has raised up for us a mighty savior,
born of the house of his servant David.

Through his holy prophets he
    promised of old
that he would save us from our enemies,
from the hands of all who hate us.

He promised to show mercy to our fathers
and to remember his holy covenant.

This was the oath he swore to our
    father Abraham:
to set us free from the hands of our enemies,
free to worship him without fear,
holy and righteous in his sight
    all the days of our life.

You, my child, shall be called the prophet of
    the Most High;
for you will go before the Lord to
    prepare his way,
to give his people knowledge of salvation
by the forgiveness of their sins.

In the tender compassion of our God
the dawn from on high shall break upon us,
to shine on those who dwell in darkness and
    the shadow of death,
and to guide our feet into the way of peace.

Glory to the Father, and to the Son,
   and to the Holy Spirit:
—as it was in the beginning, is now,
   and will be for ever. Amen.

Ant. **Blessed be the Lord our God.**

Intercessions Man was created to glorify God through his deeds. Let us earnestly pray:
May we give glory to your name, Lord.

We bless you, Creator of all things,
—for you have given us the goods of the earth and brought us to this day.

Look with favor on us as we begin our daily work,
—let us be fellow workers with you.

Make our work today benefit our brothers and sisters,
—that with them and for them we may build an earthly city, pleasing to you.

Grant joy and peace to us,
—and to all we meet this day.

The Lord's Prayer

Our Father, who art in heaven,
hallowed be thy name;
thy kingdom come,
thy will be done
on earth as it is in heaven.
Give us this day our daily bread,
and forgive us our trespasses,
as we forgive those who trespass against us;
and lead us not into temptation,
but deliver us from evil.

Pater noster, qui es in cælis:
sanctificetur nomen tuum;
adveniat regnum tuum;
fiat voluntas tua,
sicut in cælo, et in terra.
Panem nostrum cotidianum da nobis hodie;
et dimitte nobis debita nostra,
sicut et nos dimittimus debitoribus nostris;
et ne nos inducas in tentationem;
sed libera nos a malo.

Concluding Prayer

Lord God,
king of heaven and earth,
direct our minds and bodies throughout this day,
and make us holy.
Keep us faithful to your law in thought,
    word and deed.
Be our helper now and always,
free us from sin,
and bring us to salvation in that kingdom
where you live and reign with the Father and
    the Holy Spirit,
God, for ever and ever.
—Amen.

Dismissal *If praying individually, or in a group without a priest or deacon:*

May the Lord + bless us,
protect us from all evil
and bring us to everlasting life.
—Amen.

If praying with a priest or deacon, he dismisses the people:

The Lord be with you.
—And with your spirit.

May almighty God bless you,
the Father, and the Son, ✠ and the Holy Spirit.
—Amen.

Go in peace.
—Thanks be to God.

EVENING PRAYER

God, + come to my assistance.
—Lord, make haste to help me.

Glory to the Father, and to the Son,
  and to the Holy Spirit:
—as it was in the beginning, is now,
and will be for ever. Amen. Alleluia.

Hymn *Come, My Way, My Truth, My Life, p. 678*

Psalmody Ant. 1 **Our eyes are fixed intently on the Lord, waiting for his merciful help.**

EVENING PRAYER MON JULY 17

Psalm 123

To you have I lifted up my eyes,
you who dwell in the heavens:
my eyes, like the eyes of slaves
on the hand of their lords.

Like the eyes of a servant
on the hand of her mistress,
so our eyes are on the Lord our God
till he show us his mercy.

Have mercy on us, Lord, have mercy.
We are filled with contempt.
Indeed all too full is our soul
with the scorn of the rich,
with the proud man's disdain.

Glory to the Father, and to the Son,
 and to the Holy Spirit:
—as it was in the beginning, is now,
and will be for ever. Amen.

Ant.

Our eyes are fixed intently on the Lord, waiting for his merciful help.

Ant. 2

Our help is in the name of the Lord who made heaven and earth.

Psalm 124

"If the Lord had not been on our side,"
this is Israel's song.
"If the Lord had not been on our side
when men rose up against us,
then would they have swallowed us alive
when their anger was kindled.

Then would the waters have engulfed us,
the torrent gone over us;
over our head would have swept
the raging waters."

Blessed be the Lord who did not give us
as prey to their teeth!
Our life, like a bird, has escaped
from the snare of the fowler.

Indeed the snare has been broken
and we have escaped.
Our help is in the name of the Lord,
who made heaven and earth.

Glory to the Father, and to the Son,
 and to the Holy Spirit:
as it was in the beginning, is now,
and will be for ever. Amen.

Ant. **Our help is in the name of the Lord who made heaven and earth.**

Ant. 3 **God chose us in his Son to be his adopted children.**

Canticle:
Ephesians 1:3–10

Praised be the God and Father
of our Lord Jesus Christ,
who has bestowed on us in Christ
every spiritual blessing in the heavens.

God chose us in him
before the world began
to be holy
and blameless in his sight.

He predestined us
to be his adopted sons through Jesus Christ,
such was his will and pleasure,
that all might praise the glorious favor
he has bestowed on us in his beloved.

In him and through his blood, we have
  been redeemed,
and our sins forgiven,
so immeasurably generous
is God's favor to us.

God has given us the wisdom
to understand fully the mystery,
the plan he was pleased
to decree in Christ.

A plan to be carried out
in Christ, in the fullness of time,
to bring all things into one in him,
in the heavens and on earth.

Glory to the Father, and to the Son,
  and to the Holy Spirit:
—as it was in the beginning, is now,
and will be for ever. Amen.

Ant. **God chose us in his Son to be his adopted children.**

JULY 17　　MON　　　　　　　　　　EVENING PRAYER

Reading
James 4:11–12

Do not, my brothers, speak ill of one another. The one who speaks ill of his brother or judges his brother is speaking against the law. It is the law he judges. If, however, you judge the law you are no observer of the law, you are its judge. There is but one Lawgiver and Judge, one who can save and destroy. Who then are you to judge your neighbor?

Responsory

Lord, you alone can heal me, for I have grieved you by my sins.
—Lord, you alone can heal me, for I have grieved you by my sins.

Once more I say: O Lord, have mercy on me,
—for I have grieved you by my sins.

Glory to the Father, and to the Son, and to the Holy Spirit.
—Lord, you alone can heal me, for I have grieved you by my sins.

Gospel Canticle

Ant. **My soul proclaims the greatness of the Lord for he has looked with favor on his lowly servant.**

Canticle of Mary
Luke 1:46–55

My + soul proclaims the greatness of the Lord,
my spirit rejoices in God my Savior
for he has looked with favor on his
　　lowly servant.

From this day all generations will
　　call me blessed:
the Almighty has done great things for me,
and holy is his Name.

He has mercy on those who fear him
in every generation.

He has shown the strength of his arm,
he has scattered the proud in their conceit.

He has cast down the mighty from
    their thrones,
and has lifted up the lowly.

He has filled the hungry with good things,
and the rich he has sent away empty.

He has come to the help of his servant Israel
for he has remembered his promise of mercy,
the promise he made to our fathers,
to Abraham and his children for ever.

Glory to the Father, and to the Son,
    and to the Holy Spirit:
—as it was in the beginning, is now,
and will be for ever. Amen.

Ant. **My soul proclaims the greatness of the Lord for he has looked with favor on his lowly servant.**

Intercessions Christ desires to lead all men to salvation. Let us implore him with all our heart:
Draw all things to yourself, Lord.

Through your precious blood, Lord, you redeemed us from the slavery of sin,
—grant us the freedom of the sons of God.

Bestow your grace upon our bishop N., and
   upon all bishops,
—may they administer your sacraments with
   fervent joy.

Grant that all who seek the truth may find it,
—and in finding it may they desire it
   all the more.

Be present to comfort widows, orphans and
   all the abandoned, Lord,
—may they feel close to you and cling to you.

Receive our departed brethren into the
   heavenly kingdom,
—where with the Father and the Holy Spirit
   you will be all in all.

The Lord's Prayer

Our Father, who art in heaven,
hallowed be thy name;
thy kingdom come,
thy will be done
on earth as it is in heaven.
Give us this day our daily bread,
and forgive us our trespasses,
as we forgive those who trespass against us;
and lead us not into temptation,
but deliver us from evil.

Pater noster, qui es in cælis:
sanctificetur nomen tuum;
adveniat regnum tuum;
fiat voluntas tua,
sicut in cælo, et in terra.
Panem nostrum cotidianum da nobis hodie;
et dimitte nobis debita nostra,
sicut et nos dimittimus debitoribus nostris;
et ne nos inducas in tentationem;
sed libera nos a malo.

Concluding Prayer

God our Father,
at the close of day we come to you,
the light that never fades.
Shine in the darkness of our night
and forgive our sins and failings.
We ask this through our Lord Jesus Christ,
 your Son,
who lives and reigns with you and
 the Holy Spirit,
God, for ever and ever.
—Amen.

Dismissal

If praying individually, or in a group without a priest or deacon:

May the Lord + bless us,
protect us from all evil
and bring us to everlasting life.
—Amen.

If praying with a priest or deacon, he dismisses the people:

The Lord be with you.
—And with your spirit.

May almighty God bless you,
the Father, and the Son, ✠ and the Holy Spirit.
—Amen.

Go in peace.
—Thanks be to God.

NIGHT PRAYER

God, + come to my assistance.
—Lord, make haste to help me.

Glory to the Father, and to the Son,
 and to the Holy Spirit:
—as it was in the beginning, is now,
and will be for ever. Amen. Alleluia.

Examen *An optional brief examination of conscience may be made. Call to mind your sins and failings this day.*

Hymn *Before the Final Light of Day, p. 676*

Psalmody Ant. **O Lord, our God, unwearied is your love for us.**

Psalm 86 Turn your ear, O Lord, and give answer
for I am poor and needy.
Preserve my life, for I am faithful:
save the servant who trusts in you.

You are my God; have mercy on me, Lord,
for I cry to you all the day long.
Give joy to your servant, O Lord,
for to you I lift up my soul.

O Lord, you are good and forgiving,
full of love to all who call.
Give heed, O Lord, to my prayer
and attend to the sound of my voice.

In the day of distress I will call
and surely you will reply.
Among the gods there is none like you,
    O Lord;
nor work to compare with yours.

All the nations shall come to adore you
and glorify your name, O Lord:
for you are great and do marvelous deeds,
you who alone are God.

Show me, Lord, your way
so that I may walk in your truth.
Guide my heart to fear your name.

I will praise you, Lord my God, with
    all my heart
and glorify your name for ever;
for your love to me has been great:
you have saved me from the depths of
    the grave.

The proud have risen against me;
ruthless men seek my life:
to you they pay no heed.

But you, God of mercy and compassion,
slow to anger, O Lord,
abounding in love and truth,
turn and take pity on me.

JULY 17 · MON · NIGHT PRAYER

O give your strength to your servant
and save your handmaid's son.
Show me a sign of your favor
that my foes may see to their shame
that you console me and give me your help.

Glory to the Father, and to the Son,
    and to the Holy Spirit:
—as it was in the beginning, is now,
and will be for ever. Amen.

Ant. **O Lord, our God, unwearied is your love for us.**

Reading
1 Thessalonians 5:9–10

God has destined us for acquiring salvation through our Lord Jesus Christ. He died for us, that all of us, whether awake or asleep, together might live with him.

Responsory Into your hands, Lord, I commend my spirit.
—Into your hands, Lord, I commend my spirit.

You have redeemed us, Lord God of truth.
—I commend my spirit.

Glory to the Father, and to the Son,
    and to the Holy Spirit.
—Into your hands, Lord, I commend my spirit.

Gospel Canticle

Ant. Protect us, Lord, as we stay awake; watch over us as we sleep, that awake, we may keep watch with Christ, and asleep, rest in his peace.

Canticle of Simeon
Luke 2:29–32

Lord, + now you let your servant go in peace;
your word has been fulfilled:
my own eyes have seen the salvation
which you have prepared in the sight of
   every people:
a light to reveal you to the nations
and the glory of your people Israel.

Glory to the Father, and to the Son,
   and to the Holy Spirit:
—as it was in the beginning, is now,
and will be for ever. Amen.

Ant.

Protect us, Lord, as we stay awake; watch over us as we sleep, that awake, we may keep watch with Christ, and asleep, rest in his peace.

Concluding Prayer

Let us pray.
Lord,
give our bodies restful sleep
and let the work we have done today
bear fruit in eternal life.
We ask this through Christ our Lord.
—Amen.

Blessing

May the all-powerful Lord
grant us a restful night
and a peaceful death.
—Amen.

Marian Antiphon

Sing the "Salve Regina," found on p. 698, or pray a Hail Mary.

Tuesday, July 18, 2023
Tuesday of the Fifteenth Week in Ordinary Time

MORNING PRAYER

God, + come to my assistance.
—Lord, make haste to help me.

Glory to the Father, and to the Son,
  and to the Holy Spirit:
—as it was in the beginning, is now,
  and will be for ever. Amen. Alleluia.

Hymn *The Heavens Declare Your Glory, p. 704*

Psalmody Ant. 1 **Lord, you have blessed your land; you have forgiven the sins of your people.**

Psalm 85

O Lord, you once favored your land
and revived the fortunes of Jacob,
you forgave the guilt of your people
and covered all their sins.
You averted all your rage,
you calmed the heat of your anger.

Revive us now, God, our helper!
Put an end to your grievance against us.
Will you be angry with us for ever,
will your anger never cease?

Will you not restore again our life
that your people may rejoice in you?
Let us see, O Lord, your mercy
and give us your saving help.

I will hear what the Lord God has to say,
a voice that speaks of peace,
peace for his people and his friends
and those who turn to him in their hearts.
His help is near for those who fear him
and his glory will dwell in our land.

Mercy and faithfulness have met;
justice and peace have embraced.
Faithfulness shall spring from the earth
and justice look down from heaven.

The Lord will make us prosper
and our earth shall yield its fruit.
Justice shall march before him
and peace shall follow his steps.

Glory to the Father, and to the Son,
    and to the Holy Spirit:
—as it was in the beginning, is now,
and will be for ever. Amen.

Ant. **Lord, you have blessed your land; you have forgiven the sins of your people.**

Ant. 2 **My soul has yearned for you in the night, and as morning breaks I watch for your coming.**

Canticle:
Isaiah 26:1–4,
7–9, 12

A strong city have we;
he sets up walls and ramparts to protect us.
Open up the gates
to let in a nation that is just,
one that keeps faith.

A nation of firm purpose you keep in peace;
in peace, for its trust in you.
Trust in the Lord forever!
For the Lord is an eternal Rock.

The way of the just is smooth;
the path of the just you make level.
Yes, for your way and your
 judgments, O Lord,
we look to you;
your name and your title
are the desire of our souls.

My soul yearns for you in the night,
yes, my spirit within me keeps vigil for you;
when your judgment dawns upon the earth,
the world's inhabitants learn justice.

O Lord, you mete out peace to us,
for it is you who have accomplished all we
 have done.

Glory to the Father, and to the Son,
 and to the Holy Spirit:
—as it was in the beginning, is now,
and will be for ever. Amen.

Ant. **My soul has yearned for you in the night, and as morning breaks I watch for your coming.**

Ant. 3 **Lord, let the light of your face shine upon us.**

Psalm 67

O God, be gracious and bless us
and let your face shed its light upon us.
So will your ways be known upon earth
and all nations learn your saving help.

Let the peoples praise you, O God;
let all the peoples praise you.

Let the nations be glad and exult
for you rule the world with justice.
With fairness you rule the peoples,
you guide the nations on earth.

Let the peoples praise you, O God;
let all the peoples praise you.

The earth has yielded its fruit
for God, our God, has blessed us.
May God still give us his blessing
till the ends of the earth revere him.

Let the peoples praise you, O God;
let all the peoples praise you.

Glory to the Father, and to the Son,
    and to the Holy Spirit:
—as it was in the beginning, is now,
and will be for ever. Amen.

Ant. **Lord, let the light of your face shine upon us.**

JULY 18 TUE MORNING PRAYER

Reading
1 John 4:14–15

We have seen for ourselves, and can testify,
that the Father has sent the Son as savior of
   the world.
When anyone acknowledges that Jesus is the
   Son of God,
God dwells in him
and he in God.

Responsory

My God stands by me, all my trust is in him.
—My God stands by me, all my trust is in him.

I find refuge in him, and I am truly free;
—all my trust is in him.

Glory to the Father, and to the Son,
   and to the Holy Spirit.
—My God stands by me, all my trust is in him.

Gospel Canticle

Ant. **God has raised up for us a mighty Savior, as he promised of old through his holy prophets.**

*Canticle of Zechariah
Luke 1:68–79*

Blessed + be the Lord, the God of Israel;
he has come to his people and set them free.

He has raised up for us a mighty savior,
born of the house of his servant David.

Through his holy prophets he
   promised of old
that he would save us from our enemies,
from the hands of all who hate us.

He promised to show mercy to our fathers
and to remember his holy covenant.

This was the oath he swore to our
>   father Abraham:
to set us free from the hands of our enemies,
free to worship him without fear,
holy and righteous in his sight
>   all the days of our life.

You, my child, shall be called the prophet of
>   the Most High;
for you will go before the Lord to
>   prepare his way,
to give his people knowledge of salvation
by the forgiveness of their sins.

In the tender compassion of our God
the dawn from on high shall break upon us,
to shine on those who dwell in darkness and
>   the shadow of death,
and to guide our feet into the way of peace.

Glory to the Father, and to the Son,
>   and to the Holy Spirit:
—as it was in the beginning, is now,
and will be for ever. Amen.

Ant. **God has raised up for us a mighty Savior, as he promised of old through his holy prophets.**

Intercessions Lord Jesus, by your blood you have purchased for yourself a new people. We adore you and beseech you:
Remember your people, Lord.

Our King and our Redeemer, hear the praises of your Church at the beginning of this day,
—teach her to glorify your majesty without ceasing.

You are our hope and our strength, in you we trust,
—may we never despair.

Look kindly upon our weakness and hasten to our aid,
—for without you we can do nothing.

Remember the poor and the afflicted, do not let this day be a burden to them,
—but a consolation and a joy.

The Lord's Prayer

Our Father, who art in heaven,
hallowed be thy name;
thy kingdom come,
thy will be done
on earth as it is in heaven.
Give us this day our daily bread,
and forgive us our trespasses,
as we forgive those who trespass against us;
and lead us not into temptation,
but deliver us from evil.

Pater noster, qui es in cælis:
sanctificetur nomen tuum;
adveniat regnum tuum;
fiat voluntas tua,
sicut in cælo, et in terra.
Panem nostrum cotidianum da nobis hodie;
et dimitte nobis debita nostra,
sicut et nos dimittimus debitoribus nostris;
et ne nos inducas in tentationem;
sed libera nos a malo.

Concluding Prayer

God our Father,
yours is the beauty of creation
and the good things you have given us.
Help us to begin this day joyfully
    in your name
and to spend it in loving service
of you and our fellow man.
We ask this through our Lord Jesus Christ,
    your Son,
who lives and reigns with you and
    the Holy Spirit,
God, for ever and ever.
—Amen.

Dismissal

If praying individually, or in a group without a priest or deacon:

May the Lord + bless us,
protect us from all evil
and bring us to everlasting life.
—Amen.

If praying with a priest or deacon, he dismisses the people:

The Lord be with you.
—And with your spirit.

May almighty God bless you,
the Father, and the Son, ✟ and the Holy Spirit.
—Amen.

Go in peace.
—Thanks be to God.

EVENING PRAYER

God, ✟ come to my assistance.
—Lord, make haste to help me.

Glory to the Father, and to the Son,
and to the Holy Spirit:
—as it was in the beginning, is now,
and will be for ever. Amen. Alleluia.

Hymn *Immortal, Invisible, God Only Wise, p. 688*

Psalmody Ant. 1 **The Lord surrounds his people with his strength.**

Psalm 125 Those who put their trust in the Lord
are like Mount Zion, that cannot be shaken,
that stands for ever.

Jerusalem! The mountains surround her,
so the Lord surrounds his people
both now and for ever.

For the scepter of the wicked shall not rest
over the land of the just
for fear that the hands of the just
should turn to evil.

Do good, Lord, to those who are good,
to the upright of heart;
but the crooked and those who do evil,
drive them away!

On Israel, peace!

Glory to the Father, and to the Son,
    and to the Holy Spirit:
—as it was in the beginning, is now,
and will be for ever. Amen.

Ant. **The Lord surrounds his people with his strength.**

Ant. 2 **Unless you acquire the heart of a child, you cannot enter the kingdom of God.**

Psalm 131

O Lord, my heart is not proud
nor haughty my eyes.
I have not gone after things too great
nor marvels beyond me.

Truly I have set my soul
in silence and peace.
As a child has rest in its mother's arms,
even so my soul.

O Israel, hope in the Lord
both now and for ever.

Glory to the Father, and to the Son,
    and to the Holy Spirit:
—as it was in the beginning, is now,
and will be for ever. Amen.

Ant. **Unless you acquire the heart of a child, you cannot enter the kingdom of God.**

Ant. 3 **Lord, you have made us a kingdom and priests for God our Father.**

Canticle:
Revelation 4:11;
5:9, 10, 12

O Lord our God, you are worthy
to receive glory and honor and power.

For you have created all things;
by your will they came to be and were made.

Worthy are you, O Lord,
to receive the scroll and break open its seals.

For you were slain;
with your blood you purchased for God
men of every race and tongue,
of every people and nation.

You made of them a kingdom,
and priests to serve our God,
and they shall reign on the earth.

Worthy is the Lamb that was slain
to receive power and riches,
wisdom and strength,
honor and glory and praise.

Glory to the Father, and to the Son,
   and to the Holy Spirit:
—as it was in the beginning, is now,
and will be for ever. Amen.

Ant. **Lord, you have made us a kingdom and priests for God our Father.**

Reading
Romans 12:9–12

Your love must be sincere. Detest what is evil, cling to what is good. Love one another with the affection of brothers. Anticipate each other in showing respect. Do not grow slack but be fervent in spirit; he whom you serve is the Lord. Rejoice in hope, be patient under trial, persevere in prayer.

Responsory

Through all eternity, O Lord, your promise stands unshaken.
—Through all eternity, O Lord, your promise stands unshaken.

Your faithfulness will never fail;
—your promise stands unshaken.

Glory to the Father, and to the Son, and to the Holy Spirit.
—Through all eternity, O Lord, your promise stands unshaken.

Gospel Canticle

Ant. **My spirit rejoices in God my Savior.**

Canticle of Mary
Luke 1:46–55

My + soul proclaims the greatness of the Lord,
my spirit rejoices in God my Savior
for he has looked with favor on his
   lowly servant.

From this day all generations will call
   me blessed:
the Almighty has done great things for me,
and holy is his Name.

He has mercy on those who fear him
in every generation.

He has shown the strength of his arm,
he has scattered the proud in their conceit.

He has cast down the mighty from
    their thrones,
and has lifted up the lowly.

He has filled the hungry with good things,
and the rich he has sent away empty.

He has come to the help of his servant Israel
for he has remembered his promise of mercy,
the promise he made to our fathers,
to Abraham and his children for ever.

Glory to the Father, and to the Son,
    and to the Holy Spirit:
—as it was in the beginning, is now,
and will be for ever. Amen.

Ant. **My spirit rejoices in God my Savior.**

Intercessions God establishes his people in hope. Let us cry out to him with joy:
You are the hope of your people, Lord.

We thank you, Lord,
—because in Christ you have given us all the treasures of wisdom and knowledge.

O God, in your hands are the hearts of the
    powerful; bestow your wisdom upon
    government leaders,
—may they draw from the fountain
    of your counsel and please you in
    thought and deed.

The talents of artists reflect your splendor,
—may their work give the world hope and joy.

You do not allow us to be tested beyond
    our ability,
—strengthen the weak and raise up the fallen.

Through your Son you promised to raise
    men up on the Last Day,
—do not forget those who have died.

The Lord's Prayer

Our Father, who art in heaven,
hallowed be thy name;
thy kingdom come,
thy will be done
on earth as it is in heaven.
Give us this day our daily bread,
and forgive us our trespasses,
as we forgive those who trespass against us;
and lead us not into temptation,
but deliver us from evil.

Pater noster, qui es in cælis:
sanctificetur nomen tuum;
adveniat regnum tuum;
fiat voluntas tua,
sicut in cælo, et in terra.
Panem nostrum cotidianum da nobis hodie;
et dimitte nobis debita nostra,
sicut et nos dimittimus debitoribus nostris;
et ne nos inducas in tentationem;
sed libera nos a malo.

Concluding Prayer

Lord,
may our evening prayer rise up to you,
and your blessing come down upon us.
May your help and salvation be ours
now and through all eternity.
We ask this through our Lord Jesus Christ,
    your Son,
who lives and reigns with you and
    the Holy Spirit,
God, for ever and ever.
—Amen.

Dismissal

If praying individually, or in a group without a priest or deacon:

May the Lord + bless us,
protect us from all evil
and bring us to everlasting life.
—Amen.

If praying with a priest or deacon, he dismisses the people:

The Lord be with you.
—And with your spirit.

May almighty God bless you,
the Father, and the Son, ✠ and the Holy Spirit.
—Amen.

Go in peace.
—Thanks be to God.

NIGHT PRAYER

God, + come to my assistance.
—Lord, make haste to help me.

Glory to the Father, and to the Son,
and to the Holy Spirit:
—as it was in the beginning, is now,
and will be for ever. Amen. Alleluia.

Examen *An optional brief examination of conscience may be made. Call to mind your sins and failings this day.*

Hymn *O Joyful Light of God Most High, p. 693*

Psalmody **Ant. Do not hide your face from me; in you I put my trust.**

Psalm 143:1–11

Lord, listen to my prayer:
turn your ear to my appeal.
You are faithful, you are just; give answer.
Do not call your servant to judgment
for no one is just in your sight.

The enemy pursues my soul;
he has crushed my life to the ground;
he has made me dwell in darkness
like the dead, long forgotten.
Therefore my spirit fails;
my heart is numb within me.

I remember the days that are past:
I ponder all your works.
I muse on what your hand has wrought
and to you I stretch out my hands.
Like a parched land my soul thirsts for you.

Lord, make haste and answer;
for my spirit fails within me.
Do not hide your face
lest I become like those in the grave.

In the morning let me know your love
for I put my trust in you.
Make me know the way I should walk:
to you I lift up my soul.

Rescue me, Lord, from my enemies;
I have fled to you for refuge.
Teach me to do your will
for you, O Lord, are my God.
Let your good spirit guide me
in ways that are level and smooth.

For your name's sake, Lord, save my life;
in your justice save my soul from distress.

Glory to the Father, and to the Son,
    and to the Holy Spirit:
—as it was in the beginning, is now,
and will be for ever. Amen.

Ant. **Do not hide your face from me; in you I put my trust.**

Reading
1 Peter 5:8–9a

Stay sober and alert. Your opponent the devil is prowling like a roaring lion looking for someone to devour. Resist him, solid in your faith.

Responsory

Into your hands, Lord, I commend my spirit.
—Into your hands, Lord, I commend my spirit.

You have redeemed us, Lord God of truth.
—I commend my spirit.

Glory to the Father, and to the Son,
and to the Holy Spirit.
—Into your hands, Lord, I commend my spirit.

Gospel Canticle

Ant. **Protect us, Lord, as we stay awake; watch over us as we sleep, that awake, we may keep watch with Christ, and asleep, rest in his peace.**

Canticle of Simeon
Luke 2:29–32

Lord, + now you let your servant go in peace;
your word has been fulfilled:
my own eyes have seen the salvation
which you have prepared in the sight of
every people:
a light to reveal you to the nations
and the glory of your people Israel.

Glory to the Father, and to the Son,
and to the Holy Spirit:
—as it was in the beginning, is now,
and will be for ever. Amen.

JULY 18 TUE NIGHT PRAYER

Ant. **Protect us, Lord, as we stay awake; watch over us as we sleep, that awake, we may keep watch with Christ, and asleep, rest in his peace.**

Concluding Prayer
Let us pray.
Lord,
fill this night with your radiance.
May we sleep in peace and rise with joy
to welcome the light of a new day in
 your name.
We ask this through Christ our Lord.
—Amen.

Blessing
May the all-powerful Lord
grant us a restful night
and a peaceful death.
—Amen.

Marian Antiphon
Sing the "Salve Regina," found on p. 698, or pray a Hail Mary.

I HAVE FLED
TO YOU FOR
REFUGE.

TEACH ME TO
DO YOUR WILL
FOR YOU, O LORD,
ARE MY GOD.

Wednesday, July 19, 2023
Wednesday of the Fifteenth Week in Ordinary Time

MORNING PRAYER

God, ✛ come to my assistance.
—Lord, make haste to help me.

Glory to the Father, and to the Son,
   and to the Holy Spirit:
—as it was in the beginning, is now,
and will be for ever. Amen. Alleluia.

Hymn   *O Splendor of God's Glory Bright, p. 694*

Psalmody   Ant. 1 **Give joy to your servant, Lord; to you I lift up my heart.**

Psalm 86   Turn your ear, O Lord, and give answer
for I am poor and needy.
Preserve my life, for I am faithful:
save the servant who trusts in you.

You are my God, have mercy on me, Lord,
for I cry to you all the day long.
Give joy to your servant, O Lord,
for to you I lift up my soul.

O Lord, you are good and forgiving,
full of love to all who call.
Give heed, O Lord, to my prayer
and attend to the sound of my voice.

In the day of distress I will call
and surely you will reply.
Among the gods there is none like you,
    O Lord;
nor work to compare with yours.

All the nations shall come to adore you
and glorify your name, O Lord:
for you are great and do marvelous deeds,
you who alone are God.

Show me, Lord, your way
so that I may walk in your truth.
Guide my heart to fear your name.

I will praise you, Lord my God,
    with all my heart
and glorify your name for ever;
for your love to me has been great:
you have saved me from the depths of
    the grave.

The proud have risen against me;
ruthless men seek my life:
to you they pay no heed.

But you, God of mercy and compassion,
slow to anger, O Lord,
abounding in love and truth,
turn and take pity on me.

O give your strength to your servant
and save your handmaid's son.
Show me a sign of your favor
that my foes may see to their shame
that you console me and give me your help.

Glory to the Father, and to the Son,
    and to the Holy Spirit:
—as it was in the beginning, is now,
and will be for ever. Amen.

Ant. **Give joy to your servant, Lord; to you I lift up my heart.**

Ant. 2 **Blessed is the upright man, who speaks the truth.**

Canticle:
Isaiah 33:13–16

Hear, you who are far off,
what I have done;
you who are near,
acknowledge my might.

On Zion sinners are in dread,
trembling grips the impious;
"Who of us can live with the consuming fire?
Who of us can live with the everlasting flames?"

He who practices virtue and speaks honestly,
who spurns what is gained by oppression,
brushing his hands
free of contact with a bribe,
stopping his ears lest he hear of bloodshed,
closing his eyes lest he look on evil.

He shall dwell on the heights,
his stronghold shall be the rocky fastness,
his food and drink
in steady supply.

Glory to the Father, and to the Son,
    and to the Holy Spirit:
as it was in the beginning, is now,
and will be for ever. Amen.

Ant. **Blessed is the upright man, who speaks the truth.**

Ant. 3 **Let us celebrate with joy in the presence of our Lord and King.**

Psalm 98

Sing a new song to the Lord
for he has worked wonders.
His right hand and his holy arm
have brought salvation.

The Lord has made known his salvation;
has shown his justice to the nations.
He has remembered his truth and love
for the house of Israel.

All the ends of the earth have seen
the salvation of our God.
Shout to the Lord, all the earth,
ring out your joy.

Sing psalms to the Lord with the harp
with the sound of music.
With trumpets and the sound of the horn
acclaim the King, the Lord.

Let the sea and all within it thunder;
the world, and all its peoples.
Let the rivers clap their hands
and the hills ring out their joy.

Rejoice at the presence of the Lord,
for he comes to rule the earth.
He will rule the world with justice
and the peoples with fairness.

Glory to the Father, and to the Son,
    and to the Holy Spirit:
—as it was in the beginning, is now,
and will be for ever. Amen.

Ant. **Let us celebrate with joy in the presence of our Lord and King.**

Reading
Job 1:21; 2:10b

Naked I came forth from my mother's womb,
    and naked I shall go back again.
The Lord gave and the Lord has taken away;
    blessed be the name of the Lord!
We accept good things from God;
    and should we not accept evil?

Responsory

Incline my heart according to your will,
    O God.
—Incline my heart according to your will,
    O God.

Speed my steps along your path,
—according to your will, O God.

Glory to the Father, and to the Son,
>   and to the Holy Spirit.
— Incline my heart according to your will,
>   O God.

Gospel Canticle

Ant. **Show us your mercy, Lord; remember your holy covenant.**

Canticle of Zechariah
Luke 1:68–79

Blessed + be the Lord, the God of Israel;
he has come to his people and set them free.

He has raised up for us a mighty savior,
born of the house of his servant David.

Through his holy prophets he
>   promised of old
that he would save us from our enemies,
from the hands of all who hate us.

He promised to show mercy to our fathers
and to remember his holy covenant.

This was the oath he swore to our
>   father Abraham:
to set us free from the hands of our enemies,
free to worship him without fear,
holy and righteous in his sight
>   all the days of our life.

You, my child, shall be called the prophet of
>   the Most High;
for you will go before the Lord to
>   prepare his way,
to give his people knowledge of salvation
by the forgiveness of their sins.

In the tender compassion of our God
the dawn from on high shall break upon us,
to shine on those who dwell in darkness and
    the shadow of death,
and to guide our feet into the way of peace.

Glory to the Father, and to the Son,
    and to the Holy Spirit:
—as it was in the beginning, is now,
    and will be for ever. Amen.

Ant. **Show us your mercy, Lord; remember your holy covenant.**

Intercessions Christ nourishes and supports the Church
    for which he gave himself up to death. Let
    us ask him:
Remember your Church, Lord.

You are the Good Shepherd who has given
    life and light today,
—make us grateful for these gifts.

Look with mercy on the flock you have
    gathered together in your name,
—let no one whom the Father has given
    you perish.

Lead your Church in the way of your
    commandments,
—may your Holy Spirit keep her faithful.

Nourish the Church at the banquet of your
   Word and Bread,
—strengthened by this food may she follow
   you in joy.

The Lord's Prayer

Our Father, who art in heaven,
hallowed be thy name;
thy kingdom come,
thy will be done
on earth as it is in heaven.
Give us this day our daily bread,
and forgive us our trespasses,
as we forgive those who trespass against us;
and lead us not into temptation,
but deliver us from evil.

Pater noster, qui es in cælis:
sanctificetur nomen tuum;
adveniat regnum tuum;
fiat voluntas tua,
sicut in cælo, et in terra.
Panem nostrum cotidianum da nobis hodie;
et dimitte nobis debita nostra,
sicut et nos dimittimus debitoribus nostris;
et ne nos inducas in tentationem;
sed libera nos a malo.

Concluding Prayer

Lord,
as daylight fills the sky,
fill us with your holy light.
May our lives mirror our love for you
whose wisdom has brought us into being,
and whose care guides us on our way.
We ask this through our Lord Jesus Christ,
    your Son,
who lives and reigns with you and
    the Holy Spirit,
God, for ever and ever.
—Amen.

Dismissal

If praying individually, or in a group without a priest or deacon:

May the Lord ✢ bless us,
protect us from all evil
and bring us to everlasting life.
—Amen.

If praying with a priest or deacon, he dismisses the people:

The Lord be with you.
—And with your spirit.

May almighty God bless you,
the Father, and the Son, ✢ and the Holy Spirit.
—Amen.

Go in peace.
—Thanks be to God.

EVENING PRAYER

God, + come to my assistance.
—Lord, make haste to help me.

Glory to the Father, and to the Son,
 and to the Holy Spirit:
—as it was in the beginning, is now,
and will be for ever. Amen. Alleluia.

Hymn *Sing Praise to God Who Reigns Above, p. 700*

Psalmody Ant. 1 **Those who sow in tears will reap in joy.**

Psalm 126

When the Lord delivered Zion from bondage,
it seemed like a dream.
Then was our mouth filled with laughter,
on our lips there were songs.

The heathens themselves said: "What marvels
the Lord worked for them!"
What marvels the Lord worked for us!
Indeed we were glad.

Deliver us, O Lord, from our bondage
as streams in dry land.
Those who are sowing in tears
will sing when they reap.

They go out, they go out, full of tears,
carrying seed for the sowing:
they come back, they come back, full of song,
carrying their sheaves.

Glory to the Father, and to the Son,
   and to the Holy Spirit:
—as it was in the beginning, is now,
   and will be for ever. Amen.

Ant. **Those who sow in tears will reap in joy.**

Ant. 2 **May the Lord build our house and guard our city.**

Psalm 127

If the Lord does not build the house,
   in vain do its builders labor;
if the Lord does not watch over the city,
   in vain does the watchman keep vigil.

In vain is your earlier rising,
your going later to rest,
you who toil for the bread you eat:
when he pours gifts on his beloved while
   they slumber.

Truly sons are a gift from the Lord,
a blessing, the fruit of the womb.
Indeed the sons of youth
are like arrows in the hand of a warrior.

O the happiness of the man
who has filled his quiver with these arrows!
He will have no cause for shame
when he disputes with his foes in the gateways.

Glory to the Father, and to the Son,
   and to the Holy Spirit:
—as it was in the beginning, is now,
   and will be for ever. Amen.

Ant. **May the Lord build our house and guard our city.**

Ant. 3 **He is the first-born of all creation; in every way the primacy is his.**

Canticle: Colossians 1:12–20

Let us give thanks to the Father
for having made you worthy
to share the lot of the saints
in light.

He rescued us
from the power of darkness
and brought us
into the kingdom of his beloved Son.
Through him we have redemption,
the forgiveness of our sins.

He is the image of the invisible God,
the first-born of all creatures.
In him everything in heaven and on earth
　　was created,
things visible and invisible.

All were created through him;
all were created for him.
He is before all else that is.
In him everything continues in being.

It is he who is head of the body, the church!
he who is the beginning,
the first-born of the dead,
so that primacy may be his in everything.

It pleased God to make absolute fullness
   reside in him
and, by means of him, to reconcile
   everything in his person,
both on earth and in the heavens,
making peace through the blood of his cross.

Glory to the Father, and to the Son,
   and to the Holy Spirit:
—as it was in the beginning, is now,
   and will be for ever. Amen.

Ant. **He is the first-born of all creation; in every way the primacy is his.**

Reading
Ephesians 3:20–21

To God whose power now at work in us can do immeasurably more than we ask or imagine—to him be glory in the church and in Christ Jesus through all generations, world without end. Amen.

Responsory Claim me once more as your own, Lord,
   and have mercy on me.
—Claim me once more as your own, Lord,
   and have mercy on me.

Do not abandon me with the wicked;
—have mercy on me.

Glory to the Father, and to the Son,
   and to the Holy Spirit.
—Claim me once more as your own, Lord,
   and have mercy on me.

Gospel Canticle

Ant. **The Almighty has done great things for me, and holy is his Name.**

Canticle of Mary
Luke 1:46–55

My ☩ soul proclaims the greatness of the Lord,
my spirit rejoices in God my Savior
for he has looked with favor on his
    lowly servant.

From this day all generations will
    call me blessed:
the Almighty has done great things for me,
and holy is his Name.

He has mercy on those who fear him
in every generation.

He has shown the strength of his arm,
he has scattered the proud in their conceit.

He has cast down the mighty from
    their thrones,
and has lifted up the lowly.

He has filled the hungry with good things,
and the rich he has sent away empty.

He has come to the help of his servant Israel
for he has remembered his promise of mercy,
the promise he made to our fathers,
to Abraham and his children for ever.

Glory to the Father, and to the Son,
    and to the Holy Spirit:
as it was in the beginning, is now,
and will be for ever. Amen.

Ant. **The Almighty has done great things for me, and holy is his Name.**

Intercessions Let us humbly pray to God who sent his Son as the Savior and exemplar of his people:
May your people praise you, Lord.

Let us give thanks to God who chose us as the first-fruits of salvation,
—and who called us to share in the glory of our Lord Jesus Christ.

May those who confess your holy name be united in your truth,
—and fervent in your love.

Creator of all things, your Son desired to work among us with his own hands,
—be mindful of all who earn their living by the sweat of their brow.

Be mindful of those who devote themselves to the service of their brothers,
—do not let them be deterred from their goals by discouraging results or lack of support.

Be merciful to the faithful departed,
—keep them from the power of the Evil One.

The Lord's Prayer

Our Father, who art in heaven,
hallowed be thy name;
thy kingdom come,
thy will be done
on earth as it is in heaven.
Give us this day our daily bread,
and forgive us our trespasses,
as we forgive those who trespass against us;
and lead us not into temptation,
but deliver us from evil.

Pater noster, qui es in cælis:
sanctificetur nomen tuum;
adveniat regnum tuum;
fiat voluntas tua,
sicut in cælo, et in terra.
Panem nostrum cotidianum da nobis hodie;
et dimitte nobis debita nostra,
sicut et nos dimittimus debitoribus nostris;
et ne nos inducas in tentationem;
sed libera nos a malo.

Concluding Prayer

Merciful Lord,
let the evening prayer of your Church
come before you.
May we do your work faithfully;
free us from sin
and make us secure in your love.
We ask this through our Lord Jesus Christ,
    your Son,
who lives and reigns with you and
    the Holy Spirit,
God, for ever and ever.
—Amen.

JULY 19 WED NIGHT PRAYER

Dismissal *If praying individually, or in a group without a priest or deacon:*

May the Lord ✛ bless us,
protect us from all evil
and bring us to everlasting life.
—Amen.

If praying with a priest or deacon, he dismisses the people:

The Lord be with you.
—And with your spirit.

May almighty God bless you,
the Father, and the Son, ✛ and the Holy Spirit.
—Amen.

Go in peace.
—Thanks be to God.

NIGHT PRAYER

God, ✛ come to my assistance.
—Lord, make haste to help me.

Glory to the Father, and to the Son,
    and to the Holy Spirit:
—as it was in the beginning, is now,
    and will be for ever. Amen. Alleluia.

Examen *An optional brief examination of conscience may be made. Call to mind your sins and failings this day.*

Hymn Abide with Me, p. 675

Psalmody Ant. 1 **Lord God, be my refuge and my strength.**

Psalm 31:1–6

In you, O Lord, I take refuge.
Let me never be put to shame.
In your justice, set me free,
hear me and speedily rescue me.

Be a rock of refuge for me,
a mighty stronghold to save me,
for you are my rock, my stronghold.
For your name's sake, lead me and guide me.

Release me from the snares they have hidden
for you are my refuge, Lord.
Into your hands I commend my spirit.
It is you who will redeem me, Lord.

Glory to the Father, and to the Son,
 and to the Holy Spirit:
as it was in the beginning, is now,
and will be for ever. Amen.

Ant. **Lord God, be my refuge and my strength.**

Ant. 2 **Out of the depths I cry to you, Lord.**

Psalm 130

Out of the depths I cry to you, O Lord,
Lord, hear my voice!
O let your ears be attentive
to the voice of my pleading.

If you, O Lord, should mark our guilt,
Lord, who would survive?
But with you is found forgiveness:
for this we revere you.

My soul is waiting for the Lord,
I count on his word.
My soul is longing for the Lord
more than watchman for daybreak.
Let the watchman count on daybreak
and Israel on the Lord.

Because with the Lord there is mercy
and fullness of redemption,
Israel indeed he will redeem
from all its iniquity.

Glory to the Father, and to the Son,
 and to the Holy Spirit:
—as it was in the beginning, is now,
and will be for ever. Amen.

Ant. **Out of the depths I cry to you, Lord.**

Reading
Ephesians 4:26–27

If you are angry, let it be without sin. The sun must not go down on your wrath; do not give the devil a chance to work on you.

Responsory

Into your hands, Lord, I commend my spirit.
—Into your hands, Lord, I commend my spirit.

You have redeemed us, Lord God of truth.
—I commend my spirit.

Glory to the Father, and to the Son,
 and to the Holy Spirit.
—Into your hands, Lord, I commend my spirit.

Gospel Canticle

Ant. **Protect us, Lord, as we stay awake; watch over us as we sleep, that awake, we may keep watch with Christ, and asleep, rest in his peace.**

Canticle of Simeon
Luke 2:29–32

Lord, + now you let your servant go in peace;
your word has been fulfilled:
my own eyes have seen the salvation
which you have prepared in the sight of
   every people:
a light to reveal you to the nations
and the glory of your people Israel.

Glory to the Father, and to the Son,
   and to the Holy Spirit:
—as it was in the beginning, is now,
and will be for ever. Amen.

Ant. **Protect us, Lord, as we stay awake; watch over us as we sleep, that awake, we may keep watch with Christ, and asleep, rest in his peace.**

Concluding Prayer

Let us pray.
Lord Jesus Christ,
you have given your followers
an example of gentleness and humility,
a task that is easy, a burden that is light.
Accept the prayers and work of this day,
and give us the rest that will strengthen us
to render more faithful service to you
who live and reign for ever and ever.
—Amen.

Blessing May the all-powerful Lord
grant us a restful night
and a peaceful death.
—Amen.

Marian Antiphon *Sing the "Salve Regina," found on p. 698, or pray a Hail Mary.*

Thursday, July 20, 2023
Thursday of the Fifteenth Week in Ordinary Time

MORNING PRAYER

God, + come to my assistance.
—Lord, make haste to help me.

Glory to the Father, and to the Son,
  and to the Holy Spirit:
—as it was in the beginning, is now,
 and will be for ever. Amen. Alleluia.

Hymn *From All That Dwell Below the Skies, p. 679*

Psalmody Ant. 1 **Glorious things are said of you, O city of God.**

Psalm 87 On the holy mountain is his city
cherished by the Lord.
The Lord prefers the gates of Zion
to all Jacob's dwellings.
Of you are told glorious things,
O city of God!

"Babylon and Egypt I will count
among those who know me;
Philistia, Tyre, Ethiopia,
these will be her children
and Zion shall be called 'Mother'
for all shall be her children."

It is he, the Lord Most High,
who gives each his place.
In his register of peoples he writes:
"These are her children,"
and while they dance they will sing:
"In you all find their home."

Glory to the Father, and to the Son,
 and to the Holy Spirit:
—as it was in the beginning, is now,
and will be for ever. Amen.

Ant. **Glorious things are said of you,
O city of God.**

Ant. 2 **The Lord, the mighty conqueror, will come;
he will bring with him the prize of victory.**

Canticle:
Isaiah 40:10–17

Here comes with power
the Lord God,
who rules by his strong arm;
here is his reward with him,
his recompense before him.

Like a shepherd he feeds his flock;
in his arms he gathers the lambs,
carrying them in his bosom,
and leading the ewes with care.

Who has cupped in his hand the waters
   of the sea,
and marked off the heavens with a span?
Who has held in a measure the dust of
   the earth,
weighed the mountains in scales
and the hills in a balance?

Who has directed the spirit of the Lord,
or has instructed him as his counselor?
Whom did he consult to gain knowledge?
Who taught him the path of judgment,
or showed him the way of understanding?

Behold, the nations count as a drop of
   the bucket,
as rust on the scales;
the coastlands weigh no more than powder.

Lebanon would not suffice for fuel,
nor its animals be enough for holocausts.
Before him all the nations are as nought,
as nothing and void he accounts them.

Glory to the Father, and to the Son,
   and to the Holy Spirit:
—as it was in the beginning, is now,
and will be for ever. Amen.

Ant. **The Lord, the mighty conqueror, will come; he will bring with him the prize of victory.**

Ant. 3 **Give praise to the Lord our God, bow down before his holy mountain.**

Psalm 99

The Lord is king; the peoples tremble.
He is throned on the cherubim;
    the earth quakes.
The Lord is great in Zion.

He is supreme over all the peoples.
Let them praise his name, so terrible
    and great.
He is holy, full of power.

You are a king who loves what is right;
you have established equity, justice and right;
you have established them in Jacob.

Exalt the Lord our God;
bow down before Zion, his footstool.
He the Lord is holy.

Among his priests were Aaron and Moses,
among those who invoked his name
    was Samuel.
They invoked the Lord and he answered.

To them he spoke in the pillar of cloud.
They did his will; they kept the law,
which he, the Lord, had given.

O Lord our God, you answered them.
For them you were a God who forgives;
yet you punished all their offenses.

Exalt the Lord our God;
bow down before his holy mountain
for the Lord our God is holy.

Glory to the Father, and to the Son,
  and to the Holy Spirit:
—as it was in the beginning, is now,
  and will be for ever. Amen.

Ant. **Give praise to the Lord our God, bow down before his holy mountain.**

Reading
1 Peter 4:10–11a

As generous distributors of God's manifold grace, put your gifts at the service of one another, each in the measure he has received. The one who speaks is to deliver God's message. The one who serves is to do it with the strength provided by God. Thus, in all of you God is to be glorified through Jesus Christ.

Responsory

From the depths of my heart I cry to you;
  hear me, O Lord.
—From the depths of my heart I cry to you;
  hear me, O Lord.

I will do what you desire;
—hear me, O Lord.

Glory to the Father, and to the Son,
  and to the Holy Spirit.
—From the depths of my heart I cry to you;
  hear me, O Lord.

Gospel Canticle

Ant. **Let us serve the Lord in holiness, and he will save us from our enemies.**

Canticle of Zechariah
Luke 1:68–79

Blessed + be the Lord, the God of Israel;
he has come to his people and set them free.

He has raised up for us a mighty savior,
born of the house of his servant David.

Through his holy prophets he
    promised of old
that he would save us from our enemies,
from the hands of all who hate us.

He promised to show mercy to our fathers
and to remember his holy covenant.

This was the oath he swore to our
    father Abraham:
to set us free from the hands of our enemies,
free to worship him without fear,
holy and righteous in his sight
    all the days of our life.

You, my child, shall be called the prophet of
    the Most High;
for you will go before the Lord to
    prepare his way,
to give his people knowledge of salvation
by the forgiveness of their sins.

In the tender compassion of our God
the dawn from on high shall break upon us,
to shine on those who dwell in darkness and
    the shadow of death,
and to guide our feet into the way of peace.

Glory to the Father, and to the Son,
    and to the Holy Spirit:
—as it was in the beginning, is now,
and will be for ever. Amen.

Ant. **Let us serve the Lord in holiness, and he will save us from our enemies.**

Intercessions Let us joyfully cry out in thanks to God the Father whose love guides and nourishes his people:
May you be glorified, Lord, for all ages.

Most merciful Father, we praise you for your love,
—for you wondrously created us and even more wondrously restored us to grace.

At the beginning of this day fill our hearts with zeal for serving you,
—so that our thoughts and actions may redound to your glory.

Purify our hearts of every evil desire,
—make us intent on doing your will.

Open our hearts to the needs of all men,
—fill us with brotherly love.

The Lord's Prayer

Our Father, who art in heaven,
hallowed be thy name;
thy kingdom come,
thy will be done
on earth as it is in heaven.
Give us this day our daily bread,
and forgive us our trespasses,
as we forgive those who trespass against us;
and lead us not into temptation,
but deliver us from evil.

Pater noster, qui es in cælis:
sanctificetur nomen tuum;
adveniat regnum tuum;
fiat voluntas tua,
sicut in cælo, et in terra.
Panem nostrum cotidianum da nobis hodie;
et dimitte nobis debita nostra,
sicut et nos dimittimus debitoribus nostris;
et ne nos inducas in tentationem;
sed libera nos a malo.

Concluding Prayer

All-powerful and ever-living God,
shine with the light of your radiance
on a people who live in the shadow of death.
Let the dawn from on high break upon us:
your Son our Lord Jesus Christ,
who lives and reigns with you and
    the Holy Spirit,
God, for ever and ever.
—Amen.

Dismissal   *If praying individually, or in a group without a priest or deacon:*

May the Lord + bless us,
protect us from all evil
and bring us to everlasting life.
—Amen.

If praying with a priest or deacon, he dismisses the people:

The Lord be with you.
—And with your spirit.

May almighty God bless you,
the Father, and the Son, ✠ and the Holy Spirit.
—Amen.

Go in peace.
—Thanks be to God.

EVENING PRAYER

God, + come to my assistance.
—Lord, make haste to help me.

Glory to the Father, and to the Son,
  and to the Holy Spirit:
—as it was in the beginning, is now,
  and will be for ever. Amen. Alleluia.

Hymn   *Go, Labor On, p. 684*

Psalmody   Ant. 1 **Let your holy people rejoice, O Lord,
as they enter your dwelling place.**

Psalm 132

O Lord, remember David
and all the many hardships he endured,
the oath he swore to the Lord,
his vow to the Strong One of Jacob.

"I will not enter the house where I live
nor go to the bed where I rest.
I will give no sleep to my eyes,
to my eyelids I will give no slumber
till I find a place for the Lord,
a dwelling for the Strong One of Jacob."

At Ephrathah we heard of the ark;
we found it in the plains of Yearim.
"Let us go to the place of his dwelling;
let us go to kneel at his footstool."

Go up, Lord, to the place of your rest,
you and the ark of your strength.
Your priests shall be clothed with holiness:
your faithful shall ring out their joy.
For the sake of David your servant
do not reject your anointed.

Glory to the Father, and to the Son,
    and to the Holy Spirit:
as it was in the beginning, is now,
and will be for ever. Amen.

Ant. **Let your holy people rejoice, O Lord, as they enter your dwelling place.**

Ant. 2 **The Lord has chosen Zion as his sanctuary.**

Psalm 132 (continued)

The Lord swore an oath to David;
he will not go back on his word:
"A son, the fruit of your body,
will I set upon your throne.

If they keep my covenant in truth
and my laws that I have taught them,
their sons also shall rule
on your throne from age to age."

For the Lord has chosen Zion;
he has desired it for his dwelling:
"This is my resting-place for ever,
here have I chosen to live.

I will greatly bless her produce,
I will fill her poor with bread.
I will clothe her priests with salvation
and her faithful shall ring out their joy.

There David's stock will flower:
I will prepare a lamp for my anointed.
I will cover his enemies with shame
but on him my crown shall shine."

Glory to the Father, and to the Son,
and to the Holy Spirit:
—as it was in the beginning, is now,
and will be for ever. Amen.

Ant. **The Lord has chosen Zion as his sanctuary.**

Ant. 3 **The Father has given Christ all power, honor and kingship; all people will obey him.**

Canticle:
Revelation
11:17–18;
12:10b–12a

We praise you, the Lord God Almighty,
who is and who was.
You have assumed your great power,
you have begun your reign.

The nations have raged in anger,
but then came your day of wrath
and the moment to judge the dead:
the time to reward your servants
> the prophets
and the holy ones who revere you,
the great and the small alike.

Now have salvation and power come,
the reign of our God and the authority
of his Anointed One.
For the accuser of our brothers is cast out,
who night and day accused them before God.

They defeated him by the blood of the Lamb
and by the word of their testimony;
love for life did not deter them from death.
So rejoice, you heavens,
and you that dwell therein!

Glory to the Father, and to the Son,
> and to the Holy Spirit:
—as it was in the beginning, is now,
and will be for ever. Amen.

Ant.

The Father has given Christ all power, honor and kingship; all people will obey him.

Reading
1 Peter 3:8–9

All of you should be like-minded, sympathetic, loving toward one another, kindly disposed, and humble. Do not return evil for evil or insult for insult. Return a blessing instead. This you have been called to do, that you may receive a blessing as your inheritance.

Responsory

The Lord has given us food, bread of the
    finest wheat.
—The Lord has given us food, bread of the
    finest wheat.

Honey from the rock to our heart's content,
—bread of the finest wheat.

Glory to the Father, and to the Son,
    and to the Holy Spirit.
—The Lord has given us food, bread of the
    finest wheat.

Gospel Canticle

Ant. **God has cast down the mighty from their thrones, and has lifted up the lowly.**

Canticle of Mary
Luke 1:46–55

My + soul proclaims the greatness of the Lord,
my spirit rejoices in God my Savior
for he has looked with favor on his
    lowly servant.

From this day all generations will
    call me blessed:
the Almighty has done great things for me,
and holy is his Name.

He has mercy on those who fear him
in every generation.

He has shown the strength of his arm,
he has scattered the proud in their conceit.

He has cast down the mighty from
   their thrones,
and has lifted up the lowly.

He has filled the hungry with good things,
and the rich he has sent away empty.

He has come to the help of his servant Israel
for he has remembered his promise of mercy,
the promise he made to our fathers,
to Abraham and his children for ever.

Glory to the Father, and to the Son,
   and to the Holy Spirit:
—as it was in the beginning, is now,
and will be for ever. Amen.

Ant. **God has cast down the mighty from their thrones, and has lifted up the lowly.**

Intercessions Let us call upon Christ, the Good Shepherd
   who comes to the aid of his people:
Hear us, O God our refuge.

Blessed are you, Lord, for you graciously
   called us into your holy Church,
—keep us within the Church until death.

You have given the care of all the churches to
   N., our Pope,
—give him unfailing faith, lively hope and
   loving concern.

Grant the grace of conversion to all sinners,
—and the grace of true repentance to all men.

You were willing to live as a stranger in
 our world,
—be mindful of those who are separated from
 family and homeland.

To all the departed who have hoped in you,
—grant eternal peace.

The Lord's Prayer

Our Father, who art in heaven,
hallowed be thy name;
thy kingdom come,
thy will be done
on earth as it is in heaven.
Give us this day our daily bread,
and forgive us our trespasses,
as we forgive those who trespass against us;
and lead us not into temptation,
but deliver us from evil.

Pater noster, qui es in cælis:
sanctificetur nomen tuum;
adveniat regnum tuum;
fiat voluntas tua,
sicut in cælo, et in terra.
Panem nostrum cotidianum da nobis hodie;
et dimitte nobis debita nostra,
sicut et nos dimittimus debitoribus nostris;
et ne nos inducas in tentationem;
sed libera nos a malo.

Concluding Prayer

Lord,
    we thank you for guiding us
    through the course of this day's work.
    In your compassion forgive the sins
    we have committed through
        human weakness.
    We ask this through our Lord Jesus Christ,
        your Son,
    who lives and reigns with you and
        the Holy Spirit,
    God, for ever and ever.
—Amen.

Dismissal

If praying individually, or in a group without a priest or deacon:

May the Lord ✢ bless us,
protect us from all evil
and bring us to everlasting life.
—Amen.

If praying with a priest or deacon, he dismisses the people:

The Lord be with you.
—And with your spirit.

May almighty God bless you,
the Father, and the Son, ✢ and the Holy Spirit.
—Amen.

Go in peace.
—Thanks be to God.

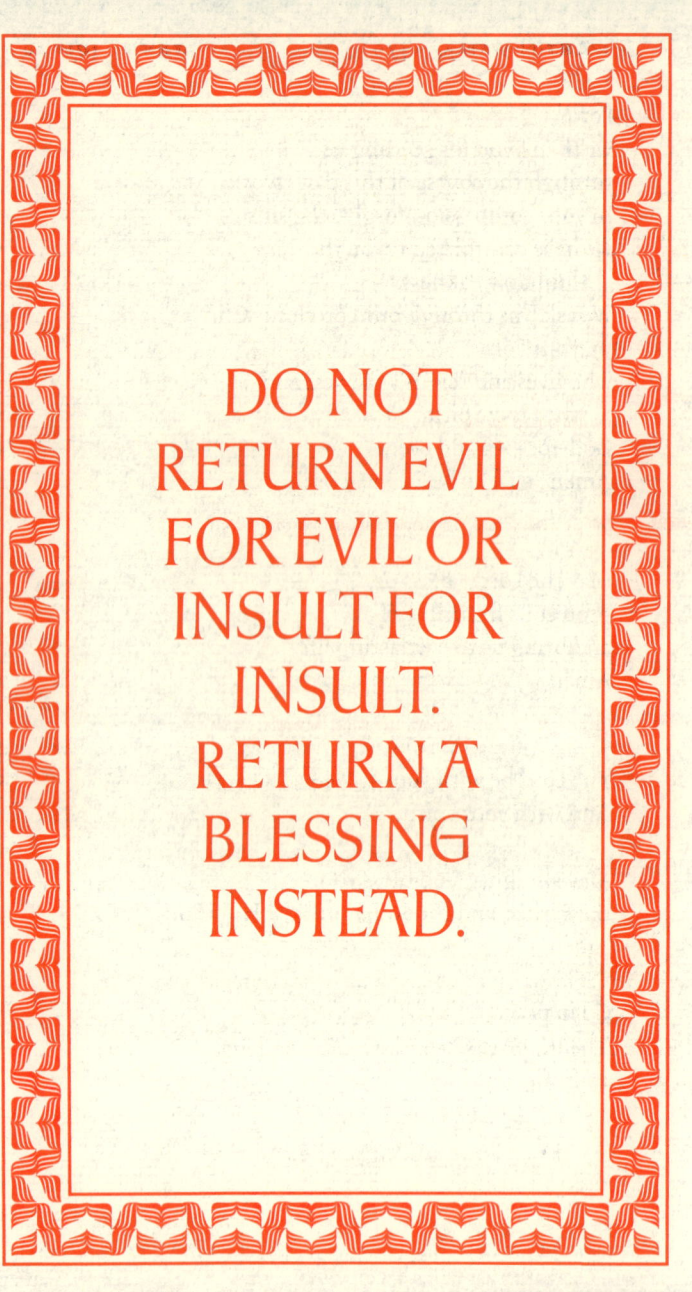

NIGHT PRAYER

God, + come to my assistance.
—Lord, make haste to help me.

Glory to the Father, and to the Son,
   and to the Holy Spirit:
—as it was in the beginning, is now,
   and will be for ever. Amen. Alleluia.

Examen *An optional brief examination of conscience may be made. Call to mind your sins and failings this day.*

Hymn *Before the Final Light of Day, p. 676*

Psalmody Ant. **In you, my God, my body will rest in hope.**

Psalm 16

Preserve me, God, I take refuge in you.
I say to the Lord: "You are my God.
My happiness lies in you alone."

He has put into my heart a marvelous love
for the faithful ones who dwell in his land.
Those who choose other gods increase
   their sorrows.
Never will I offer their offerings of blood.
Never will I take their name upon my lips.

O Lord, it is you who are my portion and cup;
it is you yourself who are my prize.
The lot marked out for me is my delight:
welcome indeed the heritage that falls to me!

I will bless the Lord who gives me counsel,
who even at night directs my heart.
I keep the Lord ever in my sight:
since he is at my right hand, I shall stand firm.

And so my heart rejoices, my soul is glad;
even my body shall rest in safety.
For you will not leave my soul
    among the dead,
nor let your beloved know decay.

You will show me the path of life,
the fullness of joy in your presence,
at your right hand happiness for ever.

Glory to the Father, and to the Son,
    and to the Holy Spirit:
—as it was in the beginning, is now,
and will be for ever. Amen.

Ant. **In you, my God, my body will rest in hope.**

Reading
1 Thessalonians 5:23

May the God of peace make you perfect in holiness. May he preserve you whole and entire, spirit, soul, and body, irreproachable at the coming of our Lord Jesus Christ.

Responsory Into your hands, Lord, I commend my spirit.
—Into your hands, Lord, I commend my spirit.

You have redeemed us, Lord God of truth.
—I commend my spirit.

Glory to the Father, and to the Son,
    and to the Holy Spirit.
—Into your hands, Lord, I commend my spirit.

Gospel Canticle

Ant. **Protect us, Lord, as we stay awake; watch over us as we sleep, that awake, we may keep watch with Christ, and asleep, rest in his peace.**

Canticle of Simeon
Luke 2:29-32

Lord, + now you let your servant go in peace;
your word has been fulfilled:
my own eyes have seen the salvation
which you have prepared in the sight of
    every people:
a light to reveal you to the nations
and the glory of your people Israel.

Glory to the Father, and to the Son,
    and to the Holy Spirit:
—as it was in the beginning, is now,
and will be for ever. Amen.

Ant.

Protect us, Lord, as we stay awake; watch over us as we sleep, that awake, we may keep watch with Christ, and asleep, rest in his peace.

Concluding Prayer

Let us pray.
Lord God,
send peaceful sleep
to refresh our tired bodies.
May your help always renew us
and keep us strong in your service.
We ask this through Christ our Lord.
—Amen.

Blessing May the all-powerful Lord
grant us a restful night
and a peaceful death.
—Amen.

Marian Antiphon *Sing the "Salve Regina," found on p. 698, or pray a Hail Mary.*

Friday, July 21, 2023
Friday of the Fifteenth Week in Ordinary Time

MORNING PRAYER

God, + come to my assistance.
—Lord, make haste to help me.

Glory to the Father, and to the Son,
and to the Holy Spirit:
—as it was in the beginning, is now,
and will be for ever. Amen. Alleluia.

Hymn *Now That the Sun Is Gleaming Bright, p. 692*

Psalmody Ant. 1 **You alone I have grieved by my sin; have pity on me, O Lord.**

Psalm 51 Have mercy on me, God, in your kindness.
In your compassion blot out my offense.
O wash me more and more from my guilt
and cleanse me from my sin.

My offenses truly I know them;
my sin is always before me.
Against you, you alone, have I sinned;
what is evil in your sight I have done.

That you may be justified when you
    give sentence
and be without reproach when you judge.
O see, in guilt I was born,
a sinner was I conceived.

Indeed you love truth in the heart;
then in the secret of my heart teach
    me wisdom.
O purify me, then I shall be clean;
O wash me, I shall be whiter than snow.

Make me hear rejoicing and gladness,
that the bones you have crushed may revive.
From my sins turn away your face
and blot out all my guilt.

A pure heart create for me, O God,
put a steadfast spirit within me.
Do not cast me away from your presence,
nor deprive me of your holy spirit.

Give me again the joy of your help;
with a spirit of fervor sustain me,
that I may teach transgressors your ways
and sinners may return to you.

O rescue me, God, my helper,
and my tongue shall ring out your goodness.
O Lord, open my lips
and my mouth shall declare your praise.

For in sacrifice you take no delight,
burnt offering from me you would refuse,
my sacrifice, a contrite spirit.
A humbled, contrite heart you will not spurn.

In your goodness, show favor to Zion:
rebuild the walls of Jerusalem.
Then you will be pleased with lawful sacrifice,
holocausts offered on your altar.

Glory to the Father, and to the Son,
    and to the Holy Spirit:
as it was in the beginning, is now,
and will be for ever. Amen.

Ant. **You alone I have grieved by my sin; have pity on me, O Lord.**

Ant. 2 **Truly we know our offenses, Lord, for we have sinned against you.**

Canticle:
Jeremiah
14:17–21

Let my eyes stream with tears
day and night, without rest,
over the great destruction which overwhelms
the virgin daughter of my people,
over her incurable wound.

If I walk out into the field,
look! those slain by the sword;
if I enter the city,
look! those consumed by hunger.
Even the prophet and the priest
forage in a land they know not.

Have you cast Judah off completely?
Is Zion loathsome to you?
Why have you struck us a blow
that cannot be healed?

We wait for peace, to no avail;
for a time of healing, but terror
   comes instead.
We recognize, O Lord, our wickedness,
the guilt of our fathers;
that we have sinned against you.

For your name's sake spurn us not,
disgrace not the throne of your glory;
remember your covenant with us, and
   break it not.

Glory to the Father, and to the Son,
   and to the Holy Spirit:
—as it was in the beginning, is now,
and will be for ever. Amen.

Ant. **Truly we know our offenses, Lord, for we have sinned against you.**

Ant. 3 **The Lord is God; we are his people, the flock he shepherds.**

Psalm 100

Cry out with joy to the Lord, all the earth.
Serve the Lord with gladness.
Come before him, singing for joy.

Know that he, the Lord, is God.
He made us, we belong to him,
we are his people, the sheep of his flock.

Go within his gates, giving thanks.
Enter his courts with songs of praise.
Give thanks to him and bless his name.

Indeed, how good is the Lord,
eternal his merciful love.
He is faithful from age to age.

Glory to the Father, and to the Son,
 and to the Holy Spirit:
—as it was in the beginning, is now,
and will be for ever. Amen.

Ant. **The Lord is God; we are his people, the flock he shepherds.**

Reading
2 Corinthians 12:9b–10

I willingly boast of my weakness that the power of Christ may rest upon me. Therefore I am content with weakness, with mistreatment, with distress, with persecutions and difficulties for the sake of Christ; for when I am powerless, it is then that I am strong.

Responsory At daybreak, be merciful to me.
—At daybreak, be merciful to me.

Make known to me the path that I must walk.
—Be merciful to me.

Glory to the Father, and to the Son,
  and to the Holy Spirit.
—At daybreak, be merciful to me.

Gospel Canticle Ant. **The Lord has come to his people and set them free.**

Canticle of Zechariah
Luke 1:68–79

Blessed + be the Lord, the God of Israel;
he has come to his people and set them free.

He has raised up for us a mighty savior,
born of the house of his servant David.

Through his holy prophets he
    promised of old
that he would save us from our enemies,
from the hands of all who hate us.

He promised to show mercy to our fathers
and to remember his holy covenant.

This was the oath he swore to our
    father Abraham:
to set us free from the hands of our enemies,
free to worship him without fear,
holy and righteous in his sight
    all the days of our life.

You, my child, shall be called the prophet of
    the Most High;
for you will go before the Lord to
    prepare his way,
to give his people knowledge of salvation
by the forgiveness of their sins.

In the tender compassion of our God
the dawn from on high shall break upon us,
to shine on those who dwell in darkness and
    the shadow of death,
and to guide our feet into the way of peace.

Glory to the Father, and to the Son,
    and to the Holy Spirit:
—as it was in the beginning, is now,
and will be for ever. Amen.

Ant. **The Lord has come to his people and set them free.**

Intercessions Raising our eyes to Christ, who was born
    and died and rose again for his people,
    let us cry out:
Save those you have redeemed by your blood, Lord.

Blessed are you, Jesus, redeemer of mankind;
    you did not hesitate to undergo your
    passion and death,
—to redeem us by your precious blood.

You promised that you would provide living
    water, the fountain of eternal life,
—pour forth your Spirit upon all men.

You send disciples to preach the Gospel to
    all nations,
—help them to extend the victory of your cross.

You have given the sick and the suffering a
    share in your cross,
—give them patience and strength.

The Lord's Prayer

Our Father, who art in heaven,
hallowed be thy name;
thy kingdom come,
thy will be done
on earth as it is in heaven.
Give us this day our daily bread,
and forgive us our trespasses,
as we forgive those who trespass against us;
and lead us not into temptation,
but deliver us from evil.

Pater noster, qui es in cælis:
sanctificetur nomen tuum;
adveniat regnum tuum;
fiat voluntas tua,
sicut in cælo, et in terra.
Panem nostrum cotidianum da nobis hodie;
et dimitte nobis debita nostra,
sicut et nos dimittimus debitoribus nostris;
et ne nos inducas in tentationem;
sed libera nos a malo.

Concluding Prayer

Father all-powerful,
let your radiance dawn in our lives,
that we may walk in the light of your law
with you as our leader.
We ask this through our Lord Jesus Christ,
    your Son,
who lives and reigns with you and
    the Holy Spirit,
God, for ever and ever.
—Amen.

Dismissal *If praying individually, or in a group without a priest or deacon:*

May the Lord + bless us,
protect us from all evil
and bring us to everlasting life.
—Amen.

If praying with a priest or deacon, he dismisses the people:

The Lord be with you.
—And with your spirit.

May almighty God bless you,
the Father, and the Son, ✠ and the Holy Spirit.
—Amen.

Go in peace.
—Thanks be to God.

EVENING PRAYER

God, + come to my assistance.
—Lord, make haste to help me.

Glory to the Father, and to the Son,
    and to the Holy Spirit:
—as it was in the beginning, is now,
    and will be for ever. Amen. Alleluia.

Hymn   *Come, My Way, My Truth, My Life, p. 678*

Psalmody   Ant. 1 **Great is the Lord, our God, transcending all other gods.**

Psalm 135

Praise the name of the Lord,
praise him, servants of the Lord,
who stand in the house of the Lord
in the courts of the house of our God.

Praise the Lord for the Lord is good.
Sing a psalm to his name for he is loving.
For the Lord has chosen Jacob for himself
and Israel for his own possession.

For I know the Lord is great,
that our Lord is high above all gods.
The Lord does whatever he wills,
in heaven, on earth, in the seas.

He summons clouds from the ends of
    the earth;
makes lightning produce the rain;
from his treasuries he sends forth the wind.

The first-born of the Egyptians he smote,
of man and beast alike.
Signs and wonders he worked
in the midst of your land, O Egypt,
against Pharaoh and all his servants.

Nations in their greatness he struck
and kings in their splendor he slew.
Sihon, king of the Amorites,
Og, the king of Bashan,
and all the kingdoms of Canaan.
He let Israel inherit their land;
on his people their land he bestowed.

Glory to the Father, and to the Son,
   and to the Holy Spirit:
—as it was in the beginning, is now,
and will be for ever. Amen.

Ant. **Great is the Lord, our God, transcending all other gods.**

Ant. 2 **House of Israel, bless the Lord! Sing psalms to him, for he is merciful.**

Psalm 135 (continued)

Lord, your name stands for ever,
unforgotten from age to age:
for the Lord does justice for his people;
the Lord takes pity on his servants.

Pagan idols are silver and gold,
the work of human hands.
They have mouths but they cannot speak;
they have eyes but they cannot see.

They have ears but they cannot hear;
there is never a breath on their lips.
Their makers will come to be like them
and so will all who trust in them!

Sons of Israel, bless the Lord!
Sons of Aaron, bless the Lord!
Sons of Levi, bless the Lord!
You who fear him, bless the Lord!

From Zion may the Lord be blessed,
he who dwells in Jerusalem!

Glory to the Father, and to the Son,
    and to the Holy Spirit:
—as it was in the beginning, is now,
and will be for ever. Amen.

Ant. **House of Israel, bless the Lord! Sing psalms to him, for he is merciful.**

Ant. 3 **All nations will come and worship before you, O Lord.**

Canticle: Revelation 15:3-4

Mighty and wonderful are your works,
Lord God Almighty!
Righteous and true are your ways,
O King of the nations!

Who would dare refuse you honor,
or the glory due your name, O Lord?

Since you alone are holy,
all nations shall come
and worship in your presence.
Your mighty deeds are clearly seen.

Glory to the Father, and to the Son,
    and to the Holy Spirit:
—as it was in the beginning, is now,
and will be for ever. Amen.

Ant. **All nations will come and worship before you, O Lord.**

Reading
James 1:2–4

My brothers, count it pure joy when you are involved in every sort of trial. Realize that when your faith is tested this makes for endurance. Let endurance come to its perfection so that you may be fully mature and lacking in nothing.

Responsory

Christ loved us and washed away our sins,
    in his own blood.
—Christ loved us and washed away our sins,
    in his own blood.

He made us a nation of kings and priests,
—in his own blood.

Glory to the Father, and to the Son,
    and to the Holy Spirit.
—Christ loved us and washed away our sins,
    in his own blood.

Gospel Canticle

Ant. **The Lord has come to the help of his servants, for he has remembered his promise of mercy.**

Canticle of Mary
Luke 1:46–55

My ✝ soul proclaims the greatness of the Lord,
my spirit rejoices in God my Savior
for he has looked with favor on his
    lowly servant.

From this day all generations will
    call me blessed:
the Almighty has done great things for me,
and holy is his Name.

He has mercy on those who fear him
in every generation.

He has shown the strength of his arm,
he has scattered the proud in their conceit.

He has cast down the mighty from
    their thrones,
and has lifted up the lowly.

He has filled the hungry with good things,
and the rich he has sent away empty.

He has come to the help of his servant Israel
for he has remembered his promise of mercy,
the promise he made to our fathers,
to Abraham and his children for ever.

Glory to the Father, and to the Son,
and to the Holy Spirit:
—as it was in the beginning, is now,
and will be for ever. Amen.

Ant. **The Lord has come to the help of his servants, for he has remembered his promise of mercy.**

Intercessions Because of our sins the Father gave the Lord Jesus up to death, and for our justification he raised him up again. Let us pray:
Have mercy on your people, Lord.

Hear our prayers and spare us as we confess our sins,
—grant us forgiveness and peace.

Your Apostle said: "Where sin abounds, grace abounds all the more,"
—forgive us our transgressions.

Lord, we have sinned, yet we have also acknowledged your infinite mercy,
—bring us to conversion.

Save your people from their sins, Lord,
—make them pleasing to you.

You opened Paradise to the thief who believed in you,
—do not close the gates of heaven to the faithful departed.

The Lord's Prayer

Our Father, who art in heaven,
hallowed be thy name;
thy kingdom come,
thy will be done
on earth as it is in heaven.
Give us this day our daily bread,
and forgive us our trespasses,
as we forgive those who trespass against us;
and lead us not into temptation,
but deliver us from evil.

Pater noster, qui es in cælis:
sanctificetur nomen tuum;
adveniat regnum tuum;
fiat voluntas tua,
sicut in cælo, et in terra.
Panem nostrum cotidianum da nobis hodie;
et dimitte nobis debita nostra,
sicut et nos dimittimus debitoribus nostris;
et ne nos inducas in tentationem;
sed libera nos a malo.

Concluding Prayer

Father,
in your loving plan
Christ your Son became the price of our salvation.
May we be united with him in his suffering
so that we may experience
the power of his resurrection
in the kingdom
where he lives and reigns with you and the Holy Spirit,
God, for ever and ever.
—Amen.

Dismissal	*If praying individually, or in a group without a priest or deacon:*

May the Lord + bless us,
protect us from all evil
and bring us to everlasting life.
—Amen.

If praying with a priest or deacon, he dismisses the people:

The Lord be with you.
—And with your spirit.

May almighty God bless you,
the Father, and the Son, + and the Holy Spirit.
—Amen.

Go in peace.
—Thanks be to God.

NIGHT PRAYER

God, + come to my assistance.
—Lord, make haste to help me.

Glory to the Father, and to the Son,
    and to the Holy Spirit:
—as it was in the beginning, is now,
and will be for ever. Amen. Alleluia.

Examen	*An optional brief examination of conscience may be made. Call to mind your sins and failings this day.*
Hymn	*O Joyful Light of God Most High, p. 693*
Psalmody	Ant. **Day and night I cry to you, my God.**

Psalm 88

Lord my God, I call for help by day;
I cry at night before you.
Let my prayer come into your presence.
O turn your ear to my cry.

For my soul is filled with evils;
my life is on the brink of the grave.
I am reckoned as one in the tomb:
I have reached the end of my strength,

like one alone among the dead;
like the slain lying in their graves;
like those you remember no more,
cut off, as they are, from your hand.

You have laid me in the depths of the tomb,
in places that are dark, in the depths.
Your anger weighs down upon me:
I am drowned beneath your waves.

You have taken away my friends
and made me hateful in their sight.
Imprisoned, I cannot escape;
my eyes are sunken with grief.

I call to you, Lord, all the day long;
to you I stretch out my hands.
Will you work your wonders for the dead?
Will the shades stand and praise you?

Will your love be told in the grave
or your faithfulness among the dead?
Will your wonders be known in the dark
or your justice in the land of oblivion?

As for me, Lord, I call to you for help:
in the morning my prayer comes before you.
Lord, why do you reject me?
Why do you hide your face?

Wretched, close to death from my youth,
I have borne your trials; I am numb.
Your fury has swept down upon me;
your terrors have utterly destroyed me.

They surround me all the day like a flood,
they assail me all together.
Friend and neighbor you have taken away:
my one companion is darkness.

Glory to the Father, and to the Son,
   and to the Holy Spirit:
—as it was in the beginning, is now,
and will be for ever. Amen.

Ant. **Day and night I cry to you, my God.**

Reading
Jeremiah 14:9a

You are in our midst, O Lord,
   your name we bear:
     do not forsake us, O Lord, our God!

Responsory

Into your hands, Lord, I commend my spirit.
—Into your hands, Lord, I commend my spirit.

You have redeemed us, Lord God of truth.
—I commend my spirit.

Glory to the Father, and to the Son,
   and to the Holy Spirit.
—Into your hands, Lord, I commend my spirit.

Gospel Canticle

Ant. **Protect us, Lord, as we stay awake; watch over us as we sleep, that awake, we may keep watch with Christ, and asleep, rest in his peace.**

Canticle of Simeon
Luke 2:29–32

Lord, + now you let your servant go in peace;
your word has been fulfilled:
my own eyes have seen the salvation
which you have prepared in the sight of
every people:
a light to reveal you to the nations
and the glory of your people Israel.

Glory to the Father, and to the Son,
and to the Holy Spirit:
—as it was in the beginning, is now,
and will be for ever. Amen.

Ant. **Protect us, Lord, as we stay awake; watch over us as we sleep, that awake, we may keep watch with Christ, and asleep, rest in his peace.**

Concluding Prayer

Let us pray.
All-powerful God,
keep us united with your Son
in his death and burial
so that we may rise to new life with him,
who lives and reigns for ever and ever.
—Amen.

Blessing

May the all-powerful Lord
grant us a restful night
and a peaceful death.
—Amen.

Marian Antiphon

Sing the "Salve Regina," found on p. 698, or pray a Hail Mary.

Saturday, July 22, 2023
St. Mary Magdalene

MORNING PRAYER

God, + come to my assistance.
—Lord, make haste to help me.

Glory to the Father, and to the Son,
 and to the Holy Spirit:
—as it was in the beginning, is now,
and will be for ever. Amen. Alleluia.

Hymn

From the Highest Heights of Glory, p. 680

Psalmody

Ant. 1 **Very early in the morning after the sabbath, Mary Magdalene came to the tomb, just as the sun was rising.**

Psalm 63:2–9

O God, you are my God, for you I long;
 for you my soul is thirsting.
My body pines for you
 like a dry, weary land without water.
So I gaze on you in the sanctuary
 to see your strength and your glory.

For your love is better than life,
my lips will speak your praise.
So I will bless you all my life,
in your name I will lift up my hands.
My soul shall be filled as with a banquet,
my mouth shall praise you with joy.

On my bed I remember you.
On you I muse through the night
for you have been my help;
in the shadow of your wings I rejoice.
My soul clings to you;
your right hand holds me fast.

Glory to the Father, and to the Son,
   and to the Holy Spirit:
as it was in the beginning, is now,
and will be for ever. Amen.

Ant. **Very early in the morning after the sabbath, Mary Magdalene came to the tomb, just as the sun was rising.**

Ant. 2 **My heart burns within me; I long to see my Lord; I look for him, but I cannot find where they have put him, alleluia.**

Canticle:
Daniel
3:57–88, 56

Bless the Lord, all you works of the Lord.
Praise and exalt him above all forever.
Angels of the Lord, bless the Lord.
You heavens, bless the Lord.
All you waters above the heavens,
    bless the Lord.
All you hosts of the Lord, bless the Lord.
Sun and moon, bless the Lord.
Stars of heaven, bless the Lord.

Every shower and dew, bless the Lord.
All you winds, bless the Lord.
Fire and heat, bless the Lord.
Cold and chill, bless the Lord.
Dew and rain, bless the Lord.
Frost and chill, bless the Lord.
Ice and snow, bless the Lord.
Nights and days, bless the Lord.
Light and darkness, bless the Lord.
Lightnings and clouds, bless the Lord.

Let the earth bless the Lord.
Praise and exalt him above all forever.
Mountains and hills, bless the Lord.
Everything growing from the earth,
    bless the Lord.
You springs, bless the Lord.
Seas and rivers, bless the Lord.
You dolphins and all water creatures,
    bless the Lord.
All you birds of the air, bless the Lord.
All you beasts, wild and tame, bless the Lord.
You sons of men, bless the Lord.

O Israel, bless the Lord.
Praise and exalt him above all forever.
Priests of the Lord, bless the Lord.
Servants of the Lord, bless the Lord.
Spirits and souls of the just, bless the Lord.
Holy men of humble heart, bless the Lord.
Hananiah, Azariah, Mishael, bless the Lord.
Praise and exalt him above all forever.

Let us bless the Father, and the Son,
    and the Holy Spirit.
Let us praise and exalt him above all forever.
Blessed are you, Lord, in the firmament
    of heaven.
Praiseworthy and glorious and exalted above
    all forever.

Ant. **My heart burns within me; I long to see my Lord; I look for him, but I cannot find where they have put him, alleluia.**

Ant. 3 **While Mary was weeping she bent down to look into the tomb; she saw two angels seated there, clothed in white, alleluia.**

Psalm 149

Sing a new song to the Lord,
his praise in the assembly of the faithful.
Let Israel rejoice in its maker,
let Zion's sons exult in their king.
Let them praise his name with dancing
and make music with timbrel and harp.

For the Lord takes delight in his people.
He crowns the poor with salvation.
Let the faithful rejoice in their glory,
shout for joy and take their rest.
Let the praise of God be on their lips
and a two-edged sword in their hand,

to deal out vengeance to the nations
and punishment on all the peoples;
to bind their kings in chains
and their nobles in fetters of iron;
to carry out the sentence pre-ordained;
this honor is for all his faithful.

Glory to the Father, and to the Son,
    and to the Holy Spirit:
—as it was in the beginning, is now,
and will be for ever. Amen.

Ant. **While Mary was weeping she bent down to look into the tomb; she saw two angels seated there, clothed in white, alleluia.**

Reading
Romans 12:1–2

Brothers, I beg you through the mercy of God to offer your bodies as a living sacrifice holy and acceptable to God, your spiritual worship. Do not conform yourselves to this age but be transformed by the renewal of your mind, so that you may judge what is God's will, what is good, pleasing and perfect.

Responsory Mary, do not weep; the Lord is risen
    from the dead.
—Mary, do not weep; the Lord is risen
    from the dead.

Go to my brothers and say to them:
—The Lord is risen from the dead.

Glory to the Father, and to the Son,
 and to the Holy Spirit.
—Mary, do not weep; the Lord is risen
 from the dead.

Gospel Canticle

Ant. **When Jesus had risen from the dead on the morning after the sabbath, he appeared first to Mary Magdalene, from whom he had cast out seven devils.**

Canticle of Zechariah
Luke 1:68–79

Blessed + be the Lord, the God of Israel;
he has come to his people and set them free.

He has raised up for us a mighty savior,
born of the house of his servant David.

Through his holy prophets he
 promised of old
that he would save us from our enemies,
from the hands of all who hate us.

He promised to show mercy to our fathers
and to remember his holy covenant.

This was the oath he swore to our
 father Abraham:
to set us free from the hands of our enemies,
free to worship him without fear,
holy and righteous in his sight
 all the days of our life.

You, my child, shall be called the prophet of
>   the Most High;
for you will go before the Lord to
>   prepare his way,
to give his people knowledge of salvation
by the forgiveness of their sins.

In the tender compassion of our God
the dawn from on high shall break upon us,
to shine on those who dwell in darkness and
>   the shadow of death,
and to guide our feet into the way of peace.

Glory to the Father, and to the Son,
>   and to the Holy Spirit:
—as it was in the beginning, is now,
and will be for ever. Amen.

Ant. **When Jesus had risen from the dead on the morning after the sabbath, he appeared first to Mary Magdalene, from whom he had cast out seven devils.**

Intercessions

My brothers, with all the holy women, let us profess our faith in our Savior and call upon him:
Come, Lord Jesus.

Lord Jesus, you forgave the sinful woman
>   because she loved much,
—forgive us who have sinned much.

Lord Jesus, the holy women ministered to
>   your needs during your journeys,
—help us to follow your footsteps.

Lord Jesus, master, Mary listened to your
   words while Martha served your needs,
—help us to serve you with love and devotion.

Lord Jesus, you call everyone who does your
   will your brother, sister and mother,
—help us to do what is pleasing to you in word
   and action.

The Lord's Prayer

Our Father, who art in heaven,
hallowed be thy name;
thy kingdom come,
thy will be done
on earth as it is in heaven.
Give us this day our daily bread,
and forgive us our trespasses,
as we forgive those who trespass against us;
and lead us not into temptation,
but deliver us from evil.

Pater noster, qui es in cælis:
sanctificetur nomen tuum;
adveniat regnum tuum;
fiat voluntas tua,
sicut in cælo, et in terra.
Panem nostrum cotidianum da nobis hodie;
et dimitte nobis debita nostra,
sicut et nos dimittimus debitoribus nostris;
et ne nos inducas in tentationem;
sed libera nos a malo.

Concluding Prayer

Father,
your Son first entrusted to Mary Magdalene
the joyful news of his resurrection.
By her prayers and example
may we proclaim Christ as our living Lord
and one day see him in glory,
for he lives and reigns with you and
 the Holy Spirit,
God, for ever and ever.
—Amen.

Dismissal

If praying individually, or in a group without a priest or deacon:

May the Lord + bless us,
protect us from all evil
and bring us to everlasting life.
—Amen.

If praying with a priest or deacon, he dismisses the people:

The Lord be with you.
—And with your spirit.

May almighty God bless you,
the Father, and the Son, ✠ and the Holy Spirit.
—Amen.

Go in peace.
—Thanks be to God.

FOR THE PEACE OF JERUSALEM PRAY: "PEACE BE TO YOUR HOMES! MAY PEACE REIGN IN YOUR WALLS, IN YOUR PALACES, PEACE!"

EVENING PRAYER
BEGINS THE SIXTEENTH SUNDAY IN ORDINARY TIME

God, + come to my assistance.
—Lord, make haste to help me.

Glory to the Father, and to the Son,
 and to the Holy Spirit:
—as it was in the beginning, is now,
 and will be for ever. Amen. Alleluia.

Hymn *Praise to the Lord, the Almighty, p. 696*

Psalmody Ant. 1 **Pray for the peace of Jerusalem.**

Psalm 122

I rejoiced when I heard them say:
"Let us go to God's house."
And now our feet are standing
within your gates, O Jerusalem.

Jerusalem is built as a city
strongly compact.
It is there that the tribes go up,
the tribes of the Lord.

For Israel's law it is,
there to praise the Lord's name.
There were set the thrones of judgment
of the house of David.

For the peace of Jerusalem pray:
"Peace be to your homes!
May peace reign in your walls,
in your palaces, peace!"

For love of my brethren and friends
I say: "Peace upon you!"
For love of the house of the Lord
I will ask for your good.

Glory to the Father, and to the Son,
  and to the Holy Spirit:
as it was in the beginning, is now,
and will be for ever. Amen.

Ant. **Pray for the peace of Jerusalem.**

Ant. 2 **From the morning watch until night, I have waited trustingly for the Lord.**

Psalm 130
Out of the depths I cry to you, O Lord,
Lord, hear my voice!
O let your ears be attentive
to the voice of my pleading.

If you, O Lord, should mark our guilt,
Lord, who would survive?
But with you is found forgiveness:
for this we revere you.

My soul is waiting for the Lord,
I count on his word.
My soul is longing for the Lord
more than watchman for daybreak.
Let the watchman count on daybreak
and Israel on the Lord.

Because with the Lord there is mercy
and fullness of redemption,
Israel indeed he will redeem
from all its iniquity.

Glory to the Father, and to the Son,
 and to the Holy Spirit:
—as it was in the beginning, is now,
and will be for ever. Amen.

Ant. **From the morning watch until night, I have waited trustingly for the Lord.**

Ant. 3 **Let everything in heaven and on earth bend the knee at the name of Jesus.**

Canticle: Philippians 2:6–11

Though he was in the form of God,
Jesus did not deem equality with God
something to be grasped at.

Rather, he emptied himself
and took the form of a slave,
being born in the likeness of men.

He was known to be of human estate,
and it was thus that he humbled himself,
obediently accepting even death,
death on a cross!

Because of this,
God highly exalted him
and bestowed on him the name
above every other name,

So that at Jesus' name
every knee must bend
in the heavens, on the earth,
and under the earth,
and every tongue proclaim
to the glory of God the Father:
JESUS CHRIST IS LORD!

Glory to the Father, and to the Son,
 and to the Holy Spirit:
—as it was in the beginning, is now,
and will be for ever. Amen.

Ant. **Let everything in heaven and on earth bend the knee at the name of Jesus.**

Reading
2 Peter 1:19–21

We possess the prophetic message as something altogether reliable. Keep your attention closely fixed on it, as you would on a lamp shining in a dark place until the first streaks of dawn appear and the morning star rises in your hearts. First you must understand this: there is no prophecy contained in Scripture which is a personal interpretation. Prophecy has never been put forward by man's willing it. It is rather that men impelled by the Holy Spirit have spoken under God's influence.

Responsory

From the rising of the sun to its setting,
may the name of the Lord be praised.
—From the rising of the sun to its setting,
may the name of the Lord be praised.

His splendor reaches far beyond the heavens;
—may the name of the Lord be praised.

Glory to the Father, and to the Son,
  and to the Holy Spirit.
—From the rising of the sun to its setting,
may the name of the Lord be praised.

Gospel Canticle

Ant. **The kingdom of heaven is like yeast which a woman took and kneaded into three measures of flour until all the dough had risen.**

Canticle of Mary
Luke 1:46–55

My + soul proclaims the greatness of the Lord,
my spirit rejoices in God my Savior
for he has looked with favor on his
  lowly servant.

From this day all generations will
  call me blessed:
the Almighty has done great things for me,
and holy is his Name.

He has mercy on those who fear him
in every generation.

He has shown the strength of his arm,
he has scattered the proud in their conceit.

He has cast down the mighty from
  their thrones,
and has lifted up the lowly.

He has filled the hungry with good things,
and the rich he has sent away empty.

He has come to the help of his servant Israel
for he has remembered his promise of mercy,
the promise he made to our fathers,
to Abraham and his children for ever.

Glory to the Father, and to the Son,
   and to the Holy Spirit:
—as it was in the beginning, is now,
and will be for ever. Amen.

Ant. **The kingdom of heaven is like yeast which a woman took and kneaded into three measures of flour until all the dough had risen.**

Intercessions Everyone who waits for the Lord finds joy.
   Now we pray to him:
Look on us with favor, Lord, and hear us.

Faithful witness, firstborn of the dead, you
   washed away our sins in your blood,
—make us always remember your
   wonderful works.

You called men to be heralds of your
   good news,
—make them strong and faithful messengers
   of your kingdom.

King of peace, send your Spirit on the leaders
   of the world,
—turn their eyes toward the poor and suffering.

Protect and defend those who are
    discriminated against because of race,
    color, class, language or religion,
—that they may be accorded the rights and
    dignity which are theirs.

May all who died in your love share in your
    happiness,
—with Mary, our mother, and all your
    holy ones.

The Lord's Prayer

Our Father, who art in heaven,
hallowed be thy name;
thy kingdom come,
thy will be done
on earth as it is in heaven.
Give us this day our daily bread,
and forgive us our trespasses,
as we forgive those who trespass against us;
and lead us not into temptation,
but deliver us from evil.

Pater noster, qui es in cælis:
sanctificetur nomen tuum;
adveniat regnum tuum;
fiat voluntas tua,
sicut in cælo, et in terra.
Panem nostrum cotidianum da nobis hodie;
et dimitte nobis debita nostra,
sicut et nos dimittimus debitoribus nostris;
et ne nos inducas in tentationem;
sed libera nos a malo.

Concluding Prayer

Lord, be merciful to your people.
Fill us with your gifts
and make us always eager to serve you
in faith, hope, and love.
Grant this through our Lord Jesus Christ,
  your Son,
who lives and reigns with you and
  the Holy Spirit,
God, for ever and ever.
—Amen.

Dismissal

If praying individually, or in a group without a priest or deacon:

May the Lord + bless us,
protect us from all evil
and bring us to everlasting life.
—Amen.

If praying with a priest or deacon, he dismisses the people:

The Lord be with you.
—And with your spirit.

May almighty God bless you,
the Father, and the Son, ✚ and the Holy Spirit.
—Amen.

Go in peace.
—Thanks be to God.

NIGHT PRAYER

God, + come to my assistance.
—Lord, make haste to help me.

Glory to the Father, and to the Son,
   and to the Holy Spirit:
—as it was in the beginning, is now,
   and will be for ever. Amen. Alleluia.

Examen *An optional brief examination of conscience may be made. Call to mind your sins and failings this day.*

Hymn *Abide with Me, p. 675*

Psalmody Ant. 1 **Have mercy, Lord, and hear my prayer.**

Psalm 4

When I call, answer me, O God of justice;
from anguish you released me; have mercy
   and hear me!

O men, how long will your hearts be closed,
will you love what is futile and seek
   what is false?

It is the Lord who grants favors to those
   whom he loves;
the Lord hears me whenever I call him.

Fear him; do not sin: ponder on your bed
   and be still.
Make justice your sacrifice and trust
   in the Lord.

"What can bring us happiness?" many say.
Let the light of your face shine on us, O Lord.

You have put into my heart a greater joy
than they have from abundance of corn
    and new wine.

I will lie down in peace and sleep
    comes at once
for you alone, Lord, make me dwell in safety.

Glory to the Father, and to the Son,
    and to the Holy Spirit:
—as it was in the beginning, is now,
and will be for ever. Amen.

Ant. **Have mercy, Lord, and hear my prayer.**

Ant. 2 **In the silent hours of night, bless the Lord.**

Psalm 134

O come, bless the Lord,
all you who serve the Lord,
who stand in the house of the Lord,
in the courts of the house of our God.

Lift up your hands to the holy place
and bless the Lord through the night.

May the Lord bless you from Zion,
he who made both heaven and earth.

Glory to the Father, and to the Son,
    and to the Holy Spirit:
—as it was in the beginning, is now,
and will be for ever. Amen.

Ant. **In the silent hours of night, bless the Lord.**

Reading
Deuteronomy 6:4–7

Hear, O Israel! The Lord is our God, the Lord alone! Therefore, you shall love the Lord, your God, with all your heart, and with all your soul, and with all your strength. Take to heart these words which I enjoin on you today. Drill them into your children. Speak of them at home and abroad, whether you are busy or at rest.

Responsory

Into your hands, Lord, I commend my spirit.
—Into your hands, Lord, I commend my spirit.

You have redeemed us, Lord God of truth.
—I commend my spirit.

Glory to the Father, and to the Son,
  and to the Holy Spirit.
—Into your hands, Lord, I commend my spirit.

Gospel Canticle

Ant. **Protect us, Lord, as we stay awake; watch over us as we sleep, that awake, we may keep watch with Christ, and asleep, rest in his peace.**

Canticle of Simeon
Luke 2:29–32

Lord, + now you let your servant go in peace;
your word has been fulfilled:
my own eyes have seen the salvation
which you have prepared in the sight of
  every people:
a light to reveal you to the nations
and the glory of your people Israel.

Glory to the Father, and to the Son,
   and to the Holy Spirit:
—as it was in the beginning, is now,
and will be for ever. Amen.

Ant. **Protect us, Lord, as we stay awake; watch over us as we sleep, that awake, we may keep watch with Christ, and asleep, rest in his peace.**

Concluding Prayer
Let us pray.
Lord,
be with us throughout this night.
When day comes may we rise from sleep
to rejoice in the resurrection of your Christ,
who lives and reigns for ever and ever.
—Amen.

Blessing
May the all-powerful Lord
grant us a restful night
and a peaceful death.
—Amen.

Marian Antiphon *Sing the "Salve Regina," found on p. 698, or pray a Hail Mary.*

Sunday, July 23, 2023
Sixteenth Sunday in Ordinary Time

MORNING PRAYER

God, + come to my assistance.
—Lord, make haste to help me.

Glory to the Father, and to the Son,
  and to the Holy Spirit:
—as it was in the beginning, is now,
and will be for ever. Amen. Alleluia.

Hymn *This Day the First of Days Was Made, p. 695*

Psalmody Ant. 1 **Praise the Lord, for his loving kindness will never fail, alleluia.**

Psalm 118

Give thanks to the Lord for he is good,
for his love endures forever.

Let the sons of Israel say:
"His love endures for ever."
Let the sons of Aaron say:
"His love endures for ever."
Let those who fear the Lord say:
"His love endures for ever."

I called to the Lord in my distress;
he answered and freed me.
The Lord is at my side; I do not fear.
What can man do against me?
The Lord is at my side as my helper:
I shall look down on my foes.

It is better to take refuge in the Lord
than to trust in men:
it is better to take refuge in the Lord
than to trust in princes.

The nations all encompassed me;
in the Lord's name I crushed them.
They compassed me, compassed me about;
in the Lord's name I crushed them.
They compassed me about like bees;
they blazed like a fire among thorns.
In the Lord's name I crushed them.

I was hard-pressed and was falling,
but the Lord came to help me.
The Lord is my strength and my song;
he is my savior.
There are shouts of joy and victory
in the tents of the just.

The Lord's right hand has triumphed;
his right hand raised me.
The Lord's right hand has triumphed;
I shall not die, I shall live
and recount his deeds.
I was punished, I was punished by the Lord,
but not doomed to die.

Open to me the gates of holiness:
I will enter and give thanks.
This is the Lord's own gate
where the just may enter.
I will thank you for you have answered
and you are my savior.

The stone which the builders rejected
has become the corner stone.
This is the work of the Lord,
a marvel in our eyes.
This day was made by the Lord;
we rejoice and are glad.

O Lord, grant us salvation;
O Lord, grant success.
Blessed in the name of the Lord
is he who comes.
We bless you from the house of the Lord;
the Lord God is our light.

Go forward in procession with branches
even to the altar.
You are my God, I thank you.
My God, I praise you.
Give thanks to the Lord for he is good;
for his love endures for ever.

Glory to the Father, and to the Son,
    and to the Holy Spirit:
as it was in the beginning, is now,
and will be for ever. Amen.

Ant. **Praise the Lord, for his loving kindness will never fail, alleluia.**

Ant. 2 **Alleluia! Bless the Lord, all you works of the Lord, alleluia!**

Canticle:
Daniel 3:52–57

Blessed are you, O Lord, the God of our fathers,
praiseworthy and exalted above all forever.

And blessed is your holy and glorious name,
praiseworthy and exalted above all
    for all ages.

Blessed are you in the temple of your
    holy glory,
praiseworthy and glorious above all forever.

Blessed are you on the throne of
    your kingdom,
praiseworthy and exalted above all forever.

Blessed are you who look into the depths
from your throne upon the cherubim,
praiseworthy and exalted above all forever.

Blessed are you in the firmament of heaven,
praiseworthy and glorious forever.

Bless the Lord, all you works of the Lord,
praise and exalt him above all forever.

Glory to the Father, and to the Son,
    and to the Holy Spirit:
—as it was in the beginning, is now,
and will be for ever. Amen.

Ant. **Alleluia! Bless the Lord, all you works of the Lord, alleluia!**

Ant. 3 **Let everything that breathes give praise to the Lord, alleluia.**

Psalm 150

Praise God in his holy place,
praise him in his mighty heavens.
Praise him for his powerful deeds,
praise his surpassing greatness.

O praise him with sound of trumpet,
praise him with lute and harp.
Praise him with timbrel and dance,
praise him with strings and pipes.

O praise him with resounding cymbals,
praise him with clashing of cymbals.
Let everything that lives and that breathes
give praise to the Lord.

Glory to the Father, and to the Son,
    and to the Holy Spirit:
—as it was in the beginning, is now,
and will be for ever. Amen.

Ant.

Let everything that breathes give praise to the Lord, alleluia.

Reading
2 Timothy 2:8, 11–13

Remember that Jesus Christ, a descendant of David, was raised from the dead. You can depend on this:
    If we have died with him,
        we shall also live with him;
    If we hold out to the end,
        we shall also reign with him.
But if we deny him he will deny us. If we are unfaithful he will still remain faithful, for he cannot deny himself.

Responsory

We give thanks to you, O God,
    as we call upon your name.
—We give thanks to you, O God,
    as we call upon your name.

We cry aloud how marvelous you are,
—as we call upon your name.

Glory to the Father, and to the Son,
    and to the Holy Spirit.
—We give thanks to you, O God,
    as we call upon your name.

Gospel Canticle

Ant. **He saw the great crowd and had pity on them, for they were like sheep without a shepherd.**

Canticle of Zechariah
Luke 1:68–79

Blessed + be the Lord, the God of Israel;
he has come to his people and set them free.

He has raised up for us a mighty savior,
born of the house of his servant David.

Through his holy prophets he
    promised of old
that he would save us from our enemies,
from the hands of all who hate us.

He promised to show mercy to our fathers
and to remember his holy covenant.

This was the oath he swore to our
    father Abraham:
to set us free from the hands of our enemies,
free to worship him without fear,
holy and righteous in his sight
    all the days of our life.

You, my child, shall be called the prophet of
    the Most High;
for you will go before the Lord to
    prepare his way,
to give his people knowledge of salvation
by the forgiveness of their sins.

In the tender compassion of our God
the dawn from on high shall break upon us,
to shine on those who dwell in darkness and
    the shadow of death,
and to guide our feet into the way of peace.

Glory to the Father, and to the Son,
    and to the Holy Spirit:
—as it was in the beginning, is now,
and will be for ever. Amen.

Ant. **He saw the great crowd and had pity on them, for they were like sheep without a shepherd.**

Intercessions Open your hearts to praise the God of power and goodness, for he loves us and knows our needs:
We praise you, Lord, and trust in you.

We bless you, almighty God, King of the
universe, because you called us while we
were yet sinners,
—to acknowledge your truth and to serve
your majesty.

O God, you opened the gates of mercy for us,
—let us never turn aside from the path of life.

As we celebrate the resurrection of your
beloved Son,
—help us to spend this day in the spirit of joy.

Give to your faithful, O Lord, a prayerful
spirit of gratitude,
—that we may thank you for all your gifts.

The Lord's Prayer Our Father, who art in heaven,
hallowed be thy name;
thy kingdom come,
thy will be done
on earth as it is in heaven.
Give us this day our daily bread,
and forgive us our trespasses,
as we forgive those who trespass against us;
and lead us not into temptation,
but deliver us from evil.

Pater noster, qui es in cælis:
sanctificetur nomen tuum;
adveniat regnum tuum;
fiat voluntas tua,
sicut in cælo, et in terra.
Panem nostrum cotidianum da nobis hodie;
et dimitte nobis debita nostra,
sicut et nos dimittimus debitoribus nostris;
et ne nos inducas in tentationem;
sed libera nos a malo.

Concluding Prayer

Lord, be merciful to your people.
Fill us with your gifts
and make us always eager to serve you
in faith, hope, and love.
Grant this through our Lord Jesus Christ,
    your Son,
who lives and reigns with you and
    the Holy Spirit,
God, for ever and ever.
—Amen.

Dismissal

If praying individually, or in a group without a priest or deacon:

May the Lord ✚ bless us,
protect us from all evil
and bring us to everlasting life.
—Amen.

If praying with a priest or deacon, he dismisses the people:

The Lord be with you.
—And with your spirit.

May almighty God bless you,
the Father, and the Son, ✚ and the Holy Spirit.
—Amen.

Go in peace.
—Thanks be to God.

EVENING PRAYER ─────────────

God, + come to my assistance.
—Lord, make haste to help me.

Glory to the Father, and to the Son,
 and to the Holy Spirit:
—as it was in the beginning, is now,
and will be for ever. Amen. Alleluia.

Hymn *Holy God, We Praise Thy Name, p. 686*

Psalmody Ant. 1 **In eternal splendor, before the dawn of light on earth, I have begotten you, alleluia.**

Psalm 110:1–5, 7 The Lord's revelation to my Master:
 "Sit on my right:
 your foes I will put beneath your feet."

The Lord will wield from Zion
your scepter of power:
rule in the midst of all your foes.

A prince from the day of your birth
on the holy mountains;
from the womb before the dawn I begot you.

The Lord has sworn an oath he will
 not change.
"You are a priest for ever,
a priest like Melchizedek of old."

The Master standing at your right hand
will shatter kings in the day of his
    great wrath.

He shall drink from the stream by
    the wayside
and therefore he shall lift up his head.

Glory to the Father, and to the Son,
    and to the Holy Spirit:
as it was in the beginning, is now,
and will be for ever. Amen.

Ant. **In eternal splendor, before the dawn of light on earth, I have begotten you, alleluia.**

Ant. 2 **Blessed are they who hunger and thirst for holiness; they will be satisfied.**

Psalm 112

Happy the man who fears the Lord,
who takes delight in all his commands.
His sons will be powerful on earth;
the children of the upright are blessed.

Riches and wealth are in his house;
his justice stands firm for ever.
He is a light in the darkness for the upright:
he is generous, merciful and just.

The good man takes pity and lends,
he conducts his affairs with honor.
The just man will never waver:
he will be remembered for ever.

He has no fear of evil news;
with a firm heart he trusts in the Lord.
With a steadfast heart he will not fear;
he will see the downfall of his foes.

Open-handed, he gives to the poor;
his justice stands firm for ever.
His head will be raised in glory.

The wicked man sees and is angry,
grinds his teeth and fades away;
the desire of the wicked leads to doom.

Glory to the Father, and to the Son,
    and to the Holy Spirit:
—as it was in the beginning, is now,
and will be for ever. Amen.

Ant. **Blessed are they who hunger and thirst for holiness; they will be satisfied.**

Ant. 3 **Praise God, all you who serve him, both great and small, alleluia.**

Canticle: See Revelation 19:1–7

Alleluia.
Salvation, glory, and power to our God:
his judgments are honest and true.
Alleluia.

Alleluia.
Sing praise to our God, all you his servants,
all who worship him reverently,
    great and small.
Alleluia.

Alleluia.
The Lord our all-powerful God is King;
let us rejoice, sing praise, and give him glory.
Alleluia.

Alleluia.
The wedding feast of the Lamb has begun,
and his bride is prepared to welcome him.
Alleluia.

Alleluia.
Glory to the Father, and to the Son,
and to the Holy Spirit:
Alleluia.

Alleluia.
as it was in the beginning, is now,
and will be for ever. Amen.
Alleluia.

Ant. **Praise God, all you who serve him, both great and small, alleluia.**

Reading
Hebrews 12:22–24

You have drawn near to Mount Zion and the city of the living God, the heavenly Jerusalem, to myriads of angels in festal gathering, to the assembly of the first-born enrolled in heaven, to God the judge of all, to the spirits of just men made perfect, to Jesus, the mediator of a new covenant, and to the sprinkled blood which speaks more eloquently than that of Abel.

Responsory Our Lord is great, mighty is his power.
—Our Lord is great, mighty is his power.

His wisdom is beyond compare,
—mighty is his power.

Glory to the Father, and to the Son,
 and to the Holy Spirit.
—Our Lord is great, mighty is his power.

Gospel Canticle Ant. **Mary has chosen the better part, and it shall not be taken from her.**

Canticle of Mary
Luke 1:46–55

My + soul proclaims the greatness of the Lord,
my spirit rejoices in God my Savior
for he has looked with favor on his
 lowly servant.

From this day all generations will
 call me blessed:
the Almighty has done great things for me,
and holy is his Name.

He has mercy on those who fear him
in every generation.

He has shown the strength of his arm,
he has scattered the proud in their conceit.

He has cast down the mighty from
 their thrones,
and has lifted up the lowly.

He has filled the hungry with good things,
and the rich he has sent away empty.

He has come to the help of his servant Israel
for he has remembered his promise of mercy,
the promise he made to our fathers,
to Abraham and his children for ever.

Glory to the Father, and to the Son,
   and to the Holy Spirit:
—as it was in the beginning, is now,
and will be for ever. Amen.

Ant. **Mary has chosen the better part, and it shall not be taken from her.**

Intercessions Rejoicing in the Lord, from whom all good things come, let us pray:
Lord, hear our prayer.

Father and Lord of all, you sent your Son into the world, that your name might be glorified in every place,
—strengthen the witness of your Church among the nations.

Make us obedient to the teachings of your apostles,
—and bound to the truth of our faith.

As you love the innocent,
—render justice to those who are wronged.

Free those in bondage and give sight to
   the blind,
—raise up the fallen and protect the stranger.

Fulfill your promise to those who already
   sleep in your peace,
—through your Son grant them a blessed
   resurrection.

The Lord's Prayer

Our Father, who art in heaven,
hallowed be thy name;
thy kingdom come,
thy will be done
on earth as it is in heaven.
Give us this day our daily bread,
and forgive us our trespasses,
as we forgive those who trespass against us;
and lead us not into temptation,
but deliver us from evil.

Pater noster, qui es in cælis:
sanctificetur nomen tuum;
adveniat regnum tuum;
fiat voluntas tua,
sicut in cælo, et in terra.
Panem nostrum cotidianum da nobis hodie;
et dimitte nobis debita nostra,
sicut et nos dimittimus debitoribus nostris;
et ne nos inducas in tentationem;
sed libera nos a malo.

Concluding Prayer

Lord, be merciful to your people.
Fill us with your gifts
and make us always eager to serve you
in faith, hope, and love.
Grant this through our Lord Jesus Christ,
   your Son,
who lives and reigns with you and
   the Holy Spirit,
God, for ever and ever.
—Amen.

Dismissal

If praying individually, or in a group without a priest or deacon:

May the Lord ✛ bless us,
protect us from all evil
and bring us to everlasting life.
—Amen.

If praying with a priest or deacon, he dismisses the people:

The Lord be with you.
—And with your spirit.

May almighty God bless you,
the Father, and the Son, ✛ and the Holy Spirit.
—Amen.

Go in peace.
—Thanks be to God.

NIGHT PRAYER

God, + come to my assistance.
—Lord, make haste to help me.

Glory to the Father, and to the Son,
 and to the Holy Spirit:
—as it was in the beginning, is now,
 and will be for ever. Amen. Alleluia.

Examen *An optional brief examination of conscience may be made. Call to mind your sins and failings this day.*

Hymn *Before the Final Light of Day, p. 676*

Psalmody Ant. **Night holds no terrors for me sleeping under God's wings.**

Psalm 91
He who dwells in the shelter of the Most High
and abides in the shade of the Almighty
says to the Lord: "My refuge,
my stronghold, my God in whom I trust!"

It is he who will free you from the snare
of the fowler who seeks to destroy you;
he will conceal you with his pinions
and under his wings you will find refuge.

You will not fear the terror of the night
nor the arrow that flies by day,
nor the plague that prowls in the darkness
nor the scourge that lays waste at noon.

A thousand may fall at your side,
ten thousand fall at your right,
you, it will never approach;
his faithfulness is buckler and shield.

Your eyes have only to look
to see how the wicked are repaid,
you who have said: "Lord, my refuge!"
and have made the Most High your dwelling.

Upon you no evil shall fall,
no plague approach where you dwell.
For you has he commanded his angels,
to keep you in all your ways.

They shall bear you upon their hands
lest you strike your foot against a stone.
On the lion and the viper you will tread
and trample the young lion and the dragon.

Since he clings to me in love, I will free him;
protect him for he knows my name.
When he calls I shall answer: "I am with you."
I will save him in distress and give him glory.

With length of life I will content him;
I shall let him see my saving power.

Glory to the Father, and to the Son,
    and to the Holy Spirit:
—as it was in the beginning, is now,
and will be for ever. Amen.

Ant. **Night holds no terrors for me sleeping under God's wings.**

Reading
Revelation 22:4–5

They shall see the Lord face to face and bear his name on their foreheads. The night shall be no more. They will need no light from lamps or the sun, for the Lord God shall give them light, and they shall reign forever.

Responsory

Into your hands, Lord, I commend my spirit.
—Into your hands, Lord, I commend my spirit.

You have redeemed us, Lord God of truth.
—I commend my spirit.

Glory to the Father, and to the Son,
    and to the Holy Spirit.
—Into your hands, Lord, I commend my spirit.

Gospel Canticle

Ant. **Protect us, Lord, as we stay awake; watch over us as we sleep, that awake, we may keep watch with Christ, and asleep, rest in his peace.**

Canticle of Simeon
Luke 2:29–32

Lord, + now you let your servant go in peace;
your word has been fulfilled:
my own eyes have seen the salvation
which you have prepared in the sight of
    every people:
a light to reveal you to the nations
and the glory of your people Israel.

Glory to the Father, and to the Son,
    and to the Holy Spirit:
—as it was in the beginning, is now,
    and will be for ever. Amen.

Ant. **Protect us, Lord, as we stay awake; watch over us as we sleep, that awake, we may keep watch with Christ, and asleep, rest in his peace.**

Concluding Prayer
Let us pray.
Lord,
we have celebrated today
the mystery of the rising of Christ to new life.
May we now rest in your peace,
safe from all that could harm us,
and rise again refreshed and joyful,
to praise you throughout another day.
We ask this through Christ our Lord.
—Amen.

Blessing
May the all-powerful Lord
grant us a restful night
and a peaceful death.
—Amen.

Marian Antiphon
Sing the "Salve Regina," found on p. 698, or pray a Hail Mary.

MAKE US KNOW
THE SHORTNESS
OF OUR LIFE
THAT WE MAY
GAIN WISDOM
OF HEART.

Monday, July 24, 2023
Monday of the Sixteenth Week in Ordinary Time

MORNING PRAYER

God, + come to my assistance.
—Lord, make haste to help me.

Glory to the Father, and to the Son,
   and to the Holy Spirit:
—as it was in the beginning, is now,
and will be for ever. Amen. Alleluia.

Hymn   *The Heavens Declare Your Glory, p. 704*

Psalmody   Ant. 1 **Each morning, Lord, you fill us with your kindness.**

Psalm 90

O Lord, you have been our refuge
from one generation to the next.
Before the mountains were born
or the earth or the world brought forth,
you are God, without beginning or end.

You turn men back to dust
and say: "Go back, sons of men."
To your eyes a thousand years
are like yesterday, come and gone,
no more than a watch in the night.

You sweep men away like a dream,
like the grass which springs up in
   the morning.
In the morning it springs up and flowers:
by evening it withers and fades.

So we are destroyed in your anger,
struck with terror in your fury.
Our guilt lies open before you;
our secrets in the light of your face.

All our days pass away in your anger.
Our life is over like a sigh.
Our span is seventy years
or eighty for those who are strong.

And most of these are emptiness and pain.
They pass swiftly and we are gone.
Who understands the power of your anger
and fears the strength of your fury?

Make us know the shortness of our life
that we may gain wisdom of heart.
Lord, relent! Is your anger for ever?
Show pity to your servants.

In the morning, fill us with your love;
we shall exult and rejoice all our days.
Give us joy to balance our affliction
for the years when we knew misfortune.

Show forth your work to your servants;
let your glory shine on their children.
Let the favor of the Lord be upon us:
give success to the work of our hands,
give success to the work of our hands.

Glory to the Father, and to the Son,
    and to the Holy Spirit:
—as it was in the beginning, is now,
and will be for ever. Amen.

Ant. **Each morning, Lord, you fill us with your kindness.**

Ant. 2 **From the farthest bounds of earth, may God be praised!**

Canticle:
Isaiah 42:10–16

Sing to the Lord a new song,
his praise from the end of the earth:

Let the sea and what fills it resound,
the coastlands, and those who dwell in them.
Let the steppe and its cities cry out,
the villages where Kedar dwells;

Let the inhabitants of Sela exult,
and shout from the top of the mountains.
Let them give glory to the Lord,
and utter his praise in the coastlands.

The Lord goes forth like a hero,
like a warrior he stirs up his ardor;
he shouts out his battle cry,
against his enemies he shows his might:

I have looked away, and kept silence,
I have said nothing, holding myself in;
but now, I cry out as a woman in labor,
gasping and panting.

I will lay waste mountains and hills,
all their herbage I will dry up;
I will turn the rivers into marshes,
and the marshes I will dry up.

I will lead the blind on their journey;
by paths unknown I will guide them.
I will turn darkness into light before them,
and make crooked ways straight.

Glory to the Father, and to the Son,
 and to the Holy Spirit:
as it was in the beginning, is now,
and will be for ever. Amen.

Ant. **From the farthest bounds of earth, may God be praised!**

Ant. 3 **You who stand in his sanctuary, praise the name of the Lord.**

Psalm 135:1-12

Praise the name of the Lord,
praise him, servants of the Lord,
who stand in the house of the Lord,
in the courts of the house of our God.

Praise the Lord for the Lord is good.
Sing a psalm to his name for he is loving.
For the Lord has chosen Jacob for himself
and Israel for his own possession.

For I know the Lord is great,
that our Lord is high above all gods.
The Lord does whatever he wills,
in heaven, on earth, in the seas.

He summons clouds from the ends of
 the earth;
makes lightning produce the rain;
from his treasuries he sends forth the wind.

The first-born of the Egyptians he smote,
of man and beast alike.
Signs and wonders he worked
in the midst of your land, O Egypt,
against Pharaoh and all his servants.

Nations in their greatness he struck
and kings in their splendor he slew.
Sihon, king of the Amorites,
Og, the king of Bashan,
and all the kingdoms of Canaan.
He let Israel inherit their land;
on his people their land he bestowed.

Glory to the Father, and to the Son,
   and to the Holy Spirit:
as it was in the beginning, is now,
and will be for ever. Amen.

Ant. **You who stand in his sanctuary, praise the name of the Lord.**

Reading
Judith 8:25–27

We should be grateful to the Lord our God, for putting us to the test, as he did our forefathers. Recall how he dealt with Abraham, and how he tried Isaac, and all that happened to Jacob in Syrian Mesopotamia while he was tending the flocks of Laban, his mother's brother. Not for vengeance did the Lord put them in the crucible to try their hearts, nor has he done so with us. It is by way of admonition that he chastises those who are close to him.

Responsory Sing for joy, God's chosen ones,
　　give him the praise that is due.
—Sing for joy, God's chosen ones,
　　give him the praise that is due.

Sing a new song to the Lord;
—give him the praise that is due.

Glory to the Father, and to the Son,
　　and to the Holy Spirit.
—Sing for joy, God's chosen ones,
　　give him the praise that is due.

Gospel Canticle Ant. **Blessed be the Lord, for he has come to his people and set them free.**

Canticle of Zechariah
Luke 1:68–79

Blessed + be the Lord, the God of Israel;
he has come to his people and set them free.

He has raised up for us a mighty savior,
born of the house of his servant David.

Through his holy prophets he
　　promised of old
that he would save us from our enemies,
from the hands of all who hate us.

He promised to show mercy to our fathers
and to remember his holy covenant.

This was the oath he swore to our
>father Abraham:
to set us free from the hands of our enemies,
free to worship him without fear,
holy and righteous in his sight
>all the days of our life.

You, my child, shall be called the prophet of
>the Most High;
for you will go before the Lord to
>prepare his way,
to give his people knowledge of salvation
by the forgiveness of their sins.

In the tender compassion of our God
the dawn from on high shall break upon us,
to shine on those who dwell in darkness and
>the shadow of death,
and to guide our feet into the way of peace.

Glory to the Father, and to the Son,
>and to the Holy Spirit:
—as it was in the beginning, is now,
and will be for ever. Amen.

Ant. **Blessed be the Lord, for he has come to his people and set them free.**

Intercessions Because Christ hears and saves those who
>hope in him, let us pray:
We praise you, Lord, we hope in you.

We thank you because you are rich in mercy,
—and for the abundant love with which you
>have loved us.

With the Father you are always at work in
 the world,
—make all things new through the power of
 your Holy Spirit.

Open our eyes and the eyes of our brothers,
—to see your wonders this day.

You call us today to your service,
—make us stewards of your many gifts.

The Lord's Prayer

Our Father, who art in heaven,
hallowed be thy name;
thy kingdom come,
thy will be done
on earth as it is in heaven.
Give us this day our daily bread,
and forgive us our trespasses,
as we forgive those who trespass against us;
and lead us not into temptation,
but deliver us from evil.

Pater noster, qui es in cælis:
sanctificetur nomen tuum;
adveniat regnum tuum;
fiat voluntas tua,
sicut in cælo, et in terra.
Panem nostrum cotidianum da nobis hodie;
et dimitte nobis debita nostra,
sicut et nos dimittimus debitoribus nostris;
et ne nos inducas in tentationem;
sed libera nos a malo.

Concluding Prayer

God our creator,
    you gave us the earth to cultivate
    and the sun to serve our needs.
    Help us to spend this day
    for your glory and our neighbor's good.
    We ask this through our Lord Jesus Christ,
        your Son,
    who lives and reigns with you and
        the Holy Spirit,
    God, for ever and ever.
—Amen.

Dismissal

If praying individually, or in a group without a priest or deacon:

May the Lord + bless us,
protect us from all evil
and bring us to everlasting life.
—Amen.

If praying with a priest or deacon, he dismisses the people:

The Lord be with you.
—And with your spirit.

May almighty God bless you,
the Father, and the Son, ✢ and the Holy Spirit.
—Amen.

Go in peace.
—Thanks be to God.

EVENING PRAYER — MON JULY 24

EVENING PRAYER ———————————

God, +come to my assistance.
—Lord, make haste to help me.

Glory to the Father, and to the Son,
    and to the Holy Spirit:
—as it was in the beginning, is now,
    and will be for ever. Amen. Alleluia.

Hymn   *Immortal, Invisible, God Only Wise, p. 688*

Psalmody   Ant. 1 **Give thanks to the Lord, for his great love is without end.**

Psalm 136

O give thanks to the Lord for he is good,
    for his love endures for ever.
Give thanks to the God of gods,
    for his love endures for ever.
Give thanks to the Lord of lords,
    for his love endures for ever;

who alone has wrought marvelous works,
    for his love endures for ever;
whose wisdom it was made the skies,
    for his love endures for ever;
who fixed the earth firmly on the seas,
    for his love endures for ever.

It was he who made the great lights,
    for his love endures for ever,
the sun to rule in the day,
    for his love endures for ever,
the moon and the stars in the night,
    for his love endures for ever.

Glory to the Father, and to the Son,
   and to the Holy Spirit:
—as it was in the beginning, is now,
and will be for ever. Amen.

Ant. **Give thanks to the Lord, for his great love is without end.**

Ant. 2 **Great and wonderful are your deeds, Lord God the Almighty.**

Psalm 136
(continued)

The first-born of the Egyptians he smote,
for his love endures for ever.
He brought Israel out from their midst,
for his love endures for ever;
arm outstretched, with power in his hand,
for his love endures for ever.

He divided the Red Sea in two,
for his love endures for ever;
he made Israel pass through the midst,
for his love endures for ever;
he flung Pharaoh and his force in the sea,
for his love endures for ever.

Through the desert his people he led,
for his love endures for ever.
Nations in their greatness he struck,
for his love endures for ever.
Kings in their splendor he slew,
for his love endures for ever.

Sihon, king of the Amorites,
for his love endures for ever;
and Og, the king of Bashan,
for his love endures for ever.

He let Israel inherit their land,
for his love endures for ever.
On his servant their land he bestowed,
for his love endures for ever.
He remembered us in our distress,
for his love endures for ever.

And he snatched us away from our foes,
for his love endures for ever.
He gives food to all living things,
for his love endures for ever.
To the God of heaven give thanks,
for his love endures for ever.

Glory to the Father, and to the Son,
  and to the Holy Spirit:
—as it was in the beginning, is now,
and will be for ever. Amen.

Ant. **Great and wonderful are your deeds, Lord God the Almighty.**

Ant. 3 **God planned in the fullness of time to restore all things in Christ.**

Canticle:
Ephesians 1:3–10

Praised be the God and Father
of our Lord Jesus Christ,
who has bestowed on us in Christ
every spiritual blessing in the heavens.

God chose us in him
before the world began
to be holy
and blameless in his sight.

He predestined us
to be his adopted sons through Jesus Christ,
such was his will and pleasure,
that all might praise the glorious favor
he has bestowed on us in his beloved.

In him and through his blood, we have
    been redeemed,
and our sins forgiven,
so immeasurably generous
is God's favor to us.

God has given us the wisdom
to understand fully the mystery,
the plan he was pleased
to decree in Christ.

A plan to be carried out
in Christ, in the fullness of time,
to bring all things into one in him,
in the heavens and on earth.

Glory to the Father, and to the Son,
    and to the Holy Spirit:
—as it was in the beginning, is now,
    and will be for ever. Amen.

Ant. **God planned in the fullness of time to restore all things in Christ.**

Reading
1 Thessalonians 3:12–13

May the Lord increase you and make you overflow with love for one another and for all, even as our love does for you. May he strengthen your hearts, making them blameless and holy before our God and Father at the coming of our Lord Jesus Christ with all his holy ones.

Responsory

Accept my prayer, O Lord,
   which rises up to you.
—Accept my prayer, O Lord,
   which rises up to you.

Like burning incense in your sight,
—which rises up to you.

Glory to the Father, and to the Son,
   and to the Holy Spirit.
—Accept my prayer, O Lord,
   which rises up to you.

Gospel Canticle

Ant. **For ever will my soul proclaim the greatness of the Lord.**

Canticle of Mary
Luke 1:46–55

My + soul proclaims the greatness of the Lord,
my spirit rejoices in God my Savior
for he has looked with favor on his
   lowly servant.

From this day all generations will
   call me blessed:
the Almighty has done great things for me,
and holy is his Name.

He has mercy on those who fear him
in every generation.

He has shown the strength of his arm,
he has scattered the proud in their conceit.

He has cast down the mighty from
   their thrones,
and has lifted up the lowly.

He has filled the hungry with good things,
and the rich he has sent away empty.

He has come to the help of his servant Israel
for he has remembered his promise of mercy,
the promise he made to our fathers,
to Abraham and his children for ever.

Glory to the Father, and to the Son,
   and to the Holy Spirit:
—as it was in the beginning, is now,
and will be for ever. Amen.

Ant. **For ever will my soul proclaim the greatness of the Lord.**

Intercessions Jesus does not abandon those who hope in him; therefore, let us humbly ask him:
Our Lord and our God, hear us.

Christ our light, brighten your Church with your splendor,
—so that it may be for the nations the great sacrament of your love.

Watch over the priests and ministers of
 your Church,
—so that after they have preached to others,
 they themselves may remain faithful in
 your service.

Through your blood you gave peace to
 the world,
—turn away the sin of strife, the scourge of war.

O Lord, help married couples with an
 abundance of your grace,
—so that they may better symbolize the
 mystery of your Church.

In your mercy forgive the sins of all the dead,
—that they may live with your saints.

The Lord's Prayer

Our Father, who art in heaven,
hallowed be thy name;
thy kingdom come,
thy will be done
on earth as it is in heaven.
Give us this day our daily bread,
and forgive us our trespasses,
as we forgive those who trespass against us;
and lead us not into temptation,
but deliver us from evil.

Pater noster, qui es in cælis:
sanctificetur nomen tuum;
adveniat regnum tuum;
fiat voluntas tua,
sicut in cælo, et in terra.
Panem nostrum cotidianum da nobis hodie;
et dimitte nobis debita nostra,
sicut et nos dimittimus debitoribus nostris;
et ne nos inducas in tentationem;
sed libera nos a malo.

Concluding Prayer

Stay with us, Lord Jesus,
for evening draws near,
and be our companion on our way
to set our hearts on fire with new hope.
Help us to recognize your presence among us
in the Scriptures we read,
and in the breaking of bread,
for you live and reign with the Father and
 the Holy Spirit,
God, for ever and ever.
—Amen.

Dismissal

If praying individually, or in a group without a priest or deacon:

May the Lord + bless us,
protect us from all evil
and bring us to everlasting life.
—Amen.

If praying with a priest or deacon, he dismisses the people:

The Lord be with you.
—And with your spirit.

May almighty God bless you,
the Father, and the Son, ✚ and the Holy Spirit.
—Amen.

Go in peace.
—Thanks be to God.

NIGHT PRAYER

God, + come to my assistance.
—Lord, make haste to help me.

Glory to the Father, and to the Son,
 and to the Holy Spirit:
—as it was in the beginning, is now,
and will be for ever. Amen. Alleluia.

Examen *An optional brief examination of conscience may be made. Call to mind your sins and failings this day.*

Hymn *O Joyful Light of God Most High, p. 693*

Psalmody Ant. **O Lord, our God, unwearied is your love for us.**

Psalm 86 Turn your ear, O Lord, and give answer
for I am poor and needy.
Preserve my life, for I am faithful:
save the servant who trusts in you.

You are my God; have mercy on me, Lord,
for I cry to you all day long.
Give joy to your servant, O Lord,
for to you I lift up my soul.

O Lord, you are good and forgiving,
full of love to all who call.
Give heed, O Lord, to my prayer
and attend to the sound of my voice.

In the day of distress I will call
and surely you will reply.
Among the gods there is none like you,
    O Lord;
nor work to compare with yours.

All the nations shall come to adore you
and glorify your name, O Lord:
for you are great and do marvelous deeds,
you who alone are God.

Show me, Lord, your way
so that I may walk in your truth.
Guide my heart to fear your name.

I will praise you, Lord my God, with
    all my heart
and glorify your name for ever;
for your love to me has been great:
you have saved me from the depths of
    the grave.

The proud have risen against me;
ruthless men seek my life:
to you they pay no heed.

But you, God of mercy and compassion,
slow to anger, O Lord,
abounding in love and truth,
turn and take pity on me.

O give your strength to your servant
and save your handmaid's son.
Show me a sign of your favor
that my foes may see to their shame
that you console me and give me your help.

Glory to the Father, and to the Son,
    and to the Holy Spirit:
—as it was in the beginning, is now,
and will be for ever. Amen.

Ant. **O Lord, our God, unwearied is your love for us.**

Reading
1 Thessalonians 5:9–10

God has destined us for acquiring salvation through our Lord Jesus Christ. He died for us, that all of us, whether awake or asleep, together might live with him.

Responsory

Into your hands, Lord, I commend my spirit.
—Into your hands, Lord, I commend my spirit.

You have redeemed us, Lord God of truth.
—I commend my spirit.

Glory to the Father, and to the Son,
    and to the Holy Spirit.
—Into your hands, Lord, I commend my spirit.

Gospel Canticle

Ant. **Protect us, Lord, as we stay awake; watch over us as we sleep, that awake, we may keep watch with Christ, and asleep, rest in his peace.**

Canticle of Simeon
Luke 2:29–32

Lord, + now you let your servant go in peace;
your word has been fulfilled:
my own eyes have seen the salvation
which you have prepared in the sight of
    every people:
a light to reveal you to the nations
and the glory of your people Israel.

Glory to the Father, and to the Son,
    and to the Holy Spirit:
—as it was in the beginning, is now,
and will be for ever. Amen.

Ant. **Protect us, Lord, as we stay awake; watch over us as we sleep, that awake, we may keep watch with Christ, and asleep, rest in his peace.**

Concluding Prayer

Let us pray.
Lord,
give our bodies restful sleep
and let the work we have done today
bear fruit in eternal life.
We ask this through Christ our Lord.
—Amen.

Blessing

May the all-powerful Lord
grant us a restful night
and a peaceful death.
—Amen.

Marian Antiphon

Sing the "Salve Regina," found on p. 698, or pray a Hail Mary.

Tuesday, July 25, 2023
St. James

MORNING PRAYER

God, + come to my assistance.
—Lord, make haste to help me.

Glory to the Father, and to the Son,
 and to the Holy Spirit:
—as it was in the beginning, is now,
 and will be for ever. Amen. Alleluia.

Hymn — *Let All on Earth Their Voices Raise, p. 690*

Psalmody — **Ant. 1 As he was walking along, Jesus saw James, the son of Zebedee, and his brother John, and he called them.**

Psalm 63:2–9

O God, you are my God, for you I long;
for you my soul is thirsting.
My body pines for you
like a dry, weary land without water.
So I gaze on you in the sanctuary
to see your strength and your glory.

For your love is better than life,
my lips will speak your praise.
So I will bless you all my life,
in your name I will lift up my hands.
My soul shall be filled as with a banquet,
my mouth shall praise you with joy.

On my bed I remember you.
On you I muse through the night
for you have been my help;
in the shadow of your wings I rejoice.
My soul clings to you;
your right hand holds me fast.

Glory to the Father, and to the Son,
    and to the Holy Spirit:
as it was in the beginning, is now,
and will be for ever. Amen.

Ant. **As he was walking along, Jesus saw James, the son of Zebedee, and his brother John, and he called them.**

Ant. 2 **Immediately they left their nets and their father and followed him.**

Canticle: Daniel 3:57–88, 56

Bless the Lord, all you works of the Lord.
Praise and exalt him above all forever.
Angels of the Lord, bless the Lord.
You heavens, bless the Lord.
All you waters above the heavens,
    bless the Lord.
All you hosts of the Lord, bless the Lord.
Sun and moon, bless the Lord.
Stars of heaven, bless the Lord.

Every shower and dew, bless the Lord.
All you winds, bless the Lord.
Fire and heat, bless the Lord.
Cold and chill, bless the Lord.
Dew and rain, bless the Lord.
Frost and chill, bless the Lord.
Ice and snow, bless the Lord.
Nights and days, bless the Lord.
Light and darkness, bless the Lord.
Lightnings and clouds, bless the Lord.

Let the earth bless the Lord.
Praise and exalt him above all forever.
Mountains and hills, bless the Lord.
Everything growing from the earth,
    bless the Lord.
You springs, bless the Lord.
Seas and rivers, bless the Lord.
You dolphins and all water creatures,
    bless the Lord.
All you birds of the air, bless the Lord.
All you beasts, wild and tame, bless the Lord.
You sons of men, bless the Lord.

O Israel, bless the Lord.
Praise and exalt him above all forever.
Priests of the Lord, bless the Lord.
Servants of the Lord, bless the Lord.
Spirits and souls of the just, bless the Lord.
Holy men of humble heart, bless the Lord.
Hananiah, Azariah, Mishael, bless the Lord.
Praise and exalt him above all forever.

Let us bless the Father, and the Son,
   and the Holy Spirit.
Let us praise and exalt him above all forever.
Blessed are you, Lord, in the firmament
   of heaven.
Praiseworthy and glorious and exalted above
   all forever.

Ant. **Immediately they left their nets and their father and followed him.**

Ant. 3 **You shall drink from the cup that I shall drink from and you shall be baptized as I am baptized.**

Psalm 149

Sing a new song to the Lord,
his praise in the assembly of the faithful.
Let Israel rejoice in its maker,
let Zion's sons exult in their king.
Let them praise his name with dancing
and make music with timbrel and harp.

For the Lord takes delight in his people.
He crowns the poor with salvation.
Let the faithful rejoice in their glory,
shout for joy and take their rest.
Let the praise of God be on their lips
and a two-edged sword in their hand,

to deal out vengeance to the nations
and punishment on all the peoples;
to bind their kings in chains
and their nobles in fetters of iron;
to carry out the sentence pre-ordained;
this honor is for all his faithful.

Glory to the Father, and to the Son,
    and to the Holy Spirit:
—as it was in the beginning, is now,
and will be for ever. Amen.

Ant. **You shall drink from the cup that I shall drink from and you shall be baptized as I am baptized.**

Reading
Ephesians 2:19–22

You are strangers and aliens no longer. No, you are fellow citizens of the saints and members of the household of God. You form a building which rises on the foundation of the apostles and prophets, with Christ Jesus himself as the capstone. Through him the whole structure is fitted together and takes shape as a holy temple in the Lord; in him you are being built into this temple, to become a dwelling place for God in the Spirit.

Responsory
You have made them rulers over all the earth.
—You have made them rulers over all the earth.

They will always remember your name, O Lord,
—over all the earth.

Glory to the Father, and to the Son,
    and to the Holy Spirit.
—You have made them rulers over all the earth.

Gospel Canticle

Ant. **Jesus took Peter, James and his brother John and led them up a high mountain where they could be alone, and he was transfigured before them.**

Canticle of Zechariah
Luke 1:68–79

Blessed + be the Lord, the God of Israel;
he has come to his people and set them free.

He has raised up for us a mighty savior,
born of the house of his servant David.

Through his holy prophets he
    promised of old
that he would save us from our enemies,
from the hands of all who hate us.

He promised to show mercy to our fathers
and to remember his holy covenant.

This was the oath he swore to our
    father Abraham:
to set us free from the hands of our enemies,
free to worship him without fear,
holy and righteous in his sight
    all the days of our life.

You, my child, shall be called the prophet of
    the Most High;
for you will go before the Lord to
    prepare his way,
to give his people knowledge of salvation
by the forgiveness of their sins.

In the tender compassion of our God
the dawn from on high shall break upon us,
to shine on those who dwell in darkness and
    the shadow of death,
and to guide our feet into the way of peace.

Glory to the Father, and to the Son,
   and to the Holy Spirit:
— as it was in the beginning, is now,
   and will be for ever. Amen.

Ant. **Jesus took Peter, James and his brother John and led them up a high mountain where they could be alone, and he was transfigured before them.**

Intercessions

Beloved friends, we have inherited heaven along with the apostles. Let us give thanks to the Father for all his gifts:
The company of apostles praises you, O Lord.

Praise be to you, Lord, for the banquet of Christ's body and blood given us through the apostles,
— which refreshes us and gives us life.

Praise be to you, Lord, for the feast of your word prepared for us by the apostles,
— giving us light and joy.

Praise be to you, Lord, for your holy Church, founded on the apostles,
— where we are gathered together into your community.

Praise be to you, Lord, for the cleansing power of baptism and penance that you have entrusted to your apostles,
— through which we are cleansed of our sins.

JULY 25 TUE MORNING PRAYER

The Lord's Prayer

Our Father, who art in heaven,
hallowed be thy name;
thy kingdom come,
thy will be done
on earth as it is in heaven.
Give us this day our daily bread,
and forgive us our trespasses,
as we forgive those who trespass against us;
and lead us not into temptation,
but deliver us from evil.

Pater noster, qui es in cælis:
sanctificetur nomen tuum;
adveniat regnum tuum;
fiat voluntas tua,
sicut in cælo, et in terra.
Panem nostrum cotidianum da nobis hodie;
et dimitte nobis debita nostra,
sicut et nos dimittimus debitoribus nostris;
et ne nos inducas in tentationem;
sed libera nos a malo.

Concluding Prayer

Almighty Father,
by the martyrdom of Saint James
you blessed the work of the early Church.
May his profession of faith give us courage
and his prayers bring us strength.
We ask this through our Lord Jesus Christ,
    your Son,
who lives and reigns with you and
    the Holy Spirit,
God, for ever and ever.
—Amen.

Dismissal *If praying individually, or in a group without a priest or deacon:*

May the Lord + bless us,
protect us from all evil
and bring us to everlasting life.
—Amen.

If praying with a priest or deacon, he dismisses the people:

The Lord be with you.
—And with your spirit.

May almighty God bless you,
the Father, and the Son, ✠ and the Holy Spirit.
—Amen.

Go in peace.
—Thanks be to God.

EVENING PRAYER

God, + come to my assistance.
—Lord, make haste to help me.

Glory to the Father, and to the Son,
    and to the Holy Spirit:
—as it was in the beginning, is now,
and will be for ever. Amen. Alleluia.

Hymn *Captains of the Saintly Band, p. 677*

Psalmody Ant. 1 **Jesus took Peter, James and John with him, and he became fearful and began to tremble.**

Psalm 116:10-19
I trusted, even when I said:
"I am sorely afflicted,"
and when I said in my alarm:
"No man can be trusted."

How can I repay the Lord
for his goodness to me?
The cup of salvation I will raise;
I will call on the Lord's name.

My vows to the Lord I will fulfill
before all his people.
O precious in the eyes of the Lord
is the death of his faithful.

Your servant, Lord, your servant am I;
you have loosened my bonds.
A thanksgiving sacrifice I make:
I will call on the Lord's name.

My vows to the Lord I will fulfill
before all his people,
in the courts of the house of the Lord,
in your midst, O Jerusalem.

Glory to the Father, and to the Son,
    and to the Holy Spirit:
—as it was in the beginning, is now,
and will be for ever. Amen.

Ant. **Jesus took Peter, James and John with him, and he became fearful and began to tremble.**

Ant. 2 **Then he said to them: Stay awake and pray that you may not be tempted.**

Psalm 126 When the Lord delivered Zion from bondage,
it seemed like a dream.
Then was our mouth filled with laughter,
on our lips there were songs.

The heathens themselves said: "What marvels
the Lord worked for them!"
What marvels the Lord worked for us!
Indeed we were glad.

Deliver us, O Lord, from our bondage
as streams in dry land.
Those who are sowing in tears
will sing when they reap.

They go out, they go out, full of tears,
carrying seed for the sowing:
they come back, they come back, full of song,
carrying their sheaves.

Glory to the Father, and to the Son,
  and to the Holy Spirit:
as it was in the beginning, is now,
and will be for ever. Amen.

Ant. **Then he said to them: Stay awake and pray that you may not be tempted.**

Ant. 3 **King Herod began persecuting certain members of the Church. He beheaded James, the brother of John.**

JULY 25 TUE   EVENING PRAYER

Canticle:
Ephesians 1:3–10

Praised be the God and Father
of our Lord Jesus Christ,
who has bestowed on us in Christ
every spiritual blessing in the heavens.

God chose us in him
before the world began
to be holy
and blameless in his sight.

He predestined us
to be his adopted sons through Jesus Christ,
such was his will and pleasure,
that all might praise the glorious favor
he has bestowed on us in his beloved.

In him and through his blood, we have
    been redeemed,
and our sins forgiven,
so immeasurably generous
is God's favor to us.

God has given us the wisdom
to understand fully the mystery,
the plan he was pleased
to decree in Christ.

A plan to be carried out
in Christ, in the fullness of time,
to bring all things into one in him,
in the heavens and on the earth.

Glory to the Father, and to the Son,
   and to the Holy Spirit:
—as it was in the beginning, is now,
and will be for ever. Amen.

Ant. **King Herod began persecuting certain members of the Church. He beheaded James, the brother of John.**

Reading
Ephesians
4:11–13

Christ gave apostles, prophets, evangelists, pastors and teachers in roles of service for the faithful to build up the body of Christ, till we become one in faith and in the knowledge of God's Son, and form that perfect man who is Christ come to full stature.

Responsory   Tell all the nations how glorious God is.
—Tell all the nations how glorious God is.

Make known his wonders to every people.
—How glorious God is.

Glory to the Father, and to the Son,
   and to the Holy Spirit.
—Tell all the nations how glorious God is.

Gospel
Canticle

Ant. **Whoever wishes to be great among you must be your servant; whoever wishes to be first among you must be the slave of all.**

Canticle of
Mary
Luke 1:46–55

My + soul proclaims the greatness of the Lord,
   my spirit rejoices in God my Savior
for he has looked with favor on his
   lowly servant.

From this day all generations will
>   call me blessed:
the Almighty has done great things for me,
and holy is his Name.

He has mercy on those who fear him
in every generation.

He has shown the strength of his arm,
he has scattered the proud in their conceit.

He has cast down the mighty from
>   their thrones,
and has lifted up the lowly.

He has filled the hungry with good things,
and the rich he has sent away empty.

He has come to the help of his servant Israel
for he has remembered his promise of mercy,
the promise he made to our fathers,
to Abraham and his children for ever.

Glory to the Father, and to the Son,
>   and to the Holy Spirit:
—as it was in the beginning, is now,
and will be for ever. Amen.

Ant. **Whoever wishes to be great among you must be your servant; whoever wishes to be first among you must be the slave of all.**

Intercessions My brothers, we build on the foundation of
the apostles. Let us pray to our almighty
Father for his holy people and say:
Be mindful of your Church, O Lord.

Father, you wanted your Son to be seen first
by the apostles after the resurrection
from the dead,
—we ask you to make us his witnesses to the
farthest corners of the world.

You sent your Son to preach the good news
to the poor,
—help us to preach this Gospel to
every creature.

You sent your Son to sow the seed of
unending life,
—grant that we who work at sowing the seed
may share the joy of the harvest.

You sent your Son to reconcile all men to you
through his blood,
—help us all to work toward achieving this
reconciliation.

Your Son sits at your right hand in heaven,
—let the dead enter your kingdom of joy.

JULY 25 TUE EVENING PRAYER

The Lord's Prayer

Our Father, who art in heaven,
hallowed be thy name;
thy kingdom come,
thy will be done
on earth as it is in heaven.
Give us this day our daily bread,
and forgive us our trespasses,
as we forgive those who trespass against us;
and lead us not into temptation,
but deliver us from evil.

Pater noster, qui es in cælis:
sanctificetur nomen tuum;
adveniat regnum tuum;
fiat voluntas tua,
sicut in cælo, et in terra.
Panem nostrum cotidianum da nobis hodie;
et dimitte nobis debita nostra,
sicut et nos dimittimus debitoribus nostris;
et ne nos inducas in tentationem;
sed libera nos a malo.

Concluding Prayer

Almighty Father,
by the martyrdom of Saint James
you blessed the work of the early Church.
May his profession of faith give us courage
and his prayers bring us strength.
We ask this through our Lord Jesus Christ,
    your Son,
who lives and reigns with you and
    the Holy Spirit,
God, for ever and ever.
—Amen.

Dismissal *If praying individually, or in a group without a priest or deacon:*

May the Lord ✠ bless us,
protect us from all evil
and bring us to everlasting life.
—Amen.

If praying with a priest or deacon, he dismisses the people:

The Lord be with you.
—And with your spirit.

May almighty God bless you,
the Father, and the Son, ✠ and the Holy Spirit.
—Amen.

Go in peace.
—Thanks be to God.

NIGHT PRAYER

God, ✠ come to my assistance.
—Lord, make haste to help me.

Glory to the Father, and to the Son,
    and to the Holy Spirit:
—as it was in the beginning, is now,
    and will be for ever. Amen. Alleluia.

Examen *An optional brief examination of conscience may be made. Call to mind your sins and failings this day.*

Hymn *Abide with Me, p. 675*

Psalmody **Ant. Do not hide your face from me; in you I put my trust.**

JULY 25   TUE   NIGHT PRAYER

Psalm 143:1–11

Lord, listen to my prayer:
turn your ear to my appeal.
You are faithful, you are just; give answer.
Do not call your servant to judgment
for no one is just in your sight.

The enemy pursues my soul;
he has crushed my life to the ground;
he has made me dwell in darkness
like the dead, long forgotten.
Therefore my spirit fails;
my heart is numb within me.

I remember the days that are past:
I ponder all your works.
I muse on what your hand has wrought
and to you I stretch out my hands.
Like a parched land my soul thirsts for you.

Lord, make haste and answer;
for my spirit fails within me.
Do not hide your face
lest I become like those in the grave.

In the morning let me know your love
for I put my trust in you.
Make me know the way I should walk:
to you I lift up my soul.

Rescue me, Lord, from my enemies;
I have fled to you for refuge.
Teach me to do your will
for you, O Lord, are my God.
Let your good spirit guide me
in ways that are level and smooth.

For your name's sake, Lord, save my life;
in your justice save my soul from distress.

Glory to the Father, and to the Son,
     and to the Holy Spirit:
—as it was in the beginning, is now,
and will be for ever. Amen.

Ant. **Do not hide your face from me; in you I put my trust.**

Reading
1 Peter 5:8–9a

Stay sober and alert. Your opponent the devil is prowling like a roaring lion looking for someone to devour. Resist him, solid in your faith.

Responsory

Into your hands, Lord, I commend my spirit.
—Into your hands, Lord, I commend my spirit.

You have redeemed us, Lord God of truth.
—I commend my spirit.

Glory to the Father, and to the Son,
     and to the Holy Spirit.
—Into your hands, Lord, I commend my spirit.

Gospel Canticle

Ant. **Protect us, Lord, as we stay awake; watch over us as we sleep, that awake, we may keep watch with Christ, and asleep, rest in his peace.**

Canticle of Simeon
Luke 2:29–32

Lord, + now you let your servant go in peace;
your word has been fulfilled:
my own eyes have seen the salvation
which you have prepared in the sight of
  every people:
a light to reveal you to the nations
and the glory of your people Israel.

Glory to the Father, and to the Son,
  and to the Holy Spirit:
—as it was in the beginning, is now,
and will be for ever. Amen.

Ant. **Protect us, Lord, as we stay awake; watch over us as we sleep, that awake, we may keep watch with Christ, and asleep, rest in his peace.**

Concluding Prayer

Let us pray.
Lord,
fill this night with your radiance.
May we sleep in peace and rise with joy
to welcome the light of a new day in
  your name.
We ask this through Christ our Lord.
—Amen.

Blessing

May the all-powerful Lord
grant us a restful night
and a peaceful death.
—Amen.

Marian Antiphon

Sing the "Salve Regina," found on p. 698, or pray a Hail Mary.

RESCUE ME, LORD, FROM MY ENEMIES; I HAVE FLED TO YOU FOR REFUGE.

Wednesday, July 26, 2023
Sts. Joachim and Anne

MORNING PRAYER —————————————

God, + come to my assistance.
—Lord, make haste to help me.

Glory to the Father, and to the Son,
   and to the Holy Spirit:
—as it was in the beginning, is now,
   and will be for ever. Amen. Alleluia.

Hymn   *Sing with All the Saints in Glory, p. 702*

Psalmody   Ant. 1 **My heart is ready, O God, my heart is ready.**

Psalm 108

My heart is ready, O God;
I will sing, sing your praise.
Awake, my soul;
awake, lyre and harp.
I will awake the dawn.

I will thank you, Lord, among the peoples,
among the nations I will praise you,
for your love reaches to the heavens
and your truth to the skies.
O God, arise above the heavens;
may your glory shine on earth!

O come and deliver your friends;
help with your right hand and reply.
From his holy place God has made
    this promise:
"I will triumph and divide the land
    of Shechem;
I will measure out the valley of Succoth.

Gilead is mine and Manasseh.
Ephraim I take for my helmet,
Judah for my commander's staff.
Moab I will use for my washbowl,
on Edom I will plant my shoe.
Over the Philistines I will shout in triumph."

But who will lead me to conquer the fortress?
Who will bring me face to face with Edom?
Will you utterly reject us, O God,
and no longer march with our armies?

Give us help against the foe:
for the help of man is vain.
With God we shall do bravely
and he will trample down our foes.

Glory to the Father, and to the Son,
    and to the Holy Spirit:
—as it was in the beginning, is now,
and will be for ever. Amen.

Ant. **My heart is ready, O God, my heart is ready.**

Ant. 2 **The Lord has robed me with grace and salvation.**

Canticle:
Isaiah 61:10–62:5

I rejoice heartily in the Lord,
in my God is the joy of my soul;
for he has clothed me with a robe of salvation,
and wrapped me in a mantle of justice,
like a bridegroom adorned with a diadem,
like a bride bedecked with her jewels.

As the earth brings forth its plants,
and a garden makes its growth spring up,
so will the Lord God make justice and praise
spring up before all the nations.

For Zion's sake I will not be silent,
for Jerusalem's sake I will not be quiet,
until her vindication shines forth
    like the dawn
and her victory like a burning torch.

Nations shall behold your vindication,
and all kings your glory;
you shall be called by a new name
pronounced by the mouth of the Lord.
You shall be a glorious crown in the hand
    of the Lord,
a royal diadem held by your God.

No more shall men call you "Forsaken,"
or your land "Desolate,"
but you shall be called "My delight,"
and your land "Espoused."
For the Lord delights in you,
and makes your land his spouse.

As a young man marries a virgin,
your Builder shall marry you;
and as a bridegroom rejoices in his bride
so shall your God rejoice in you.

Glory to the Father, and to the Son,
    and to the Holy Spirit:
—as it was in the beginning, is now,
and will be for ever. Amen.

Ant. **The Lord has robed me with grace and salvation.**

Ant. 3 **I will praise my God all the days of my life.**

Psalm 146

My soul, give praise to the Lord;
I will praise the Lord all my days,
make music to my God while I live.

Put no trust in princes,
in mortal men in whom there is no help.
Take their breath, they return to clay
and their plans that day come to nothing.

He is happy who is helped by Jacob's God,
whose hope is in the Lord his God,
who alone made heaven and earth,
the seas and all they contain.

It is he who keeps faith for ever,
who is just to those who are oppressed.
It is he who gives bread to the hungry,
the Lord, who sets prisoners free,

the Lord who gives sight to the blind,
who raises up those who are bowed down,
the Lord, who protects the stranger
and upholds the widow and orphan.

It is the Lord who loves the just
but thwarts the path of the wicked.
The Lord will reign for ever,
Zion's God, from age to age.

Glory to the Father, and to the Son,
    and to the Holy Spirit:
—as it was in the beginning, is now,
and will be for ever. Amen.

Ant. **I will praise my God all the days of my life.**

Reading
Isaiah 55:3

Come to me heedfully,
    listen that you may have life.
I will renew with you the everlasting covenant,
    the benefits assured to David.

Responsory

In the tender compassion of our God,
    the Lord has come to us.
—In the tender compassion of our God,
    the Lord has come to us.

He has raised up Jesus, our savior.
—The Lord has come to us.

Glory to the Father, and to the Son,
    and to the Holy Spirit.
—In the tender compassion of our God,
    the Lord has come to us.

Gospel Canticle

Ant. **Blessed be the Lord, the God of Israel; he has raised up for us a mighty savior, born of the house of his servant David.**

Canticle of Zechariah
Luke 1:68–79

Blessed + be the Lord, the God of Israel;
he has come to his people and set them free.

He has raised up for us a mighty savior,
born of the house of his servant David.

Through his holy prophets he
   promised of old
that he would save us from our enemies,
from the hands of all who hate us.

He promised to show mercy to our fathers
and to remember his holy covenant.

This was the oath he swore to our
   father Abraham:
to set us free from the hands of our enemies,
free to worship him without fear,
holy and righteous in his sight
   all the days of our life.

You, my child, shall be called the prophet of
   the Most High;
for you will go before the Lord to
   prepare his way,
to give his people knowledge of salvation
by the forgiveness of their sins.

In the tender compassion of our God
the dawn from on high shall break upon us,
to shine on those who dwell in darkness and
the shadow of death,
and to guide our feet into the way of peace.

Glory to the Father, and to the Son,
and to the Holy Spirit:
—as it was in the beginning, is now,
and will be for ever. Amen.

Ant. **Blessed be the Lord, the God of Israel; he has raised up for us a mighty savior, born of the house of his servant David.**

Intercessions My brothers, let us praise Christ, asking to serve him and to be holy and righteous in his sight all the days of our life. Let us acclaim him:
Lord, you alone are the holy one.

You desired to experience everything we experience but sin,
—have mercy on us, Lord Jesus.

You called us to love perfectly,
—make us holy, Lord Jesus.

You commissioned us to be the salt of the earth and the light of the world,
—let your light shine on us, Lord Jesus.

You desired to serve, not to be served,
—help us, Lord Jesus, to give humble service to
    you and to our neighbors.

You are in the form of God sharing in the
    splendor of the Father,
—Lord Jesus, let us see the glory of your face.

The Lord's Prayer

Our Father, who art in heaven,
hallowed be thy name;
thy kingdom come,
thy will be done
on earth as it is in heaven.
Give us this day our daily bread,
and forgive us our trespasses,
as we forgive those who trespass against us;
and lead us not into temptation,
but deliver us from evil.

Pater noster, qui es in cælis:
sanctificetur nomen tuum;
adveniat regnum tuum;
fiat voluntas tua,
sicut in cælo, et in terra.
Panem nostrum cotidianum da nobis hodie;
et dimitte nobis debita nostra,
sicut et nos dimittimus debitoribus nostris;
et ne nos inducas in tentationem;
sed libera nos a malo.

Concluding Prayer

God of our fathers,
you gave Saints Joachim and Ann
the privilege of being the parents of Mary,
the mother of your incarnate Son.
May their prayers help us to attain
the salvation you have promised to
    your people.
Grant this through our Lord Jesus Christ,
    your Son,
who lives and reigns with you and
    the Holy Spirit,
God, forever and ever.
—Amen.

Dismissal

If praying individually, or in a group without a priest or deacon:

May the Lord + bless us,
protect us from all evil
and bring us to everlasting life.
—Amen.

If praying with a priest or deacon, he dismisses the people:

The Lord be with you.
—And with your spirit.

May almighty God bless you,
the Father, and the Son, ✠ and the Holy Spirit.
—Amen.

Go in peace.
—Thanks be to God.

EVENING PRAYER ——————————

God, + come to my assistance.
—Lord, make haste to help me.

Glory to the Father, and to the Son,
    and to the Holy Spirit:
—as it was in the beginning, is now,
and will be for ever. Amen. Alleluia.

Hymn   *Jesus, Eternal Truth Sublime, p. 689*

Psalmody   Ant. 1 **Lord, how wonderful is your wisdom, so far beyond my understanding.**

Psalm 139

O Lord, you search me and you know me,
you know my resting and my rising,
you discern my purpose from afar.
You mark when I walk or lie down,
all my ways lie open to you.

Before ever a word is on my tongue
you know it, O Lord, through and through.
Behind and before you besiege me,
your hand ever laid upon me.
Too wonderful for me, this knowledge,
too high, beyond my reach.

O where can I go from your spirit,
or where can I flee from your face?
If I climb the heavens, you are there.
If I lie in the grave, you are there.

If I take the wings of the dawn
and dwell at the sea's furthest end,
even there your hand would lead me,
your right hand would hold me fast.

If I say: "Let the darkness hide me
and the light around me be night,"
even darkness is not dark for you
and the night is as clear as the day.

Glory to the Father, and to the Son,
    and to the Holy Spirit:
as it was in the beginning, is now,
and will be for ever. Amen.

Ant. **Lord, how wonderful is your wisdom, so far beyond my understanding.**

Ant. 2 **I am the Lord: I search the mind and probe the heart; I give to each one as his deeds deserve.**

Psalm 139
(continued)

For it was you who created my being,
knit me together in my mother's womb.
I thank you for the wonder of my being,
for the wonders of all your creation.

Already you knew my soul,
my body held no secret from you
when I was being fashioned in secret
and molded in the depths of the earth.

Your eyes saw all my actions,
they were all of them written in your book;
every one of my days was decreed
before one of them came into being.

To me, how mysterious your thoughts,
the sum of them not to be numbered!
If I count them, they are more than the sand;
to finish, I must be eternal, like you.

O search me, God, and know my heart.
O test me and know my thoughts.
See that I follow not the wrong path
and lead me in the path of life eternal.

Glory to the Father, and to the Son,
    and to the Holy Spirit:
as it was in the beginning, is now,
and will be for ever. Amen.

Ant. **I am the Lord: I search the mind and probe the heart; I give to each one as his deeds deserve.**

Ant. 3 **Through him all things were made; he holds all creation together in himself.**

Canticle:
Colossians
1:12–20

Let us give thanks to the Father
for having made you worthy
to share the lot of the saints
in light.

He rescued us
from the power of darkness
and brought us
into the kingdom of his beloved Son.
Through him we have redemption,
the forgiveness of our sins.

He is the image of the invisible God,
the first-born of all creatures.
In him everything in heaven and on earth
　　was created,
things visible and invisible.

All were created through him;
all were created for him.
He is before all else that is.
In him everything continues in being.

It is he who is head of the body, the church!
he who is the beginning,
the first-born of the dead,
so that primacy may be his in everything.

It pleased God to make absolute fullness
　　reside in him
and, by means of him, to reconcile
　　everything in his person,
both on earth and in the heavens,
making peace through the blood of his cross.

Glory to the Father, and to the Son,
　　and to the Holy Spirit:
as it was in the beginning, is now,
and will be for ever. Amen.

Ant. **Through him all things were made; he holds all creation together in himself.**

Evening Prayer — WED JULY 26

Reading
Romans 9:4–5

To the Israelites belonged the adoption, the glory, the covenants, the law-giving, the worship, and the promises; theirs were the patriarchs, and from them came the Messiah (I speak of his human origins). Blessed forever be God who is over all! Amen.

Responsory

He has come to the help of his servant Israel;
  he has remembered his promise of mercy.
—He has come to the help of his servant Israel;
  he has remembered his promise of mercy.

According to the promise he made to
  our fathers,
—he has remembered his promise of mercy.

Glory to the Father, and to the Son,
  and to the Holy Spirit.
—He has come to the help of his servant Israel;
  he has remembered his promise of mercy.

Gospel Canticle

Ant. **From the noble stem of Jesse a branch has sprung, and from this branch a beautiful flower, rich in scent, has blossomed.**

Canticle of Mary
Luke 1:46–55

My + soul proclaims the greatness of the Lord,
my spirit rejoices in God my Savior
for he has looked with favor on his
    lowly servant.

From this day all generations will
    call me blessed:
the Almighty has done great things for me,
and holy is his Name.

He has mercy on those who fear him
in every generation.

He has shown the strength of his arm,
he has scattered the proud in their conceit.

He has cast down the mighty from
   their thrones,
and has lifted up the lowly.

He has filled the hungry with good things,
and the rich he has sent away empty.

He has come to the help of his servant Israel
for he has remembered his promise of mercy,
the promise he made to our fathers,
to Abraham and his children for ever.

Glory to the Father, and to the Son,
   and to the Holy Spirit:
as it was in the beginning, is now,
and will be for ever. Amen.

Ant. **From the noble stem of Jesse a branch has sprung, and from this branch a beautiful flower, rich in scent, has blossomed.**

Intercessions Let us pray to the Father, the source of all holiness, and ask him to lead us to holiness of life through the example and intercession of his saints:
May we be holy as you are holy.

Holy Father, you want us to be called your
    sons and truly to be such,
—grant that your holy Church may proclaim
    you throughout the world.

Holy Father, you want us to walk worthily
    and please you in all we do,
—let us abound in doing good works.

Holy Father, you have reconciled us to
    yourself through Christ,
—preserve us in your name so that all
    may be one.

Holy Father, you have called us to a
    heavenly banquet,
—through the bread that came down from
    heaven make us worthy to grow in
    perfect love.

Holy Father, forgive the offenses of
    every sinner,
—let the dead perceive the light of your
    countenance.

The Lord's Prayer

Our Father, who art in heaven,
hallowed be thy name;
thy kingdom come,
thy will be done
on earth as it is in heaven.
Give us this day our daily bread,
and forgive us our trespasses,
as we forgive those who trespass against us;
and lead us not into temptation,
but deliver us from evil.

Pater noster, qui es in cælis:
sanctificetur nomen tuum;
adveniat regnum tuum;
fiat voluntas tua,
sicut in cælo, et in terra.
Panem nostrum cotidianum da nobis hodie;
et dimitte nobis debita nostra,
sicut et nos dimittimus debitoribus nostris;
et ne nos inducas in tentationem;
sed libera nos a malo.

Concluding Prayer

God of our fathers,
you gave Saints Joachim and Ann
the privilege of being the parents of Mary,
the mother of your incarnate Son.
May their prayers help us to attain
the salvation you have promised to
    your people.
Grant this through our Lord Jesus Christ,
    your Son,
who lives and reigns with you and
    the Holy Spirit,
God, forever and ever.
—Amen.

Dismissal *If praying individually, or in a group without a priest or deacon:*

May the Lord + bless us,
protect us from all evil
and bring us to everlasting life.
—Amen.

If praying with a priest or deacon, he dismisses the people:

The Lord be with you.
—And with your spirit.

May almighty God bless you,
the Father, and the Son, ✠ and the Holy Spirit.
—Amen.

Go in peace.
—Thanks be to God.

NIGHT PRAYER

God, ✠ come to my assistance.
—Lord, make haste to help me.

Glory to the Father, and to the Son,
   and to the Holy Spirit:
—as it was in the beginning, is now,
   and will be for ever. Amen. Alleluia.

Examen *An optional brief examination of conscience may be made. Call to mind your sins and failings this day.*

Hymn *Before the Final Light of Day, p. 676*

Psalmody Ant. 1 **Lord God, be my refuge and my strength.**

Psalm 31:1–6

In you, O Lord, I take refuge.
Let me never be put to shame.
In your justice, set me free,
hear me and speedily rescue me.

Be a rock of refuge for me,
a mighty stronghold to save me,
for you are my rock, my stronghold.
For your name's sake, lead me and guide me.

Release me from the snares they have hidden
for you are my refuge, Lord.
Into your hands I commend my spirit.
It is you who will redeem me, Lord.

Glory to the Father, and to the Son,
 and to the Holy Spirit:
as it was in the beginning, is now,
and will be for ever. Amen.

Ant. **Lord God, be my refuge and my strength.**

Ant. 2 **Out of the depths I cry to you, Lord.**

Psalm 130
Out of the depths I cry to you, O Lord,
Lord, hear my voice!
O let your ears be attentive
to the voice of my pleading.

If you, O Lord, should mark our guilt,
Lord, who would survive?
But with you is found forgiveness:
for this we revere you.

My soul is waiting for the Lord,
I count on his word.
My soul is longing for the Lord
more than watchman for daybreak.
Let the watchman count on daybreak
and Israel on the Lord.

Because with the Lord there is mercy
and fullness of redemption,
Israel indeed he will redeem
from all its iniquity.

Glory to the Father, and to the Son,
    and to the Holy Spirit:
—as it was in the beginning, is now,
    and will be for ever. Amen.

Ant. **Out of the depths I cry to you, Lord.**

Reading
Ephesians 4:26–27

If you are angry, let it be without sin. The sun must not go down on your wrath; do not give the devil a chance to work on you.

Responsory

Into your hands, Lord, I commend my spirit.
—Into your hands, Lord, I commend my spirit.

You have redeemed us, Lord God of truth.
—I commend my spirit.

Glory to the Father, and to the Son,
    and to the Holy Spirit.
—Into your hands, Lord, I commend my spirit.

Gospel Canticle

Ant. **Protect us, Lord, as we stay awake; watch over us as we sleep, that awake, we may keep watch with Christ, and asleep, rest in his peace.**

Canticle of Simeon
Luke 2:29–32

Lord, + now you let your servant go in peace;
your word has been fulfilled:
my own eyes have seen the salvation
which you have prepared in the sight of
    every people:
a light to reveal you to the nations
and the glory of your people Israel.

Glory to the Father, and to the Son,
   and to the Holy Spirit:
—as it was in the beginning, is now,
and will be for ever. Amen.

Ant. **Protect us, Lord, as we stay awake; watch over us as we sleep, that awake, we may keep watch with Christ, and asleep, rest in his peace.**

Concluding Prayer

Let us pray.
Lord Jesus Christ,
you have given your followers
an example of gentleness and humility,
a task that is easy, a burden that is light.
Accept the prayers and work of this day,
and give us the rest that will strengthen us
to render more faithful service to you
who live and reign for ever and ever.
—Amen.

Blessing

May the all-powerful Lord
grant us a restful night
and a peaceful death.
—Amen.

Marian Antiphon

Sing the "Salve Regina," found on p. 698, or pray a Hail Mary.

Thursday, July 27, 2023
Thursday of the Sixteenth Week in Ordinary Time

MORNING PRAYER

God, + come to my assistance.
—Lord, make haste to help me.

Glory to the Father, and to the Son,
    and to the Holy Spirit:
—as it was in the beginning, is now,
and will be for ever. Amen. Alleluia.

Hymn   *O Splendor of God's Glory Bright, p. 694*

Psalmody   Ant. 1 **At daybreak, be merciful to me, O Lord.**

Psalm 143:1–11

Lord, listen to my prayer:
turn your ear to my appeal.
You are faithful, you are just; give answer.
Do not call your servant to judgment
for no one is just in your sight.

The enemy pursues my soul;
he has crushed my life to the ground;
he has made me dwell in darkness
like the dead, long forgotten.
Therefore my spirit fails;
my heart is numb within me.

I remember the days that are past:
I ponder all your works.
I muse on what your hand has wrought
and to you I stretch out my hands.
Like a parched land my soul thirsts for you.

Lord, make haste and answer;
for my spirit fails within me.
Do not hide your face
lest I become like those in the grave.

In the morning let me know your love
for I put my trust in you.
Make me know the way I should walk:
to you I lift up my soul.

Rescue me, Lord, from my enemies;
I have fled to you for refuge.
Teach me to do your will
for you, O Lord, are my God.
Let your good spirit guide me
in ways that are level and smooth.

For your name's sake, Lord, save my life;
in your justice save my soul from distress.

Glory to the Father, and to the Son,
    and to the Holy Spirit:
—as it was in the beginning, is now,
and will be for ever. Amen.

Ant. **At daybreak, be merciful to me, O Lord.**

Ant. 2 **The Lord will make a river of peace flow through Jerusalem.**

Canticle:
Isaiah 66:10–14a

Rejoice with Jerusalem and be glad
    because of her,
all you who love her;
exult, exult with her,
all you who were mourning over her!

Oh, that you may suck fully
of the milk of her comfort,
that you may nurse with delight
at her abundant breasts!

For thus says the Lord:
Lo, I will spread prosperity over her
    like a river,
and the wealth of the nations like an
    overflowing torrent.

As nurslings, you shall be carried in her arms,
and fondled in her lap;
as a mother comforts her son,
so will I comfort you;
in Jerusalem you shall find your comfort.

When you see this, your heart shall rejoice,
and your bodies flourish like the grass.

Glory to the Father, and to the Son,
    and to the Holy Spirit:
as it was in the beginning, is now,
and will be for ever. Amen.

Ant. **The Lord will make a river of peace flow through Jerusalem.**

Ant. 3 **Let us joyfully praise the Lord our God.**

Psalm 147:1-11

Praise the Lord for he is good;
sing to our God for he is loving:
to him our praise is due.

The Lord builds up Jerusalem
and brings back Israel's exiles,
he heals the broken-hearted,
he binds up all their wounds.
He fixes the number of the stars;
he calls each one by its name.

Our Lord is great and almighty;
his wisdom can never be measured.
The Lord raises the lowly;
he humbles the wicked to the dust.
O sing to the Lord, giving thanks;
sing psalms to our God with the harp.

He covers the heavens with clouds;
he prepares the rain for the earth,
making mountains sprout with grass
and with plants to serve man's needs.
He provides the beasts with their food
and young ravens that call upon him.

His delight is not in horses
nor his pleasure in warriors' strength.
The Lord delights in those who revere him,
in those who wait for his love.

Glory to the Father, and to the Son,
    and to the Holy Spirit:
—as it was in the beginning, is now,
and will be for ever. Amen.

Ant. **Let us joyfully praise the Lord our God.**

Reading
Romans 8:18–21

The sufferings of the present are as nothing compared with the glory to be revealed in us. Indeed, the whole created world eagerly awaits the revelation of the sons of God. Creation was made subject to futility, not of its own accord but by him who once subjected it; yet not without hope, because the world itself will be freed from its slavery to corruption and share in the glorious freedom of the children of God.

Responsory

In the early hours of the morning, I think of you, O Lord.
—In the early hours of the morning, I think of you, O Lord.

Always you are there to help me,
—I think of you, O Lord.

Glory to the Father, and to the Son, and to the Holy Spirit.
—In the early hours of the morning, I think of you, O Lord.

Gospel Canticle

Ant. **Give your people knowledge of salvation, Lord, and forgive us our sins.**

Canticle of Zechariah
Luke 1:68–79

Blessed + be the Lord, the God of Israel;
he has come to his people and set them free.

He has raised up for us a mighty savior,
born of the house of his servant David.

Through his holy prophets he
    promised of old
that he would save us from our enemies,
from the hands of all who hate us.

He promised to show mercy to our fathers
and to remember his holy covenant.

This was the oath he swore to our
    father Abraham:
to set us free from the hands of our enemies,
free to worship him without fear,
holy and righteous in his sight
    all the days of our life.

You, my child, shall be called the prophet of
    the Most High;
for you will go before the Lord to
    prepare his way,
to give his people knowledge of salvation
by the forgiveness of their sins.

In the tender compassion of our God
the dawn from on high shall break upon us,
to shine on those who dwell in darkness and
    the shadow of death,
and to guide our feet into the way of peace.

Glory to the Father, and to the Son,
    and to the Holy Spirit:
—as it was in the beginning, is now,
and will be for ever. Amen.

Ant. **Give your people knowledge of salvation, Lord, and forgive us our sins.**

Intercessions Let us pray to God, who gives salvation to his people:
You are our life, O Lord.

Blessed are you, Father of our Lord Jesus Christ, for by your mercy we have been reborn to a living hope,
—through the resurrection of Jesus Christ from the dead.

You made man in your image and renewed him in Christ,
—mold us into the likeness of your Son.

Pour out your love through the Holy Spirit,
—heal our hearts, wounded by hatred and jealousy.

Today grant work to laborers, bread to the hungry, joy to the sorrowful,
—grace and redemption to all men.

The Lord's Prayer
Our Father, who art in heaven,
hallowed be thy name;
thy kingdom come,
thy will be done
on earth as it is in heaven.
Give us this day our daily bread,
and forgive us our trespasses,
as we forgive those who trespass against us;
and lead us not into temptation,
but deliver us from evil.

Pater noster, qui es in cælis:
sanctificetur nomen tuum;
adveniat regnum tuum;
fiat voluntas tua,
sicut in cælo, et in terra.
Panem nostrum cotidianum da nobis hodie;
et dimitte nobis debita nostra,
sicut et nos dimittimus debitoribus nostris;
et ne nos inducas in tentationem;
sed libera nos a malo.

Concluding Prayer

Lord,
let the knowledge of salvation
enlighten our hearts,
so that, freed from fear and from the power
of our enemies,
we may serve you faithfully all the days
of our life.
We ask this through our Lord Jesus Christ,
your Son,
who lives and reigns with you and
the Holy Spirit,
God, for ever and ever.
—Amen.

Dismissal

If praying individually, or in a group without a priest or deacon:

May the Lord + bless us,
protect us from all evil
and bring us to everlasting life.
—Amen.

If praying with a priest or deacon, he dismisses the people:

The Lord be with you.
—And with your spirit.

May almighty God bless you,
the Father, and the Son, ✠ and the Holy Spirit.
—Amen.

Go in peace.
—Thanks be to God.

EVENING PRAYER

God, + come to my assistance.
—Lord, make haste to help me.

Glory to the Father, and to the Son,
    and to the Holy Spirit:
—as it was in the beginning, is now,
and will be for ever. Amen. Alleluia.

Hymn *Sing Praise to God Who Reigns Above, p. 700*

Psalmody Ant. 1 **He is my comfort and my refuge. In him I put my trust.**

Psalm 144 Blessed be the Lord, my rock
who trains my arms for battle,
who prepares my hands for war.

He is my love, my fortress;
he is my stronghold, my savior,
my shield, my place of refuge.
He brings peoples under my rule.

Lord, what is man that you care for him,
mortal man, that you keep him in mind;
man, who is merely a breath,
whose life fades like a shadow?

Lower your heavens and come down;
touch the mountains; wreathe
 them in smoke.
Flash your lightnings; rout the foe,
shoot your arrows and put them to flight.

Reach down from heaven and save me;
draw me out from the mighty waters,
from the hands of alien foes
whose mouths are filled with lies,
whose hands are raised in perjury.

Glory to the Father, and to the Son,
 and to the Holy Spirit:
as it was in the beginning, is now,
and will be for ever. Amen.

Ant. **He is my comfort and my refuge. In him I put my trust.**

Ant. 2 **Blessed are the people whose God is the Lord.**

Psalm 144 (continued)

To you, O God, will I sing a new song;
I will play on the ten-stringed harp
to you who give kings their victory,
who set David your servant free.

You set him free from the evil sword;
you rescued him from alien foes
whose mouths were filled with lies,
whose hands were raised in perjury.

Let our sons then flourish like saplings
grown tall and strong from their youth:
our daughters graceful as columns,
adorned as though for a palace.

Let our barns be filled to overflowing
with crops of every kind;
our sheep increasing by thousands,
myriads of sheep in our fields,
our cattle heavy with young,

no ruined wall, no exile,
no sound of weeping in our streets.
Happy the people with such blessings;
happy the people whose God is the Lord.

Glory to the Father, and to the Son,
    and to the Holy Spirit:
—as it was in the beginning, is now,
and will be for ever. Amen.

Ant. **Blessed are the people whose God is the Lord.**

Ant. 3 **Now the victorious reign of our God has begun.**

Canticle: Revelation 11:17–18; 12:10b–12a

We praise you, the Lord God Almighty,
who is and who was.
You have assumed your great power,
you have begun your reign.

The nations have raged in anger,
but then came your day of wrath
and the moment to judge the dead:
the time to reward your servants
    the prophets
and the holy ones who revere you,
the great and the small alike.

Now have salvation and power come,
The reign of our God and the authority
of his Anointed One.
For the accuser of our brothers is cast out,
who night and day accused them before God.

They defeated him by the blood of the Lamb
and by the word of their testimony;
love for life did not deter them from death.
So rejoice, you heavens,
and you that dwell therein!

Glory to the Father, and to the Son,
    and to the Holy Spirit:
—as it was in the beginning, is now,
and will be for ever. Amen.

Ant. **Now the victorious reign of our God has begun.**

Reading *See Colossians 1:23*

You must hold fast to faith, be firmly grounded and steadfast in it, unshaken in the hope promised you by the gospel you have heard. It is the gospel which has been announced to every creature under heaven.

Responsory

The Lord is my shepherd,
   I shall want for nothing.
—The Lord is my shepherd,
   I shall want for nothing.

He has brought me to green pastures.
—I shall want for nothing.

Glory to the Father, and to the Son,
   and to the Holy Spirit.
—The Lord is my shepherd,
   I shall want for nothing.

Gospel Canticle

Ant. **If you hunger for holiness, God will satisfy your longing, good measure, and flowing over.**

Canticle of Mary
Luke 1:46–55

My + soul proclaims the greatness of the Lord,
my spirit rejoices in God my Savior
for he has looked with favor on his
   lowly servant.

From this day all generations will
   call me blessed:
the Almighty has done great things for me,
and holy is his Name.

He has mercy on those who fear him
in every generation.

He has shown the strength of his arm,
he has scattered the proud in their conceit.

He has cast down the mighty from
    their thrones,
and has lifted up the lowly.

He has filled the hungry with good things,
and the rich he has sent away empty.

He has come to the help of his servant Israel
for he has remembered his promise of mercy,
the promise he made to our fathers,
to Abraham and his children for ever.

Glory to the Father, and to the Son,
    and to the Holy Spirit:
—as it was in the beginning, is now,
and will be for ever. Amen.

Ant. **If you hunger for holiness, God will satisfy your longing, good measure, and flowing over.**

Intercessions Let us pray to Christ, the light of the nations
    and the joy of every living creature:
Give us light, peace and security, Lord.

Brilliant Light, Word of the Father, you came
    to save all men,
—lead the catechumens of your Church into
    your marvelous light.

Overlook our sins, Lord,
—for you are the source of forgiveness.

Lord, it is your will that men use their minds
> to unlock nature's secrets and master
> the world,
—may the arts and sciences advance your glory
> and the happiness of all peoples.

Look kindly on those who have dedicated
> themselves to the service of their fellow men,
—may they fulfill their work freely and completely.

Lord, you open the way and no one can close it,
—lead into your light those who have fallen
> asleep in the hope of resurrection.

The Lord's Prayer

Our Father, who art in heaven,
hallowed be thy name;
thy kingdom come,
thy will be done
on earth as it is in heaven.
Give us this day our daily bread,
and forgive us our trespasses,
as we forgive those who trespass against us;
and lead us not into temptation,
but deliver us from evil.

Pater noster, qui es in cælis:
sanctificetur nomen tuum;
adveniat regnum tuum;
fiat voluntas tua,
sicut in cælo, et in terra.
Panem nostrum cotidianum da nobis hodie;
et dimitte nobis debita nostra,
sicut et nos dimittimus debitoribus nostris;
et ne nos inducas in tentationem;
sed libera nos a malo.

Concluding Prayer

Lord,
hear the evening prayers we bring before you:
help us to follow in the footsteps of your Son
so that we may produce an abundant harvest
  of goodness
in patience and in faith.
We ask this through our Lord Jesus Christ,
  your Son,
who lives and reigns with you and
  the Holy Spirit,
God, for ever and ever.
—Amen.

Dismissal

If praying individually, or in a group without a priest or deacon:

May the Lord ✚ bless us,
protect us from all evil
and bring us to everlasting life.
—Amen.

If praying with a priest or deacon, he dismisses the people:

The Lord be with you.
—And with your spirit.

May almighty God bless you,
the Father, and the Son, ✚ and the Holy Spirit.
—Amen.

Go in peace.
—Thanks be to God.

I KEEP THE LORD EVER IN MY SIGHT: SINCE HE IS AT MY RIGHT HAND, I SHALL STAND FIRM.

NIGHT PRAYER

God, + come to my assistance.
—Lord, make haste to help me.

Glory to the Father, and to the Son,
    and to the Holy Spirit:
—as it was in the beginning, is now,
and will be for ever. Amen. Alleluia.

Examen *An optional brief examination of conscience may be made. Call to mind your sins and failings this day.*

Hymn *O Joyful Light of God Most High, p. 693*

Psalmody Ant. **In you, my God, my body will rest in hope.**

Psalm 16

Preserve me, God, I take refuge in you.
I say to the Lord: "You are my God.
My happiness lies in you alone."

He has put into my heart a marvelous love
for the faithful ones who dwell in his land.
Those who choose other gods increase
    their sorrows.
Never will I offer their offerings of blood.
Never will I take their name upon my lips.

O Lord, it is you who are my portion and cup;
it is you yourself who are my prize.
The lot marked out for me is my delight:
welcome indeed the heritage that falls to me!

I will bless the Lord who gives me counsel,
who even at night directs my heart.
I keep the Lord ever in my sight:
since he is at my right hand, I shall stand firm.

And so my heart rejoices, my soul is glad;
even my body shall rest in safety.
For you will not leave my soul
    among the dead,
nor let your beloved know decay.

You will show me the path of life,
the fullness of joy in your presence,
at your right hand happiness for ever.

Glory to the Father, and to the Son,
    and to the Holy Spirit:
—as it was in the beginning, is now,
and will be for ever. Amen.

Ant. **In you, my God, my body will rest in hope.**

Reading (1 Thessalonians 5:23)

May the God of peace make you perfect in holiness. May he preserve you whole and entire, spirit, soul, and body, irreproachable at the coming of our Lord Jesus Christ.

Responsory

Into your hands, Lord, I commend my spirit.
—Into your hands, Lord, I commend my spirit.

You have redeemed us, Lord God of truth.
—I commend my spirit.

JULY 27   THU   NIGHT PRAYER

>   Glory to the Father, and to the Son,
>   and to the Holy Spirit.
> —Into your hands, Lord, I commend my spirit.

Gospel Canticle

Ant. Protect us, Lord, as we stay awake; watch over us as we sleep, that awake, we may keep watch with Christ, and asleep, rest in his peace.

Canticle of Simeon
Luke 2:29–32

Lord, + now you let your servant go in peace;
your word has been fulfilled:
my own eyes have seen the salvation
which you have prepared in the sight of
    every people:
a light to reveal you to the nations
and the glory of your people Israel.

Glory to the Father, and to the Son,
    and to the Holy Spirit:
—as it was in the beginning, is now,
and will be for ever. Amen.

Ant. **Protect us, Lord, as we stay awake; watch over us as we sleep, that awake, we may keep watch with Christ, and asleep, rest in his peace.**

Concluding Prayer

Let us pray.
Lord God,
send peaceful sleep
to refresh our tired bodies.
May your help always renew us
and keep us strong in your service.
We ask this through Christ our Lord.
—Amen.

Blessing May the all-powerful Lord
grant us a restful night
and a peaceful death.
—Amen.

Marian Antiphon *Sing the "Salve Regina," found on p. 698, or pray a Hail Mary.*

Friday, July 28, 2023
Friday of the Sixteenth Week in Ordinary Time

MORNING PRAYER

God, + come to my assistance.
—Lord, make haste to help me.

Glory to the Father, and to the Son,
  and to the Holy Spirit:
—as it was in the beginning, is now,
  and will be for ever. Amen. Alleluia.

Hymn *From All That Dwell Below the Skies, p. 679*

Psalmody Ant. 1 **Create a clean heart in me, O God; renew in me a steadfast spirit.**

Psalm 51 Have mercy on me, God, in your kindness.
In your compassion blot out my offense.
O wash me more and more from my guilt
and cleanse me from my sin.

My offenses truly I know them;
my sin is always before me.
Against you, you alone, have I sinned;
what is evil in your sight I have done.

That you may be justified when you
    give sentence
and be without reproach when you judge.
O see, in guilt I was born,
a sinner was I conceived.

Indeed you love truth in the heart;
then in the secret of my heart teach
    me wisdom.
O purify me, then I shall be clean;
O wash me, I shall be whiter than snow.

Make me hear rejoicing and gladness,
that the bones you have crushed may revive.
From my sins turn away your face
and blot out all my guilt.

A pure heart create for me, O God,
put a steadfast spirit within me.
Do not cast me away from your presence,
nor deprive me of your holy spirit.

Give me again the joy of your help;
with a spirit of fervor sustain me,
that I may teach transgressors your ways
and sinners may return to you.

O rescue me, God, my helper,
and my tongue shall ring out your goodness.
O Lord, open my lips
and my mouth shall declare your praise.

For in sacrifice you take no delight,
burnt offering from me you would refuse,
my sacrifice, a contrite spirit.
A humbled, contrite heart you will not spurn.

In your goodness, show favor to Zion:
rebuild the walls of Jerusalem.
Then you will be pleased with lawful sacrifice,
holocausts offered on your altar.

Glory to the Father, and to the Son,
 and to the Holy Spirit:
as it was in the beginning, is now,
and will be for ever. Amen.

Ant. **Create a clean heart in me, O God; renew in me a steadfast spirit.**

Ant. 2 **Rejoice, Jerusalem, for through you all men will be gathered to the Lord.**

Canticle:
Tobit 13:8–11,
13–15

Let all men speak of the Lord's majesty,
and sing his praises in Jerusalem.

O Jerusalem, holy city,
he scourged you for the works of your hands,
but will again pity the children of the
 righteous.

Praise the Lord for his goodness,
and bless the King of the ages,
so that his tent may be rebuilt in
    you with joy.

May he gladden within you all who
    were captives;
all who were ravaged may he cherish
    within you
for all generations to come.

A bright light will shine to all parts of
    the earth;
many nations shall come to you from afar,
and the inhabitants of all the limits of
    the earth,
drawn to you by the name of the Lord God,
bearing in their hands their gifts for the King
    of heaven.

Every generation shall give joyful
    praise in you,
and shall call you the chosen one,
through all ages forever.

Go, then, rejoice over the children of the
    righteous,
who shall all be gathered together
and shall bless the Lord of the ages.

Happy are those who love you,
and happy those who rejoice in your
    prosperity.

Happy are all the men who shall
   grieve over you,
over all your chastisements,

for they shall rejoice in you
as they behold all your joy forever.

My spirit blesses the Lord, the great King.

Glory to the Father, and to the Son,
   and to the Holy Spirit:
as it was in the beginning, is now,
and will be for ever. Amen.

Ant. **Rejoice, Jerusalem, for through you all men will be gathered to the Lord.**

Ant. 3 **Zion, praise your God, who sent his Word to renew the earth.**

Psalm 147:12–20

O praise the Lord, Jerusalem!
Zion, praise your God!

He has strengthened the bars of your gates,
he has blessed the children within you.
He established peace on your borders,
he feeds you with finest wheat.

He sends out his word to the earth
and swiftly runs his command.
He showers down snow white as wool,
he scatters hoar-frost like ashes.

He hurls down hailstones like crumbs.
The waters are frozen at his touch;
he sends forth his word and it melts them:
at the breath of his mouth the waters flow.

He makes his word known to Jacob,
to Israel his laws and decrees.
He has not dealt thus with other nations;
he has not taught them his decrees.

Glory to the Father, and to the Son,
    and to the Holy Spirit:
—as it was in the beginning, is now,
and will be for ever. Amen.

Ant. **Zion, praise your God, who sent his Word to renew the earth.**

Reading
Galatians 2:19b–20

I have been crucified with Christ, and the life I live now is not my own; Christ is living in me. I still live my human life, but it is a life of faith in the Son of God, who loved me and gave himself for me.

Responsory

The Lord, the Most High, has done good
    things for me.
In need I shall cry out to him.
—The Lord, the Most High, has done good
    things for me.
In need I shall cry out to him.

May he send his strength to rescue me.
—In need I shall cry out to him.

Glory to the Father, and to the Son,
   and to the Holy Spirit.
—The Lord, the Most High, has done good
   things for me.
In need I shall cry out to him.

Gospel Canticle

Ant. **Through the tender compassion of our God the dawn from on high shall break upon us.**

Canticle of Zechariah
Luke 1:68–79

Blessed + be the Lord, the God of Israel;
he has come to his people and set them free.

He has raised up for us a mighty savior,
born of the house of his servant David.

Through his holy prophets he
   promised of old
that he would save us from our enemies,
from the hands of all who hate us.

He promised to show mercy to our fathers
and to remember his holy covenant.

This was the oath he swore to our
   father Abraham:
to set us free from the hands of our enemies,
free to worship him without fear,
holy and righteous in his sight
   all the days of our life.

You, my child, shall be called the prophet of
    the Most High;
for you will go before the Lord to
    prepare his way,
to give his people knowledge of salvation
by the forgiveness of their sins.

In the tender compassion of our God
the dawn from on high shall break upon us,
to shine on those who dwell in darkness and
    the shadow of death,
and to guide our feet into the way of peace.

Glory to the Father, and to the Son,
    and to the Holy Spirit:
—as it was in the beginning, is now,
and will be for ever. Amen.

Ant. **Through the tender compassion of our God the dawn from on high shall break upon us.**

Intercessions We trust in God's concern for every person he has created and redeemed through his Son. Let us, therefore, renew our prayer to him:
Fulfill the good work you have begun in us, Lord.

O God of mercy, guide us toward
    spiritual growth,
—fill our minds with thoughts of truth,
    justice and love.

For your name's sake, do not abandon
> us for ever,
—and do not annul your covenant.

Accept us, for our hearts are humble and our
> spirits contrite,
—and those who trust in you shall not be
> put to shame.

You have called us to a prophetic vocation
> in Christ,
—help us proclaim your mighty deeds.

The Lord's Prayer

Our Father, who art in heaven,
hallowed be thy name;
thy kingdom come,
thy will be done
on earth as it is in heaven.
Give us this day our daily bread,
and forgive us our trespasses,
as we forgive those who trespass against us;
and lead us not into temptation,
but deliver us from evil.

Pater noster, qui es in cælis:
sanctificetur nomen tuum;
adveniat regnum tuum;
fiat voluntas tua,
sicut in cælo, et in terra.
Panem nostrum cotidianum da nobis hodie;
et dimitte nobis debita nostra,
sicut et nos dimittimus debitoribus nostris;
et ne nos inducas in tentationem;
sed libera nos a malo.

Concluding Prayer

Lord,
fill our hearts with your love
as morning fills the sky.
By living your law may we have
your peace in this life
and endless joy in the life to come.
We ask this through our Lord Jesus Christ,
    your Son,
who lives and reigns with you and
    the Holy Spirit,
God, for ever and ever.
—Amen.

Dismissal

If praying individually, or in a group without a priest or deacon:

May the Lord + bless us,
protect us from all evil
and bring us to everlasting life.
—Amen.

If praying with a priest or deacon, he dismisses the people:

The Lord be with you.
—And with your spirit.

May almighty God bless you,
the Father, and the Son, ✠ and the Holy Spirit.
—Amen.

Go in peace.
—Thanks be to God.

EVENING PRAYER ——————————————

God, + come to my assistance.
—Lord, make haste to help me.

Glory to the Father, and to the Son,
    and to the Holy Spirit:
—as it was in the beginning, is now,
    and will be for ever. Amen. Alleluia.

Hymn   Go, Labor On, p. 684

Psalmody   Ant. 1 **Day after day I will bless you, Lord; I will tell of your marvelous deeds.**

Psalm 145

I will give you glory, O God my King,
I will bless your name for ever.

I will bless you day after day
and praise your name for ever.
The Lord is great, highly to be praised,
his greatness cannot be measured.

Age to age shall proclaim your works,
shall declare your mighty deeds,
shall speak of your splendor and glory,
tell the tale of your wonderful works.

They will speak of your terrible deeds,
recount your greatness and might.
They will recall your abundant goodness;
age to age shall ring out your justice.

The Lord is kind and full of compassion,
slow to anger, abounding in love.
How good is the Lord to all,
compassionate to all his creatures.

All your creatures shall thank you, O Lord,
and your friends shall repeat their blessing.
They shall speak of the glory of your reign
and declare your might, O God,

to make known to men your mighty deeds
and the glorious splendor of your reign.
Yours is an everlasting kingdom;
your rule lasts from age to age.

Glory to the Father, and to the Son,
 and to the Holy Spirit:
as it was in the beginning, is now,
and will be for ever. Amen.

Ant. **Day after day I will bless you, Lord; I will tell of your marvelous deeds.**

Ant. 2 **To you alone, Lord, we look with confidence; you are ever close to those who call upon you.**

Psalm 145
(continued)

The Lord is faithful in all his words
and loving in all his deeds.
The Lord supports all who fall
and raises all who are bowed down.

The eyes of all creatures look to you
and you give them their food in due time.
You open wide your hand,
grant the desires of all who live.

The Lord is just in all his ways
and loving in all his deeds.
He is close to all who call him,
who call on him from their hearts.

He grants the desires of those who fear him,
he hears their cry and he saves them.
The Lord protects all who love him;
but the wicked he will utterly destroy.

Let me speak the praise of the Lord,
let all mankind bless his holy name
for ever, for ages unending.

Glory to the Father, and to the Son,
   and to the Holy Spirit:
—as it was in the beginning, is now,
and will be for ever. Amen.

Ant. **To you alone, Lord, we look with confidence; you are ever close to those who call upon you.**

Ant. 3 **King of all the ages, your ways are perfect and true.**

Canticle:
Revelation
15:3–4

Mighty and wonderful are your works,
Lord God Almighty!
Righteous and true are your ways,
O King of the nations!

Who would dare refuse you honor,
or the glory due your name, O Lord?

Since you alone are holy,
all nations shall come
and worship in your presence.
Your mighty deeds are clearly seen.

Glory to the Father, and to the Son,
   and to the Holy Spirit:
—as it was in the beginning, is now,
and will be for ever. Amen.

Ant. **King of all the ages, your ways are perfect and true.**

Reading
Romans 8:1–2

There is no condemnation now for those who are in Christ Jesus. The law of the spirit, the spirit of life in Christ Jesus, has freed you from the law of sin and death.

Responsory

Christ died for our sins to make of us an offering to God.
—Christ died for our sins to make of us an offering to God.

He died to this world of sin, and rose in the power of the Spirit,
—to make of us an offering to God.

Glory to the Father, and to the Son,
and to the Holy Spirit.
—Christ died for our sins to make of us an offering to God.

Gospel Canticle

Ant. **Remember your mercy, Lord, the promise of mercy you made to our fathers.**

Canticle of Mary
Luke 1:46–55

My ✠ soul proclaims the greatness of the Lord,
my spirit rejoices in God my Savior
for he has looked with favor on his
    lowly servant.

From this day all generations will
    call me blessed:
the Almighty has done great things for me,
and holy is his Name.

He has mercy on those who fear him
in every generation.

He has shown the strength of his arm,
he has scattered the proud in their conceit.

He has cast down the mighty from
    their thrones,
and has lifted up the lowly.

He has filled the hungry with good things,
and the rich he has sent away empty.

He has come to the help of his servant Israel
for he has remembered his promise of mercy,
the promise he made to our fathers,
to Abraham and his children for ever.

Glory to the Father, and to the Son,
    and to the Holy Spirit:
—as it was in the beginning, is now,
and will be for ever. Amen.

Ant. **Remember your mercy, Lord, the promise of mercy you made to our fathers.**

Intercessions Let us pray to Christ, the source of hope for all who know his name:
Lord, have mercy.

Christ, our frail humanity is prone to fall,
—strengthen us through your help.

Left to itself, our nature is inclined to sin,
—let your love always restore it to grace.

Lord, sin offends you, repentance pleases you,
—do not punish us in your wrath even when we have sinned.

You forgave the penitent woman, and placed the wandering sheep on your shoulders,
—do not deprive us of your mercy.

By your death on the cross you opened the gates of heaven,
—admit into your kingdom all who hoped in you.

The Lord's Prayer
Our Father, who art in heaven,
hallowed be thy name;
thy kingdom come,
thy will be done
on earth as it is in heaven.
Give us this day our daily bread,
and forgive us our trespasses,
as we forgive those who trespass against us;
and lead us not into temptation,
but deliver us from evil.

Pater noster, qui es in cælis:
sanctificetur nomen tuum;
adveniat regnum tuum;
fiat voluntas tua,
sicut in cælo, et in terra.
Panem nostrum cotidianum da nobis hodie;
et dimitte nobis debita nostra,
sicut et nos dimittimus debitoribus nostris;
et ne nos inducas in tentationem;
sed libera nos a malo.

Concluding Prayer

God our Father,
you brought salvation to all mankind
through the suffering of Christ your Son.
May your people strive to offer themselves to
    you as a living sacrifice
and be filled with the abundance of your love.
We ask this through our Lord Jesus Christ,
    your Son,
who lives and reigns with you and
    the Holy Spirit,
God, for ever and ever.
—Amen.

Dismissal

If praying individually, or in a group without a priest or deacon:

May the Lord + bless us,
protect us from all evil
and bring us to everlasting life.
—Amen.

If praying with a priest or deacon, he dismisses the people:

The Lord be with you.
—And with your spirit.

May almighty God bless you,
the Father, and the Son, ✠ and the Holy Spirit.
—Amen.

Go in peace.
—Thanks be to God.

NIGHT PRAYER

God, + come to my assistance.
—Lord, make haste to help me.

Glory to the Father, and to the Son,
and to the Holy Spirit:
—as it was in the beginning, is now,
and will be for ever. Amen. Alleluia.

Examen *An optional brief examination of conscience may be made. Call to mind your sins and failings this day.*

Hymn *Abide with Me, p. 675*

Psalmody Ant. **Day and night I cry to you, my God.**

Psalm 88 Lord my God, I call for help by day;
I cry at night before you.
Let my prayer come into your presence.
O turn your ear to my cry.

For my soul is filled with evils;
my life is on the brink of the grave.
I am reckoned as one in the tomb:
I have reached the end of my strength,

like one alone among the dead;
like the slain lying in their graves;
like those you remember no more,
cut off, as they are, from your hand.

You have laid me in the depths of the tomb,
in places that are dark, in the depths.
Your anger weighs down upon me:
I am drowned beneath your waves.

You have taken away my friends
and made me hateful in their sight.
Imprisoned, I cannot escape;
my eyes are sunken with grief.

I call to you, Lord, all the day long;
to you I stretch out my hands.
Will you work your wonders for the dead?
Will the shades stand and praise you?

Will your love be told in the grave
or your faithfulness among the dead?
Will your wonders be known in the dark
or your justice in the land of oblivion?

As for me, Lord, I call to you for help:
in the morning my prayer comes before you.
Lord, why do you reject me?
Why do you hide your face?

Wretched, close to death from my youth,
I have borne your trials; I am numb.
Your fury has swept down upon me;
your terrors have utterly destroyed me.

They surround me all the day like a flood,
they assail me all together.
Friend and neighbor you have taken away:
my one companion is darkness.

Glory to the Father, and to the Son,
   and to the Holy Spirit:
—as it was in the beginning, is now,
and will be for ever. Amen.

Ant. **Day and night I cry to you, my God.**

Reading
Jeremiah 14:9a

You are in our midst, O Lord,
   your name we bear:
      do not forsake us, O Lord, our God!

Responsory   Into your hands, Lord, I commend my spirit.
—Into your hands, Lord, I commend my spirit.

You have redeemed us, Lord God of truth.
—I commend my spirit.

Glory to the Father, and to the Son,
   and to the Holy Spirit.
—Into your hands, Lord, I commend my spirit.

Gospel Canticle   Ant. **Protect us, Lord, as we stay awake; watch over us as we sleep, that awake, we may keep watch with Christ, and asleep, rest in his peace.**

Canticle of Simeon
Luke 2:29–32

Lord, + now you let your servant go in peace;
your word has been fulfilled:
my own eyes have seen the salvation
which you have prepared in the sight of
    every people:
a light to reveal you to the nations
and the glory of your people Israel.

Glory to the Father, and to the Son,
    and to the Holy Spirit:
—as it was in the beginning, is now,
and will be for ever. Amen.

Ant. **Protect us, Lord, as we stay awake; watch over us as we sleep, that awake, we may keep watch with Christ, and asleep, rest in his peace.**

Concluding Prayer

Let us pray.
All-powerful God,
keep us united with your Son
in his death and burial
so that we may rise to new life with him,
who lives and reigns for ever and ever.
—Amen.

Blessing

May the all-powerful Lord
grant us a restful night
and a peaceful death.
—Amen.

Marian Antiphon

Sing the "Salve Regina," found on p. 698, or pray a Hail Mary.

Saturday, July 29, 2023
Sts. Martha, Mary, and Lazarus

MORNING PRAYER

God, + come to my assistance.
—Lord, make haste to help me.

Glory to the Father, and to the Son,
    and to the Holy Spirit:
—as it was in the beginning, is now,
and will be for ever. Amen. Alleluia.

Hymn   *Sing with All the Saints in Glory, p. 702*

Psalmody   Ant. 1 **We do well to sing to your name, Most High, and proclaim your mercy at daybreak.**

Psalm 92   It is good to give thanks to the Lord,
to make music to your name, O Most High,
to proclaim your love in the morning
and your truth in the watches of the night,
on the ten-stringed lyre and the lute,
with the murmuring sound of the harp.

Your deeds, O Lord, have made me glad;
for the work of your hands I shout with joy.
O Lord, how great are your works!
How deep are your designs!
The foolish man cannot know this
and the fool cannot understand.

Though the wicked spring up like grass
and all who do evil thrive:
they are doomed to be eternally destroyed.
But you, Lord, are eternally on high.
See how your enemies perish;
all doers of evil are scattered.

To me you give the wild-ox's strength;
you anoint me with the purest oil.
My eyes looked in triumph on my foes;
my ears heard gladly of their fall.
The just will flourish like the palm-tree
and grow like a Lebanon cedar.

Planted in the house of the Lord,
they will flourish in the courts of our God,
still bearing fruit when they are old,
still full of sap, still green,
to proclaim that the Lord is just.
In him, my rock, there is no wrong.

Glory to the Father, and to the Son,
   and to the Holy Spirit:
—as it was in the beginning, is now,
and will be for ever. Amen.

Ant. **We do well to sing to your name, Most High, and proclaim your mercy at daybreak.**

Ant. 2 **I will create a new heart in you, and breathe into you a new spirit.**

Canticle:
Ezekiel 36:24-28

I will take you away from among the nations,
gather you from all the foreign lands,
and bring you back to your own land.

I will sprinkle clean water upon you
to cleanse you from all your impurities,
and from all your idols I will cleanse you.

I will give you a new heart
and place a new spirit within you,
taking from your bodies your stony hearts
and giving you natural hearts.

I will put my spirit within you
and make you live by my statutes,
careful to observe my decrees.

You shall live in the land I gave your fathers;
you shall be my people,
and I will be your God.

Glory to the Father, and to the Son,
    and to the Holy Spirit:
—as it was in the beginning, is now,
and will be for ever. Amen.

Ant. **I will create a new heart in you, and breathe into you a new spirit.**

Ant. 3 **On the lips of children and infants you have found perfect praise.**

Psalm 8

How great is your name, O Lord our God,
through all the earth!

Your majesty is praised above the heavens;
on the lips of children and of babes
you have found praise to foil your enemy,
to silence the foe and the rebel.

When I see the heavens, the work of
    your hands,
the moon and the stars which you arranged,
what is man that you should keep
    him in mind,
mortal man that you care for him?

Yet you have made him little less than a god;
with glory and honor you crowned him,
gave him power over the works of
    your hands,
put all things under his feet.

All of them, sheep and cattle,
yes, even the savage beasts,
birds of the air, and fish
that make their way through the waters.

How great is your name, O Lord our God
through all the earth!

Glory to the Father, and to the Son,
    and to the Holy Spirit:
—as it was in the beginning, is now,
and will be for ever. Amen.

Ant. **On the lips of children and infants you have found perfect praise.**

Reading
Romans 12:1–2

Brothers, I beg you through the mercy of God to offer your bodies as a living sacrifice holy and acceptable to God, your spiritual worship. Do not conform yourselves to this age but be transformed by the renewal of your mind, so that you may judge what is God's will, what is good, pleasing and perfect.

Responsory

Let the just rejoice in the presence of God.
—Let the just rejoice in the presence of God.

Let them be filled with gladness,
—in the presence of God.

Glory to the Father, and to the Son,
   and to the Holy Spirit.
—Let the just rejoice in the presence of God.

Gospel Canticle

Ant. Blessed are the peace makers, and blessed are the pure of heart; they shall see God.

Canticle of Zechariah
Luke 1:68–79

Blessed + be the Lord, the God of Israel;
he has come to his people and set them free.

He has raised up for us a mighty savior,
born of the house of his servant David.

Through his holy prophets he
   promised of old
that he would save us from our enemies,
from the hands of all who hate us.

He promised to show mercy to our fathers
and to remember his holy covenant.

This was the oath he swore to our
    father Abraham:
to set us free from the hands of our enemies,
free to worship him without fear,
holy and righteous in his sight
    all the days of our life.

You, my child, shall be called the prophet of
    the Most High;
for you will go before the Lord to
    prepare his way,
to give his people knowledge of salvation
by the forgiveness of their sins.

In the tender compassion of our God
the dawn from on high shall break upon us,
to shine on those who dwell in darkness and
    the shadow of death,
and to guide our feet into the way of peace.

Glory to the Father, and to the Son,
    and to the Holy Spirit:
—as it was in the beginning, is now,
and will be for ever. Amen.

Ant. **Blessed are the peace makers, and blessed are the pure of heart; they shall see God.**

Intercessions My brothers, let us praise Christ, asking to serve him and to be holy and righteous in his sight all the days of our life. Let us acclaim him:
Lord, you alone are the holy one.

You desired to experience everything we experience but sin,
—have mercy on us, Lord Jesus.

You called us to love perfectly,
—make us holy, Lord Jesus.

You commissioned us to be the salt of the earth and the light of the world,
—let your light shine on us, Lord Jesus.

You desired to serve, not to be served,
—help us, Lord Jesus, to give humble service to you and to our neighbors.

You are in the form of God sharing in the splendor of the Father,
—Lord Jesus, let us see the glory of your face.

The Lord's Prayer Our Father, who art in heaven,
hallowed be thy name;
thy kingdom come,
thy will be done
on earth as it is in heaven.
Give us this day our daily bread,
and forgive us our trespasses,
as we forgive those who trespass against us;
and lead us not into temptation,
but deliver us from evil.

Pater noster, qui es in cælis:
sanctificetur nomen tuum;
adveniat regnum tuum;
fiat voluntas tua,
sicut in cælo, et in terra.
Panem nostrum cotidianum da nobis hodie;
et dimitte nobis debita nostra,
sicut et nos dimittimus debitoribus nostris;
et ne nos inducas in tentationem;
sed libera nos a malo.

Concluding Prayer

Grant, we pray, almighty God,
that the example of your saints may spur us
on to a better life,
so that we, who celebrate the memory of
Saints Martha, Mary and Lazarus,
may also imitate without ceasing their deeds.
Through our Lord Jesus Christ,
your Son,
who lives and reigns with you in the unity of
the Holy Spirit,
God, for ever and ever.
—Amen.

Dismissal

If praying individually, or in a group without a priest or deacon:

May the Lord + bless us,
protect us from all evil
and bring us to everlasting life.
—Amen.

If praying with a priest or deacon, he dismisses the people:

The Lord be with you.
—And with your spirit.

May almighty God bless you,
the Father, and the Son, ✠ and the Holy Spirit.
—Amen.

Go in peace.
—Thanks be to God.

EVENING PRAYER

BEGINS SEVENTEENTH SUNDAY IN ORDINARY TIME

God, + come to my assistance.
—Lord, make haste to help me.

Glory to the Father, and to the Son,
    and to the Holy Spirit:
—as it was in the beginning, is now,
    and will be for ever. Amen. Alleluia.

Hymn *Praise to the Lord, the Almighty, p. 696*

Psalmody Ant. 1 **Like burning incense, Lord, let my prayer rise up to you.**

Psalm 141:1–9 I have called to you, Lord; hasten to help me!
Hear my voice when I cry to you.
Let my prayer arise before you like incense,
the raising of my hands like an
    evening oblation.

Set, O Lord, a guard over my mouth;
keep watch at the door of my lips!
Do not turn my heart to things that
    are wrong,
to evil deeds with men who are sinners.

Never allow me to share in their feasting.
If a good man strikes or reproves me it
    is kindness;
but let the oil of the wicked not
    anoint my head.
Let my prayer be ever against their malice.

Their princes were thrown down by the side
    of the rock:
then they understood that my words
    were kind.
As a millstone is shattered to pieces on
    the ground,
so their bones were strewn at the mouth of
    the grave.

To you, Lord God, my eyes are turned:
in you I take refuge; spare my soul!
From the trap they have laid for me
    keep me safe:
keep me from the snares of those who do evil.

Glory to the Father, and to the Son,
    and to the Holy Spirit:
— as it was in the beginning, is now,
and will be for ever. Amen.

Ant. **Like burning incense, Lord, let my prayer rise up to you.**

Ant. 2 **You are my refuge, Lord; you are all that I desire in life.**

JULY 29 SAT EVENING PRAYER

Psalm 142

With all my voice I cry to the Lord,
with all my voice I entreat the Lord.
I pour out my trouble before him;
I tell him all my distress
while my spirit faints within me.
But you, O Lord, know my path.

On the way where I shall walk
they have hidden a snare to entrap me.
Look on my right and see:
there is not one who takes my part.
I have no means of escape,
not one who cares for my soul.

I cry to you, O Lord.
I have said: "You are my refuge,
all I have left in the land of the living."
Listen then to my cry
for I am in the depths of distress.

Rescue me from those who pursue me
for they are stronger than I.
Bring my soul out of this prison
and then I shall praise your name.
Around me the just will assemble
because of your goodness to me.

Glory to the Father, and to the Son,
    and to the Holy Spirit:
—as it was in the beginning, is now,
and will be for ever. Amen.

Ant. **You are my refuge, Lord; you are all that I desire in life.**

Ant. 3 **The Lord Jesus humbled himself, and God exalted him for ever.**

Canticle:
Philippians
2:6–11

Though he was in the form of God,
Jesus did not deem equality with God
something to be grasped at.

Rather, he emptied himself
and took the form of a slave,
being born in the likeness of men.

He was known to be of human estate,
and it was thus that he humbled himself,
obediently accepting even death,
death on a cross!

Because of this,
God highly exalted him
and bestowed on him the name
above every other name,

So that at Jesus' name
every knee must bend
in the heavens, on the earth,
and under the earth,
and every tongue proclaim
to the glory of God the Father:
JESUS CHRIST IS LORD!

Glory to the Father, and to the Son,
    and to the Holy Spirit:
as it was in the beginning, is now,
and will be for ever. Amen.

JULY 29   SAT   EVENING PRAYER

Ant.   **The Lord Jesus humbled himself, and God exalted him for ever.**

Reading
Romans 11:33–36

How deep are the riches and the wisdom and the knowledge of God! How inscrutable his judgments, how unsearchable his ways! For "who has known the mind of the Lord? Or who has been his counselor? Who has given him anything so as to deserve return?" For from him and through him and for him all things are. To him be glory forever. Amen.

Responsory

Our hearts are filled with wonder as we contemplate your works, O Lord.
— Our hearts are filled with wonder as we contemplate your works, O Lord.

We praise the wisdom which wrought them all,
— as we contemplate your works, O Lord.

Glory to the Father, and to the Son, and to the Holy Spirit.
— Our hearts are filled with wonder as we contemplate your works, O Lord.

Gospel Canticle

Ant. The kingdom of heaven is like a merchant in search of fine pearls; when he found one of great value, he sold everything he had and bought it.

Canticle of Mary
Luke 1:46–55

My ✙ soul proclaims the greatness of the Lord,
my spirit rejoices in God my Savior
for he has looked with favor on his
    lowly servant.

From this day all generations will
    call me blessed:
the Almighty has done great things for me,
and holy is his Name.

He has mercy on those who fear him
in every generation.

He has shown the strength of his arm,
he has scattered the proud in their conceit.

He has cast down the mighty from
    their thrones,
and has lifted up the lowly.

He has filled the hungry with good things,
and the rich he has sent away empty.

He has come to the help of his servant Israel
for he has remembered his promise of mercy,
the promise he made to our fathers,
to Abraham and his children for ever.

Glory to the Father, and to the Son,
    and to the Holy Spirit:
as it was in the beginning, is now,
and will be for ever. Amen.

Ant. **The kingdom of heaven is like a merchant in search of fine pearls; when he found one of great value, he sold everything he had and bought it.**

Intercessions We give glory to the one God—Father,
Son and Holy Spirit—and in our
weakness we pray:
Lord, be with your people.

Holy Lord, Father all-powerful, let justice
spring up on the earth,
—then your people will dwell in the
beauty of peace.

Let every nation come into your kingdom,
—so that all peoples will be saved.

Let married couples live in your peace,
—and grow in mutual love.

Reward all who have done good to us, Lord,
—and grant them eternal life.

Look with compassion on victims of
hatred and war,
—grant them heavenly peace.

The Lord's Prayer Our Father, who art in heaven,
hallowed be thy name;
thy kingdom come,
thy will be done
on earth as it is in heaven.
Give us this day our daily bread,
and forgive us our trespasses,
as we forgive those who trespass against us;
and lead us not into temptation,
but deliver us from evil.

Pater noster, qui es in cælis:
sanctificetur nomen tuum;
adveniat regnum tuum;
fiat voluntas tua,
sicut in cælo, et in terra.
Panem nostrum cotidianum da nobis hodie;
et dimitte nobis debita nostra,
sicut et nos dimittimus debitoribus nostris;
et ne nos inducas in tentationem;
sed libera nos a malo.

Concluding Prayer

God our Father and protector,
without you nothing is holy,
nothing has value.
Guide us to everlasting life
by helping us to use wisely
the blessings you have given to the world.
We ask this through our Lord Jesus Christ,
    your Son,
who lives and reigns with you and
    the Holy Spirit,
God, for ever and ever.
—Amen.

Dismissal

If praying individually, or in a group without a priest or deacon:

May the Lord + bless us,
protect us from all evil
and bring us to everlasting life.
—Amen.

If praying with a priest or deacon, he dismisses the people:

The Lord be with you.
—And with your spirit.

May almighty God bless you,
the Father, and the Son, ✢ and the Holy Spirit.
—Amen.

Go in peace.
—Thanks be to God.

NIGHT PRAYER

God, + come to my assistance.
—Lord, make haste to help me.

Glory to the Father, and to the Son,
   and to the Holy Spirit:
—as it was in the beginning, is now,
   and will be for ever. Amen. Alleluia.

Examen *An optional brief examination of conscience may be made. Call to mind your sins and failings this day.*

Hymn Before the Final Light of Day, p. 676

Psalmody Ant. 1 **Have mercy, Lord, and hear my prayer.**

Psalm 4

When I call, answer me, O God of justice;
from anguish you released me; have mercy
   and hear me!

O men, how long will your hearts be closed,
will you love what is futile and seek
   what is false?

It is the Lord who grants favors to those
   whom he loves;
the Lord hears me whenever I call him.

Fear him; do not sin: ponder on your bed
    and be still.
Make justice your sacrifice and trust
    in the Lord.

"What can bring us happiness?" many say.
Let the light of your face shine on us, O Lord.

You have put into my heart a greater joy
than they have from abundance of corn
    and new wine.

I will lie down in peace and sleep
    comes at once
for you alone, Lord, make me dwell in safety.

Glory to the Father, and to the Son,
    and to the Holy Spirit:
as it was in the beginning, is now,
and will be for ever. Amen.

Ant.   **Have mercy, Lord, and hear my prayer.**

Ant. 2   **In the silent hours of night, bless the Lord.**

Psalm 134

O come, bless the Lord,
all you who serve the Lord,
who stand in the house of the Lord,
in the courts of the house of our God.

Lift up your hands to the holy place
and bless the Lord through the night.

May the Lord bless you from Zion,
he who made both heaven and earth.

Glory to the Father, and to the Son,
>   and to the Holy Spirit:
—as it was in the beginning, is now,
and will be for ever. Amen.

Ant. **In the silent hours of night, bless the Lord.**

Reading
Deuteronomy 6:4-7

Hear, O Israel! The Lord is our God, the Lord alone! Therefore, you shall love the Lord, your God, with all your heart, and with all your soul, and with all your strength. Take to heart these words which I enjoin on you today. Drill them into your children. Speak of them at home and abroad, whether you are busy or at rest.

Responsory

Into your hands, Lord, I commend my spirit.
—Into your hands, Lord, I commend my spirit.

You have redeemed us, Lord God of truth.
—I commend my spirit.

Glory to the Father, and to the Son,
>   and to the Holy Spirit.
—Into your hands, Lord, I commend my spirit.

Gospel Canticle

Ant. **Protect us, Lord, as we stay awake; watch over us as we sleep, that awake, we may keep watch with Christ, and asleep, rest in his peace.**

Canticle of Simeon
Luke 2:29–32

Lord, + now you let your servant go in peace;
your word has been fulfilled:
my own eyes have seen the salvation
which you have prepared in the sight of
  every people:
a light to reveal you to the nations
and the glory of your people Israel.

Glory to the Father, and to the Son,
  and to the Holy Spirit:
—as it was in the beginning, is now,
and will be for ever. Amen.

Ant.

Protect us, Lord, as we stay awake; watch over us as we sleep, that awake, we may keep watch with Christ, and asleep, rest in his peace.

Concluding Prayer

Let us pray.
Lord,
be with us throughout this night.
When day comes may we rise from sleep
to rejoice in the resurrection of your Christ,
who lives and reigns for ever and ever.
—Amen.

Blessing

May the all-powerful Lord
grant us a restful night
and a peaceful death.
—Amen.

Marian Antiphon

Sing the "Salve Regina," found on p. 698, or pray a Hail Mary.

MY SOUL SHALL BE FILLED AS WITH A BANQUET, MY MOUTH SHALL PRAISE YOU WITH JOY.

Sunday, July 30, 2023
Seventeenth Sunday in Ordinary Time

MORNING PRAYER

God, + come to my assistance.
—Lord, make haste to help me.

Glory to the Father, and to the Son,
    and to the Holy Spirit:
—as it was in the beginning, is now,
    and will be for ever. Amen. Alleluia.

Hymn   *This Day the First of Days Was Made, p. 695*

Psalmody   Ant. 1 **As morning breaks I look to you, O God, to be my strength this day, alleluia.**

Psalm 63:2–9

O God, you are my God, for you I long;
for you my soul is thirsting.
My body pines for you
like a dry, weary land without water.
So I gaze on you in the sanctuary
to see your strength and your glory.

For your love is better than life,
my lips will speak your praise.
So I will bless you all my life,
in your name I will lift up my hands.
My soul shall be filled as with a banquet,
my mouth shall praise you with joy.

On my bed I remember you.
On you I muse through the night
for you have been my help;
in the shadow of your wings I rejoice.
My soul clings to you;
your right hand holds me fast.

Glory to the Father, and to the Son,
    and to the Holy Spirit:
—as it was in the beginning, is now,
and will be for ever. Amen.

Ant.   **As morning breaks I look to you, O God, to be my strength this day, alleluia.**

Ant. 2   **From the midst of the flames the three young men cried out with one voice: Blessed be God, alleluia.**

Canticle: Daniel 3:57–88, 56

Bless the Lord, all you works of the Lord.
Praise and exalt him above all forever.
Angels of the Lord, bless the Lord.
You heavens, bless the Lord.
All you waters above the heavens,
    bless the Lord.
All you hosts of the Lord, bless the Lord.
Sun and moon, bless the Lord.
Stars of heaven, bless the Lord.

Every shower and dew, bless the Lord.
All you winds, bless the Lord.
Fire and heat, bless the Lord.
Cold and chill, bless the Lord.
Dew and rain, bless the Lord.
Frost and chill, bless the Lord.
Ice and snow, bless the Lord.
Nights and days, bless the Lord.
Light and darkness, bless the Lord.
Lightnings and clouds, bless the Lord.

Let the earth bless the Lord.
Praise and exalt him above all forever.
Mountains and hills, bless the Lord.
Everything growing from the earth,
    bless the Lord.
You springs, bless the Lord.
Seas and rivers, bless the Lord.
You dolphins and all water creatures,
    bless the Lord.
All you birds of the air, bless the Lord.
All you beasts, wild and tame, bless the Lord.
You sons of men, bless the Lord.

O Israel, bless the Lord.
Praise and exalt him above all forever.
Priests of the Lord, bless the Lord.
Servants of the Lord, bless the Lord.
Spirits and souls of the just, bless the Lord.
Holy men of humble heart, bless the Lord.
Hananiah, Azariah, Mishael, bless the Lord.
Praise and exalt him above all forever.

Let us bless the Father, and the Son,
  and the Holy Spirit.
Let us praise and exalt him above all forever.
Blessed are you, Lord, in the firmament
  of heaven.
Praiseworthy and glorious and exalted above
  all forever.

Ant.   **From the midst of the flames the three young men cried out with one voice: Blessed be God, alleluia.**

Ant. 3   **Let the people of Zion rejoice in their King, alleluia.**

Psalm 149

Sing a new song to the Lord,
  his praise in the assembly of the faithful.
Let Israel rejoice in its maker,
  let Zion's sons exult in their king.
Let them praise his name with dancing
  and make music with timbrel and harp.

For the Lord takes delight in his people.
He crowns the poor with salvation.
Let the faithful rejoice in their glory,
  shout for joy and take their rest.
Let the praise of God be on their lips
  and a two-edged sword in their hand,

to deal out vengeance to the nations
  and punishment on all the peoples;
to bind their kings in chains
  and their nobles in fetters of iron;
to carry out the sentence pre-ordained;
  this honor is for all his faithful.

Glory to the Father, and to the Son,
> and to the Holy Spirit:
—as it was in the beginning, is now,
and will be for ever. Amen.

Ant. **Let the people of Zion rejoice in their King, alleluia.**

Reading
Revelation 7:10, 12

Salvation is from our God, who is seated on the throne, and from the Lamb! Praise and glory, wisdom and thanksgiving and honor, power and might, to our God forever and ever. Amen!

Responsory

Christ, Son of the living God,
> have mercy on us.
—Christ, Son of the living God,
> have mercy on us.

You are seated at the right hand of the Father,
—have mercy on us.

Glory to the Father, and to the Son,
> and to the Holy Spirit.
—Christ, Son of the living God,
> have mercy on us.

Gospel Canticle

Ant. **When those men saw the signs Jesus performed, they said: Surely this is the Prophet who is to come into the world.**

Canticle of Zechariah Luke 1:68–79

Blessed + be the Lord, the God of Israel;
he has come to his people and set them free.

He has raised up for us a mighty savior,
born of the house of his servant David.

Through his holy prophets he
 promised of old
that he would save us from our enemies,
from the hands of all who hate us.

He promised to show mercy to our fathers
and to remember his holy covenant.

This was the oath he swore to our
 father Abraham:
to set us free from the hands of our enemies,
free to worship him without fear,
holy and righteous in his sight
 all the days of our life.

You, my child, shall be called the prophet of
 the Most High;
for you will go before the Lord to
 prepare his way,
to give his people knowledge of salvation
by the forgiveness of their sins.

In the tender compassion of our God
the dawn from on high shall break upon us,
to shine on those who dwell in darkness and
 the shadow of death,
and to guide our feet into the way of peace.

Glory to the Father, and to the Son,
 and to the Holy Spirit:
—as it was in the beginning, is now,
 and will be for ever. Amen.

Ant. **When those men saw the signs Jesus performed, they said: Surely this is the Prophet who is to come into the world.**

Intercessions Christ is the sun that never sets, the true light that shines on every man. Let us call out to him in praise:
Lord, you are our life and our salvation.

Creator of the stars, we thank you for your gift, the first rays of the dawn,
—and we commemorate your resurrection.

May your Holy Spirit teach us to do your will today,
—and may your Wisdom guide us always.

Each Sunday give us the joy of gathering as your people,
—around the table of your Word and your Body.

From our hearts we thank you,
—for your countless blessings.

The Lord's Prayer
Our Father, who art in heaven,
hallowed be thy name;
thy kingdom come,
thy will be done
on earth as it is in heaven.
Give us this day our daily bread,
and forgive us our trespasses,
as we forgive those who trespass against us;
and lead us not into temptation,
but deliver us from evil.

Pater noster, qui es in cælis:
sanctificetur nomen tuum;
adveniat regnum tuum;
fiat voluntas tua,
sicut in cælo, et in terra.
Panem nostrum cotidianum da nobis hodie;
et dimitte nobis debita nostra,
sicut et nos dimittimus debitoribus nostris;
et ne nos inducas in tentationem;
sed libera nos a malo.

Concluding Prayer

God our Father and protector,
without you nothing is holy,
nothing has value.
Guide us to everlasting life
by helping us to use wisely
the blessings you have given to the world.
We ask this through our Lord Jesus Christ,
 your Son,
who lives and reigns with you and
 the Holy Spirit,
God, for ever and ever.
—Amen.

Dismissal

If praying individually, or in a group without a priest or deacon:

May the Lord ✛ bless us,
protect us from all evil
and bring us to everlasting life.
—Amen.

If praying with a priest or deacon, he dismisses the people:

The Lord be with you.
—And with your spirit.

May almighty God bless you,
   the Father, and the Son, ✠ and the Holy Spirit.
—Amen.

Go in peace.
—Thanks be to God.

EVENING PRAYER

God, ✠ come to my assistance.
—Lord, make haste to help me.

Glory to the Father, and to the Son,
   and to the Holy Spirit:
—as it was in the beginning, is now,
   and will be for ever. Amen. Alleluia.

Hymn *Holy God, We Praise Thy Name, p. 686*

Psalmody Ant. 1 **The Lord will stretch forth his mighty scepter from Zion, and he will reign for ever, alleluia.**

Psalm 110:1–5, 7
The Lord's revelation to my Master:
   "Sit on my right:
   your foes I will put beneath your feet."

The Lord will wield from Zion
your scepter of power:
rule in the midst of all your foes.

A prince from the day of your birth
on the holy mountains;
from the womb before the dawn I begot you.

The Lord has sworn an oath he will
    not change.
"You are a priest for ever,
a priest like Melchizedek of old."

The Master standing at your right hand
will shatter kings in the day of his
    great wrath.

He shall drink from the stream by
    the wayside
and therefore he shall lift up his head.

Glory to the Father, and to the Son,
    and to the Holy Spirit:
as it was in the beginning, is now,
and will be for ever. Amen.

Ant. **The Lord will stretch forth his mighty scepter from Zion, and he will reign for ever, alleluia.**

Ant. 2 **The earth is shaken to its depths before the glory of your face.**

Psalm 114

When Israel came forth from Egypt,
Jacob's sons from an alien people,
Judah became the Lord's temple,
Israel became his kingdom.

The sea fled at the sight:
the Jordan turned back on its course,
the mountains leapt like rams
and the hills like yearling sheep.

Why was it, sea, that you fled,
that you turned back, Jordan, on
    your course?
Mountains, that you leapt like rams,
hills, like yearling sheep?

Tremble, O earth, before the Lord,
in the presence of the God of Jacob,
who turns the rock into a pool
and flint into a spring of water.

Glory to the Father, and to the Son,
    and to the Holy Spirit:
—as it was in the beginning, is now,
and will be for ever. Amen.

Ant. **The earth is shaken to its depths before the glory of your face.**

Ant. 3 **All power is yours, Lord God, our mighty King, alleluia.**

Canticle: See Revelation 19:1–7

Alleluia.
Salvation, glory, and power to our God:
his judgments are honest and true.
Alleluia.

Alleluia.
Sing praise to our God, all you his servants,
all who worship him reverently,
    great and small.
Alleluia.

Alleluia.
The Lord our all-powerful God is King;
let us rejoice, sing praise, and give him glory.
Alleluia.

Alleluia.
The wedding feast of the Lamb has begun,
and his bride is prepared to welcome him.
Alleluia.

Alleluia.
Glory to the Father, and to the Son,
and to the Holy Spirit:
Alleluia.

Alleluia.
as it was in the beginning, is now,
and will be for ever. Amen.
Alleluia.

Ant. **All power is yours, Lord God, our mighty King, alleluia.**

Reading
2 Corinthians
1:3–4

Praised be God, the Father of our Lord Jesus Christ, the Father of mercies and the God of all consolation! He comforts us in all our afflictions and thus enables us to comfort those who are in trouble, with the same consolation we have received from him.

Responsory The whole creation proclaims the greatness
of your glory.
—The whole creation proclaims the greatness
of your glory.

Eternal ages praise
—the greatness of your glory.

Glory to the Father, and to the Son,
and to the Holy Spirit.
—The whole creation proclaims the greatness
of your glory.

Gospel Canticle Ant. **Ask and you will receive, seek and you will find, knock and the door will be opened to you.**

Canticle of Mary Luke 1:46–55

My ☩ soul proclaims the greatness of the Lord,
my spirit rejoices in God my Savior
for he has looked with favor on his
lowly servant.

From this day all generations will
call me blessed:
the Almighty has done great things for me,
and holy is his Name.

He has mercy on those who fear him
in every generation.

He has shown the strength of his arm,
he has scattered the proud in their conceit.

He has cast down the mighty from
    their thrones,
and has lifted up the lowly.

He has filled the hungry with good things,
and the rich he has sent away empty.

He has come to the help of his servant Israel
for he has remembered his promise of mercy,
the promise he made to our fathers,
to Abraham and his children for ever.

Glory to the Father, and to the Son,
    and to the Holy Spirit:
— as it was in the beginning, is now,
and will be for ever. Amen.

Ant. **Ask and you will receive, seek and you will find, knock and the door will be opened to you.**

Intercessions Christ the Lord is our head; we are his members. In joy let us call out to him:
Lord, may your kingdom come.

Christ our Savior, make your Church a more vivid symbol of the unity of all mankind,
— make it more effectively the sacrament of salvation for all peoples.

Through your presence, guide the college of bishops in union with the Pope,
— give them the gifts of unity, love and peace.

Bind all Christians more closely to yourself,
    their divine Head,
—lead them to proclaim your kingdom by the
    witness of their lives.

Grant peace to the world,
—let every land flourish in justice and security.

Grant to the dead the glory of resurrection,
—and give us a share in their happiness.

The Lord's Prayer

Our Father, who art in heaven,
hallowed be thy name;
thy kingdom come,
thy will be done
on earth as it is in heaven.
Give us this day our daily bread,
and forgive us our trespasses,
as we forgive those who trespass against us;
and lead us not into temptation,
but deliver us from evil.

Pater noster, qui es in cælis:
sanctificetur nomen tuum;
adveniat regnum tuum;
fiat voluntas tua,
sicut in cælo, et in terra.
Panem nostrum cotidianum da nobis hodie;
et dimitte nobis debita nostra,
sicut et nos dimittimus debitoribus nostris;
et ne nos inducas in tentationem;
sed libera nos a malo.

Concluding Prayer

God our Father and protector,
without you nothing is holy,
nothing has value.
Guide us to everlasting life
by helping us to use wisely
the blessings you have given to the world.
We ask this through our Lord Jesus Christ,
  your Son,
who lives and reigns with you and
  the Holy Spirit,
God, for ever and ever.
—Amen.

Dismissal

If praying individually, or in a group without a priest or deacon:

May the Lord ✚ bless us,
protect us from all evil
and bring us to everlasting life.
—Amen.

If praying with a priest or deacon, he dismisses the people:

The Lord be with you.
—And with your spirit.

May almighty God bless you,
the Father, and the Son, ✚ and the Holy Spirit.
—Amen.

Go in peace.
—Thanks be to God.

NIGHT PRAYER

God, + come to my assistance.
—Lord, make haste to help me.

Glory to the Father, and to the Son,
  and to the Holy Spirit:
—as it was in the beginning, is now,
  and will be for ever. Amen. Alleluia.

Examen — *An optional brief examination of conscience may be made. Call to mind your sins and failings this day.*

Hymn — *O Joyful Light of God Most High, p. 693*

Psalmody — Ant. **Night holds no terrors for me sleeping under God's wings.**

Psalm 91

He who dwells in the shelter of
    the Most High
and abides in the shade of the Almighty
says to the Lord: "My refuge,
my stronghold, my God in whom I trust!"

It is he who will free you from the snare
of the fowler who seeks to destroy you;
he will conceal you with his pinions
and under his wings you will find refuge.

You will not fear the terror of the night
nor the arrow that flies by day,
nor the plague that prowls in the darkness
nor the scourge that lays waste at noon.

A thousand may fall at your side,
ten thousand fall at your right,
you, it will never approach;
his faithfulness is buckler and shield.

Your eyes have only to look
to see how the wicked are repaid,
you who have said: "Lord, my refuge!"
and have made the Most High your dwelling.

Upon you no evil shall fall,
no plague approach where you dwell.
For you has he commanded his angels,
to keep you in all your ways.

They shall bear you upon their hands
lest you strike your foot against a stone.
On the lion and the viper you will tread
and trample the young lion and the dragon.

Since he clings to me in love, I will free him;
protect him for he knows my name.
When he calls I shall answer: "I am with you."
I will save him in distress and give him glory.

With length of life I will content him;
I shall let him see my saving power.

Glory to the Father, and to the Son,
    and to the Holy Spirit:
—as it was in the beginning, is now,
and will be for ever. Amen.

Ant. **Night holds no terrors for me sleeping under God's wings.**

Reading
Revelation 22:4–5

They shall see the Lord face to face and bear his name on their foreheads. The night shall be no more. They will need no light from lamps or the sun, for the Lord God shall give them light, and they shall reign forever.

Responsory

Into your hands, Lord, I commend my spirit.
—Into your hands, Lord, I commend my spirit.

You have redeemed us, Lord God of truth.
—I commend my spirit.

Glory to the Father, and to the Son,
    and to the Holy Spirit.
—Into your hands, Lord, I commend my spirit.

Gospel Canticle

Ant. **Protect us, Lord, as we stay awake; watch over us as we sleep, that awake, we may keep watch with Christ, and asleep, rest in his peace.**

Canticle of Simeon
Luke 2:29–32

Lord, + now you let your servant go in peace;
your word has been fulfilled:
my own eyes have seen the salvation
which you have prepared in the sight of
    every people:
a light to reveal you to the nations
and the glory of your people Israel.

Glory to the Father, and to the Son,
    and to the Holy Spirit:
—as it was in the beginning, is now,
    and will be for ever. Amen.

Ant. **Protect us, Lord, as we stay awake; watch over us as we sleep, that awake, we may keep watch with Christ, and asleep, rest in his peace.**

Concluding Prayer

Let us pray.
Lord,
we have celebrated today
the mystery of the rising of Christ to new life.
May we now rest in your peace,
safe from all that could harm us,
and rise again refreshed and joyful,
to praise you throughout another day.
We ask this through Christ our Lord.
—Amen.

Blessing

May the all-powerful Lord
grant us a restful night
and a peaceful death.
—Amen.

Marian Antiphon

Sing the "Salve Regina," found on p. 698, or pray a Hail Mary.

Monday, July 31, 2023
St. Ignatius of Loyola

MORNING PRAYER

God, + come to my assistance.
—Lord, make haste to help me.

Glory to the Father, and to the Son,
   and to the Holy Spirit:
—as it was in the beginning, is now,
and will be for ever. Amen. Alleluia.

Hymn *Sing with All the Saints in Glory, p. 702*

Psalmody Ant. 1 **I lift up my heart to you, O Lord, and you will hear my morning prayer.**

Psalm 5:2–10, 12–13

To my words give ear, O Lord,
give heed to my groaning.
Attend to the sound of my cries,
my King and my God.

It is you whom I invoke, O Lord.
In the morning you hear me;
in the morning I offer you my prayer,
watching and waiting.

You are no God who loves evil;
no sinner is your guest.
The boastful shall not stand their ground
before your face.

You hate all who do evil;
you destroy all who lie.
The deceitful and bloodthirsty man
the Lord detests.

But I through the greatness of your love
have access to your house.
I bow down before your holy temple,
filled with awe.

Lead me, Lord, in your justice,
because of those who lie in wait;
make clear your way before me.

No truth can be found in their mouths,
their heart is all mischief,
their throat a wide-open grave,
all honey their speech.

All those you protect shall be glad
and ring out their joy.
You shelter them; in you they rejoice,
those who love your name.

It is you who bless the just man, Lord:
you surround him with favor as with a shield.

Glory to the Father, and to the Son,
    and to the Holy Spirit:
—as it was in the beginning, is now,
and will be for ever. Amen.

Ant. **I lift up my heart to you, O Lord, and you will hear my morning prayer.**

Ant. 2 **We praise your glorious name, O Lord, our God.**

Canticle:
1 Chronicles
29:10–13

Blessed may you be, O Lord,
God of Israel our father,
from eternity to eternity.

Yours, O Lord, are grandeur and power,
majesty, splendor, and glory.

For all in heaven and on earth is yours;
yours, O Lord, is the sovereignty:
you are exalted as head over all.

Riches and honor are from you,
and you have dominion over all.
In your hand are power and might;
it is yours to give grandeur and
    strength to all.

Therefore, our God, we give you thanks
and we praise the majesty of your name.

Glory to the Father, and to the Son,
    and to the Holy Spirit:
—as it was in the beginning, is now,
and will be for ever. Amen.

Ant. **We praise your glorious name, O Lord, our God.**

Ant. 3 **Adore the Lord in his holy court.**

JULY 31   MON   MORNING PRAYER

Psalm 29

O give the Lord, you sons of God,
give the Lord glory and power;
give the Lord the glory of his name.
Adore the Lord in his holy court.

The Lord's voice resounding on the waters,
the Lord on the immensity of waters;
the voice of the Lord, full of power,
the voice of the Lord, full of splendor.

The Lord's voice shattering the cedars,
the Lord shatters the cedars of Lebanon;
he makes Lebanon leap like a calf
and Sirion like a young wild-ox.

The Lord's voice flashes flames of fire.

The Lord's voice shaking the wilderness,
the Lord shakes the wilderness of Kadesh;
the Lord's voice rending the oak tree
and stripping the forest bare.

The God of glory thunders.
In his temple they all cry: "Glory!"
The Lord sat enthroned over the flood;
the Lord sits as king for ever.

The Lord will give strength to his people,
the Lord will bless his people with peace.

Glory to the Father, and to the Son,
   and to the Holy Spirit:
—as it was in the beginning, is now,
and will be for ever. Amen.

Ant.	**Adore the Lord in his holy court.**
Reading Hebrews 13:7–9a	Remember your leaders who spoke the word of God to you; consider how their lives ended, and imitate their faith. Jesus Christ is the same yesterday, today, and forever. Do not be carried away by all kinds of strange teaching.
Responsory	On your walls, Jerusalem, I have set my watchmen to guard you. —On your walls, Jerusalem, I have set my watchmen to guard you. Day or night, they will not cease to proclaim the name of the Lord. —I have set my watchmen to guard you. Glory to the Father, and to the Son, and to the Holy Spirit. —On your walls, Jerusalem, I have set my watchmen to guard you.
Gospel Canticle	Ant. **Would that I might know Christ and the power of his resurrection and that I might share in his sufferings.**
Canticle of Zechariah Luke 1:68–79	Blessed + be the Lord, the God of Israel; he has come to his people and set them free. He has raised up for us a mighty savior, born of the house of his servant David.

Through his holy prophets he
    promised of old
that he would save us from our enemies,
from the hands of all who hate us.

He promised to show mercy to our fathers
and to remember his holy covenant.

This was the oath he swore to our
    father Abraham:
to set us free from the hands of our enemies,
free to worship him without fear,
holy and righteous in his sight
    all the days of our life.

You, my child, shall be called the prophet of
    the Most High;
for you will go before the Lord to
    prepare his way,
to give his people knowledge of salvation
by the forgiveness of their sins.

In the tender compassion of our God
the dawn from on high shall break upon us,
to shine on those who dwell in darkness and
    the shadow of death,
and to guide our feet into the way of peace.

Glory to the Father, and to the Son,
    and to the Holy Spirit:
as it was in the beginning, is now,
and will be for ever. Amen.

Ant. **Would that I might know Christ and the power of his resurrection and that I might share in his sufferings.**

Intercessions Christ is the Good Shepherd who laid down his life for his sheep. Let us praise and thank him as we pray:
Nourish your people, Lord.

Christ, you decided to show your merciful love through your holy shepherds,
— let your mercy always reach us through them.

Through your vicars you continue to perform the ministry of shepherd of souls,
— direct us always through our leaders.

Through your holy ones, the leaders of your people, you served as physician of our bodies and our spirits,
— continue to fulfill your ministry of life and holiness in us.

You taught your flock through the prudence and love of your saints,
— grant us continual growth in holiness under the direction of our pastors.

The Lord's Prayer

Our Father, who art in heaven,
hallowed be thy name;
thy kingdom come,
thy will be done
on earth as it is in heaven.
Give us this day our daily bread,
and forgive us our trespasses,
as we forgive those who trespass against us;
and lead us not into temptation,
but deliver us from evil.

Pater noster, qui es in cælis:
sanctificetur nomen tuum;
adveniat regnum tuum;
fiat voluntas tua,
sicut in cælo, et in terra.
Panem nostrum cotidianum da nobis hodie;
et dimitte nobis debita nostra,
sicut et nos dimittimus debitoribus nostris;
et ne nos inducas in tentationem;
sed libera nos a malo.

Concluding Prayer

Father,
you gave Saint Ignatius of Loyola to
    your Church
to bring greater glory to your name.
May we follow his example on earth
and share the crown of life in heaven.
We ask this through our Lord Jesus Christ,
    your Son,
who lives and reigns with you and
    the Holy Spirit,
God, for ever and ever.
—Amen.

Dismissal *If praying individually, or in a group without a priest or deacon:*

May the Lord + bless us,
protect us from all evil
and bring us to everlasting life.
—Amen.

If praying with a priest or deacon, he dismisses the people:

The Lord be with you.
—And with your spirit.

May almighty God bless you,
the Father, and the Son, ✠ and the Holy Spirit.
—Amen.

Go in peace.
—Thanks be to God.

EVENING PRAYER

God, + come to my assistance.
—Lord, make haste to help me.

Glory to the Father, and to the Son,
    and to the Holy Spirit:
—as it was in the beginning, is now,
and will be for ever. Amen. Alleluia.

Hymn   *Jesus, Eternal Truth Sublime, p. 689*

Psalmody   Ant. 1 **The Lord looks tenderly on those who are poor.**

JULY 31 MON EVENING PRAYER

Psalm 11

In the Lord I have taken my refuge.
How can you say to my soul:
"Fly like a bird to its mountain.

See the wicked bracing their bow;
they are fixing their arrows on the string
to shoot upright men in the dark.
Foundations once destroyed, what can
    the just do?"

The Lord is in his holy temple,
the Lord, whose throne is in heaven.
His eyes look down on the world;
his gaze tests mortal men.

The Lord tests the just and the wicked:
the lover of violence he hates.
He sends fire and brimstone on the wicked;
he sends a scorching wind as their lot.

The Lord is just and loves justice:
the upright shall see his face.

Glory to the Father, and to the Son,
    and to the Holy Spirit:
as it was in the beginning, is now,
and will be for ever. Amen.

Ant.   **The Lord looks tenderly on those who are poor.**

Ant. 2   **Blessed are the pure of heart, for they shall see God.**

EVENING PRAYER   MON JULY 31

Psalm 15

Lord, who shall be admitted to your tent
and dwell on your holy mountain?

He who walks without fault:
he who acts with justice
and speaks the truth from his heart;
he who does not slander with his tongue;

he who does no wrong to his brother,
who casts no slur on his neighbor,
who holds the godless in disdain,
but honors those who fear the Lord;

he who keeps his pledge, come what may;
who takes no interest on a loan
and accepts no bribes against the innocent.
Such a man will stand firm for ever.

Glory to the Father, and to the Son,
 and to the Holy Spirit:
—as it was in the beginning, is now,
and will be for ever. Amen.

Ant.

Blessed are the pure of heart, for they shall see God.

Ant. 3

God chose us in his Son to be his adopted children.

Canticle:
Ephesians 1:3–10

Praised be the God and Father
of our Lord Jesus Christ,
who has bestowed on us in Christ
every spiritual blessing in the heavens.

God chose us in him
before the world began
to be holy
and blameless in his sight.

He predestined us
to be his adopted sons through Jesus Christ,
such was his will and pleasure,
that all might praise the glorious favor
he has bestowed on us in his beloved.

In him and through his blood, we have
 been redeemed,
and our sins forgiven,
so immeasurably generous
is God's favor to us.

God has given us the wisdom
to understand fully the mystery,
the plan he was pleased
to decree in Christ.

A plan to be carried out
in Christ, in the fullness of time,
to bring all things into one in him,
in the heavens and on earth.

Glory to the Father, and to the Son,
 and to the Holy Spirit:
—as it was in the beginning, is now,
and will be for ever. Amen.

Ant. **God chose us in his Son to be his adopted children.**

EVENING PRAYER MON JULY 31

Reading
1 Peter 5:1–4

To the elders among you I, a fellow elder, a witness of Christ's sufferings and sharer in the glory that is to be revealed, make this appeal. God's flock is in your midst; give it a shepherd's care. Watch over it willingly as God would have you do, not under constraint; and not for shameful profit either, but generously. Be examples to the flock, not lording it over those assigned to you, so that when the chief Shepherd appears you will win for yourselves the unfading crown of glory.

Responsory

This is a man who loved his brethren and
  ever prayed for them.
—This is a man who loved his brethren and
  ever prayed for them.

He spent himself in their service,
—and ever prayed for them.

Glory to the Father, and to the Son,
  and to the Holy Spirit.
—This is a man who loved his brethren and
  ever prayed for them.

Gospel Canticle

Ant. **Of what use is it to a man to gain the whole world, if he pays for it by losing his soul?**

Canticle of Mary
Luke 1:46–55

My + soul proclaims the greatness of the Lord,
my spirit rejoices in God my Savior
for he has looked with favor on his
  lowly servant.

From this day all generations will
    call me blessed:
the Almighty has done great things for me,
and holy is his Name.

He has mercy on those who fear him
in every generation.

He has shown the strength of his arm,
he has scattered the proud in their conceit.

He has cast down the mighty from
    their thrones,
and has lifted up the lowly.

He has filled the hungry with good things,
and the rich he has sent away empty.

He has come to the help of his servant Israel
for he has remembered his promise of mercy,
the promise he made to our fathers,
to Abraham and his children for ever.

Glory to the Father, and to the Son,
    and to the Holy Spirit:
as it was in the beginning, is now,
and will be for ever. Amen.

Ant. **Of what use is it to a man to gain the whole world, if he pays for it by losing his soul?**

Intercessions Jesus Christ is worthy of all praise, for he was appointed high priest among men and their representative before God. We honor him and in our weakness we pray:
Bring salvation to your people, Lord.

You marvelously illuminated your Church through distinguished leaders and holy men and women,
—let Christians rejoice always in such splendor.

You forgave the sins of your people when their holy leaders like Moses sought your compassion,
—through their intercession continue to purify and sanctify your holy people.

In the midst of their brothers and sisters you anointed your holy ones and filled them with the Holy Spirit,
—fill all the leaders of your people with the same Spirit.

You yourself are the only visible possession of our holy pastors,
—let none of them, won at the price of your blood, remain far from you.

The shepherds of your Church keep your flock from being snatched out of your hand. Through them you give your flock eternal life,
—save those who have died, those for whom you gave up your life.

The Lord's Prayer

Our Father, who art in heaven,
hallowed be thy name;
thy kingdom come,
thy will be done
on earth as it is in heaven.
Give us this day our daily bread,
and forgive us our trespasses,
as we forgive those who trespass against us;
and lead us not into temptation,
but deliver us from evil.

Pater noster, qui es in cælis:
sanctificetur nomen tuum;
adveniat regnum tuum;
fiat voluntas tua,
sicut in cælo, et in terra.
Panem nostrum cotidianum da nobis hodie;
et dimitte nobis debita nostra,
sicut et nos dimittimus debitoribus nostris;
et ne nos inducas in tentationem;
sed libera nos a malo.

Concluding Prayer

Father,
you gave Saint Ignatius of Loyola to
    your Church
to bring greater glory to your name.
May we follow his example on earth
and share the crown of life in heaven.
We ask this through our Lord Jesus Christ,
    your Son,
who lives and reigns with you and
    the Holy Spirit,
God, for ever and ever.
—Amen.

Dismissal *If praying individually, or in a group without a priest or deacon:*

May the Lord + bless us,
protect us from all evil
and bring us to everlasting life.
—Amen.

If praying with a priest or deacon, he dismisses the people:

The Lord be with you.
—And with your spirit.

May almighty God bless you,
the Father, and the Son, ✠ and the Holy Spirit.
—Amen.

Go in peace.
—Thanks be to God.

NIGHT PRAYER

God, + come to my assistance.
—Lord, make haste to help me.

Glory to the Father, and to the Son,
    and to the Holy Spirit:
—as it was in the beginning, is now,
and will be for ever. Amen. Alleluia.

Examen *An optional brief examination of conscience may be made. Call to mind your sins and failings this day.*

Hymn *Abide with Me, p. 675*

Psalmody Ant. **O Lord, our God, unwearied is your love for us.**

JULY 31   MON   NIGHT PRAYER

Psalm 86

Turn your ear, O Lord, and give answer
for I am poor and needy.
Preserve my life, for I am faithful:
save the servant who trusts in you.

You are my God; have mercy on me, Lord,
for I cry to you all day long.
Give joy to your servant, O Lord,
for to you I lift up my soul.

O Lord, you are good and forgiving,
full of love to all who call.
Give heed, O Lord, to my prayer
and attend to the sound of my voice.

In the day of distress I will call
and surely you will reply.
Among the gods there is none like you, O Lord;
nor work to compare with yours.

All the nations shall come to adore you
and glorify your name, O Lord:
for you are great and do marvelous deeds,
you who alone are God.

Show me, Lord, your way
so that I may walk in your truth.
Guide my heart to fear your name.

I will praise you, Lord my God,
    with all my heart
and glorify your name for ever;
for your love to me has been great:
you have saved me from the depths of the grave.

The proud have risen against me;
ruthless men seek my life:
to you they pay no heed.

But you, God of mercy and compassion,
slow to anger, O Lord,
abounding in love and truth,
turn and take pity on me.

O give your strength to your servant
and save your handmaid's son.
Show me a sign of your favor
that my foes may see to their shame
that you console me and give me your help.

Glory to the Father, and to the Son,
    and to the Holy Spirit:
—as it was in the beginning, is now,
and will be for ever. Amen.

Ant. **O Lord, our God, unwearied is your love for us.**

Reading
1 Thessalonians 5:9–10

God has destined us for acquiring salvation through our Lord Jesus Christ. He died for us, that all of us, whether awake or asleep, together might live with him.

Responsory

Into your hands, Lord, I commend my spirit.
—Into your hands, Lord, I commend my spirit.

You have redeemed us, Lord God of truth.
—I commend my spirit.

Glory to the Father, and to the Son,
    and to the Holy Spirit.
—Into your hands, Lord, I commend my spirit.

Gospel Canticle

Ant. **Protect us, Lord, as we stay awake; watch over us as we sleep, that awake, we may keep watch with Christ, and asleep, rest in his peace.**

Canticle of Simeon
Luke 2:29-32

Lord, + now you let your servant go in peace;
your word has been fulfilled:
my own eyes have seen the salvation
which you have prepared in the sight of
    every people:
a light to reveal you to the nations
and the glory of your people Israel.

Glory to the Father, and to the Son,
    and to the Holy Spirit:
—as it was in the beginning, is now,
and will be for ever. Amen.

Ant. **Protect us, Lord, as we stay awake; watch over us as we sleep, that awake, we may keep watch with Christ, and asleep, rest in his peace.**

Concluding Prayer

Let us pray.
Lord,
give our bodies restful sleep
and let the work we have done today
bear fruit in eternal life.
We ask this through Christ our Lord.
—Amen.

Blessing May the all-powerful Lord
grant us a restful night
and a peaceful death.
—Amen.

Marian Antiphon *Sing the "Salve Regina," found on p. 698, or pray a Hail Mary.*

Hymns

Abide with Me

A-bide with me! fast falls the e-ven-tide;
Swift to its close ebbs out life's lit-tle day;
I fear no foe with thee at hand to bless:
Hold thou thy cross be-fore my clos-ing eyes;

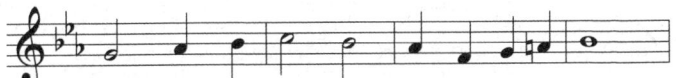

The dark-ness deep-ens; Lord, with me a-bide.
Earth's joys grow dim, its glo-ries pass a-way;
Ills have no weight, and tears no bit-ter-ness.
Shine through the gloom, and point me to the skies;

When oth-er help-ers fail, and com-forts flee,
Change and de-cay in all a-round I see;
Where is death's sting? where, grave, thy vic-to-ry?
Heaven's morn-ing breaks, and earth's vain shad-ows flee:

Help of the help-less, O a-bide with me!
O thou who chang-est not, a-bide with me!
I tri-umph still if thou a-bide with me.
In life, in death, O Lord, a-bide with me!

Text: Henry Francis Lyte
Tune: EVENTIDE, William Henry Monk
10.10.10.10

Before the Final Light of Day

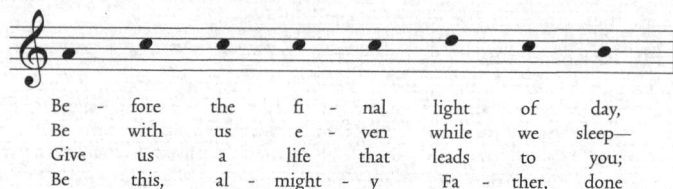

1. Before the final light of day,
2. Be with us even while we sleep—
3. Give us a life that leads to you;
4. Be this, almighty Father, done

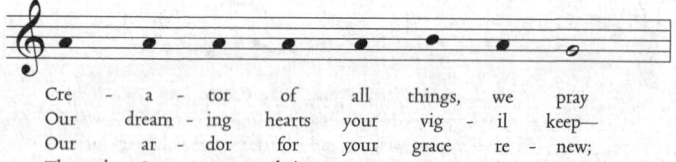

1. Creator of all things, we pray
2. Our dreaming hearts your vigil keep—
3. Our ardor for your grace renew;
4. Through Jesus Christ, your only Son,

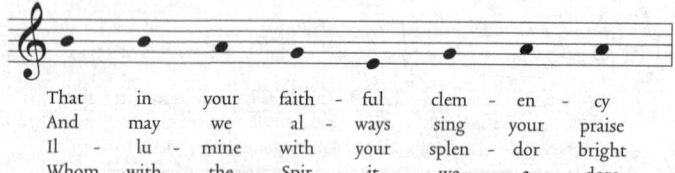

1. That in your faithful clemency
2. And may we always sing your praise
3. Illumine with your splendor bright
4. Whom with the Spirit we adore

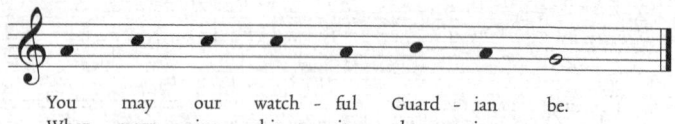

1. You may our watchful Guardian be.
2. When morning shines its dawning rays.
3. The deepest darkness of the night.
4. Forever and forevermore.

Text: *Te lucis ante terminum*, translated by Kathleen Pluth (Creative Commons BY-NC-ND 4.0)
Tune: TE LUCIS, Latin hymn tune
Long Meter, 8.8.8.8

Captains of the Saintly Band

Captains of the saintly band,
Lights who lighten every land,
Princes who with Jesus dwell,
Judges of his Israel:

On the nations sunk in night
You have shed the Gospel light;
Sin and error flee away;
Truth reveals the promised day.

Earth, that long in sin and pain
Groaned in Satan's deadly chain,
Now to serve its God is free
In the law of liberty.

Distant lands with one acclaim
Tell the honor of your name
Who, wherever man has trod,
Teach the mysteries of God.

Glory to the Three-in-One
While eternal ages run,
Who from deepest shades of night
Called us to his glorious light.

Text: *Cælestis aulæ principes*, Jean-Baptiste de Santeuil, translated by Henry W. Baker
Tune: NUN KOMM DER HEIDEN HEILAND, from *Geistliche Gesangbüchlein*
7.7.7.7

Come, My Way, My Truth, My Life

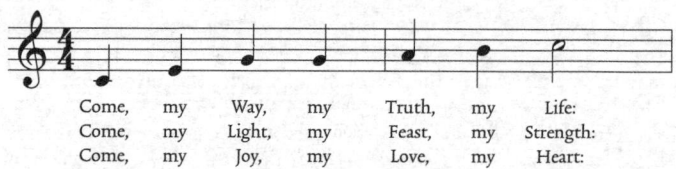

Come, my Way, my Truth, my Life:
Come, my Light, my Feast, my Strength:
Come, my Joy, my Love, my Heart:

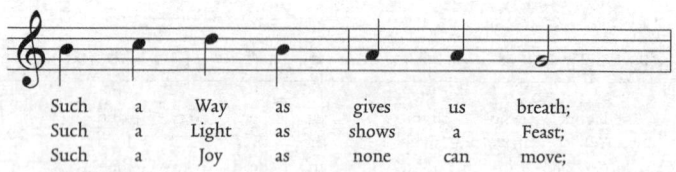

Such a Way as gives us breath;
Such a Light as shows a Feast;
Such a Joy as none can move;

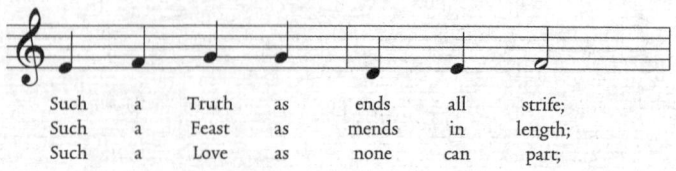

Such a Truth as ends all strife;
Such a Feast as mends in length;
Such a Love as none can part;

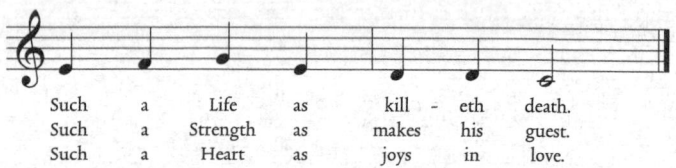

Such a Life as kill-eth death.
Such a Strength as makes his guest.
Such a Heart as joys in love.

Text: George Herbert
Tune: GOTT SEI DANK, Johann Anastasius Freylinghausen
7.7.7.7

HYMNS

From All That Dwell Below the Skies

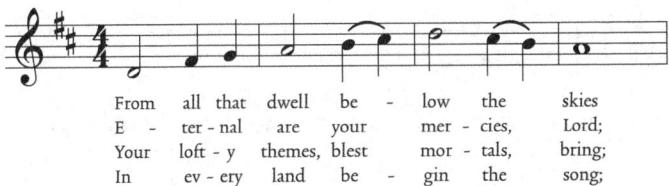

From all that dwell be - low the skies
E - ter - nal are your mer - cies, Lord;
Your loft - y themes, blest mor - tals, bring;
In ev - ery land be - gin the song;

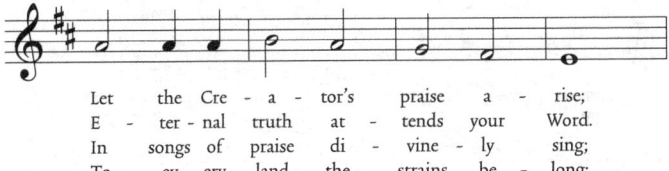

Let the Cre - a - tor's praise a - rise;
E - ter - nal truth at - tends your Word.
In songs of praise di - vine - ly sing;
To ev - ery land the strains be - long;

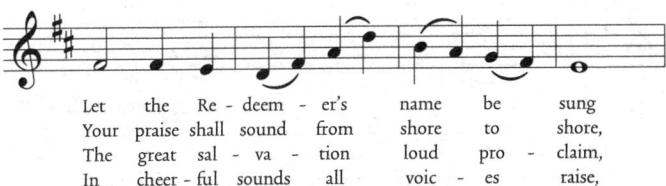

Let the Re - deem - er's name be sung
Your praise shall sound from shore to shore,
The great sal - va - tion loud pro - claim,
In cheer - ful sounds all voic - es raise,

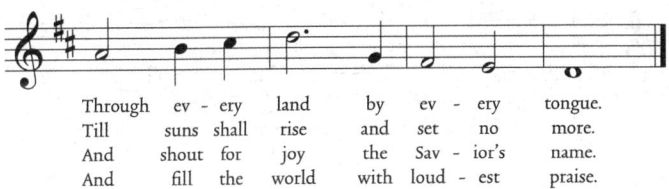

Through ev - ery land by ev - ery tongue.
Till suns shall rise and set no more.
And shout for joy the Sav - ior's name.
And fill the world with loud - est praise.

Text: Isaac Watts
Tune: DUKE STREET, John Hatton
Long Meter, 8.8.8.8

From the Highest Heights of Glory

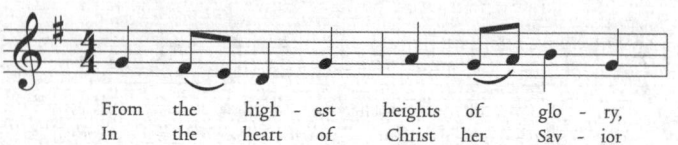

From the highest heights of glory,
In the heart of Christ her Savior

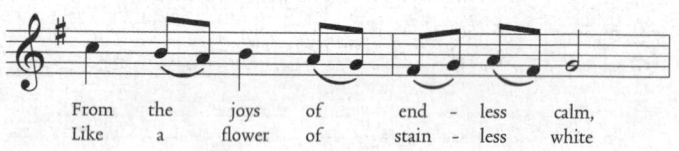

From the joys of endless calm,
Like a flower of stainless white

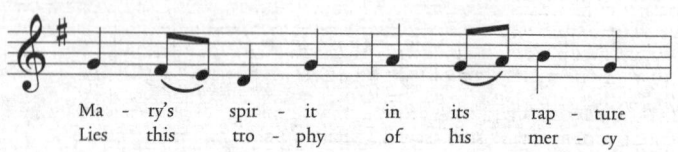

Mary's spirit in its rapture
Lies this trophy of his mercy

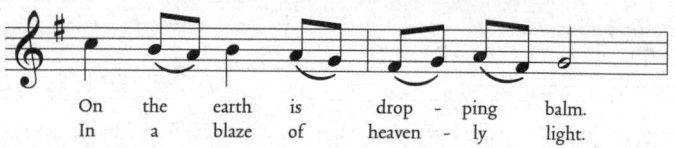

On the earth is dropping balm.
In a blaze of heavenly light.

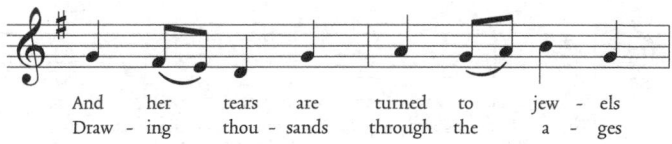

Text: Frederick W. Faber, alt.
Tune: IN BABILONE, from *Oude en Nieuwe Hollantse Boerenlieties en Contredansen*
8.7.8.7 D

God Who Made Both Earth and Heaven

1. God who made both earth and heaven,
   Father, Son, and Holy Ghost,
   Who the day and night have given,
   Sun and moon and starry host,

2. God, I thank thee: in thy keeping
   Safely have I slumbered here;
   Thou hast guarded me while sleeping
   From all danger, pain, and fear.

3. Let the night of sin that shrouded
   Former days with this depart;
   Shine on me with beams unclouded:
   Jesus, in thy loving heart

4. O my God, I now commend me
   Wholly to thy mighty hand:
   All the powers that thou dost lend me
   Let me use at thy command;

5. Thus afresh with each new morning
   Save me from the power of sin;
   Hourly let me feel thy warning
   Ruling, prompting all within,

Text: *Gott des Himmels und der Erden*, Heinrich Albert, translated by Catherine Winkworth
Tune: ZEUCH MICH, ZEUCH MICH, from *Geistreiches Gesangbuch*
8.7.8.7

Go, Labor On

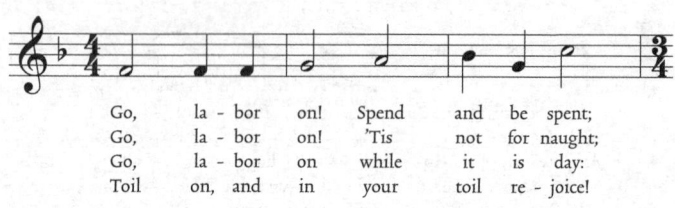

Go, labor on! Spend and be spent;
Go, labor on! 'Tis not for naught;
Go, labor on while it is day:
Toil on, and in your toil rejoice!

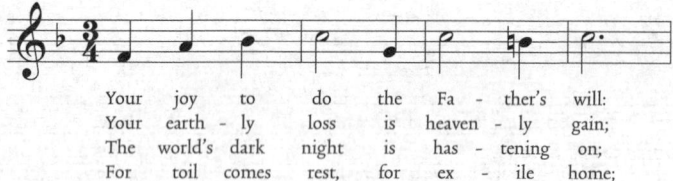

Your joy to do the Father's will:
Your earthly loss is heavenly gain;
The world's dark night is hastening on;
For toil comes rest, for exile home;

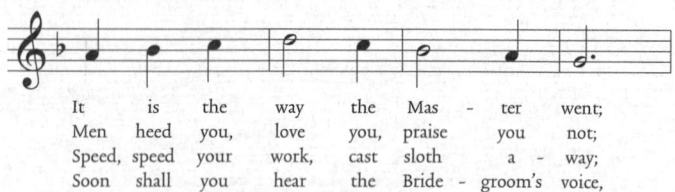

It is the way the Master went;
Men heed you, love you, praise you not;
Speed, speed your work, cast sloth away;
Soon shall you hear the Bridegroom's voice,

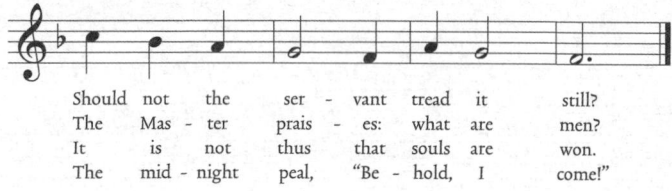

Should not the servant tread it still?
The Master praises: what are men?
It is not thus that souls are won.
The midnight peal, "Behold, I come!"

Text: Horatius Bonar
Tune: SONG 34, Orlando Gibbons
Long Meter, 8.8.8.8

High Let Us All Our Voices Raise

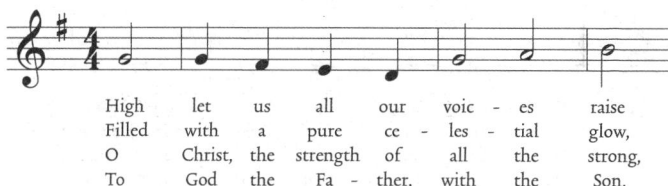

High let us all our voices raise
Filled with a pure celestial glow,
O Christ, the strength of all the strong,
To God the Father, with the Son,

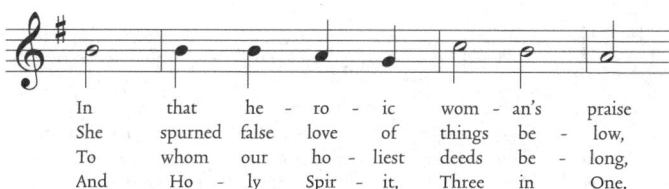

In that heroic woman's praise
She spurned false love of things below,
To whom our holiest deeds belong,
And Holy Spirit, Three in One,

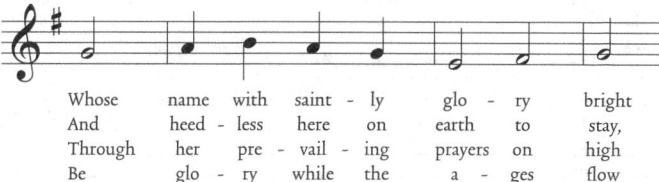

Whose name with saintly glory bright
And heedless here on earth to stay,
Through her prevailing prayers on high
Be glory while the ages flow

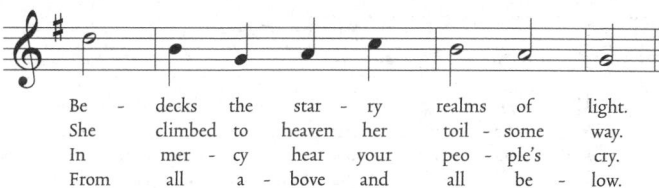

Bedecks the starry realms of light.
She climbed to heaven her toilsome way.
In mercy hear your people's cry.
From all above and all below.

Text: *Fortem virili pectore*, Silvio Antoniano, translated by Edward Caswall
Tune: OLD HUNDREDTH, Louis Bourgeois
Long Meter, 8.8.8.8

Holy God, We Praise Thy Name

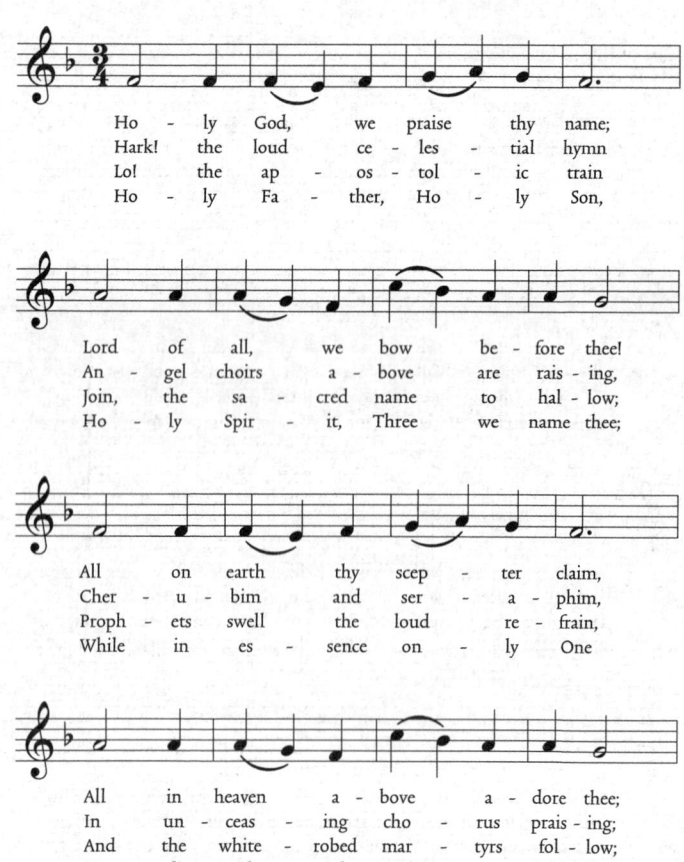

Text: *Te Deum*, paraphrased by Ignaz Franz, translated by Clarence Walworth
Tune: GROSSER GOTT, from *Katholisches Gesangbuch*
7.8.7.8.7.7.7.7

Immortal, Invisible, God Only Wise

Immortal, invisible, God only wise,
Unresting, unhasting, and silent as light,
To all, life thou givest, to both great and small.
Great God of all glory, great God of all light,

In light inaccessible, hid from our eyes,
Nor wanting, nor wasting, thou rulest in might,
In all life thou livest, the true Life of all.
Thine angels adore thee, all veiling their sight.

Most blessed, most glorious, the Ancient of Days,
Thy justice like mountains high soaring above
We blossom and flourish as leaves on the tree,
All praise we would render; O help us to see

Almighty, victorious, thy great name we praise.
Thy clouds, which are fountains of goodness and love.
And wither and perish, but naught changeth thee.
'Tis only the splendor of light hideth thee.

Text: Walter Chalmers Smith
Tune: ST. DENIO, Welsh melody
11.11.11.11

Jesus, Eternal Truth Sublime

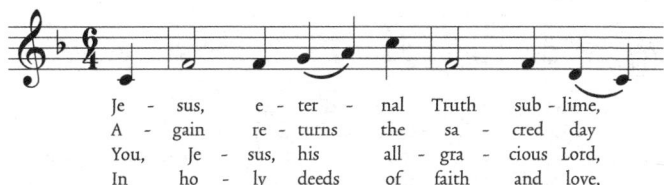
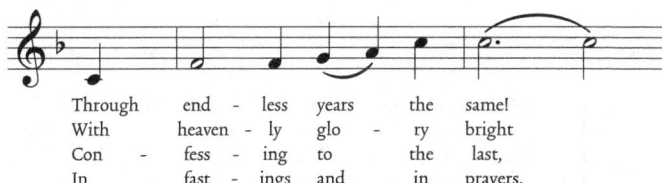

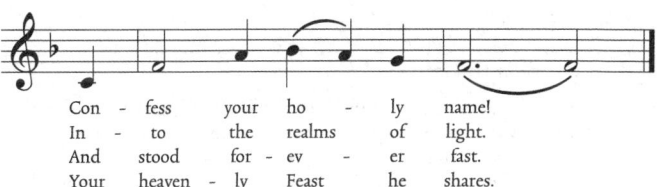

1. Jesus, eternal Truth sublime, Through endless years the same! O Crown of those who through all time Confess your holy name!

2. Again returns the sacred day With heavenly glory bright Which saw your saint go on his way Into the realms of light.

3. You, Jesus, his all-gracious Lord, Confessing to the last, He trod beneath him Satan's fraud, And stood forever fast.

4. In holy deeds of faith and love, In fastings and in prayers, His days were spent, and now above Your heavenly Feast he shares.

Text: *Iesu, Corona celsior*, translated by Edward Caswall
Tune: LAND OF REST, American folk melody
Common Meter, 8.6.8.6

Let All on Earth Their Voices Raise

Let all on earth their voices raise,
Re-echoing heaven's triumphant praise
To him who gave th'apostles grace
To run on earth their glorious race.

Lord, at whose word they bore the light
Of gospel truth o'er heathen night,
To us that heavenly light impart
To glad our eyes and cheer our heart.

Lord, at whose will to them was given
To bind and loose in earth and heaven,
Our chains unbind, our sins undo,
And in our hearts your grace renew.

Lord, in whose might they spoke the word
That cured disease and health restored,
To us its healing power prolong;
Support the weak, confirm the strong.

And when the thrones are set on high,
And judgment's awful hour draws nigh,
Then, Lord, with them pronounce us blest,
And take us to your endless rest.

Text: Richard Mant
Tune: TALLIS' CANON, Thomas Tallis
Long Meter, 8.8.8.8

Let Heaven Highest Praises Bring

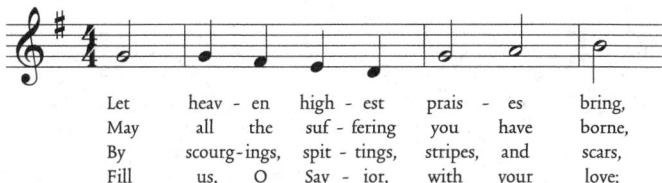

Let heav-en high-est prais-es bring,
May all the suf-fering you have borne,
By scourg-ings, spit-tings, stripes, and scars,
Fill us, O Sav-ior, with your love;

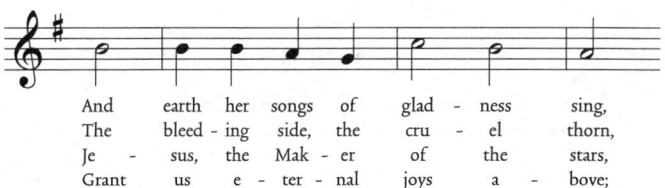

And earth her songs of glad-ness sing,
The bleed-ing side, the cru-el thorn,
Je-sus, the Mak-er of the stars,
Grant us e-ter-nal joys a-bove;

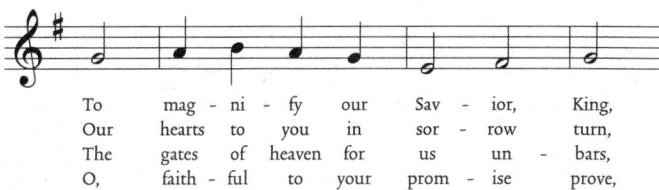

To mag-ni-fy our Sav-ior, King,
Our hearts to you in sor-row turn,
The gates of heaven for us un-bars,
O, faith-ful to your prom-ise prove,

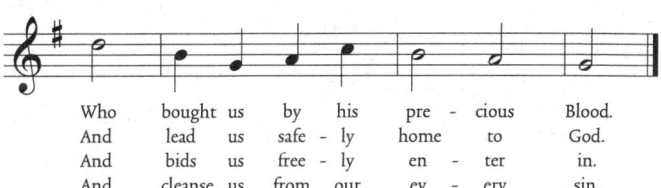

Who bought us by his pre-cious Blood.
And lead us safe-ly home to God.
And bids us free-ly en-ter in.
And cleanse us from our ev-ery sin.

Text: St. Bonaventure, translated by Heloise Soule
Tune: OLD HUNDREDTH, Louis Bourgeois
Long Meter, 8.8.8.8

Now That the Sun Is Gleaming Bright

Now that the sun is gleam-ing bright,
Im-plore we, bend-ing low,
That he, the un-cre-at-ed Light
May guide us as we go.

No sin-ful word, nor deed of wrong,
Nor thoughts that id-ly rove,
But sim-ple truth be on our tongue,
And in our hearts be love.

And while the hours in or-der flow,
O Christ, se-cure-ly fence
Our gates, be-lea-guered by the foe:
The gate of ev-ery sense.

And grant that to your hon-or, Lord,
Our dai-ly toil may tend:
That we be-gin it at your word,
And in your fa-vor end.

Text: *Iam lucis orto sidere*, translated by St. John Henry Newman
Tune: NEW BRITAIN, from *Virginia Harmony*
Common Meter, 8.6.8.6

O Joyful Light of God Most High

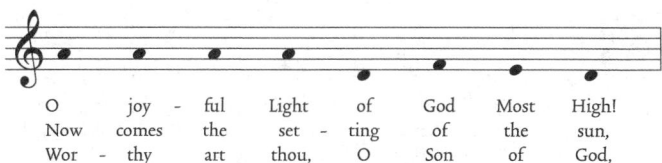

O joy-ful Light of God Most High!
Now comes the set-ting of the sun,
Wor-thy art thou, O Son of God,

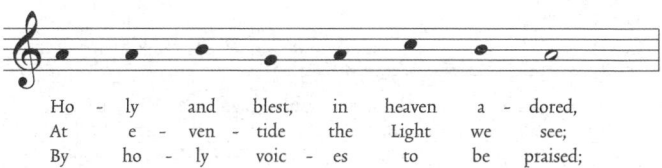

Ho-ly and blest, in heaven a-dored,
At e-ven-tide the Light we see;
By ho-ly voic-es to be praised;

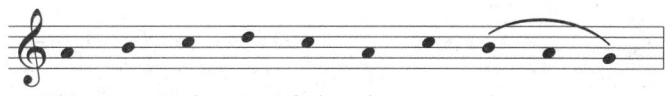

The im-mor-tal Fa-ther's Glo-ry: thee
O Fa-ther, Son, and Spir-it blest,
There-fore to thee, who give all life,

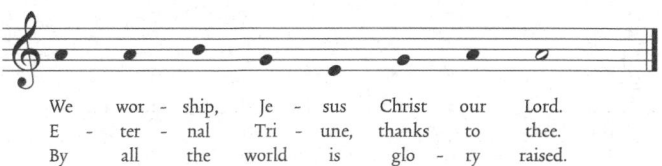

We wor-ship, Je-sus Christ our Lord.
E-ter-nal Tri-une, thanks to thee.
By all the world is glo-ry raised.

Text: Φῶς Ἱλαρόν, translated by William Chatterton Dix
Tune: JESU DULCIS MEMORIA, Latin hymn tune
Long Meter, 8.8.8.8

O Splendor of God's Glory Bright

O Splendor of God's glory bright,
O you who bring forth light from light,
O Light of Light, light's living Spring,
O Day, all days illumining.

O Christ true Sun, on us your glance
Let fall in royal radiance;
The Spirit's sanctifying beam
Upon our earthly senses stream.

The Father, too, our prayers implore,
Father of glory evermore;
The Father of all grace and might,
To banish sin from our delight.

Morn in her rosy car is borne;
Let him come forth, our perfect Morn,
The Word in God the Father one,
The Father perfect in the Son.

All laud to God the Father be;
All praise, eternal Son, to thee;
All glory, as is ever meet,
To God the holy Paraclete.

Text: *Splendor Paternæ gloriæ*, by St. Ambrose, translated by Robert Bridges
Tune: PUER NOBIS NASCITUR, folk melody collected in a Trier
manuscript, adapted by Michael Praetorius
Long Meter, 8.8.8.8

This Day the First of Days Was Made

This day the first of days was made,
When God in light the world arrayed,
And when his Word arose again,
And, conquering death, gave life to men.

Slumber and sloth drive far away;
Early arise to greet the day;
And ere its dawn in heaven unfold,
The heart's desire to God be told.

That us, who here this day repair
To keep the apostles' time of prayer
And hymn the quiet hours of morn,
With blessed gifts he may adorn.

For this, Redeemer, you we pray
That you will wash our sins away,
And of your lovingkindness grant
Whatever good our spirits want.

That, exiles here a while in flesh,
Some whisper may our souls refresh
Of that pure life for which we long:
Some foretaste of the heavenly song.

All glory to the Father be,
And to his Son eternally,
Whom with the Spirit we adore
Forever and forevermore.

Text: *Primo dierum omnium*, attributed to Pope St. Gregory the Great,
translated by Robert Bridges
Tune: PUER NOBIS NASCITUR
Long Meter, 8.8.8.8

Praise to the Lord, the Almighty

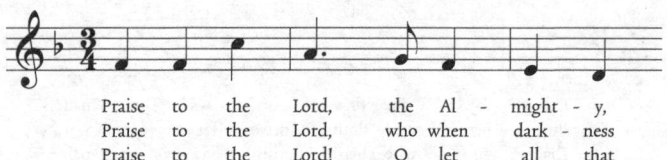
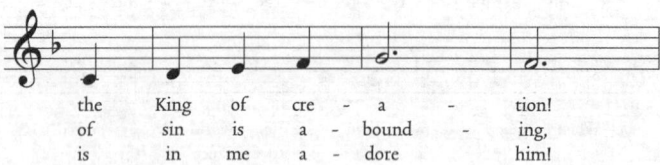
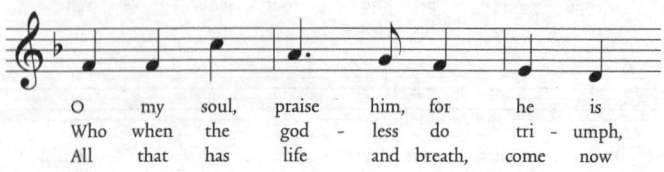
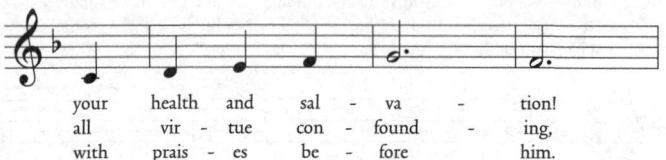

All you who hear, now to his tem-ple draw near;
Sheds forth his light, chas-es the hor-rors of night,
Let the "A-men" sound from his peo-ple a-gain;

Praise him in glad ad-o-ra-tion.
Saints with his mer-cy sur-round-ing.
Glad-ly for-e'er we a-dore him.

Text: Joachim Neander, translated by Catherine Winkworth
Tune: LOBE DEN HERREN
14.14.4.7.8

HYMNS

Salve Regina

Sal-ve, Re-gi-na, Ma-ter mi-se-ri-cor-di-æ,

vi-ta, dul-ce-do, et spes no-stra, sal-ve.

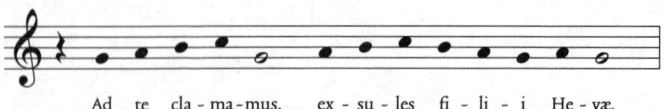
Ad te cla-ma-mus, ex-su-les fi-li-i He-væ.

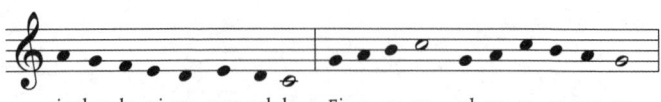
Ad te sus-pi-ra-mus, ge-men-tes et flen-tes

in hac la-cri-ma-rum val-le. Ei-a er-go, ad-vo-ca-ta nos-tra,

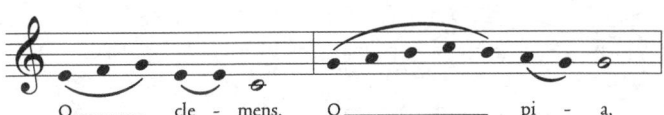

Text: Latin, 11th century
Tune: SALVE REGINA
Irregular meter

Sing Praise to God Who Reigns Above

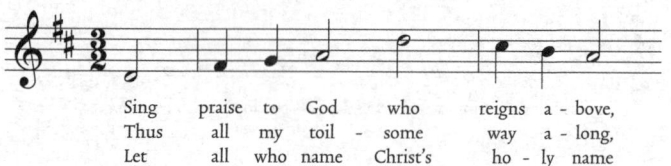
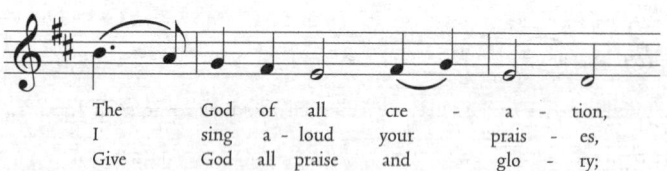
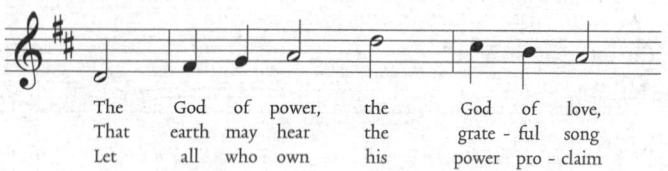
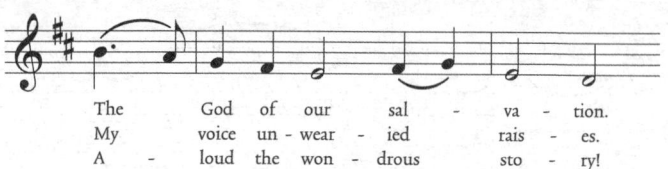

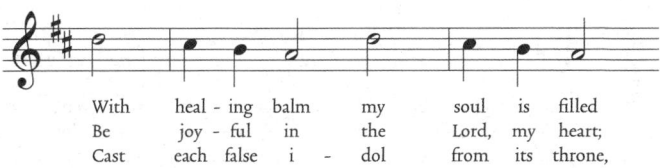

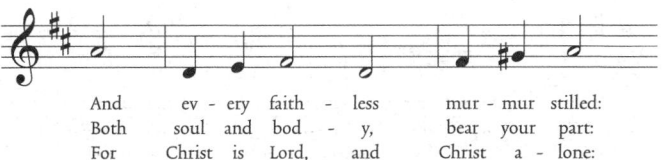

Text: Johann J. Schütz, translated by Frances E. Cox
Tune: MIT FREUDEN ZART
8.7.8.7.8.8.7

Sing with All the Saints in Glory

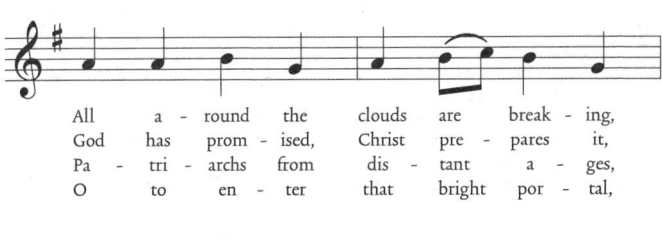
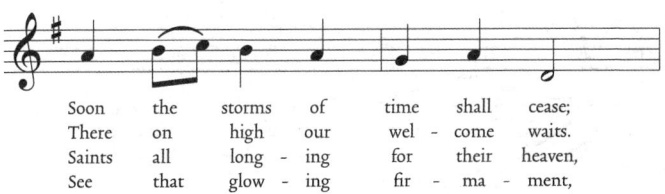
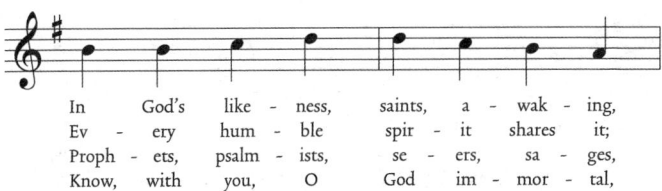
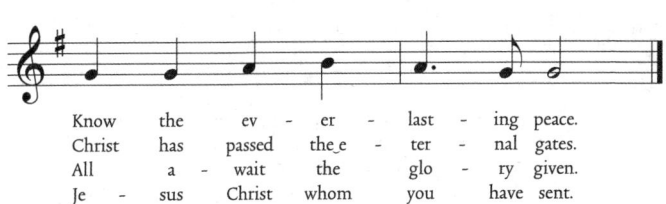

Text: William J. Irons
Tune: HYMN TO JOY, arranged from Ludwig van Beethoven
8.7.8.7 D

The Heavens Declare Your Glory

The heavens declare your glory,
The firmament your power;
Day unto day the story
Repeats from hour to hour.

The sun with royal splendor
Goes forth to chant your praise;
And moonbeams soft and tender
Their gentler anthem raise.

How perfect, just, and holy
The precepts you have given!
Still making wise the lowly,
They lift the thoughts to heaven.

All heaven on high rejoices
To do its Maker's will;
The stars with solemn voices
Resound your praises still;

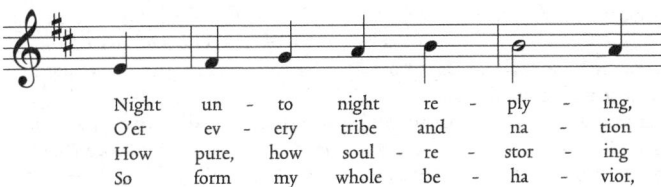

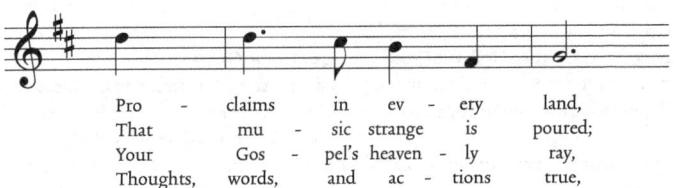

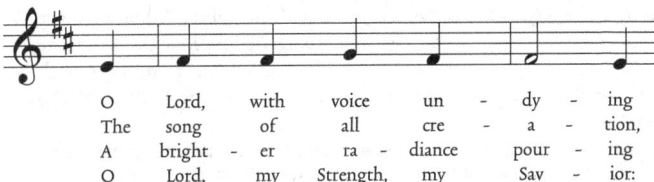

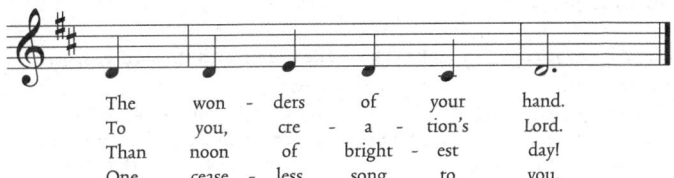

Text: Thomas R. Birks
Tune: AURELIA, Samuel S. Wesley
7.6.7.6 D

Abide with Me (p. 675)
Alternate melodies: God of Our Fathers (National Hymn); Soul of My Savior

Before the Final Light of Day (p. 676)
Alternate melodies: All Hail, Adored Trinity; All People That on Earth Do Dwell; Creator of the Stars of Night; From All That Dwell Below the Skies; Jesus Shall Reign; I Know That My Redeemer Lives; Lift Up Your Heads; O Radiant Light; O Salutaris Hostia (O Saving Victim); Take Up Your Cross; The God Whom Earth and Sea and Sky; When I Survey the Wondrous Cross

Captains of the Saintly Band (p. 677)
This melody is also sung with the text "Savior of the Nations, Come."
Alternate melody: On This Day, the First of Days

Come, My Way, My Truth, My Life (p. 678)
This melody is also sung with the text "On This Day, the First of Days."
Alternate melody: Savior of the Nations, Come

From All That Dwell Below the Skies (p. 679)
This melody is also sung with the texts "Jesus Shall Reign" and "I Know That My Redeemer Lives."
Alternate melodies: All Hail, Adored Trinity; All People That on Earth Do Dwell; Creator of the Stars of Night; Lift Up Your Heads; O Radiant Light; O Salutaris Hostia (O Saving Victim); Take Up Your Cross; The God Whom Earth and Sea and Sky; When I Survey the Wondrous Cross

From the Highest Heights of Glory (p. 680)
This melody is also sung with the texts "Blessed Feasts of Blessed Martyrs" and "There's a Wideness in God's Mercy."
Alternate melodies: God, We Praise You; Joyful, Joyful, We Adore Thee; Love Divine, All Loves Excelling; Praise the Lord! Ye Heavens Adore Him; Sing with All the Saints in Glory

Go, Labor On (p. 684)
Alternate melodies: All Hail, Adored Trinity; All People That on Earth Do Dwell; Creator of the Stars of Night; From All That Dwell Below the Skies; Jesus Shall Reign; I Know That My Redeemer Lives; Lift Up Your Heads; O Radiant Light; O Salutaris Hostia (O Saving Victim); Take Up Your Cross; The God Whom Earth and Sea and Sky; When I Survey the Wondrous Cross

God Who Made Both Earth and Heaven (p. 682)
Alternate melodies: Light Serene of Holy Glory

High Let Us All Our Voices Raise (p. 685)
This melody is also sung with the texts "All Hail, Adored Trinity" and "All People That on Earth Do Dwell."
Alternate melodies: Creator of the Stars of Night; From All That Dwell Below the Skies; Jesus Shall Reign; I Know That My Redeemer Lives; Lift Up Your Heads; O Radiant Light; O Salutaris Hostia (O Saving Victim); Take Up Your Cross; The God Whom Earth and Sea and Sky; When I Survey the Wondrous Cross

Holy God, We Praise Thy Name (p. 686)

Immortal, Invisible, God Only Wise (p. 688)
This melody is by far the most common melody in its meter.

Jesus, Eternal Truth Sublime (p. 689)
This melody is also sung with the text "Jerusalem, My Happy Home."
Alternate melodies: Amazing Grace; The Head That Once Was Crowned with Thorns; The King of Love My Shepherd Is; The King Shall Come When Morning Dawns; We Walk by Faith

Let All on Earth Their Voices Raise (p. 690)
This melody is also sung with the text "All Praise to Thee, My God, This Night."
Alternate melodies: All Hail, Adored Trinity; All People That on Earth Do Dwell; Creator of the Stars of Night; From All That Dwell Below the Skies; Jesus Shall Reign; I Know That My Redeemer Lives; Lift Up Your Heads; O Radiant Light; O Salutaris Hostia (O Saving Victim); Take Up Your Cross; The God Whom Earth and Sea and Sky; When I Survey the Wondrous Cross

Let Heaven Highest Praises Bring (p. 691)
This melody is also sung with the texts "All Hail, Adored Trinity" and "All People That on Earth Do Dwell."
Alternate melodies: Creator of the Stars of Night; From All That Dwell Below the Skies; Jesus Shall Reign; I Know That My Redeemer Lives; Lift Up Your Heads; O Radiant Light; O Salutaris Hostia (O Saving Victim); Take Up Your Cross; The God Whom Earth and Sea and Sky; When I Survey the Wondrous Cross

Now That the Sun Is Gleaming Bright (p. 692)
This melody is also sung with the text "Amazing Grace."
Alternate melodies: Jerusalem, My Happy Home; The Head That Once Was Crowned with Thorns; The King of Love My Shepherd Is; The King Shall Come When Morning Dawns; We Walk by Faith

O Joyful Light of God Most High (p. 693)
This melody is also sung with the texts "Around the Throne a Glorious Band" and "O Radiant Light."
Alternate melodies: All Hail, Adored Trinity; All People That on Earth Do Dwell; Creator of the Stars of Night; From All That Dwell Below the Skies; Jesus Shall Reign; I Know That My Redeemer Lives; Lift Up Your Heads; O Radiant Light; O Salutaris Hostia (O Saving Victim); Take Up Your Cross; The God Whom Earth and Sea and Sky; When I Survey the Wondrous Cross

HYMNS

O Splendor of God's Glory Bright
(p. 694)
This melody is also sung with the text "That Eastertide with Joy Was Bright."
Alternate melodies: All Hail, Adored Trinity; All People That on Earth Do Dwell; Creator of the Stars of Night; From All That Dwell Below the Skies; Jesus Shall Reign; I Know That My Redeemer Lives; Lift Up Your Heads; O Radiant Light; O Salutaris Hostia (O Saving Victim); Take Up Your Cross; The God Whom Earth and Sea and Sky; When I Survey the Wondrous Cross

This Day the First of Days Was Made
(p. 695)
This melody is also sung with the text "That Eastertide with Joy Was Bright."
Alternate melodies: All Hail, Adored Trinity; All People That on Earth Do Dwell; Creator of the Stars of Night; From All That Dwell Below the Skies; Jesus Shall Reign; I Know That My Redeemer Lives; Lift Up Your Heads; O Radiant Light; O Salutaris Hostia (O Saving Victim); Take Up Your Cross; The God Whom Earth and Sea and Sky; When I Survey the Wondrous Cross

Praise to the Lord, the Almighty
(p. 696)
This melody is by far the most common melody in its meter.

Salve Regina (p. 698)
This melody is one of a kind and does not have an alternative. The text may be recited if not sung, or a Hail Mary may be said.

Sing Praise to God Who Reigns Above (p. 700)
This melody is by far the most common melody in its meter.

Sing with All the Saints in Glory
(p. 702)
This melody is also sung with the text "Joyful, Joyful, We Adore Thee."
Alternate melodies: God, We Praise You; Love Divine, All Loves Excelling; Praise the Lord! Ye Heavens Adore Him; There's a Wideness in God's Mercy

The Heavens Declare Your Glory
(p. 704)
This melody is also sung with the text "The Church's One Foundation."
Alternate melodies: All Glory, Laud, and Honor; From All Your Saints in Warfare (By All Your Saints Still Striving); Go Make of All Disciples; O Sacred Head, Surrounded

Pray with the Church.

*Subscribe at wordonfire.org/pray
and receive a new Liturgy of the Hours
booklet each month.*

*To update your address or modify your account,
simply go to account.wordonfire.org/loth*

The Liturgy of the Hours (issn 2771-1285) is published monthly by
Word on Fire Catholic Ministries, 25 Northwest Point Blvd,
Suite 1025, Elk Grove Village, IL 60007. Periodicals Postage Paid at
Elk Grove Village, IL, and at additional mailing offices.

POSTMASTER: Send address changes to
The Liturgy of the Hours, PO Box 170, Des Plaines, IL 60016.

Issue 14

JULY 2023   2771-1285